Power, Gender
and Social Change in Africa

Power, Gender and Social Change in Africa

Edited by

Muna Ndulo and Margaret Grieco

CAMBRIDGE SCHOLARS
PUBLISHING

Power, Gender and Social Change in Africa, Edited by Muna Ndulo and Margaret Grieco

This book first published 2009

Cambridge Scholars Publishing

12 Back Chapman Street, Newcastle upon Tyne, NE6 2XX, UK

British Library Cataloguing in Publication Data
A catalogue record for this book is available from the British Library

Copyright © 2009 by Muna Ndulo and Margaret Grieco and contributors

All rights for this book reserved. No part of this book may be reproduced, stored in a retrieval system, or transmitted, in any form or by any means, electronic, mechanical, photocopying, recording or otherwise, without the prior permission of the copyright owner.

ISBN (10): 1-4438-0582-3, ISBN (13): 978-1-4438-0582-7

TABLE OF CONTENTS

List of Tables vii

List of Figures ix

Foreword x

Acknowledgements xv

Acronyms xvi

Introduction: Power, Gender and Social Change in Africa 1

Part I: Gender Mainstreaming, Politics, and Participation

1. Taking the Fast Track to Parliament:
   Comparing Electoral Gender Quotas in Eastern and Southern Africa
   Gretchen Bauer 8

2. Women's Rights Advocacy versus Gender and Development Programming:
   Complementary or Alternative Strategies?
   Marcia Greenberg 26

3. Radical Citizenship: Powerful Mothers and Equal Rights
   Judith Van Allen 60

4. The Economic Roots of African Women's Political Participation
   Claire Robertson 77

Part II: Activisim, Scholarship and Gender

5. Mobilizing for Change Locally and Globally
   African Women as Scholar-Activists in Feminist and Gender Studies
   Mary J. Osirim 94

6. The Anthropological Collaborator:
   Feminist Scholarship and Activism in Africa
   Diana J. Fox 112

Part III: Health, Education and Culture

7. Maternal Mortality and Transport:
Africa's Burden
Margaret Grieco 144

8. Women in Chinsapo, Malawi
Vulnerability and Risk of HIV/AIDS
Jayati Ghosh and Ezekiel Kalipeni 155

9. Islam and Girl's Schooling in Sub-Saharan Africa:
Exploring the Size and Sources of the Gender Gap in Education
Fatou Jah 177

10. Gender Equity in African Tertiary Education Systems
A Critical Look at Women's Progress
Philomina Okeke-Ihejirika 207

Part IV: Legal Framework, Human Rights, Conflict, and Economic Empowerment

11. Imagine All the Women
Power, Gender and the Transformative Possibilities of the South African Constitution
Penelope E. Andrews 232

12. Women and Inheritance under Customary Law:
The Response of the Courts
Muna Ndulo 251

13. Land Reforms, Land Titling and Gender Dilemmas In Africa
An Exploration of Issues
Susie Jacobs 271

14. Empowering Women in the African Entrepreneurial Landscape
Micro-entrepreneurs to Business Globalists in the Formal and Informal Sectors
Anita Spring 293

15. Armed Conflict, Displacement, Gender-based Violence in Africa and *Anomie*
The Case of Darfur
Kabahenda Nyakabwa 327

Bibliography 341

Notes on Contributors 377

Index 385

LIST OF TABLES

Table 1-1.
Women in Lower or Single Houses of Parliament in African Countries in Top 35 Worldwide: Pre- and Post-Transition Elections 22

Table 2-2.
Becoming a Human Rights Advocate Step by Step 35

Table 8-1.
Questions on gender issues: leaving husband or doing things without husband's knowledge 173

Table 8-2.
Questions on gender issues: certain actions that can or cannot be taken by a woman 173

Table 8-3.
General knowledge and attitudes about AIDS and condoms 174

Table 8-4.
Which of the following ways in which women might get infected with the AIDS virus are you most worried about for yourself? And how worried are you that you might catch AIDS? 175

Table 8-5.
What do you think is the best way to protect yourself from getting AIDS? 176

Table 9-1.
Estimates of the effect of Muslim composition (sq. rt. of % Muslims on the female to male ratio; i.e. size of the gender gap, in schooling) 187

Table 9-2.
Estimates of the effect of Muslim composition (sq. rt. of % Muslim) on the sources of the female to male ratio (i.e. size of gender gap) in schooling 197

Table 9-3.
Estimate of the effect of Muslim composition on the size of the female to male ratio in primary schooling (i.e. gender gap), SSA 199

Table 9-4.
Estimate of the effect of Muslim composition on the size of the female to male ratio in secondary schooling (i.e. gender gap), SSA 201

Table 9-5.
Estimates of the effect of Muslim composition on the sources of the female to male ratio in schooling (i.e. gender gap), SSA 202

Table 9-6.
Estimates of the effect of Muslim composition on the sources of female to male ratio in schooling. 203

Table 14-1.
Spatial and Operational Features of the Small Informal Sector in Harare 316

Table 14-2:
Informal and Formal Financial Activities for a Kenyan Woman 317

Table 14-3.
NGAE Members Interviewed by Business Position and Business Acquisition ... 318

LIST OF FIGURES

Figure 8-1.
Location of Chinsapo on the Southwestern Periphery of the City of
Lilongwe. Source: Authors.. 156

Figure 9-1.
Gross and net effects of religion on female-male ratio in schooling, SSA 194

Figure 9-2.
Gross and net effects of religion on the sources of the gender gap, SSA. 195

Figure 14-1.
Movement within and between sectors by size/type of business 319

Figure 14-2.
Some demographic characteristics 320

Figure 14-3.
Types of Enterprise/Firms (excludes e-commerce) 321

Figure 14-4.
Formalized-Informal Sector: Microcredit/finance, Sites and Services 322

Figure 14-5.
E-Commerce Categories, Use of Internet, Family, Shipping 323

Figure 14-6.
Sources of Start-up Capital by Informal and Formal Sector 324

Figure 14-7.
Sourcing and Markets by Informal and Formal Sector   325

Figure 14-8.
Membership in Networks and Associations by Informal and Formal Sector 326

FOREWORD

Adrien K. Wing

The problems facing African women in the twenty-first century are daunting. As has been the case for centuries, they continue to be suppressed in reactionary patriarchal cultures that limit their ability to thrive in both the public and private sectors. The global economic crisis is only the latest in the phenomena that disproportionally affect them. The burdens are enormous. As the Chinese proverb says: "women hold up more than half the sky."[1] I have termed the culmination of the denial of women's rights in all spheres "spirit injury," which envisions physical, psychological, spiritual, and cultural harm.[2] The effects can be "as devastating, as costly, and as physically obliterating as robbery or assault."[3] Symptoms of spirit injury, which can occur on an individual or group level, include "defilement, silence, denial, shame, guilt, fear, blaming the victim, violence, self-destructive behaviors, acute despair/emotional death, emasculation, trespass, and pollution."[4] Even when progressive international and national laws are drafted and policies are developed, little actually penetrates into the day-to-day lives of women.

The Cornell University Institute for African Development has contributed to our understanding of the issues affecting African women in the new millennium by producing this important collection. I was delighted to be the keynote speaker at the event that generated the chapters of this book—the April, 2006 conference on Power, Gender, and Social Change in Africa. Institute Director and volume editor Muna Ndulo and co-editor Margaret Grieco must be congratulated for gathering the distinguished group of multidisciplinary authors, who have written pieces that carefully excavate the myriad complexities of African women's lives. The coverage of the book is both broad and deep, including political participation, academe, law, health, education, culture, and economic empowerment.

I regard the problems concerning African women's issues as intersectional and multidimensional in nature.[5] In other words, the matters intertwine and cannot be regarded in isolation. Moreover, the issues are not additive in scope, but multiplicative. For example, underdevelopment is not a singular concern, but reflective of the overlap of educational, health, economic, and environmental factors. The contributions to this book are impressive because taken together, they educate us about the interwoven nature of oppression.

Detailing the impoverished status of African women's existence can be extraordinarily depressing. Many of us in the global north often regard African women with profound pity, sometimes bordering on condescension. We may slip into essentializing the women as global victims with little to no agency.

We forget that wonderful South African saying which is also the name of a modern play, "You strike the woman, you strike the rock."[6] Despite daunting circumstances, many African women exemplify strength and power. The first female President, Ellen Johnson Sirleaf of Liberia, has joined the boys' club of leaders. Courageous human rights advocate Unity Dow augmented the all-male ranks of the Botswana Supreme Court. Baleka Mbete was South African Speaker of the National Assembly. Annonciata Mukamugema of Rwanda has played a leadership role with AVEGA, the widow's network in a country still coping with the ravaging effects of the 1994 genocide. She has been given the African Women of Empowerment Project Award. Navanethen Pillay of South Africa has been appointed the United Nations High Commissioner of Human Rights. In Nigeria, Safiya Husseini and Amina Lawal dared challenge an Islamic law that would have resulted in their stoning for being pregnant outside of wedlock. Mamphela Ramphele, who began her career as an anti-apartheid activist, has been a managing director of the World Bank and Vice Chancellor of the University of Cape Town. As a result of her path-breaking environmental rights activism, Wangari Maathai became the first African woman to win the Nobel Peace Prize. There are undoubtedly countless unknown women who are on the forefront of implementing societal change in their own communities.

If we listen to African women's voices and needs as portrayed directly and indirectly in this book, we can gain information suitable to working together *with* them, rather than merely on their behalf. "Spirit warming" can replace spirit injury as we strive for a brighter future for Africa and the rest of the world.

If we respect the knowledge gleaned from the text of each author, we may be able to learn some lessons applicable for western society as well. For example, the U.S. has much to learn from the South African experience described in Professor Andrews' chapter *Imagine All the Women: Power, Gender and Transformative Possibilities of the South*

African Constitution. Perhaps one day, the U.S. will have an equality clause that includes gender and sexual orientation as South Africa does.[7] The South African equality clause also covers race, sex, pregnancy, marital status, ethnic or social origin, color, age, disability, religion, conscience, belief, culture, language and birth.[8] Maybe the U.S. could aim, as South Africa does, to provide substantive justice, not merely procedural justice.

In my own work, I have illustrated how Africa has made a critical contribution to the development of women's rights[9] by devising the Women's Protocol[10] of the African Charter on Human and People's Rights.[11] The Banjul Charter's protocol is the first regional treaty devoted specifically to women's rights. It is the first covenant to explicitly mention abortion, and to call for the legal prohibition of female genital surgery. Thus, Africans did not limit themselves to the contours of what other treaties had already said. They have pushed the envelope in ways that may show a path for other parts of the world.

In reviewing the major challenges confronting African women, this book gives us cause for hope in the twenty-first century. A progressive agenda for social change can be culled from the contributions—an agenda that represents the need for multifaceted solutions for the multifaceted problems.

More African women must have the opportunity to become nation-builders as well as world-builders. Those women who are already doing so, such as those mentioned above, need to become more well-known on the global stage. Educational levels for females must approach international standards to enable girls and women to fully participate in all arenas.

On the constitutional level, I have been deeply honored to work with the founding mothers of two African countries—South Africa and Rwanda. Electoral quota systems discussed herein are one way to jump-start the kind of participation in the legislative sector that is needed to implement even the best constitution. Putting women in governmental positions in all three branches is a necessary piece of the development puzzle.

Additionally, more women must become involved outside the government sector in *both* women's rights advocacy and in gender and development planning. Customary norms that impede women, such as the inability to own or inherit land, coupled with polygamy and low marriage ages, must be tackled to permit participation in the private sector. While microfinance projects are important, more women must reap the benefits of national agribusiness and natural resources development. Why should women receive $500 loans, while men receive and often mismanage 5 million to 5 billion?

A vibrant academic sector for women can create the space for theorizing about Africa's problems and solutions in ways that are not possible in other areas. Internet resources can make massive collections of data available in Burundi. Videoconferencing can connect Iowa City to Harare. More opportunities for academic exchanges, rather than one way brain drain are essential to enhance the creation of future lecturers and the ongoing support of beleaguered professors.

None of the accomplishments in other areas are possible if health care for women is not prioritized, whether it be prenatal visits or pap smears. HIV rates cannot come down unless the ability to say no to unprotected sex is culturally and personally possible. Gender-based violence cannot be reduced unless every culture around the world combats cultural norms and teaches that violence is not an acceptable way to deal with loved ones. Just as you would not want someone to hurt your mother or sister, so you should not hurt someone else's mother or sister.

Any ambitious agenda for social change cannot advance the cause of women's rights unless men are as involved as women in that struggle. Women's issues cannot afford to be tokenized or ghettoized. It will take male Presidents, legislators, business people, doctors, farmers, and activists to work alongside women to craft and implement the solutions addressed and implied by this book. It will take husbands and fathers as well as wives and mothers to talk to their sons and daughters about gender-based violence. It will take men and women to value the birth of female children as much as that of male children.

Finally, great perseverance will be required to advance women beyond token numbers in all the sectors mentioned in this volume. It will not happen to the degree that we would like in most of our lifetimes. Problems of patriarchy and misogyny have existed for centuries. Victory cannot be judged by arrival at some preset finish line, but in the quality of the journey to get there. We must pace ourselves for a marathon, not a sprint. Nelson Mandela has an autobiography entitled "The struggle is my Life." The battle for gender justice must be part of all of our lives, whether in Africa or America. "Power, Gender and Social Change in Africa" makes a vital contribution to that struggle.

Notes

Many thanks to Professor Muna Ndulo for inviting me to do the keynote for the conference. Also, thanks to my research assistant Peter Nadimi for his help with this foreword.

[1] See Anna Han, "Women Holding Up more than Half the Sky," in *Global Critical Race Feminism: An International Reader,* 392 (Adrien Katherine Wing ed., NYU Press 2000).

[2] See Adrien Katherine Wing, "Women's Rights and Africa's Evolving Landscape: The Women's Protocol of the Banjul Charter," in *Africa: Mapping New Boundaries in International Law* 13 (Jeremy Levitt ed., Hart 2008).

[3] See Patricia Williams, "Spirit-Murdering the Messenger: The Discourse of Finger-Pointing as the Law's Response to Racism," 42 U. *Miami L. Rev.* 127, 129 (1987).

[4] See Adrien Katherine Wing & Richard Johnson, The Promise of the Post-Genocide Constitution: Healing Rwandan Spirit Injuries, 7 Mich. J. Race & L. 247, 289 (2002).

[5] See Adrien Katherine Wing, *Introduction to Global Critical Race Feminism: An International Reader* 1 (Adrien Katherine Wing ed., NYU Press 2000).

[6] See Strike the Rock Foundation, available at: http://striketherock.isat.co.za/Index_files/page0001.htm.

[7] See Adrien Katherine Wing and Samuel Nielson, "An Agenda for the Obama Administration on Gender Equality: Lessons from Abroad," 107 *Mich. L. Rev.* First Impressions 124 (2009), available at: http://www.michiganlawreview.org/first impressions/vol107/wing&nielson.pdf; Adrien Katherine Wing, "Race Across Boundaries: the South African Constitution Role Models for the U.S.," 24 *Harvard Blackletter J.* 73 (2008); Adrien Katherine Wing, "The Fifth Anniversary of the South African Constitution: a Role Model on Sexual Orientation," 26 *Vermont L. Rev.* 821 (2002).

[8] South African Const. art. 9 (1996).

[9] Wing, supra note 2.

[10] See Protocol to the *African Charter on Human and People's Rights* on the Rights of Women in Africa (11 July 2003), http://www.africa-union.org/home/ Welcome.htm.

[11] See African Charter on Human and People's Rights (adopted 27 June 1981, entered into force 21 October 1986), OAU Doc CAB/LEG/67/3/rev.5 (1982) 21ILM 58.

ACKNOWLEDGEMENTS

This book is based on papers presented at a conference organized by the Institute for African Development (IAD) from 21–22 April, 2006. We would like to acknowledge and thank those who made this conference possible through financial assistance and otherwise: Ravi Kanbur (T.H. Lee Professor of World Affairs, Cornell University) and Cornell University departments and units including the Einaudi Center for International Studies; the Africana Studies and Research Center; Cornell Institute for Public Affairs (CIPA); the Department of History; the Feminist, Gender, and Sexuality Studies Program; and the Gender and Global Change Program. Thanks also to the Conference Committee composed of Josephine Allen, Margaret Washington, Mechthild Nagel, Judith Van Allen and Margaret Grieco. The conference would not have been possible without the hard work of IAD staff Jackie Sayegh, Program Manager, and Alexis Boyce, Assistant Program Coordinator. They handled the logistics of the conference efficiently, with patience and unconditional support. I would also like to thank the contributors and Evangeline Ray, Assistant Program Coordinator, IAD, who painstakingly edited the manuscript and remained unfailingly committed to the project throughout its preparation for publication. Thanks goes also to Anna Herforth for providing the cover photo. Sincere thanks to our publishers, Cambridge scholars, for their inputs and for publishing this book.

ACRONYMS

AAWORD	Association of African Women for Research and Development
ABC	AIDS prevention strategy: A=Abstinence; B=Be Faithful; C= Condoms
ACB	Anti-Corruption Bureau
AFWE	African Federation of Women Entrepreneurs
AIDS	Acquired immunodeficiency syndrome
ANC	African National Congress
ASCA	Accumulating Savings and Credit Associations
ASA	African Studies Association
AWID	Association for Women's Rights in Development
BAOBAB	Organization for women's human rights in Nigeria
BDP	Botswana Democratic Party
BFA	Black Feminist Anthropology
CAR	Central African Republic
CEDAW	Convention on the Elimination of Discrimination against Women
CEDPA	Center for Development and Population Activities
CEELI	Central European And Eurasian Law Initiative
CPA	Community Property Association
CSW	Commercial sex worker
DAWN	Development Alternatives with Women for a New Era
DHS	Demographic and Health Surveys
DTS	Development and Training Systems
ECOWAS	Economic Community of West African States
EISA	European Institute for Sustainable Development in Agriculture
FGM/FC	Female genital mutilation / female cutting
FIDA	Federation of Women Lawyers Kenya
FMRA	World Forum on Agrarian Reform
FTPT	First past the post (electoral system)
GAD	Gender and Development
GAWE	Ghanaian Association of Women Entrepreneurs
GDA	Gender and Development Approaches
GDI	Gender-related Development Index of UNDP
GEE	Generalized estimating equation
GEM	Gender Empowerment Index
GLTF	Gender Land Task Force

GWIP	Global Women in Politics
GWS Africa	Gender and Women's Studies for Africa's Transformation Project
HBE	Home-based Enterprises
HDI	Human Development Index of UNDP
HIV	Juman immunodeficiency virus
HPI	Human Poverty Index of UNDP
HRBA	Human Rights-Based Approach
HRW	Human Rights Watch
ICCPR	International Covenant on Civil and Political Rights
ICESCR	International Covenant on Economic, Social and Cultural Rights
ICG	International Crisis Group
IDP	Internally Displaced Persons
IDS	Institute of Development Studies
IDW	Internally Displaced Women
IPU	Inter-Parliamentary Union
IFI	International Financial Institutions
IPPF	International Planned Parenthood Federation
JEM	Justice Equality Movement
MDG	Millenium Development Goals
MDICP	Malawi Diffusion and Ideational Change Project
MMR	Maternal Mortality Rate
MP	Members of Parliament
MSF	Médecins sans frontiers
MST	Landless People's Movement
NDI	National Democratic Institute
NEPAD	New Partnership for Africa's Development
NGAE	New Generation of African Entrepreneurs
NGO	Non-government organization
OCHA	Office for the Coordination of Humanitarian Affairs
OECD	Organization for Economic Cooperation and Development
OHCHR	Office of the United Nations High Commissioner for Human Rights
PR	Proportional Representation
PRDs	Pregnancy-related dropouts
ROSCA	Informal Rotating Savings and Credit Associations
SADC	Southern African Development Community
SAEN	South Africa Enterprise Network

SAP	Structural Adjustment Program
SGBV	Sexual and Gender-Based Violence
SID	Society for International Development
SLA	Sudan Liberation Army
SME	Small to Medium Enterprise
SOE	State-owned Enterprise
SSA	Sub-Saharan Africa
TFNs	transnational feminist networks
TWLA	Tanzania Women Lawyers Association
UDF	United Democratic Front (political party, Malawi)
UNDP	United Nations Development Program
UNFPA	United National Population Fund
UNHCR	UN High Commission for Refugees
UNRISD	UN Research Institute for Social Development
UOA	Ukimwi Orphans Assistance
USAID	U.S. Agency for International Development
UWEL	Uganda Women Entrepreneurs Ltd.
WID	Women in Development
WAD	Women and Development
WAEN	West Africa Enterprise Network
WiLDAF	Women in Law and Development in Africa
WLRI	Women's Legal Rights Initiative
WLSA	Women and Law in Southern Africa
WLUML	Women Living Under Muslim Laws
WTO	World Trade Organization

INTRODUCTION: POWER, GENDER AND SOCIAL CHANGE IN AFRICA

Muna Ndulo and Margaret Grieco

The importance of recognizing the significance of gender in assessing power relationships and access to resources—including education, wage-based employment, mental and physical health, health care, adequate nutrition, and housing—cannot be overemphasized. According to a recent World Bank report, Engendering Development through Gender Equality in Rights, Resources, and Voice,[1] careful attention must be given in several critical areas.

Central to this discussion is the fact that enormous disparities exist between men and women in basic rights, access to resources, and the power to determine the future in Africa and around the globe. Understanding and accounting for the links among gender, public policy and development outcomes can improve the effectiveness of policy formulation and development. It has been well documented that poverty—especially extreme poverty all over the world—is a very serious and complex issue and that gender is one of its most critical dimensions.

A review of progress since the 1985 Nairobi UN World Conference on Women highlights areas of particular urgency that stand out as priorities for action. The 1995 Beijing UN World Conference—Beijing Plus Five—and the Millennium Development Goals again highlight gender as both a central and critical component to the alleviation of poverty.

In providing for the lack of policy options on critical issues facing societies and the world, the Institute for African Development and Cornell are greatly influenced by the Land Grant University philosophy, where service is a priority. This book proceeds on the assumption that academia matters when it comes to knowledge and analytical skills in addressing societal problems. Issues such as the ones dealt with in this book recognize the importance of gender in assessing power relationships, access to resources, wage-based employment, mental and physical health, and adequate nutrition or housing.

The importance and timeliness of the issues addressed in this book in the context of today's world are not debatable. A number of conventions and declarations have been adopted over the years to deal with such issues: the Convention for the Elimination of all forms of Discrimination Against Women,[2] the 1993 International Conference on Human Rights in Vienna[3] where the mantra, "Women's Rights are Human Rights," was coined; the Nairobi Conference; the Fourth World on Women in Beijing and the Millennium Development Goals (2000), to name a few. Many countries have adopted progressive domestic legal frameworks. Yet women's rights are flouted and women remain the majority of the poor, the unemployed, and the dispossessed.

Since their adoption the Millennium Development Goals (or MDGs) have taken center stage in the development discourse. Progress in every sector is measured against the eight world targets to reduce poverty and hunger, disease, child mortality, maternal mortality; HIV/AIDS, malaria and other diseases while promoting gender equality, education, and sustainable development. The interconnected world we live in demands a standard set of measures to keep us focused on the common goals of humanity.

It is now 2009, twenty-four years after the Nairobi Conference, fourteen years after the Beijing Conference and well over half-way to the target date for reaching the Millennium Development Goals. In relation to the goal of promoting gender equality, the score card does not look good. The Secretary-General in his report to the 2006 Commission on the Status of Women pointed out that "in no country in the world has women's full de jure and de facto equality been achieved."[4] A Gender Links Publication,[5] "Missing the Mark? Audit of the Southern African Development Community's Declaration on Gender and Development: Women in Decision-Making" has observed that laws, systems and services for addressing gender violence are inadequate. New forms of gender violence, such as human trafficking, are on the rise. HIV/AIDS, the pandemic which more than any other has preyed on the gender disparities in Africa, is negatively impacting on positive gains made. The current food and financial crisis is exacerbating an already critical situation. In most countries poverty is on the rise and increasingly it has a feminine face. While there has been some progress in raising awareness and challenging gender stereotypes in the media and popular culture, as well as in engaging men as partners, the battle to change the mind-set is still far from won. The number one lesson learned is that there is a propensity on the part of leaders to sign declarations and commitments without any intention or plan for delivering on these promises. As a result the effective implementation, monitoring and evaluation of gender policies, programs and activities continue to elude those charged with the responsibility of accounting to the public as the gap between policy and practice widens.

The failure to make progress is apparent not only within countries but in the international system as well. At a conference on UN reform and human rights, Stephen Lewis, the UN Special Envoy for HIV/AIDS in Africa, lamented on how the multilateral system is disgorging a high-level panel of fifteen people to look at the redesign of all those areas of the United Nations system which so significantly address the lives of women, yet only three members of the panel are women.[6] He remarked that when he read the composition of the High Level Panel, the natural instinct was to throw up one's hands in dismay and ask: "When will things ever change? What do you have to do to get multilateralism to embrace even the simplest element of gender equality: the element called parity?" He said he was reminded by extension of the Commission on Africa appointed by the British Prime Minister Tony Blair, with three women among seventeen men.[7] He observed that it was no coincidence to find the weakest part of the Commission's report was the way it dealt with—or more accurately failed to deal with—the women of Africa.

On the question of strategies to be employed in the achievement of gender equality, as Kofi Annan has observed in the report "In Larger Freedom: towards Development, Security and Human Rights for All,"[8] "The world must advance the causes of security, development and human rights together, otherwise none will succeed. Humanity will not enjoy security without development; it will not enjoy development without security; and it will not enjoy either without respect for human rights." In other words, gender equality is intrinsic to security and development. Unless women are able to exercise their human rights freely in societies in which they live, true development will not take place. As a leading South African NGO, Gender Links has observed that many processes are in place which aim at targets, measures and practical indicators. Some of these processes were in place before the MDGs, and what is particularly important about these global efforts is the increasing emphasis placed on women's rights being at the core of any strategy to achieve equality between women and men, in other words, prioritizing the strategic over the practical. Thus, for example, it is pointless to talk about women's empowerment when women do not have access to land, property and credit. Similarly, there is little point in talking about ABC in relation to AIDS when women do not have the choice to abstain.

This book contains chapters from an interdisciplinary group of scholars, including sociologists, economists, political scientists, anthropologists, historians and others to discuss these important issues. The chapters of the book include analysis of strategic gender initiatives, case studies, research, and policies as well as conceptual and theoretical pieces. Chapter one addresses promoting gender equality and women's participation in parliament and political efficacy; chapter two looks at mobilization and activism and gender mainstreaming. Chapter three, while taking a case study perspective, discusses political leadership and social transformation. Chapter four examines gender and its importance in the development process by looking at the economic roots of African women's political participation; Chapter five revisits the issue of mobilization by looking at it through scholarship and gender studies. Chapter six continues the debate on mobilization and scholarship. Chapters seven and eight take on the issue of health and gender by looking at maternal mortality and transport, and women's vulnerability and risk of AIDS infection. Chapters nine and ten address the issue of education by looking at Islam and gender inequality in education and access and representation in higher education. Chapters eleven and twelve examine gender, human rights, customary law and the impact of traditional values on gender relations. Women face some of the greatest challenges in the labor and production sectors. Chapters thirteen and fourteen focus on land rights and agricultural sustainability and women's contributions. The final chapter, fifteen, looks at how conflict and its attendant effects—displacement and violence—impact on women.

This book will have achieved its purpose if through its discussion of the challenges, achievements and lessons learned in efforts to attain gender equality it contributes to research, informs teaching and activism, and encourages the exchange of ideas, resources and recorded experiences as well as sharing theoretical models and best practices for engaging the issues of power, gender and social change in Africa and around the world.

Notes

[1] Engendering Development through Gender Equality in Rights, Resource, and Voice. Mason, Andrew D., King, Elizabeth M., 2001/01/31. Report # 21776, Volume 1.

[2] Convention for the elimination of all forms of discrimination against women, adopted by the UN General Assembly 1979.

[3] 1993 World Conference on Human Rights, June 14–15, 1993, Vienna, Austria.

[4] Secretary General's Report, 2006, Commission on the Status of Women, UN Division for the Advancement of Women.

[5] Gender Links. http://www.genderlinks.org.za

[6] http://www.choike.org/nuevo_eng/informes/5439.html

[7] In early 2004, the British Prime Minister, Tony Blair, established the Commission for Africa. The 17 members of the Commission published their report "Our Common Interest" in March 2005.

[8] 'In Larger Freedom': Towards Development, Security and Human Rights For All. *UN Publications,* July 25, 2005.

Part I

Gender Mainstreaming, Politics, and Participation

CHAPTER ONE
TAKING THE FAST TRACK TO PARLIAMENT:
Comparing Electoral Gender Quotas in Eastern and Southern Africa

Gretchen Bauer

Introduction

During the past fifteen years large numbers of women have entered parliaments in several east and southern African countries. As of mid-2006 Burundi, Rwanda, Tanzania, Uganda, Mozambique, Namibia, South Africa and Seychelles all had national legislatures that included from 25 to nearly 50 percent women, placing them in the top 30 nations worldwide in terms of numbers of women in national legislatures. This is far above the African regional and world averages of about 17 percent women in a single or lower house of parliament (www.ipu.org/wmn-e/classif.htm). This development is part of a global trend whereby women are using gender-based electoral quotas to take a "fast track" to equal legislative representation (Dahlerup and Freidenvall 2005). Rather than following the example of Scandinavia, where decades of socio-economic development and changes in cultural attitude finally allowed large numbers of women to enter the national legislature, women around the world are using a variety of gender-based electoral quotas to gender their parliaments, sometimes 'overnight' (in one election).[1]

Several Asian, European and Latin American countries have utilized gender-based electoral quotas with similar success, though nowhere in the world has the rate of increase in women's representation matched that of Africa (Dahlerup and Freidenvall 2005, 33; Tripp 2004, 72). The increased use of quotas across Africa reflects a renewed interest in formal politics and political institutions among African women's movements. Shireen Hassim and Sheila Meintjes (2005, 4) argue that efforts to break down the barriers to women's equal political participation "signal that there is room for women's agency to shape politics, and that formal political rights are an important precondition for advancing equitable social policies" for women. Bringing African women into national legislatures in significant numbers is one part of this effort.

A few recent studies have examined this phenomenon of increasing numbers of women in several African parliaments. Three of these comparative studies identify a similar set of factors accounting for the rise in women's legislative presence. Gretchen Bauer and Hannah E. Britton (2006a), in the introduction to a book based on dozens of interviews with women members of parliament (MPs) in five countries, find that these success stories share common characteristics. All have experienced a political transition following a period of prolonged conflict in the past twenty years (civil war, liberation struggle, genocide, guerilla insurgency). These conflicts—and the roles women played in them at home and abroad—contributed to an available cadre of capable women candidates to stand for public office. Moreover, during the political transitions in the post-conflict period, women activists and their organizations inserted themselves into the processes of crafting new constitutions and drafting new laws that provided the legal foundations and political frameworks for the institutions and mechanisms to bring more women into political office (namely, the use of certain types of electoral systems and gender quotas). Critical to this process were national women's movements and organizations and the pressure they exerted on (usually dominant) political parties to adopt the strategies and mechanisms that led to women's increased representation. Finally, a global women's movement, to which many African women were exposed in the course of conflict (and to which they contributed substantially in a variety of international forums such as the United Nations conferences on women), has also played a significant role.

International IDEA's (Ballington 2004a) study of women's increased electoral representation across Africa draws many of the same conclusions. In the final chapter, Ballington identifies the use of specific electoral systems and quotas, the strength and cohesion of national women's movements, pressure exerted by international women's movements and organizations, and the strategic use of windows of political opportunity as the factors giving rise to women's increased political representation in Africa in the 1990s and 2000s. A Gender Links survey of six southern African countries ties women's increased representation to a proportional representation (PR) electoral system and party-based gender quotas or reserved seats for women. Moreover, the survey also finds that the countries with the highest proportion of women in politics have recently emerged from struggle or conflict situations, or have ruling parties with social democratic inclinations, or both (Morna 2004b).[2]

Clearly, gender-based electoral quotas are key to increasing women's legislative representation with the factors cited in the studies above determining *whether or not* quotas will be adopted—and *what types* of quotas will be adopted. For purposes of comparison, it is interesting to note that the percentages of women in national parliaments in several Southern African Development Community (SADC) countries that do not utilize quotas are merely at or well below the African (and world) average for single or lower houses of parliament: Mauritius' parliament is composed of 17.1 percent women, Zimbabwe's of 16.7 percent (since 2005), Botswana's of 11.1 percent, and Malawi's of 13.9 percent (since 2004). Women comprise 10.8 percent of Swaziland's parliament (since 2003), 11.7 percent of Lesotho's (since 2002), and 12.7 percent of Zambia's (since 2001) (see www.ipu.org). (Angola and the Democratic Republic of Congo are still in transition; Angola is yet to schedule parliamentary elections and the DRC has just held them.) This poor showing is despite a declaration signed by all SADC heads of state in 1997 committing themselves and their countries to 30 percent women in positions of political power and decision-making by 2005 (with a clear emphasis on national legislatures). The four countries that met or nearly met the SADC target (included among the six below) all use some kind of voluntary party-based quota or special seats.

The six countries discussed in this chapter more or less conform to the trajectory described in the studies above, with one interesting difference.[3] The three southern African cases have all increased the number of women MPs using a PR electoral system and voluntary political party-based quotas. The three east African cases have utilized a mix of electoral systems and mandatory 'special' or 'reserved' seats for women. Indeed, gender-based electoral quotas may take different forms. In Africa they have largely been of two kinds: reserved or appointed seats intended to determine at least a minimum number of seats to be held by women, or measures adopted voluntarily by political parties aimed at influencing the number of women candidates (Tripp 2004, 73).[4] While the former are nearly always legal quotas, the latter may be voluntary or mandatory. The remainder of this chapter elaborates the two regionally-based alternatives and discusses their implications for women's political empowerment and social and economic advancement.

The Southern African Cases: Mozambique, Namibia and South Africa

Mozambique, Namibia and South Africa all emerged from conflict situations in the early 1990s—Mozambique from decades of civil war, Namibia from decades of war for political independence, and South Africa from decades of struggle for a democratic and non-racial South Africa.[5] In all three cases women were part and parcel of the conflicts (Urdang 1989, Becker 1995, Britton 2005). In the latter two cases thousands of women spent decades in exile, in some cases fighting alongside male counterparts as armed combatants, in other cases gaining critical skills and experience at schools and universities abroad. Upon their return many of these women, well versed in feminist theory and praxis from experience overseas and well aware of the pitfalls of national independence from experience elsewhere in Africa, joined forces with women at home to press for new gender dispensations in the post-conflict period, including a formal role for women in the political process (Seidman 1995). In Namibia a small number of women members of the Constituent Assembly played a key role in shaping Namibia's gender-progressive constitution, and one woman MP was largely responsible for the adoption of a gender quota for local elections shortly after independence (Bauer 2006, 100-101). In South Africa women activists and exiles came together in the early 1990s to form a national women's organization, develop a national plan of action and ultimately influence the unfolding constitutional negotiations such that South Africa too has one of the most gender-progressive constitutions in the world today (Britton 2006, 64-65). In Mozambique too, women fought alongside male counterparts both from without (in exile) and within the rebel movement (Morna 2004b, 53). In Mozambique in the early 1990s women began to organize themselves into many new groups with the express purpose of educating women voters at the grassroots level to participate effectively in all phases of the electoral process (Abreu 2004b, 62).

With independence in Namibia, democratic rule in South Africa and an end to war and transition to multiparty politics in Mozambique, PR electoral systems were adopted in all three countries for national legislative elections. In South Africa this was done with the recognition that PR systems are more favorable to women (though there were other reasons as well for adopting the system).[6] While there is no evidence that women's electoral outcomes figured into the choice of a PR system at the national level in Namibia, the decision in 2002 to retain a PR system for local legislative elections was made in part on the argument that PR systems favor women (Britton 2006, 65-66; Bauer 2006, 91). In South Africa and Mozambique, meanwhile, the two ruling parties—the African National Congress (ANC) and the Front for the Liberation of Mozambique (Frelimo) respectively—adopted 30 percent quotas for their candidate lists for National Assembly elections, the ANC before the 1994 election and Frelimo at its sixth party congress in 1992 (Myakayaka-Manzini 2004; Abreu 2004b). Subsequently, both parties committed themselves to the equal distribution of women's names (every third name a woman's) throughout their candidate lists (Myakayaka 2004; Disney 2006). Colleen Lowe Morna (2004, 62) argues that internal struggles to secure the ANC's 30 percent quota have been "a key mobilizing tool for women, and a critical component of transforming the attitudes of men within the party." In Namibia, meanwhile, women's organizations have exerted considerable pressure on political parties since before the 1999 election. Like South Africa, Namibia has an active 50/50 campaign, and a 50/50 bill has been drafted and presented to parliament. Still, political parties have not formally adopted gender quotas, though for the last two elections most candidate lists have been at or close to 30 percent women. But women's names have not always been well distributed throughout party lists with the result that women's representation in the National Assembly has stagnated at 25 percent.

The East African Cases: Rwanda, Tanzania and Uganda

Rwanda, Tanzania and Uganda have also experienced transitions in the past two decades. Uganda was first, with the National Resistance Movement (NRM) wresting power from the last in a series of dictatorial and military regimes in 1986. Tanzania followed a more peaceful path to political transition with amendments to its constitution in 1992 that proscribed a one-party political system and commenced the transition to a multiparty political system. Rwanda's transition came on the heels of an aborted democratic opening, war, and the genocide of up to one million people. In these cases too, it has been argued, women's enhanced participation in the political process in the post-conflict and post-transition period stems in part from their participation in the conflicts. In Uganda, with already-existing contacts in the NRM, women activists in the late 1980s were invited by the new president to identify women leaders for leadership positions in government (Tripp 2006, 112). Sylvia Tamale (1999) argues that President Yoweri Museveni was receptive to women's increased participation in politics in part because of their participation in the armed struggle that brought him and his movement to power. In Rwanda, women were prominent among the civil society activists who pressured government for reform beginning in 1989; indeed, they were specifically targeted during the 1994 genocide. Women's groups took a leading role in the post-genocide period, helping Rwandans to reconstruct their lives. Over time they experienced growing public influence which they were able to translate into political power (Longman 2006, 138). In Tanzania, not marked by the kind of conflict experienced in Uganda or Rwanda, women activists from the Tanzania Gender Networking Project have monitored closely the reserved seat system, put in place following the 1992 political transition, for its impact on women MPs and women's representation (Morna 2004b, 60).

In east Africa the mechanisms used to gender parliaments have differed from those in southern Africa. In Uganda a first-past-the-post electoral system (FPTP) has been utilized for directly elected 'constituency' MPs since the country's first post-transition election in 1989. In addition, reserved 'district' seats for women were introduced during that election by expanding the Ugandan parliament to include extra seats for women only (one from each district in the country). In 1995 a revised constitution institutionalized the quota system by providing for a number of reserved seats in the national parliament equal to the number of districts in the country.[7] The women MPs from the district seats are now elected from all-female lists of candidates by male-dominated electoral colleges whose members are drawn from local councils and women's councils; by contrast the constituency MPs are elected by universal adult suffrage (Tamale 2004, 38). The constitution also provides for reserved seats for workers, the youth, the disabled and the army, of which five out of 25 must also be women (www.ipu.org/parlinee/reports/ 2329_A.htm).

In Rwanda, as in southern Africa, the critical moment for increasing women's national legislative representation came with the drawing up of a new constitution. According to Judith Kanakuze (2004, 96), a transition government in power from July 1994 to May 2003 had the "political will" to establish institutional mechanisms to promote gender equality. The government was responding in part to pressure from women's organizations and networks that conducted a multi-pronged campaign to increase awareness, conduct training, evaluate indicators of equality and equity and strengthen the advocacy and lobbying skills of women (Kanakuze 2004, 96).[8] Mona Lena Krook (2005) suggests that the RPF government was also positively influenced by its exile experiences in Uganda and its contacts with South Africa's ANC.[9] Rwanda now elects its lower house of parliament using a PR electoral system but with reserved seats, appointed separately by electoral colleges, for women (and, as in Uganda, a few other groups). Article 76 of the constitution mandates that the Chamber of Deputies be composed of 80 members—53 elected by universal suffrage plus 24 women members (30 percent of the total) elected from the provinces and the city of Kigali (two representatives from each); in addition two seats are reserved for the youth and one for the handicapped. Interestingly, in the first election (2003) under the new constitution 48.8 percent of members elected to the Chamber of Deputies were women, meaning that women won many more than just the seats reserved for women (Longman 2006, 141).

In Tanzania, a small number of 'special' seats for women existed during the single-party era, though not for the purpose of redressing historic imbalances, but rather with the goal of enhancing the representation of varied interests in a one-party regime (Meena 2004, 82-83). Since the political transition in the early 1990s Tanzania has continued to set aside seats for women; 15 percent of parliamentary seats were reserved in 1995, increased to 20 percent for the 2000 election, and women were to comprise "not less than 30 percent of all members" for the 2005 election.[10] The move to increase the number of reserved seats for women in 2005 was intended to ensure that Tanzania met the Southern African Development Community's 30 percent target by 2005.[11] For the legislature's 232 directly elected seats, a first-past-the-post electoral system is utilized. Seventy-five additional seats are reserved for women; they are elected by political parties on the basis of proportional representation among the parties. [In addition, five seats are indirectly elected from Zanzibar, of which two must be women; and ten appointed by the president, of which five must be women.] With 30.4 percent women in its National Assembly since the 2005 election, Tanzania has reached the highest percentage of women in parliament ever achieved under a majoritarian electoral system (IPU 2006).

Cases Compared: Party-based Quotas versus Reserved Seats for Women

What do we find when we compare the types of quotas used—party-based gender quotas in southern Africa and reserved seats for women in east Africa?[12] Rwanda has the greatest number of women in parliament of any country in the world—48.8 percent—since its 2003 election, the first election to use electoral gender quotas. In Mozambique and South Africa, Tanzania and Uganda, the progress for women in parliament has been steady over the last three national elections (see Table 1-1), with Mozambique and South Africa above 30 percent women and Uganda and Tanzania approaching or at 30 percent women in parliament at mid-decade. In Namibia the percentage of women MPs doubled from the 1994 to 1999 election and then remained the same for the 2004 election (25 percent of voting members). In terms of which type of quota is more effective in sending significant numbers of women to parliament, the answer appears to be that steady increments have been made under both systems. Only Namibia, with no formally adopted or legislated quotas, lags behind the other five.

Party-based voluntary quotas

Looking in more detail at party-based quotas, we note that in Mozambique and South Africa a specific combination has led to the achievement of more than 30 percent women in national legislatures: voluntary (though internally-mandated) 30 percent quotas on the part of the dominant party in each country, with women required by the parties to be evenly dispersed throughout candidate lists (and the use of closed list PR electoral systems). In Namibia, by contrast, a number of political parties have aimed for, but have not required, 30 percent women on their candidate lists; moreover they have not mandated that the women be dispersed throughout the lists, with the result that the same percentage of women—5 percent less than the SADC goal—were elected in the 1999 and 2004 elections (LeBeau and Dima 2005). In Namibia there has been some 'contagion' in the sense of smaller parties following the ruling party's lead in 'aiming' for more women, though in Mozambique and South Africa other parties have generally not followed the ruling parties' leads. [At the same time, it has been suggested that in Mozambique and South Africa other parties have sought to 'headhunt' individual women candidates, thereby showing the power of the quota idea, while not embracing it fully (Morna 2004b).] Clearly, if party-based quotas are not nationally legislated (or at least internally mandated by all political parties), their use will be uneven. Moreover, the placement of women's names on candidate lists is critical; therefore a 'placement mandate' must also be specified (Matland 2006, 283). Finally, though this has not been an issue to date in Mozambique or South Africa, sanctions for non-compliance are generally recognized as essential for political party-based quotas to be effective (Matland 2006, 283).

All three southern African cases represent dominant-party political systems. Paradoxically, this factor has contributed to the high representation of women; in all three cases the dominant parties have been the ones most willing to slate women candidates and, with their large majorities in parliament, they have significantly raised the percentage of women MPs. Indeed, Hassim and Meintjes (2005, 21) argue that bringing more women into parliament is "relatively costless electorally" when a PR electoral system is combined with a dominant party political system. Dominant-party systems make gender quotas "politically cheap (and therefore politically saleable)" in that "extending a quota to women does mean that some men will not get onto party lists, but with sufficient power a dominant party can in any case exert control over the women they place on party lists." Proportional-representation electoral systems, as many have observed, also mean that individual MPs—male or female—lack constituencies. Rather, the only constituency to which the MP is accountable is the political party. All of this leads to concerns about party paternalism and concerns about women MPs' abilities to push for gender equality platforms. Under such circumstances, the question follows, will gender ever supersede party? Parliamentary women's caucuses that bring together women MPs across party lines have been mooted as one response to this concern. In all three countries, however, they have floundered. In Namibia a caucus has been formed, though how effective it has been is highly debatable (Bauer 2006). In South Africa the parliamentary women's group has been superseded by another body, the Joint Monitoring Committee (Britton 2006, 73), while in Mozambique a six-member team of women MPs (three each from the two main parties) has been working since 1997 to form a parliamentary women's caucus.[13]

Special or reserved seats

Turning to special or reserved seats, in Uganda by the time of the 2006 election there were 74 reserved seats for women out of a total 322 seats (a 22.9 percent quota)—69 district-based seats and five seats from among the 25 reserved for workers, the youth, the disabled and the army (Bauer forthcoming). In addition to those 74 seats, women in Uganda were directly elected to 14 constituency seats in the national legislature and one more woman was elected to an additional seat for the army for a total of 89 parliamentary seats (27.6 percent). Interestingly, there was fierce competition for some of the reserved district seats, with some prominent women MPs losing to lesser known women candidates. This prompted speculation that more women might be persuaded in the future to run for the directly elected seats, although the challenges of doing so remain many (Muhumuza 2006).

At the same time, many problems with the reserved seat system in Uganda, in particular with the way that district women MPs are elected, have been identified. At a most fundamental level, Anne Marie Goetz argues, the 'add-on' mechanism used in Uganda, whereby "new public space reserved exclusively for women..." is created, is highly problematic

(2003, 118). Rather than "giving women advantages in political contests with men," thereby allowing them to compete on an equal footing with men, district-based reserved seats for women only "have negative implications for the perceived legitimacy, and ultimately the political effectiveness, of women politicians" (2003, 118). The add-on mechanism, in Goetz's view, reinforces a politics of patronage: it is based "on a principle of extending patronage to a new clientele, and indeed of 'extending the state.'" Former Ugandan MP Miria Matembe (2006, 9) confirms this view: as a patronage opportunity, she argues, the quota system "does not necessarily attract qualified and competent women to espouse the cause of gender equality...but any woman who needs employment." Goetz also contends that the 'add-on mechanism' used to elect district MPs influences the relationship between the Ugandan women's movement and women in office. Goetz argues that the electoral college process for electing women to reserved seats requires "no further screening processes beyond ascertaining the candidate's gender, no process of winnowing out likely candidates according to their effectiveness in promoting any particular party platform or social program, and no process to enable the women's movement to review candidates" (2003, 120).

Aili Mari Tripp finds several disadvantages as well to the use of electoral colleges for selecting women to the district seats. For example, she cites one critic of the system who argues that "women MPs cannot legitimately speak on behalf of their constituents if they only represent the views of the electoral college" that elected them. Others critics argue that a small body such as an electoral college is especially susceptible to bribery and intimidation and other corrupt methods of persuasion. Moreover, there is a widespread feeling that the bodies from which the electoral college members are drawn are dominated by the ruling NRM and thus, the district women MPs are essentially a gift to the ruling party (Tripp 2000, 231-232).

Tanzania's late 2005 election brought 97 women into parliament out of 319 (30.4 percent): 75 to seats reserved for women, 17 to directly-elected constituency-based seats, two to reserved seats from Zanzibar and three appointed by the president (there should be two more women appointed).[14] And while "not less that 30 percent of all members of the National Assembly must be women" in Tanzania (www.ipu.org/parline-e/reports/2337_A.htm), the seats reserved for women only total 82—a 25.3 percent quota. In Tanzania too, there is concern about the mechanism by which women are elected into reserved seats. For example, the methods by which parties select women to their reserved seats vary and are not necessarily included in party constitutions. According to Ruth Meena (2004, 84), in 2000 only the ruling Chama Cha Mapinduzi "made its mechanism a little more competitive by allowing women party members to elect their representatives and also by broadening the base of representation also to include, for example, representatives of NGOs [non-governmental organizations] and female intellectuals." Opposition parties, by contrast, did not define a mechanism for selecting women to their reserved seats, according to Meena, leaving open the possibility of abuse: "This introduces into the political system the potential for corruption, including sexual corruption, thereby undermining the integrity of female candidates, even those who entered via a more transparent system" (2004, 84). As in Uganda, there is also the question of whose interests are served by the women in reserved seats. As Meena (2004, 85) asks, "When women and gender-related issues are in conflict with the party interest, what position will these women [in reserved seats] take?"

A concern expressed by many women activists in Tanzania is the potential for a two-tiered system of legislators when reserved seats are used to elect the majority of women MPs. According to Richard Matland (2006, 289) this is a general risk of reserved seat systems—that the system relegates representatives in women's seats to an inferior status and diminishes their legislative accomplishments. Anna Makinda, Chairperson of the Tanzania Parliamentary Women's Group, worries that reserved seats have created a hierarchy among women politicians in her country, "with those who contested elections being more highly regarded than those who came in through the 'special seats'" (Morna 2004b, 73). For Rwanda, Hella Schwartz (2004, 38-40) found in a survey of all 80 Rwandan MPs that the majority of MPs knew exactly which women MPs were elected by quota and which were elected by party list. In general, she also finds that the women MPs elected from the provinces and Kigali on the gender quota were far less experienced ("new to the political arena") than the party-list women MPs (who were more likely to have served in the transitional parliament), were considered "grassroots politicians" because they were likely to know well the problems of women and children at the local level, and were considered more likely to represent "women in particular."

In Tanzania and Uganda there is a concern about the impact of reserved seats on women's chances of winning directly elected constituency seats. Indeed, the availability of plenty of reserved seats takes the pressure off political parties to nominate women to stand in constituency seats. As such, reserved seats run the risk of becoming a ceiling rather than a floor, according to Matland (2006, 189). Activists with the Tanzania Gender Networking Project, for example, fear that in the long term reserved seats could have a "crippling effect because women can become scared to stand on their own in constituencies" (Morna 2004b, 60). More optimistically, women MPs in Tanzania also argue that women who enter the Bunge through special seats "can be groomed to stand as future constituency candidates" (Morna 2004b, 117). In Uganda over the last two elections the number of women in constituency seats has reached a plateau—thirteen in 2001 and fourteen in 2006—with the percentage falling as the size of the National Assembly has increased (Bauer forthcoming). In Tanzania over the last two elections, the number of women in constituency seats has declined. By contrast, in Rwanda women in constituency seats make up nearly half of all women in the Chamber of Deputies (15 of 39), bringing the percentage of women far above the country's 30 percent quota to almost 50 percent.

Still for Rwanda, Longman (2006, 148-149) also reports a perception that women MPs are serving the ruling party rather than the women's groups that support them. One informant told him: "The RPF [Rwandan Patriotic Front] focuses on diversity so that they can appear democratic even though they control all power. They put women in the National Assembly because they know they [the women] will not challenge them." Similarly, former Ugandan MP Matembe argues that women in Uganda "have been trapped and have become hostages to the quota system, which was originally introduced to liberate them" (2006, 8). In Matembe's view, Ugandan women have failed to embrace their seats in parliament as a political right; rather they perceive them as a privilege bestowed by a benevolent president. As a consequence, Matembe continues, women activists and politicians are unwilling to interrogate or challenge President Museveni and his government. Moreover, an increasingly authoritarian political climate in Rwanda is further restricting the impact of women legislators. Finally, Longman charges that the lack of political freedom at all levels of government in Rwanda limits the ability of women to influence policy. "Until the Rwandan government shows greater tolerance for human rights in general," Longman concludes, "the impressive representation of women in Rwanda's parliament and other government institutions will have only a limited impact on the lives of Rwandan women" (Longman 2006, 148-149).[15]

Other Considerations

Another way of comparing the effectiveness of the two types of quotas is to look at the accomplishments of women MPs in the different parliaments. In Mozambique, Namibia and South Africa, authors in the Bauer and Britton (2006b) volume point to a long list of legislative accomplishments despite women's greater presence in those parliaments for only a decade or so. In Namibia, women MPs have taken credit for the 1996 Married Persons Equality Act that makes women and men equal before the law in marriage, the 2000 Combating of Rape Act that prescribes minimum sentences for rape and places more emphasis on the rights of rape victims, and the 2002 Communal Land Reform Bill that protects women wishing to remain on their land in the event of their husband's death. In South Africa women MPs have similarly provided the leadership for a range of legislative acts: the 1996 Choice on the Termination of Pregnancy Act that extends the right to abortion on demand to all women, the 1996 Films and Publications Act that provides protections against the degradation of women and children, and the 1998 Domestic Violence Act that increases the legal and institutional protection for victims of domestic violence, among many others. In Mozambique, women legislators and women's organizations came together to play a crucial role in the passage of the 2003 New Family Law. Women MPs and their allies in civil society have also been instrumental in creating a range of state institutions—national machineries—for the advancement of women and the achievement of gender equality.

In Tanzania, according to Meena (2004), women MPs tabled and defended a bill providing maternity leave for married and unmarried women. They also pushed a bill that allowed female students to enter university directly after high school, rather than having to wait two years as in the past. With the strong support of women's organizations, Tanzanian women MPs also successfully supported legislation that increased the severity of punishment for sexual offences and ensured that a land reform bill incorporated a clause that customary practices discriminating against women be declared unconstitutional. Schwartz (2004, 43, 62) found for Rwanda that in general women MPs, however elected, were far more likely than men MPs to consider women's interests "important duties" and therefore, she concludes, the use of the gender quota has "contributed to the presence of MPs with a strong commitment to representing women."[16] Further, according to Longman (2006), women MPs in Rwanda have actively promoted legislation that serves the interests of women, including revisions to inheritance laws, a law banning discrimination against women, and a strengthening of rape laws. In Tripp's view, as already noted, women MPs in Uganda can claim some important legislative accomplishments, though fewer than might have been expected. Matembe argues that despite so many women in parliament, the body has failed to enact "good laws" on marriage, divorce or inheritance, domestic violence, and sexual offenses or to establish an Equal Opportunities

Commission as mandated by the constitution (2006, 8). Still, measured successes have been recorded in all cases.

Reserved seat systems as used in east Africa have the benefit of also allowing for women to be directly elected to constituency-based seats, in addition to their special seats, though those numbers remain very small and seem to grow at a snail's pace. In the meantime, they also create a two-tiered system of women's representation with those in special seats often considered second-class citizens (while at the same time at least some consider women's interests their special mandate). With party-based quota systems as used in southern Africa there are no such distinctions; indeed no MPs—male or female—are directly elected and none has a constituency beyond the party. In both cases, women MPs and women activists worry about the power of political parties—ever the gatekeepers—in determining which women are elected to parliament and what they will do once they get there.

In all cases then, strong national women's movements and traditions of political advocacy and mobilization are necessary to counter the influence and power of political parties, whether women are elected on party lists or in special seats. All too often actual political strategies are collapsed into a single demand for a quota (Hassim and Meintjes 2005, 21). Moreover it is also clear, as the Rwandan and Ugandan cases demonstrate especially well, that a democratic dispensation is essential for gender-based electoral quotas to have meaning; if all MPs are silenced then no one—male or female—will have the opportunity to advance an equality agenda for women.

A revision of this chapter was originally published as Bauer, Gretchen: "Fifty/Fifty by 2020" in *International Feminist Journal of Politics* (2008) vol. 10 no. 3, Taylor & Francis Ltd. Reprinted by permission of the publisher.

Table 1-1
Women in Lower or Single Houses of Parliament in African Countries in Top 35 Worldwide: Pre- and Post-Transition Elections*

Country	Pre-Transition Election	Mid-1990s Election	1999/00 Election	Mid-2000s Election
Mozambique (none appointed)	Not Available	Oct 1994 63/250 **25.2%**	Dec 1999 75/250 **30.0%**	Dec 2004 87/250 **34.8%**
Namibia (excludes non-voting appointed)**	Not Available	Dec 1994 9/72 **12.5%**	Nov 1999 18/72 **25.0%**	Nov 2004 18/72 **25.0%**
South Africa (none appointed)	Sept 1989 5/178 **2.8%**	April 1994 100/400 **25.0%**	June 1999 120/400 **30.0%**	April 2004 131/400 **32.8%**
Rwanda (includes reserved)	Sept 1988 12/70 **17.1%**			Sept 2003 39/80 **48.8%**
Tanzania (includes special seats)	Oct 1990 28/249 **11.2%**	Oct 1995 45/275 **16.4%**	Oct 2000 61/275 **22.2%**	Dec 2005 97/319 **30.4%**
Uganda (includes reserved)	1980 1/126 **0.7%**	June 1996 50/276 **18.1%**	June 2001 75/305 **24.6%**	Feb 2006 89/322 **27.6%**
Burundi	June 1993 8/81 **9.9%**			July 2005 36/118 **30.5%**

*Seychelles, which has not experienced a political transition, is not included.
**The IPU includes non-voting members for Namibia, bringing the percentage of women MPs to 26.9 percent (21/78).

Source: Inter-Parliamentary Union: women in parliaments, women in politics database, parline database; www.ipu.org. Does not take into account changes subsequent to an election, except for some appointed or designated members.

Notes

[1] Many observers have attributed Scandinavia's high representation of women since the 1970s to the use of quotas. Dahlerup (2004, 18) notes, however, that in Scandinavia quotas were never mandated by law; rather they were adopted by political parties (and not all parties used them). Further, these party-based quotas were not introduced until women had already acquired around 25 percent of seats in parliament, a result of socio-economic developments over time.

[2] In a new study, Tripp (forthcoming) finds that the most important factor accounting for high percentages of national-level women legislators is whether the country was involved in a conflict that came to an end after 1986, followed by use of some type of quota and membership in the Southern African Development Community.

[3] As mentioned, the two other African countries in the top 30 worldwide are Burundi and the Seychelles, neither of which is treated in detail in this chapter. Burundi also recently emerged from a conflict situation, approving a new constitution by referendum in February 2005 and electing just over 30 percent women to parliament in July 2005. Prior to the July 2005 election, the last election had been held in 1993 (shortly after which the parliament was dissolved). Burundi also utilizes a 30 percent quota for women (in both houses of parliament); while 100 of 118 members of the lower house are directly elected, the rest are members 'co-opted' to ensure that the 30 percent quota for women (and a 60/40 Hutu/Tutsi split) has been met. In the event, 24 women were directly elected and 12 more co-opted (www.ipu.org/parline-e/reports/2049.htm). Seychelles is another interesting case. In 2002, 29.4 percent of those elected to parliament were women; in 1998, 23.5 percent and in 1993, 27.2 percent–all without any kind of gender-based quota. According to Morna (2004b, 250), "the reason Seychelles is different is [that] its particular history has led to a more open society in which women have traditionally played an active role in public affairs. Simply put, the 'face' of politics is not quite as masculine as it is in every other southern African country."

[4] Tripp (forthcoming) identifies four types of quotas used in Africa: reserved seats which determine the number of women to hold seats from the outset, measures adopted voluntarily by parties to influence the number of women candidates, measures determined through national legislation or constitutional mandates requiring a certain percentage of women candidates, or executive appointments.

[5] Angola is another country in the region to emerge from war in the early 1990s but, unlike the others, has not yet experienced a democratic political transition.

[6] PR systems are considered more favorable toward women because under them political parties seek to compose inclusive party lists that will attract as many voters as possible. (With plurality-majority systems each party nominates only one candidate in each constituency and women candidates are typically viewed as more risky than men candidates.) Quotas are more easily implemented under PR systems

than under plurality-majority systems, and 'contagion'–parties adopting each other's policies–is more likely under a PR system.

[7] The constitution also provides for a gender quota at the local level–one-third of seats for women (Tamale 2004, 38).

[8] Schwartz (2004, 11-12) suggests that there is no conclusive evidence for why the gender quota was included in the constitution or "whether it was implemented mainly from above or below." She observes that some have attributed the quota to pressure from women's organizations while others such as Elisabeth Powley (2004) have argued that "the government could be using the inclusion of women and youth as a means of diverting attention from the absence of ethnic pluralism."

[9] Longman (2006, 140-141) also suggests that the Ugandan origins of the RPF have deeply influenced its policies since taking power, including its policies on women's rights and inclusion at the local and national level.

[10] According to the Inter-Parliamentary Union (IPU), of the 324 members in Tanzania's Bunge, 232 are directly elected, 75 are in seats reserved for women, 5 are in seats indirectly elected from Zanzibar, of which 2 are reserved for women, 10 are appointed by the president, of which 5 are women, and the last 2 are the Attorney General and Speaker. www.ipu.org/parline-e/reports/2337_A.htm.

[11] Pius Msekwa, Speaker of the National Assembly and chair of the committee that proposed the changes for the 2005 election, observed that Tanzania was keen to involve women in politics and felt compelled to implement Commonwealth and SADC commitments (Faustine Rwambali, 2004). Tanzania aims for 100 Female MPs by 2005 (*The East African*, 18 May) www.fairvote.org/pr/global/tanzania women.htm.

[12] In many ways, Burundi is an interesting combination of both systems. The country has a bicameral parliament with a 30 percent gender quota for both houses (as well as ethnic quotas). As noted above, in the National Assembly 100 members are elected using a proportional representation electoral system; each party's candidate list must have at least 20 percent women with one woman's name included in every five names on the list. 'Co-opted' members assure the fulfillment of the 30 percent women MPs if 30 percent are not directly elected. In the July 2005 election 24 women were elected out of 100 and 12 co-opted women were added after the election for a total 30.51 percent women members. www.ipu.org/parline-e/reports/2049.htm.

[13] Gender Links. Nd. 'Profile: Angelina Enoque—an MP growing in her job.' www.genderlinks.org.za/page.php?p_id=164.

[14] According to the IPU (www.ipu.org/parline-e/reports/2337_A.htm) there are statutorily 323 members of the Bunge, though currently only 319 are filled.

[15] Schwartz (2004, 62) expresses the same concerns about "authoritarian tendencies" in Rwanda. And while Uganda made the transition from a no-party to a multiparty political system in early 2006, in mid-2005 it abolished term limits for the presidency, thereby introducing the possibility of a return to "presidents for life."

[16] 97 percent of women MPs found women's interests to be very important, while only 60 percent of men MPs found women's interests to be very important. Differences between 'quota women' and 'party women' were minimal (100 percent versus 93 percent). By contrast 83 percent of men MPs found political party interests to be very important while only 54 percent of women MPs found them to be very important (Schwartz 2004, 43).

CHAPTER TWO
WOMEN'S RIGHTS ADVOCACY VERSUS GENDER AND DEVELOPMENT PROGRAMMING:
Complementary or Alternative Strategies?

Marcia Greenberg

Challenging the Accepted Approach

The primary purpose of this chapter is to apply some analytical tools from the fields of law and development to assess common practices of women's rights advocacy. The initial hypothesis is that generally accepted legalistic approaches for ensuring respect of women's rights may be rooted in expectations that do not hold true in all contexts. This chapter explores how women's rights programs typically rely on activities grounded in liberal legal assumptions. The alternative, it suggests, is to re-frame the objective: from one that is technical, i.e. "fixing" legal systems to incorporate laws and improve enforcement, to one that is transformative, i.e. seeking through gender and development projects to build societies that recognize and practice gender equality.

A Growing Concern about the Results from Common Approaches

The advocacy tactics in vogue over the past two decades for the enhancement and protection of women's rights have been less effective and sustainable at the national and local levels than many had expected. Continued reliance on those approaches may be ineffective at best, and at worst may also squander limited resources and generate negative reactions, thereby preventing greater progress toward the goal of worldwide gender equality.

Out of concern about the existing paradigms, this author proposes two hypotheses: (1) that the dominance of American lawyer-type approaches have led to excessive reliance in women's rights advocacy on drafting and passing protective new laws (or removing discriminatory ones), pressing cases in the courts, and removing gender bias from legal and judicial institutions; and (2) that alternative guiding principles and action tools may be found within the realm of "gender and development."

The analysis for this chapter stems from cautions regarding the lure of liberal legalist assumptions, and the privileging of lawyers' guidance. This chapter is an attempt to apply some of the concepts of "law and development," primarily the domain of lawyers, to international experiences in women's rights, often undertaken by advocates not guided by or rooted in western concepts of law. It suggests an opportunity to apply the thinking from one field (law and development) to experience in another (gender and development). In some ways, the alternative ways of thinking about the challenges and approaches do not introduce much that is new for those engaged in gender and development or in feminist approaches to social transformation. But this chapter seeks primarily to address western legal specialists directly, to remove their often unconscious reliance on legalistic approaches and to introduce them to the need to give greater attention to alternatives.

A number of years ago, the Washington chapter of the Society for International Development (SID) hosted a gathering of lawyers and development specialists. A couple of dynamics were noteworthy: First, the lawyers did most of the talking. Development professionals otherwise known to be quite forthcoming with richness of experience somehow did not speak up very often within the debate. Second, the focus was particularly "legalistic"—ignoring in many ways some fundamental lessons of development, such as being needs-driven, seeking to build capacity, and concerns for sustainability. Third, and most importantly, because the two groups spoke somewhat different languages using somewhat different concepts, there seemed to be limited penetration of thinking (more talking at or past one another)—and therefore a missed opportunity for real growth. Though there has been some progress between these two groups, the lawyers' terminology, concepts and approaches tend to be a starting point, imbued with the very assumptions this chapter seeks to challenge.

The Historical Context: Two Steps Forward but One Step Back?

This chapter takes as a given the global objective of realizing respect for women's rights and gender equality.[1] The issue under examination is not the goal, but rather *the means of achieving that goal:* women's rights legal advocacy—particularly in Africa, but with some reflection on how that may reflect on practices here in the United States.

The question arises within the "Post-Beijing context": the Fourth World Conference on Women, held in Beijing in 1995, was a historic milestone in global efforts for women's rights. The global scope, the level of participation, and the consensus on recognizing and respecting women's rights were perhaps unanticipated and certainly unparalleled. International endorsement of the Platform for Action (the "Platform") seemed to establish long-sought recognition of a simple proposition: Women's rights are Human rights. Yet "Post-Beijing" actions at the national and local levels have been problematic, with the Five-Year Review of the Platform (2000) revealing that resources and implementation had posed greater challenges than anticipated, and more importantly, the Ten-Year Review (2005) revealing that women's rights seem to be ever more under attack and at risk not only in such countries as Iran and Afghanistan, but also in Poland and the United States.[2]

Further, the global shift of commitments from agreements such as the environmental agreements in Rio, the population and development agreements in Cairo, and the gender equality agreements in Beijing, to the Millennium Development Goals ("MDGs") has taken focus away from the express women's rights targets of the Platform. Rather than seeking on a national level to ensure that governments meet their Beijing pledges (as well as commitments under the Convention on the Elimination of all Forms of Discrimination against Women [CEDAW]), feminists and gender equality advocates now find themselves struggling not only to ensure achievement of Millennium Development Goal #3 on Gender Equality and Women's Empowerment, but also that women's needs, rights and gender equality are built into the MDG standards and programs.

Before addressing the issue, a critical distinction must be emphasized: This chapter is not about *global* advocacy for women's rights. The achievements in Beijing, on the other hand, were most certainly a result of women's rights advocacy around the world. From the International Women's Year conference in Mexico City in 1975 that launched the Decade of Women, to Nairobi to Kuala Lumpur to the Fourth World Conference on Women in 1995, it had been along and purposeful campaign.[3] In contrast, this chapter focuses on achieving respect for women's rights and gender equality *at the national level*. This is about women's rights activists working within their own countries to change laws, implementation and practices. This is about translating international and regional declarations of norms, treaties, covenants or protocols into positive social, economic and political changes in women's lives.[4] The question, therefore, addresses the methods utilized by national and local rights advocates: Is a law-focused women's rights advocacy the right tool, or the only tool, for achieving *de facto* respect for women's rights in Africa at the national and local levels?[5]

Targeted women's rights advocacy is one approach, while seeking opportunities to promote new roles, the allocation of resources and power, and gender equality within development programs—such as those focused on governance, economic growth, health issues or natural resource management[6]—may be another.[7]

A sub-hypothesis of this chapter is that Americans (and some Europeans) who are either lawyers or are infected by their own legal systems have promoted "women's rights advocacy," and African women leaders (some of whom have been trained as lawyers) and women's right organizations have *adopted* it. As will be explained below, the primary concern is that the liberal legal model fails to take account of cultural differences. Examples taken from African women's organizations show how components of their programs reflect an approach that others have encouraged. Just as African law schools may teach methods promoted by American law schools that assume an American model and legal culture, women's legal rights organizations may utilize methods promoted by American or European NGOs that assume legal and political contexts like their own.

Readers' responses to this chapter will differ depending on their national and cultural frameworks: For Americans, the chapter urges caution and some re-thinking of the appropriateness and effectiveness of the prescribed approach; for Africans, it suggests some questioning of what may be touted as universal approaches to achieving gender equality and encourages the design and use of approaches based on African-specific social, cultural and political challenges. For the Diaspora, a call to re-assess the efficacy of an accepted methodology abroad presents an opportunity to reflect on whether those methods have in fact achieved the results promised for African-Americans (and others) in the United States.

When advocates for women's rights recognize that law-focused programs may not be the right approach for all circumstances, they may be prepared to consider alternatives. Thus the chapter concludes by presenting illustrations of how a gender and development approach—one that is broadly development-oriented rather than narrowly "rights-based"—may be more effective and sustainable than a western law-influenced model. Ultimately, advocates within each community or country ought to have the intellectual freedom and knowledge with which to assess and choose women's rights advocacy or gender mainstreaming options. To ensure the exercise of that latitude and agency, donors and advisors need to be freed of assumptions and paradigms that inadvertently narrow the range of possibilities and effectively limit progress toward the shared goal of achieving gender equality.

Structure of the Chapter

The chapter is presented in four parts. The first situates the problem professionally, noting where the issues are not only programmatic but also disciplinary as they arise from the roles played by lawyers engaged in the field of international development. Some personal reflections that illustrate the contradictions between the worlds of lawyers and development professionals, and between Americans and local advocates, help to clarify the professional problem.[8] To lay the foundations for the technical aspects of the discussion, the term "women's rights advocacy" is defined for the purposes of this chapter.

The second section introduces *three conceptual frameworks* from the field of law and development: 1) the liberal legal model, 2) the three components of a legal system, and 3) "reglementation" relating laws and behavior, with which many women's rights advocates are not familiar. Predicated on a concern that advocacy is often undertaken with the assumption that it will achieve similar results in a wide range of contexts, these frameworks offer a way to consider the appropriateness and effectiveness of western-style advocacy techniques in Africa.

The third part of the chapter explores examples of common women's advocacy practices through the new lenses proposed earlier in the work. These examples illustrate the hypothesis and model ways in which commonly accepted practices may rely on questionable assumptions regarding context and appropriate models.

The chapter concludes with examples suggesting how gender-and-development approaches may offer effective alternatives for changing attitudes and behaviors. The final section also posits that lessons learned by critiquing the effectiveness of legalistic women's advocacy in Africa may be helpful in other parts of the world as well; if approaches outside the advocacy model are perceived as effective, this may similarly lead to reconsideration of the role of women's rights advocacy in the United States.

Personal Reflections: Law *versus* Development Perspectives

Three situations—from 1991, 1998, and 2001—lay the foundations for this author's reflections. In each case, something about the work or approach just did not seem right, but it was difficult to identify where the problem lay.

The first arose in the course of research for a consultancy in Mali in 2001,[9] when the author learned of efforts by women's organizations to enact a new family law. Women's rights advocates had worked on drafting the law and on gaining government support. Pursuant to the process recommended to them, they held a large public meeting to introduce the draft law. To their astonishment, the reactions were vehement anger—particularly from Islamic clerics. The women, not believing that they were proposing a law that defied or undermined their own Islamic beliefs, were quite taken aback. Moreover, they had "followed instructions," i.e. they had used the process they had learned (possibly from American or French technical assistance), but it did not work for achieving their objective.

> My puzzlement, which has been bothering me now for several years, was this: Was it possible that the women's organizations had been misadvised? Was the advocacy approach not the right one for their context, and should they perhaps have approached the social change objective, changing women's standing and status within the family, differently?

The second situation involved participation in a team of gender and development specialists focused on bilateral assistance within a Women's Legal Rights program. In the midst of efforts to "reinvent government" and to "manage for results," a team was to identify indicators for assessing the "results." Typically, members of the team suggested indicators such as "number of new laws passed to protect women's rights" or "number of laws repealed that had authorized or allowed discrimination against women." Such indicators raised concerns, however, in that they created pressure to get results in legislatures—which in the worst cases would mean that US NGO-implementing partners might feel compelled to lobby in foreign legislatures for new laws (though such "lobbying" does happen as American organizations work with elected officials, staff, members of the judiciary, etc.). The push for quick results also contradicted development experience, paralleling the fable of the tortoise and the hare: that quickly-passed laws may be just as quickly revoked (or ignored), while those that slowly make their way through the process may be more sustainable. Acknowledging that possibility, the team stressed the importance of building capacity among members of civil society, e.g. women's organizations, for them to advocate for law reform. Yet problems may arise when new laws become the primary focus.[10]

> While that was better, it still struck me that it was not good enough. It seemed still that pressures to achieve measurable changes within the funding periods risked distorting the approaches or sacrificing longer-term, more sustainable impacts for short term results. Women's organizations might be empowered, but Americans would still be teaching them "our tricks", i.e. those that are employed and work (we think) in the United States.

The last reflection dates back a full decade. For a student at the Fletcher School of Law and Diplomacy, it was difficult to resolve a personal commitment to women's rights and a professional commitment to culturally sensitive development. A potential clash of norms arose: norms of an American, politically liberal woman, that women are equal to men and that their rights ought to be respected, *versus* norms of cultural sensitivity, that an outsider supporting social and economic development should not impose his or her own norms and expectations, but should instead respect local practices, history and objectives.

In fact, over the years that ideal of "cultural sensitivity" that had seemed to be a development imperative, has become "politically correct" and somewhat of a "knee-jerk" response, losing its original intent and meaning. In some instances the charge of "relativism" is levied against those who do not firmly insist upon the absolutes of rights.

Further, the women's conference in Beijing in 1995 seemed to dispel the idea that feminism and goals of women's equality were western or northern notions, because women from around the world found consensus regarding the social economic disadvantages they experienced and their desire to end discrimination. If one consulted a broader spectrum of society than had historically been the practice, i.e. if one asked women to identify their cultural aspirations, respecting women's rights was not an ideal of the "north" or the "rich" only.

> My reconciling of the two views has evolved. Now, again, I am beginning to think of it differently—and am back to seeing differences between north and south. At this stage, however, I do not see a conflict, i.e. women's rights versus culture. Rather, the question has become: How does one achieve respect for women's rights *within* culture? I wonder about how the means, effectiveness and sustainability depend on understanding and reflecting tradition and culture.

Those three sources of reflection have led, therefore, to questions regarding methods of advancing the respect for and enjoyment of women's rights. Might the approach of advocacy be a mechanism that does not operate effectively everywhere? The issue is how *best* to achieve dignity and equal opportunities for women *within* families, communities, nations ... and "best" means achieving broad-based, sustainable changes in attitudes and behaviors among urban and rural men and women, young and old.

Thus it is the "how" that introduces the questions and concepts of "law and development", i.e. of how law-related advocacy functions in contexts different from that of America or [Western] Europe. Is it possible that there is an "American approach" that is predicated on frequent litigation to assert individual rights, and on a family culture that encourages challenge, debate, and efforts to convince others—even around the dinner table?[11] Women's empowerment and advocacy projects may be promoting a model, a "Standard Operating Procedure," for women, women activists, and women's NGOs; and that model may allow for organizing and getting out the word (educating), but at the same time it stresses advocacy for legislation as the *primary* tool with which to achieve social change.

In fact, the advocacy approach may over-credit the power of positive law: presuming a role for state-enacted legislation or a capacity to implement and enforce. Some practices and behaviors may not be determined by laws (even in the United States). In Africa, there are historic strata: norms and practices that date back centuries; customary law reflecting interpretations and colonial laws; and, more recently, norms and laws promoted by multilateral and bilateral donors. Placing primary attention on state-enacted laws tends to ignore the fact that people can always continue practices despite laws (such as in rural areas where there is little awareness of, or compliance with, the laws). Further, since it is always possible to change the laws back again, the ultimate objective is not to change laws, but to change norms and behaviors.[12] If the objective is to change discriminatory behavior and practices, such emphasis on laws may lead to excluding other factors—such as education, religion, family norms—that may be more effective. The focus on advocacy—building individual and organizational capacity—may be a heavily legalistic approach that is particularly suited to the context of the United States but is oddly out of place elsewhere. At best, it may be ineffective; at worst, it may be counter-productive.

Clarifying the Term "Women's Rights Advocacy"

The focal concern of this chapter is *advocacy* initiatives relating to *rights*. Advocacy may entail efforts to pass new laws protecting women's rights or to repeal discriminatory ones; it may involve public demonstrations, awareness and teaching, and use of efforts to challenge practices and enforce the law. In nearly all cases, however, laws are pivotal—passing, changing, building awareness of, applying or enforcing them.

Some typical scenarios:

- A women's bar association works with MPs in Parliament to change legislation relating to AIDS.
- Women's organizations work together on a new Family Law, and through their contacts succeed in gaining the President's agreement to support it.
- After the Fourth World Conference on Women in 1995, a group of women organizes a legal literacy program to teach women in rural areas about their rights, and their Ministry for Women, Children and Family publishes a pamphlet about the Convention on the Elimination of All Forms of Discrimination (CEDAW) using pictures rather than words.
- A women's clinic takes up a case of a widow thrown out of her home by relatives after her husband dies.

For the purposes of this chapter, women's rights advocacy may mean a range of activities—from the legal literacy workshops and publications referenced above, to legal cases, lobbying for new laws, and demonstrations. The results of such initiatives have, in fact, led to some acknowledgement of the limitations of new laws.[13] Following the successful passage of new laws, many women's rights advocates deplore the lack of implementation. They call for better enforcement and question the degree of political will. In other cases, the establishment of legal protections has little impact because women are not aware of their rights or lack access to mechanisms by which to assert them. This has led to increased initiatives for women's legal literacy in an effort to expand the constituency for new laws or for their implementation and enforcement. Programs have also evolved to use not just modern media, but theater; to include men in organizing and marching against violence (see, e.g. South Africa), and to focus legal literacy beyond individual awareness to group awareness and political action.

Further, this chapter recognizes an expansive understanding of women's rights advocacy developed by Marge Schuler:[14]
1) Naming or defining a right,
2) Lobbying for legislation that recognizes and protects that right, and
3) Ongoing education and monitoring to ensure implementation and respect for that right.

Table 2-2 Becoming a Human Rights Advocate Step by Step

GOALS	Name the human	Gain acceptance of the right by inclusion	Assure the right's
METHODS	Research & fact-finding to:	Political action through:	Monitoring and litigation to:
	Identify violations	Public education	Hold states account-able for violations
	Show the right was violated	Constituency building	Seek redress for victims
		Lobbying	Assure that the system "works"
		Mobilization	

Yet while there have been thoughtful and useful extensions beyond some traditional views of rights advocacy, such approaches still target state-recognized rights passed by government bodies—with the goal of removing laws that violate women's rights or enacting laws that name and protect women's rights, be it by an executive or legislative body, at the national or local level. Typically the targets of such initiatives are the executive (and his/her staff), and elected or appointed legislators (and their staff). The objective is to achieve a change in positive, government-enacted law. The advocacy approaches are grounded in assumptions regarding the centrality of government-made laws for achieving the changes in attitudes and behavior needed to achieve gender equality.

Whether a right stems from what has been articulated in international agreements or takes effect because a nation has agreed as party to a treaty or covenant, this chapter focuses on advocacy as an accepted means of ensuring the enjoyment of that right, especially when civil society (legal professionals or citizen activists) works with representatives of an executive branch or with members of a legislative body to gain the enactment of new laws, edicts, legislation or regulations.[15]

An Illustration from Uganda, UWONET's Policy Advocacy Program[16]

The Policy Advocacy program is UWONET's core program

> It seeks to include women as a key constituency in the formulation and implementation of any laws, policies, programs and practices to the end that women's and society's status improves, thus contributing to the vision of a prosperous Uganda. UWONET's policy advocacy program targets policy and decision makers at the national level, i.e. Parliament, government ministries and the donor community...

The *Key Activities* under the Policy Advocacy program will include:
- Monitoring International and Regional women's rights conventions, especially tracking CEDAW
- Advocacy for the ratification of international and regional conventions
- Gender Audit of laws and key policies and instruments relating to women
- Advocacy for the Enactment of the Sexual Offences Bill, Domestic Relations Bill and the Domestic Violence Act

Key expected *outputs/outcomes* of the Policy Advocacy program include:

- Women's concerns incorporated into laws and policies (like the health policy and land policy)
- An engendered law, policy-making and implementation process in Uganda
- Signature and ratification of the Additional Protocol on the African Charter on People and Human Rights and the ILO Convention on workers with family responsibility
- Women's political, social, health and economic rights promoted and protected
- Government adherence to and implementation of women's rights as contained in regional and international treaties and conventions such as CEDAW through UWONET's monitoring.

The suggestion here is not that it is always or entirely or even fundamentally wrong to strive for laws that recognize and protect women's rights. They can, in some instances, establish new norms, provide a mechanism to help some women, or mark an expectation for government action. Yet as Lisa VeneKlasen and her colleagues have articulated, many rights advocacy programs also entail risks:

> "[P]eople understand rights in different ways. The concept often conjures up the image of a legalistic approach that is more technical than empowering. The legalistic approach to rights all too often focuses on "what-the-law-says" and downplays the dynamic aspect of the political process that shapes the extent to which rights are enforced and realized in people's lives. This legalistic view plays out in legal education efforts that essentially teach people (through workshops and pamphlets) a simplified version of laws, and in advocacy efforts that focus exclusively on legal reform in order to "deliver rights" (IDS, p. 7).

Thus law-focused programs may crowd out other options. Donors and implementers may privilege such programs over others. Each time an organization selects a law-focused program, there may be opportunity costs for having foregone an alternative approach.

The Conceptual Frameworks of Law and Development

All too often, academic disciplines and professional collaboration fail to link or exchange thinking. Complaints about sectoral "stove-piping" abound within international development agencies—from the U.S. Agency for International Development (USAID) to the United Nations Development Program (UNDP). This chapter strives to achieve some new ways of thinking about women's rights advocacy by linking two strands: the first of lawyers and women's rights advocates, with the second of development specialists—including those focused on law and development, and those focused on gender and development. It also encourages attention to three themes this author underscores when teaching Americans about international work: the need to pay careful attention to *unrecognized assumptions*, the importance of *context*, and the dangers of *supply-driven assistance* (as compared with that identified and provided in response to particular needs).

From the field of Law and Development, three concepts shed new light on how one views women's rights legal advocacy: 1) The liberal legal model, 2) legal culture, and 3) "reglementation" regarding law and behavior. Each is helpful in revealing what may be unstated and unrecognized assumptions regarding the effectiveness of "western" [very often U.S.] approaches to law reform and to the use of law for social change.

The Liberal Legal Model

Within the field of Law and Development, David Trubek and Marc Galanter wrote a seminal article in the 1970s, thereby taking the unusual step of publishing a paper that questioned what they and others were doing abroad.[17] Entitled "Scholars in Self-Estrangement," the article sought to raise questions about the methods utilized in law and development projects —primarily in Latin America and often funded by the U.S. government and by the Ford Foundation. Believing that they and their colleagues sincerely intended to address poverty and inequality, and to work for social change to improve the lives of the most marginalized, Trubek and Galanter wondered "aloud" whether their methods were in fact achieving those objectives. Worse still, they worried that perhaps they were inadvertently strengthening the rich, reinforcing the status quo, and worsening the prospects for the poor.

Trying to reflect on their approach, they suggested that American lawyers were exporting a "liberal legal model," meaning a model legal system that looked like that of the United States, and were expecting that it was possible to graft it onto social, economic, cultural and historic contexts that were vastly different from ours. The model also assumed a kind of evolution of legal systems—from weak or primitive systems of social order to institutions and laws much like our own. There was also an expectation that all aspects of "the model" either exist or are about to come into being—so reformers can focus on one piece without worrying about the other necessary changes. The elements included the centrality of the State, the State as primary agent of social control and change, and a focus on higher agencies such as legislatures and courts—with little interest in non-state forms of legal and social ordering. A central question was therefore whether Americans were assuming both an idealized outcome—and the viability of others adopting or evolving into it.[18]

When considering common women's rights advocacy programs, one finds that they do seem to adopt much of the aforementioned model and many of the said assumptions. In fact, they focus a great deal on higher-level agencies like courts and parliaments. They assume the centrality of the State for social control and change related to gender equality. Programs tend to assume that, as courts strengthen and access improves, women will seek help and judges will work to apply State-generated law without regard to other normative systems. There has been a tendency to downgrade or even ignore non-state forms of legal and social ordering such as religion.

Legal Culture

Around the same time that Trubek and Galanter were publishing their work, Lawrence Friedman and Steward Macaulay suggested a way of thinking about legal systems that sought to unpack and explain the failings of the liberal-legal model.[19] They suggested that a legal system is not comprised of only two commonly recognized parts—the substance of law and the structures of institutions; rather, they urged consideration of a third part: legal culture. "Legal culture" reflected the idea that within their broader culture, societies have attitudes, values and behaviors *relating particularly to "law."*[20] And for their purposes, "law" referred to positivist, government-based law.

Friedman and Macaulay's article helps us to realize that while people of one community or state may recognize and respect state law, people elsewhere may ignore, scorn and avoid it. In some contexts, citizens may regard law as only a tool of oppression, or may deem it an illegitimate irritation and obstacle to "normal" social and economic processes. While it may be somewhat easy to export the language of laws, or the structures and processes of institutions, neither will take hold or be effective if society largely ignores legal culture.[21] Yet most often technical assistance focuses on the law and the institutions—and there is then some bewilderment about why changes in the law do not stop "corruption," illegal or extra-legal activities.

There may be many African contexts for legal culture—ranging from reliance on dispute resolution by a chief or other respected person in a village, to rent-seeking by African civil servants that Africans may accept as normal supplementation of inadequate or irregularly paid wages (while Americans quite automatically regard it as *illegal* corruption). A black Namibian woman in Parliament has been quoted as saying:

> Sometimes people adhere to outdated notions even though the real lives they live have changed. Some people call in the aid of customary law when it suits them, well aware that such laws are flexible, unwritten and can be manipulated by those who have the power and authority ... I am afraid that culture and religion are conveniently used as instruments by those who want to subject women to all forms of inequality.[22]

Thus, while women's organizations might successfully pass laws and train judges, it is possible that this kind of legal advocacy—inherently part of American legal culture—might lack the same resonance or impact in other settings. Perhaps the outcomes of advocacy, such as the passage of new laws, and the impacts of advocacy, such as respect for those laws, are dependent upon a legal culture such as that in the U.S.—a nation highly conscious of and unusually respectful of state law. It is possible that the persuasive power of state-enacted laws and the legitimacy of state laws to set norms are tied to American legal culture but are not compatible by comparison with the way many Africans establish norms and rules, educate young people and resolve disputes.

Law and Behavior: "Reglementation"

Thirdly, there is a commonly held expectation that the passage of new laws is an instrument by which to change people's attitudes and behavior. In part, this stems from real success in the United States, particularly with regard to the Civil Rights movement.[23] Anthropologists like Sally Falk Moore,[24] however, have pointed to a range of "reglementation" that affects behavior. Robert and Ann Seidman emphasize that laws may seek to influence the behavior of two different groups of "role occupants"— citizens (directly) *and* people within the various implementing agencies responsible for applying and enforcing laws. When anticipating the need to change behaviors, the second group may remind those drafting laws to consider the fact that various interests (economic, social, etc.) and ideology may prove more influential than the State's law. Extending such thinking about how social norms or signals may affect people's attitudinal or behavioral choices opens the way to considering norms from social institutions like families and schools, expectations from "corporate groups" like labor unions or clubs, and of course religious institutions.[25]

Concerns here about social and cultural contexts do not militate for cultural relativism. Rather, they are reminders of a tendency to pass over the fundamentals of if, how, and when "law" or "reglementation" affects people's behaviors—perhaps competing with the expected response to state-based, positive law. It is important to remember the extent to which people respond to their peers and respected leaders, work within contexts and environments, act according to what they recognize as their self-interest, and follow codes and norms from non-statutory sources, such as tradition, custom and religion. For many people, state-enacted law does not "trump" other reglementation.

Viewing advocacy programs through such law and development lenses raises questions about whether such efforts unduly rely on rights advocacy. This view challenges those choosing positive law as the primary tool for change to check their presumptions about state-enacted law having the power to affect behavior and attitudes—to counter or have greater sway than other normative sources—of diverse nations and communities of Africans.

Re-Viewing Women's Rights Advocacy in Africa through a Law and Development Lens

There is some likelihood, therefore, that practitioners' use of women's rights advocacy is predicated on legal-liberal models, assumes a legal culture or a standardized path of evolution for legal culture, and ignores or minimizes the power of other systems of reglementation. To the extent that this is the case, advocacy-related training, technical assistance and practice may have only limited impacts. Worse, there are opportunity costs of investing human and financial resources in those approaches rather than others that might be more effective—and worst of all, these approaches may generate misunderstandings and backlash.

This section illustrates how the law and development lenses bring some common practices into focus—revealing flaws in their basic assumptions and questions about their results. The referenced activities are drawn from organizations that are either American (in origin and personnel) or multilateral (but arguably substantially influenced by American- and Western-trained lawyers).[26] They encompass those focused particularly on women's rights advocacy and those who promote advocacy when it is then applied to women's rights issues.[27]

An important extension of this study would be to consider the work and initiatives of African organizations. Such organizations are often staffed by lawyers who have been trained in the U.S. or Europe or through American/European organizations, and they have often adopted practices touted as effective in other contexts. The author has done cursory reviews of the African programs of two regional organizations, Women in Law and Development in Africa (WiLDAF) and Women and Law in Southern Africa (WLSA). These organizations' legal programs, while sometimes introducing context-driven innovations, tend to parallel those of American-staffed and financed organizations.[28] While African organizations of lawyers may readily adopt many approaches predicated on liberal-legal models, women's advocacy organizations with fewer ties to law and lawyers may enjoy somewhat greater freedom from such practices.

Illustrative Activities

To explore how law and development critiques shed light on common activities, we will use a typology of women's rights advocacy activities drawn from the four focal areas of a recent USAID-funded Women's Legal Rights Initiative (WLRI): 1) constructing a *legislative framework*, 2) enhancing *justice sector capability*, 3) strengthening the *ability of civil society organizations to advocate* for women's legal rights, and 4) expanding *public awareness*.[29] The project pillars for the World Bank's Women and the Law in Africa similarly focus on government institutions and state-based law: *1) institutional strengthening* (primarily capacity of and partnerships among women-oriented ministries and NGOs), *2) legal literacy* (strengthening women's knowledge/awareness of their rights), and *3) access to legal and judicial services* (strengthening women's ability to enforce their rights).

Focusing on laws and legislative frameworks

Often a first step for women's rights advocates is to assess and address the "legislative frameworks," nearly always referencing the laws of national governments. Thus, for example, the National Democratic Institute (NDI) has noted: "In many countries the laws ensuring women's equal participation do not exist or are weak. NDI has assisted in constitutional reform programs that help ensure equality under the law." Similarly, the WLRI "advances the legal, civil, property, and human rights of women." It touts as best-practice accomplishments relating to domestic violence in South Africa, noting that it strengthened legislation by expanding the term "abuse" to include more than physical abuse and addressed the responsibilities of the police. In Botswana, the Department of Women's Affairs in the Ministry of Labor and Home Affairs undertook a review of all laws affecting the status of women in Botswana. The review resulted in amendments to the Penal Code, Criminal Code, Employment Act, Citizenship Act, and Public Service Act (WLRI, p. 11). In USAID's earlier women's rights program, Global Women in Politics (GWIP) reported that its partners were "instrumental in shaping the laws and institutions addressing domestic violence at the national level. The role each partner plays in the policy arena responds to country-specific constituency needs."

In many ways, such programs may be regarded as positive interventions on behalf of women. The laws do mark two important accomplishments: establishing *some* statements of new norms and providing legal recourse for *some*. Yet recalling the Law and Development concepts, such foci are limited. First, the programs assume that state-enacted laws are of central importance in people's lives. They put the State in the center and expect, even when legal systems are weak, that they are evolving into primary and controlling systems for people's behavior. Thus, while laws are statements of norms, they take primary attention as compared with the many other statements and sources of norms. The privileging of that system of "reglementation" tends to minimize the extent to which other social fields influence people's attitudes and behavior, including associations that may be "traditional," religious, or familial, among others.

From the Center for Development and Population Activities (CEDPA's) work in Bahrain[30]

In 2004, the Moroccan government adopted the landmark Family Law supporting women's equality and granting them new rights in marriage and divorce. Several women's organization members who lobbied the government to sign the law shared their advocacy efforts during one of the conference panels. [One leader] noted that these women were successful particularly because they developed strategies that respected the Shari'a, or Islamic law.

Second, the legal recourse is limited, as recognized now by many programs, by issues of access—and access depends upon knowledge, economic resources, physical proximity and transportation (among other constraints). Typically the legal recourse is available to women in capital cities who are well-educated and relatively affluent. Legal recourse also depends upon knowledge of law, which drives legal literacy projects. Yet proponents of legal literacy programs also assume that once women become aware of such positive laws, ranging from the national to the international, they will attribute central meaning to them.

Further, those who from their own cultural and professional background respect and rely on state laws inadvertently denigrate existing normative systems, seeking to overcome them as somehow primitive or outdated.

"Unfortunately, legal and customary barriers often prevent women from exercising their full legal rights and utilizing existing laws and protections. Many citizens—both men and women— are unaware of existing laws and legislation that are designed to ensure equally rights and protections to women in society."[31] —*USAID's Women's Legal Rights Initiative*

Thus, while women's rights advocates increasingly parrot the truism that "laws on the books alone do not suffice," they continue to invest a great deal of energy and resources in the passage of those laws. They then focus on failures of implementation or enforcement, thereby blaming a lack of resources or a failure of political will, rather than reconsidering whether the laws themselves are the most effective way for African women to change thinking and practices. They also emphasize the "substantive" component of legal systems, i.e. laws, with attention to the institutional components out of concern for the effectiveness of the laws—but give little consideration to "legal culture."

Applying the Law and Development concepts should generate some debate regarding the time and resources invested in state-enacted law—not ignoring it as one mechanism, but putting it in perspective, within a broader range of norm-focused, behavior-changing approaches.

Improving justice and legal sector capabilities, particularly through training

As the focus on enacting and reforming laws has produced outputs (laws) but limited impacts (changes in behavior), many women's rights programs have shifted their focus to the people within the institutions who must implement and enforce the laws. By necessity, programs must look beyond laws, awareness- and capacity-building to the legal and judicial institutions—Friedman and Macaulay's second component of legal systems. The problems experienced when relying on state laws are real and pervasive. Hence more and more projects target the people responsible for applying the laws—the judges and magistrates, lawyers and paralegals, court clerks and police. The WLRI's first annual report notes that "implementation of women's human rights lies with the judiciary and within the wider judicial/legal system. The existence of laws does not in itself mean that women's legal rights will be implemented and enforced. It is only when the courts as well as other judicial players...fully understand the rights of women that they can be expected to enforce these rights through the judicial and legal process." Similarly, guidelines for the World Bank's assessment of its Women and Law in Africa program give primary importance to "enhancement of the reported *capacity* of selected government agencies and civil society organizations to prepare, draft, advocate for, adopt and implement gender-responsive legislation, regulation and policy documents."

In fact, much work in South Africa has gone into building such capacity—in relation to, for example, cases of violence against women.[32] For a 1992 volume on women's legal literacy, Akua Kuenyehia of Ghana wrote a piece explaining the impediments to implementation of laws protecting women when magistrates, judges, banks and police do not recognize women's property rights, question their ability to provide bail, regard violence against women as a "family matter," and further victimize a victim of rape. In each case, the officials' biases and attitudes (stemming from custom, practice and competing normative frameworks) preclude honest implementation and enforcement of the laws.[33] Each illustration of how people within legal institutions undercut the purpose and effect of the law rings true for experience throughout Africa—and elsewhere as well. The WLRI's cited best practices from Southern Africa include a Legal Aid and Counseling program in Botswana, as well as legal aid services and a pre-trial handbook to help women understand the court process in cases of rape in South Africa. Recognizing, perhaps, the limitations of the law, however, they have also provided some alternative dispute resolution within families and places of employment in Mozambique.

Yet even when programs extend beyond passage of laws to their application, there remains the risk that they are not facing the problem squarely: that they still emphasize high-level institutions, focus too much on courts, and assume an evolution toward a liberal-legal model as the mechanism for defining and enforcing rules. There is still frustration with those who, instead of trusting state-enacted law and turning to it as a just, reliable and socially acceptable source of redress, seek support elsewhere. The WLRI has reported that in Malawi, traditional practices and customary law remain obstacles to women's rights, and that in 1995-96 the government abolished traditional courts—but today those courts continue to exist. Instead of recognizing and working with the existing "legal culture," some programs may regard those who do not want to turn to the courts as uninformed, fearful, or uncooperative.

How women deal with family violence, perhaps the most universally targeted women's rights issue, illustrates this: In all sorts of families—from urban to rural, educated to illiterate—accounts indicate that women do not want to go to court over such issues. Most often, they utilize other coping strategies—from turning to neighbors and friends, to seeking a Shelter, to leaving altogether in search of a new life. While passage of laws forbidding gender-based violence does establish new norms, and can provide recourse for some, it is also possible that social reglementation and legal culture preclude reliance on public legal mechanisms to stop, punish or get away from violence. It is perhaps in recognition of such limitations that communities are now seeking to work with the men to change their behaviors—and not just threatening them with legal or judicial sanctions.

Strengthening the advocacy skills of civil society organizations

Another common approach is to focus on strengthening the organizations seeking the passage and enforcement of laws. While some civil society, nongovernmental or community-based organizations deliver services, others engage in advocacy. "Advocacy" is widely regarded as a critical means of educating the public, protesting policies, holding government accountable, and pressuring for new legislation.

There are many examples among organizations focused on whole ranges of issues, and among the subset of organizations working on women's rights. Thus the WLRI seeks to build the capacity of NGOs to advocate for new laws and women's rights. In one report, it states that increased access to communications and *the globalization of strategies and campaigns have made NGOs increasingly effective. Yet many NGOs need further development ..."* (WLRI, p. 13]. The NDI trains all sorts of NGOs in advocacy, lobbying skills and "strategies for citizen participation." The GWIP programs were to "impart key skills for women and women's organizations to engage in political processes broadly, including public education, public dialogue, media campaigns, constituency building, policy advocacy and legal reform, and regional exchange."

NDI has stated a "philosophy that supporting nongovernmental organizations and their efforts to conduct advocacy-related programs is critical to giving community groups and key NGOs the power to keep pace with government." In Namibia, NDI had a program to "strengthen the Parliament by encouraging greater public participation in the legislative process and making transparency, accountability and responsiveness a top concern to members of Parliament and staff." "In some countries where women's voting rights have been limited by law or tradition, NDI has worked with NGOs on voter education campaigns to break those patterns." In Mozambique there was a T-Shirt campaign in support of a new Family Law.

The idea of organizations in which people work together and thus have more influence than if working individually does not seem so culturally-specific. Throughout West Africa there are "groupement de femmes" who provide mutual support, share information, and have the opportunity to address issues together. They are genuine groups. In contrast, there is frequent criticism that women's NGOs do not have real grassroots membership, i.e. connections to the very women who might rely on the new laws. Along with this there is the common failing of legislators who are not connected or accountable to their constituencies. Often strengthening the advocacy skills of an organization presupposes social ordering, such as constituencies, of a liberal-legal model. When such assumed connections do not exist, the meaning of advocacy, i.e. advocacy on behalf of whom, feeds the cynicism of those agreeing to the laws.

Insofar as the groups are representative, the women's rights programs promote "advocacy" and particular "skills." Advocacy implies persuasion—either person-to-person, such as lobbying, or in large, public venues, such as demonstrations. In how many African nations have programs encouraged women activists in the capital cities to lobby Presidents, members of Parliament, party leaders and legislatures, for passage of new legislation? Sometimes they succeed, and a new law appears on the books. Yet, as was discussed above, the institutions are often ineffective. Sometimes inadvertently, but potentially quite purposefully, there may not be resources with which to implement the new laws. Even when political leaders agree to revoking or passing laws, there is little reason to expect that they themselves are changing their attitudes or behavior. They, like so many outside of Africa, have learned how to be "politically correct." According to their legal culture, those laws may not have substantial meaning or traction within their lives.

Again, there are certainly times when those approaches are warranted. But with regard to women's rights—for which the ultimate objective is to *change attitudes and behaviors* and establish gender equality—it is possible that where the liberal legal model does not fit the context, such law and policy-focused approaches may not lead to effective and sustainable change. Advocacy, as other societies practice it, may not fit the "legal culture" and may therefore not be the most effective way to change people's attitudes and behaviors in Africa. If the objective is to change how people regard women, treat them and relate to them, perhaps "advocacy," political persuasion, and legalistic approaches lack the meaning in African settings that they may have in the West.

In a 1995 regional Civic Education and Advocacy workshop delivered by NDI in the Gambia, participants engaged in a role-playing exercise in advocacy. They were expected to organize an advocacy campaign—taking into account their socio-economic, cultural and political perspectives—to include strategies, activities and budgets. Sample examples included voter education and encouragement of women's participation. The workshop evaluations show that 39 percent found developing a civic advocacy strategy "most enriching"; but 10 percent found it least interesting *because outreach and advocacy activities were "not linked to the Gambian context"* (emphasis added).

It is possible, therefore, that such programs assume a familiarity with, a comfort with, and a confidence with using state-enacted laws and institutions. Another example from NDI suggests that the systems and culture may not be as well-established as presumed: "In 1996, NDI-Malawi sponsored an advocacy skills-building workshop for women parliamentarians, women chiefs and representatives from women's organizations. The intent of the workshop was to try and assist each of the three groups with possible skills that would help them find more effective ways to lobby for legal reform in the area of wills and inheritance, marriage, divorce, citizenship and affiliation." Reportedly, the mixing of the three groups was not at all successful. The MPs lacked the background and knowledge of the key bills and so were caught looking uninformed—even if, in fact, they were informed! The NGO representatives reacted angrily to unsatisfactory MP responses, which in turn upset the chiefs. Typically, the assessment would be that the failure of the meeting was a matter of difficult personalities, or perhaps a simple "lesson learned" about preparing and organizing such workshops. Possibly, however, there was something more going on.

In strengthening civil society organizations for advocacy, there are assumptions that the organizations are connected to and working with (and for) women, that there is a functioning and meaningful liberal legal model being addressed and influenced by advocacy, and that those to whom advocacy is addressed have the power and resources to change behaviors. There is also some danger of pitting women with some advocacy tactics against men—when there may in fact be ways to address common goals.

Expanding public awareness

The last area is that of public awareness. In nearly every nation of Africa some ministry, such as a Ministry for Gender or a Ministry for Women and Family Affairs or some women's rights organization, has published a booklet on CEDAW "in simple language" and targeted to people in rural areas (see, e.g. WLR, p. 12]. Untold numbers of projects do legal literacy training for women in cities and in rural areas, for women with education and women who are illiterate.

Finding that "public awareness" targeted at women seemed to have limited impacts, the focus shifted to the audience, namely questioning *whose* awareness to target. Within the last ten years, there has been increased recognition of the importance of reaching men as well as women. Hence there has been an expanding focus—from seeking to build women's awareness of their rights to "public awareness." In relation to its Increased Public Awareness of Women's Legal Rights, the WLR states "Women need to be trained in legal and political participation, advocacy, coalition-building, and networking *to ensure that the general public becomes more aware of women's legal rights*" (WLR, p. 16). There is a range of mechanisms used to advise "the public" of women's rights, including television and radio programs, pamphlets, T-shirts, and others.

Yet seen through the lens of law and development critiques, there may be issues not only of whom to target, but also of what is brought to people's attention. Here again there is a fundamental assumption—primarily that if people are aware of state-enacted laws, those laws will have meaning in their lives and will influence their behaviors. There is a risk that by addressing norms and behaviors within a western rights-framework, the campaigns implicitly embed their discussions within a liberal legal model. By focusing on substantive law and institutions of which people should be aware, the campaign organizers fail to understand and address legal culture, that is, the use (or nonuse) of state law and public institutions.

Further, there is an assumption—as much in the West as in Africa—that awareness changes behaviors. It is expected that by announcing or stating or disseminating information, such programs can counter the many other sources of reglementation in Africa—including but not limited to customary law. Even when civic education or awareness-oriented programs go beyond the "modern" media of newspapers, radio and television (such as using theatre), the presumption is still that announcements or advice will change people's norms and behavior. To the World Bank's credit, its current evaluation of the Women and Law in Africa program seeks to assess "enhancement of public awareness of women's rights *and changing behaviors of both women and men.*" By framing the issue as going beyond assessing outputs of public awareness to questions of changing behaviors, the World Bank may have opened the investigation to probe the actual impacts of public awareness.

It may well be possible within the particular cultural contexts of Africa that other mechanisms would be more effective. Efforts to identify and explain "positive deviation," as has been undertaken by CEDPA, may help to understand why norms and behaviors change in some places or contexts, contrary to the normal trends—and presumably not simply in response to public awareness campaigns.[34]

Uncertainties Generated

Thus by using the law and development critiques to review some standard components of women's rights advocacy, we may find there are some overarching questions:

- Might women's rights advocacy assume a liberal legal model? Is it predicated on legal systems that are not the current, nor perhaps the future, legal frameworks in some areas of Africa?
- Might the advocacy part of women's rights advocacy constitute an additional part of the liberal legal model, relating perhaps more to legal culture than to the laws and institutions? Even if not intentional, do women's rights programs seek to export a process that is foreign, and that fails to take account of local legal culture?
- Does women's rights advocacy assume a particular legal culture, without which there may be laws and institutions but people who do not rely on them?
- Might women's rights advocacy expect too much of state-enacted, positive law for changing norms, attitudes and behaviors relating to women's status (the attitudes of men as men), and forget the powerful roles of other sorts of reglementation?

Using Gender and Development Approaches to Achieve Respect for Women's Rights and Gender Equality: Preliminary Thoughts on Alternatives to Women's Rights Advocacy

Clarifying the Goals and Shifting Focus

This chapter suggests that when re-viewed through the lenses of law and development critiques, law-focused programming for women's rights advocacy no longer seems an effective or sustainable way to bring about lasting social change—to achieve gender equality. When these approaches target women, rights, and advocacy for the recognition and enforcement of rights within a state-sponsored system of laws and institutions, they tend to adhere to a liberal-legal model. Typically, they therefore ignore legal culture and existing reglementation. Women's rights advocates tend to adopt the liberal-legal model and assumptions regarding reglementation and legal culture. They have lost sight of important issues relating to culture and relationships. Were they, however, to take a contextualized view of gender relations, law and social change in Africa, they might recognize some challenges and opportunities not revealed when using liberal legal templates.

If, once grounded in the realities of most lives in Africa, we reject the assumptions that the State is the primary agent of social control and change, and that the State will use law to transform society, then there is a rationale for shifting from law-related tactics that target legal systems to development-related approaches focused on attitudes and behaviors. Further, if there is clarity of purpose in recognizing that the goal is not a legalistic one of women's rights, but instead a social one of gender equality, this also shifts the focus from law to norms and behavior. Once the true goal is gender equality and the primary focus is behaviors, then initiatives must target men as well as women—and strive for the transformation of socially-constructed roles, responsibilities and power.

Recognizing the need to use different sorts of programs

On a programmatic level, therefore, there is a need for a broad range of initiatives—including those that work primarily with men *and* those that present opportunities to change how women and men function together. Rather than creating isolated activities, often involving women only, programs seeking to achieve gender equality might find gender and development approaches (GAD) more effective ways to promote and achieve the enjoyment of basic rights by women in Africa.

Up to this time, most approaches have reflected a women-in-development (WID) perspective—concerned with women's needs and deficits, and encouraging women as protagonists and activists. Programs focus on women's rights within laws, women's legal literacy, and advocacy by women's organizations in civil society. Women activists promote new laws, lobby men in power to agree to new laws, and monitor men in enforcement positions to ensure that they respect the new laws. Limited success with the passage of laws has led to workshops to educate men (and women) who must implement and enforce the laws. Gender budgets have enabled women's rights advocates to ensure that resources are allocated for women's needs. The WID approach and a "rights-based approach" to development fit comfortably with liberal-legal approaches to law reform and democracy-building, focusing primarily on the two recognized components of a legal system, substantive law and institutions.

The alternative of GAD approaches may lead to either different or complementary tactics. In the early years, some believed GAD meant simply recognizing that men have particular needs and deficits as well as women.[35] Yet definitions of "gender" that refer to socially constructed roles, responsibilities, and power move development thinking away from biological attributes (sex) and "head-counting" toward looking at how men and women relate to one another—in families, communities and nations.[36] A GAD perspective should mean more than "men as well as women," or even women along with men; it should seek to achieve gender equality by recognizing how women and men *relate to one another*. This, in turn, involves attitudes and behaviors.

A Gender and Development Approach…
• Shifts attention to context, both social and cultural • Looks at relations between women and men • Focuses on power • Seeks to understand, and then change, the ways in which women and men relate to one another.

An additional benefit of a GAD approach to women's rights and women's legal rights advocacy might be that GAD would require greater attention to understanding context, both social and cultural.[37] This also opens the way to thinking more purposefully about power: who wields it, limits it and shares it—and how that may restrain or enable women's enjoyment of their rights in private as well as public spaces. Much of this is normative, is socially and "culturally" embedded, and relates closely to the realm of "reglementation".

In addition, paying more explicit attention to existing roles and responsibilities, to power and power-sharing, and to influence within families and communities, might generate a new array of activities oriented toward changing attitudes and behaviors. Rather than using social marketing like slogans, billboards, and jingles, and rather than promoting lobbying and public demonstrations, GAD might lead women's organizations to identify and use existing methods of transmitting or changing family relations. It might enable program designers to challenge the liberal-legal model, to investigate legal culture, and to recognize the many sorts of "reglementation" that define and direct the roles and responsibilities of boys and girls, old and young, women and men.

Illustrations of GAD Approaches to Gender Equality

A couple of examples may help: In the course of its AIDS program in Africa, UNDP has launched "community conversations." Through such facilitated discussions, men are learning more about AIDS, about experiences of young women (including their daughters and sisters), and about how their lives might be enriched by more open and respectful relations between men and women. Those conversations have the potential to change behaviors more effectively than laws passed in Addis Ababa.

Similarly, in Senegal the "Tostan" program almost accidentally addressed female genital cutting within the course of a women's health and literacy program. When women learned about the health risks, they began questioning the practice among themselves—and with the men in their families and communities. The women did not focus on changing laws. It was people at the local level, women along with men, who rejected the practice and sought new rituals.

"Gender Budget" initiatives have taken hold in South Africa and Tanzania, among other countries. This approach engages women as civil society watchdogs, questioning how government is spending scarce resources. Typically, groups of women-as-citizens work with men-as-government to analyze budgets and determine who benefits from the resource allocations. Such programs are valuable as mechanisms for government accountability and transparency. In addition, however, they engage men and women in processes that build the visibility and effectiveness of women, bridge the power differentials, and establish respect through civil and professional interactions. The projects may not be labeled "women's rights," but their impact is to accord women greater rights and responsibilities within social and political settings.

Lastly, while this is an example in South Asia rather than Africa, there are comparable examples in Africa as well in which post-disaster or in this case pre-disaster programming focuses on improving respectful collaboration among women and men. Following the extraordinary destruction of a super-cyclone in Ossetia, India, UNDP volunteers sought a way to improve disaster preparation. The objective was to improve the capacity of small, rural villages to prepare and mobilize in the face of approaching natural disasters. The programs could have been structured within existing gender roles, such as working with women on preparing children and food, and with men on transportation. Instead, the program initiated emergency teams that included women with men, and mock-drills that engaged whole villages. Faced with the threat of cyclones and other natural disasters, men and women have made incremental progress toward respectful, collaborative relationships – perhaps promising more respect for women's rights in a rural area where State-enacted law and courts are unlikely to provide much protection.

The Challenge for Women's Rights Advocates

This chapter has raised questions regarding the tactics or approaches widely undertaken to achieve the goals of gender equality and respect for women's rights. Drawing on some conceptual frameworks from the field of Law and Development—especially those challenging the models and assumptions underlying many programs on access to justice, rule of law and democracy-building—this chapter posits that perhaps the standardized approaches to women's legal rights advocacy are more rooted in American/western legal culture than is generally recognized. Observing that lobbying and law-reform focuses of women's rights advocacy at the national and local levels may not be effective, either short-term or more especially long-term, the author has suggested that gender and development approaches may open space and creativity to design more appropriate tactics with more sustainable results.

For earnest, skilled and well-intended professionals engaged in "women's rights advocacy," this chapter may seem harsh and over-reaching. Their responses will surely include a number of valid points:

- But the law is just one tool among many, no one has ever suggested otherwise.
- Achieving passage of a new law should never be viewed as the end of a lobbying process.
- Even when people do not fully know or use the law, legal statements have power beyond their actual use. Law may still be respected as a source of authority.
- Even if they are not yet ready to use it, women may benefit from knowing that [state] law is there as another or ultimate resource. When laws are not widely used, the opportunity for some to use them may lead the way for others.

Each of such reactions seems valid, in and of itself. What they do not address, however, are several dynamics of development work, project design and resource allocation. As long as law is one tool, and lawyers are articulate, there is potential (and substantial evidence backs this up) that it may be a preferred tool more than warranted. Though laws should not be the end of a lobbying process, the resources and energy often run out; and hopes remain that the law itself may eventually gain credence. While state-enacted laws may have power and respect, attention focused on them tends to divert attention from other sources of reglementation that command greater respect and frame norms more powerfully. Lastly, while the use by some women may inspire others, such expectations tend to minimize the potential of alternative systems while downplaying the bias of legal systems towards those with money and education.

This chapter puts forward a challenge—to women's rights advocates and lawyers, along with development professionals still prone to gender-blindness—to focus on accomplishing the goal rather than using the "tried-and-true" approaches. Similarly, donors must be willing to support new approaches, different from those that are familiar, but targeted on the real problems of attitudes and behaviors. For southern women and lawyers who have ably mastered much of the law reform and advocacy tactics as "the" way to promote rights and achieve social change, this challenge may be discouraging, but should also be empowering, allowing for greater attention to gender relations within local contexts and experimentation with new approaches. It is hoped that such cross-disciplinary and cross-regional dialogue may promote sustainable social change through context-relevant, meaningful transformation of norms, attitudes and behaviors, resulting in respect for women's rights and gender equality.

Notes

[1] Beyond the women's suffrage movements in the United States and in the United Kingdom that date back to the nineteenth century, the 1948 United Nations Universal Declaration of Human Rights expresses an ideal of achieving "the dignity and worth of the human person *and the equal rights of men and women.*" Since then, there have been repeated international guarantees for all people to exercise universal rights *without discrimination of any kind as to race, color, sex, ...*" (International Covenant on Economic, Social and Cultural Rights) or to enjoy rights and freedoms "*without distinction of any kind such as race, ethnic group, sex, ...*" (African Charter on Human and People's Rights). The 2000 Constitutive Act of the African Union states that the Union shall function in accordance with principles that include "promotion of gender equality." In 2003, African Union Heads of State and Government adopted the African Women's Protocol (www.achpr.org/english/_info/women_en.html) and it came into force (with 15 countries' ratification) in 2005. The Protocol addresses "specific problems and issues that have been major constraints and hindrances for African women in the past," including "the right to inheritance, widowhood, affirmative action to promote equal access and participation in politics and decision-making; and rights of particularly vulnerable groups of women." (Gladys Mutukwa, regional coordinator of WiLDAF, from a paper presented to the SADC regional women's parliamentary caucus in May 2005.)

[2] The concerns of the five-year review were confirmed by the UNDP's recent completion of independent evaluation of gender mainstreaming over the last 10 years—stemming from strong concerns by members of the Executive Board that UNDP had not been effective, and that women [and development] were losing along the way. The ten-year review context was reflected in the AWID biannual meetings in Bangkok in Oct. 2005 with the theme, "What have we changed, and how"? There was a call for more analysis on how to solve problems and create change, adding to our strengths in identifying the need for change. We need to think about how change happens—whether it is via actions such as movement and alliance building, non-violent action or strategic spaces within institutions."

[3] For more on the global movement, see *The Global Women's Movement: Origins, Issues and Strategies*, Peggy Atrobus, Zed Books, 2004.

[4] The author does not suggest that the international norms drive women's rights advocates, i.e. that their work for change is because of international pressure. She does, however, question whether some of the tactics are driven by the international community, particularly by donors.

[5] Others, too, are searching for ways to understand limited impacts and improve results: "[M]ore systematic thinking and ongoing dialogue is urgently needed to clarify the meanings of participation and rights, and related terms of empowerment and rights-based development, including their relationships to one another and their implication for practice." Institute of Development Studies (IDS) Working Paper 235, "Rights-based approaches and Beyond: Challenges of Linking Rights and Participation," p.3 (2004).

[6] Gender mainstreaming, if undertaken effectively—which is also not always a given.

[7] "By failing to break down the boxes that have separated rights and development, NGOs lose the potential dynamism and power that such integration offers." IDS, p. 3.

[8] As will be noted below, this chapter paper is in part "inspired" by Trubek and Galanter's 1973 paper entitled "Scholars in Self-Estrangement"—so this one may be "Women's Rights Advocate in Reflection."

[9] For purposes of introducing the tensions or issues, they do not follow chronologically.

[10] These concerns do not belie the fact that there may be positive outcomes from the lobbying process, even when it does not result in a new law because the discussions may lead to incremental changes in attitudes. There are risks, however, that aggressive lobbying may have the opposite effect, driving some people away with pressure rather than engaging them in conversations.

[11] This may not be "American" across the board, as there are such variations culturally and geographically within the United States. I suspect, for example, that such "dinner table culture" may be more northeastern than southern!

[12] See, e.g. the impending reversal of *Roe v. Wade*, U.S. Supreme Court. While the law has yet to be fully reversed, the process of changing attitudes has taken place more outside the courts than within and then using the law to impose an extended thinking by some upon the broader population.

[13] In fact some readers of this chapter may find that rather than raising an unknown or unrecognized issue, its contribution is more to underscore or support those observations.

[14] See "Introduction" by Marge Schuler in *Becoming a Human Rights Advocate Step by Step,* Women, Law and Development International, 2000, pp. 2-16.

[15] We might also look to "gender budgets" projects to consider efforts to ensure that resources are allocated for implementation and for meeting the needs of women—but I shall leave that discussion to our later comparison with "gender mainstreaming."

[16] Note that this is an edited list, and there are some activities and outcomes that go a bit farther toward the recommended approach, but these do appear to be major drivers of the program.

[17] "Scholars in Self-Estrangement: Some Reflections on the Crisis in Law and Development Studies in the United States," Trubek D. and M. Galanter, *Wisconsin Law Review*, vol. 1974 (1975): pp. 1062-1102. See also the unpublished paper by Meagher and Silverstein that suggests three levels of input from local people and culture—core conception (liberal legal), middle level hypothesis, and culturally sensitive—and illustrates the preferred approach with a case study from Ethiopia.

[18] The result, in part, was a period of little work on law followed by a sort of resurgence within work in Central and Eastern Europe, but now with the label "Rule of Law" instead of "Law and Development." Twenty years later, and now based on similar concerns stemming from the Eastern European work, Tom Carothers and others affiliated with the Carnegie Institute's Rule of Law project are raising stunningly similar concerns. "Promoting the Rule of Law Abroad: The Problem of Knowledge," Thomas Carothers, Working Paper (2003), Carnegie Endowment for International Peace. See also "International Support for Civil Justice Reform in Developing and Transition Countries: An Overview and Evaluation," presentation by Richard E. Messick, Senior Public Sector Specialist, The World Bank (2000): pp. 1-13.

[19] "Legal Culture and Social Development" in *Law and the Behavioral Sciences*, Lawrence Friedman and Stewart Macaulay (1970): pp. 1000-1017.

[20] There are those who recognize the importance of culture, but do not focus on *legal* culture in particular. For example, Lisa VeneKlasen et al. go well beyond the legalistic practitioners when they note: "Changes in the substance of the law and policy or in the behavior and practice of enforcing structures (e.g. the courts, police, hospitals) have little impact on [domestic violence] abuse unless complemented by cultural changes (personal empowerment, education and the development of critical thinking and skills). Economic development alone, which is often seen as the solution to inequality, will not automatically lead to the improvement of governance systems or the advancement and exercise of rights" (IDS 40-41). Still, the solution is assumed to lie within perfecting and gaining access to a liberal legal system.

[21] One example might be Japanese culture: that until recently, resolving disputes and maintaining social order may have depended more on striving for harmony ("wa") than on vindicating individual rights. In the former Soviet system, predicated on Karl Marx's expectation that the State would wither away and law become unnecessary, laws were in fact used as mechanisms for control and oppression, and not so much regarded as socially agreed-upon guidelines to be respected for the social good.

[22] Cited by Dianne Hubbard, coordinator of the Gender Research & Advocacy Project in Namibia.

[23] Though, in the context of a conference focus that extends beyond Africa to the Diaspora, I would venture to challenge the extent to which laws alone have in

fact changed attitudes and behavior—as well as the extent to which attitudes and behaviors have in fact changed!

[24] "Law and Social Change: The Semi-Autonomous social field as an appropriate subject of study," Sally Falk Moore in *Law as Process*, Routledge & Kegan, Paul (1978): pp. 54-81. The chapter includes discussion of Tanzanian society, mixing customary and communist reglementation within communities.

[25] A comparable concept would be the "Arenas of Choice" that Robert and Ann Seidman suggest for "role occupants" expected to comply with or follow government imposed rules. *Legislative Drafting for Democratic Social Change: A Manual for Drafters,* Ann Seidman, Robert B. Seidman and Nalin Abeysekere, Kluwer Law International (2001).

[26] The multilateral example of the World Bank's project on Women and the Law in Africa may illustrate how American/western approaches have become standardized, or how a more international organization may take a somewhat more varied or culturally-appropriate approach.

[27] They include a program of the Asia Foundation in the 1990s, the Global Women in Politics (GWIP) program; the Women's Legal Rights Initiative (WLRI) implemented by Chemonics International, along with the Center for Development and Population Activities (CEDPA), Development and Training Services (DTS) and several other organizations; the American Bar Association's Central European and Eurasian Law Initiative (CEELI) and Africa Programs; Minnesota Advocates Women's Program; and the National Democratic Institute's work on advocacy. As Minnesota Advocates' Women's Human Rights Program has not worked in Africa (it has partnered with organizations in Central and Eastern Europe, the Commonwealth of Independent States, Nepal, Mexico and Haiti), we shall not consider it here. Their approach, however, is to document violations of women's rights, such as domestic violence, rape, employment discrimination, and sexual harassment in the workplace. Their staff and volunteers conduct in-country research through close collaboration with local women's non-governmental organizations, and their reports include analyses of a country's legislation related to women's rights and of the local law enforcement system, as well as recommendations on bringing laws and practice into conformity with international human rights obligations. The National Democratic Institute (NDI) is a U.S. nongovernmental organization engaged in democracy building around the world. NDI's Global Programs include civic advocacy and education, political party reform, assisting women candidates, training elected women leaders, and strengthening legal frameworks. In the 1990s, NDI's work with women was limited to activities such as supporting a women's political caucus in South Africa; it has since increased until today it has a "Win with Women" program.

[28] It might also be instructive to consider a number of organizations associated with Georgetown University's Women in Law and Public Policy program: Leadership and Advocacy for Women in Africa-Ghana (LAWA-Ghana); Law and Advocacy for Women-Uganda (LAW-Uganda); the Women's Legal Aid Centre in Tanzania; and the Women's Rights and Protection Alternative (WRAPA) in

Nigeria, recognizing that each has involved leadership by women who are 1) lawyers and 2) were influenced by their programs at a U.S. law school.

[29] WLR Annual Report on Best Practices, Lessons Learned and Success Stories, Chemonics International Inc., and Development & Training Services Inc., February 2004, p. 7. http://womensnet.org.za/WLRI/index.shtml.

[30] www.CEDPA.org

[31] WLR Annual Report, p. 9.

[32] While South Africa certainly belongs within the ambit of this analysis geographically, it is not always helpful to rely on it as an illustration for Africa, as its history—including the legal system of laws, institutions and legal culture—differs so substantially from that of other African nations. In many parts of Africa, the western colonial law did not reach beyond a limited geographic and demographic range—leaving the rest of the population to continue using and relying on customary law or other sources of reglementation.

[33] "Legal Literacy and Law Enforcement Agencies in Ghana," Akua Kuenyehia, in *Legal Literacy: A Tool for Women's Empowerment*," Eds. Margaret Schuler & Sakuntala Kadirgamar-Rajasingham; Women, Law and Development International, UNIFEM 1992.

[34] See, for example, the Tostan program in Senegal that has focused on Female Genital Cutting—but not as a legal program. Rather, it emerged from a women's legal literacy program and a health unit within it, and it grew as a result of women taking leadership to raise the issue and seek change at the local level.

[35] The classic example was concern for the increase in men's alcoholism and decreased life expectancies in the former Soviet Union in the late 1990s.

[36] As well as in workforce offices, organizations, teams, etc.

[37] It is this author's belief that the evolving understanding of gender and development was not only generated by experience, but also enriched and strengthened by inclusion of voices and leadership from the South.

CHAPTER THREE
RADICAL CITIZENSHIP: POWERFUL
MOTHERS AND EQUAL RIGHTS

Judith Van Allen

Liberal democratic citizenship, in many times and places rather taken for granted, is today widely contested as globalizing capitalism drives increasing migration and new communities challenge old assumptions about "belonging" and rights. When the denial of citizenship is perceived not only as the denial of civil and political rights, but also as the denial of personhood itself, claims about citizenship can become passionate. In Africa's environment of "new democracies" and new constitutions, "citizenship"—as a claim to rights, to entitlements, to civic participation—takes on salience and offers political traction for both "outsiders" and "insiders," those who seek to open as well as those who seek to narrow the boundaries of belonging (See *African Studies Review* 2006).

In this moment of passionate contestation over citizenship, women in Africa are pressing their demands for entrance into the political sphere—spaces and practices that have been historically gendered as male. Feminists have analyzed and brought into visibility the false universalism of liberal democratic citizenship—a citizenship implicitly understood as the privilege of men and for generations legally restricted to white, propertied male heads of households, who were construed as "representing" women, children, apprentices, servants and slaves. Only the propertied or "free" man was considered a proper citizen. It took long political struggles for other groups to claim formal citizenship, and their political struggles for equal substantive citizenship and for social citizenship continue (Friedman 2005; Hobson, Lewis and Simm 2002; Lister 1997; Molyneux and Razavi 2002; Orleck 1997; Pateman 1988; Voet 1998; Vogel 1991; Werbner and Yuval-Davis 1999).

This male European construction of the political was carried by colonialism to African societies through law and missionary practices, where it merged and interconnected with African structuring of leadership as "male," systems in which male elders are construed as "representing" the whole of their kinship units. As many scholars and activists have argued, in African pre-colonial dual systems, women had their own political sphere, and in patrilineal as well as in matrilineal societies, women in ruling lineages often had authority over women in many respects, but these forms of female political authority tended to be suppressed by colonialism's "unification" of political authority into male-gendered political institutions (Clark 1980; Mba 1982; O'Barr 1975-76; Okonjo 1976; Presley 1986; Ritzenthaler 1960; Shanklin 1990; Van Allen 1976; Wipper 1982).

African women attempting to exercise citizenship rights or claim citizenship entitlements today must engage these African/European constructions—of political membership and citizenship, and especially of political leadership—as "male," that is, as something only men "properly" engage in, because only men are seen as the "proper" representatives of "all" citizens, and because the socially constructed as well as the narrowly biological demands of family responsibility placed upon women pose serious barriers to their participation and active leadership.[1]

As a strategy for making government policy more "woman-friendly, African women activists are using various party and electoral mechanisms to get more women into government" (Bauer, this volume; Bauer and Taylor 2005; Britton 2005; Geisler 2004; Goetz and Hassim 2003; Hassim 2006; Selolwane 2006; Tripp 2000). But when women enter parliaments and cabinets, we must still ask: "What as?" If women challenge the false universalism of citizenship, what do they (what should they) put in its place? Is it possible to create new constructions of citizenship and political leadership that capture the particularities of female gender as currently constructed socially, and yet hold onto the visionary and emotive qualities of "universal citizenship"?

In Western politics—perhaps especially in Britain and the U.S.—the "solution" that has been pursued by feminists focused on electoral politics in recent decades was to assimilate the male model of "universal" citizenship and leadership, abstracting the qualities of active citizens and leaders from gender, that is, treating gender differences as irrelevant to citizenship and leadership. Women seeking political leadership have generally argued that women are equally good legislators and executives, that their "femaleness" does not interfere with their capacities for leadership, and that they should be judged on the same criteria as men. This strategy preserves the emotive qualities of the universalist citizenship vision, but jostles uncomfortably with the expectations of some feminist theorists and women voters that women legislators will be particularly sensitive to women's rights and women's needs. Women politicians seeking leadership positions in fact often seem to have been concerned with proving that they are as tough and un-nurturing as the boys—*pace* Margaret Thatcher or Golda Meir or Indira Ghandi or Condoleeza Rice.

In contrast, African political contexts and history potentially offer a very different "solution" for women challenging the false universalism of citizenship and the strongly male-gendered construct of leadership—one based on "embodied" citizenship and leadership. Some feminist theorists argue for an "embodied" citizenship as a replacement for the abstract universal "citizen," as a way of recognizing the male-gendered historical construction of citizenship and of expanding "citizenship" to include female as well as male bodies (Elshtain 1981; Lister 1989; Pateman 1992; Phillips 1991; Young 1989). But what does it mean to "embody" citizenship? For women to engage in the practices of citizenship and of political leadership as "embodied" actors? Judith Butler argues that there is no such thing as a "prediscursive" body: "…there is no recourse to a body that has not always already been interpreted by cultural meanings" (Butler 1990: 8). Since those cultural meanings differ among societies and over time, shouldn't strategies for "embodying" citizenship also differ?

The attempt to "embody" citizenship can lead to feminist arguments for the transformation of gender constructs and the gendered division of labor, reducing differential embodied citizenship by reducing gender differentials, for example, constructing both women and men as "parents" who equally support and care for children, instead of as "mothers" and "fathers" with differential responsibilities. But such a strategy misses the emotive traction of the particular constructs of "mothers" right now in many African societies—strong constructions of women as mothers, as well as wives and grandmothers and mothers-in-law, and, in many societies, strong histories of women's political leadership and mobilization as "mothers." Can African women effectively claim citizenship and leadership as embodied *mothers*?

There is an extensive (mostly Western) feminist literature on women acting politically from their positions as mothers, covering many countries and historical periods, and taking a variety of positions about how to characterize such action. Women's political mobilization to protect their children, rather than to seek their own rights, is generally labeled "motherist," and evaluations of motherist activism vary widely: from its dismissal as serious female politics to arguments that motherist activism often transforms into either feminist activism (for women's own rights) or into national or international activism (for peace or environmentalism or human rights) and so should be understood as a political gateway for women, to arguments that all forms of "political motherhood" are equally valuable, or that the qualities of "motherist" politics have transformed politics itself into a more "caring" mode. Feminists often warn against the potential dangers in appeals to motherhood and the historical manipulation of motherhood in nationalism—the mothers of the nation whose duty is to produce children, especially soldiers for the nation's armies, and to be proud to sacrifice those children in the nation's name (for example, Albanese 2006; Gaitskell and Unterhalter, 1989; Hobson, et. al, 2002; Jetter et. al, 1997; Kaplan 1982; Lister, 1997; Orleck 1997; Ruddick, 1980; Werbner, 1999; Yuval-Davis and Werbner, 1999).

This literature offers valuable analysis and many useful warnings, but I am struck by the extent to which so many scholars with otherwise differing evaluations of "motherist" politics employ constructions of "motherhood" that seem to reflect Western (white) constructions of "mothers," even when making international or even specifically African claims. "Motherist" politics is seen as expressing nurturance and caring, including the need to feed one's children and keep them safe, certainly characteristics of motherhood shared by African mothers. But with the exception of Deborah Gaitskell's and Elaine Unterhalter's useful analysis of an ANC discourse of mothers as "powerful" emerging in the 1980s (Gaitskell and Unterhalter 1989: 69-75), the discourse of powerful mothers that runs through African history is missing from these analyses of "motherist" politics. Also missing is discussion of the ways in which African women have deployed powerful links between the fertility of women and the fertility of the land to assert their own interests against colonial authorities. That is, African constructions of women as "mothers" have historically been sources of power for women to use to protect their own interests as "women," as well as acting as "mothers" to protect their children, and African women in many societies have acted as "powerful mothers" against threats to their interests—against colonialism, against their "own" national governments, against white settler regimes, against soldiers in genocidal and civil wars, and today against oil companies and other forms of globalizing capitalism.

Various nationalist forces may construct women as "mothers of the nation," but that construction doesn't negate the nascent possibilities of powerful mothers claiming their own rights as mothers and as women. Nor does the construction of women as liberal democratic citizens negate possibilities for women to push for self-definitions of female citizenship. It is crucial to understand that women are "constituted" as citizens, as Linzi Manicom argues:

> Rather than assuming that women exist as political subjects a priori, that is, outside of their representation in political forms, processes and discourses, I am wanting to explore how 'women' are fashioned as different kinds of

gendered political subjects when they are constituted as democratic citizens with rights…(2005: 24)

It is also important to understand the ways in which women's rights organizations become part of a liberal democratic "gender industry" and employ "technologies of citizenship"—the workshops and trainings and conferences that teach women how to enter politics and thereby "constitute" women as liberal democratic citizens and leaders. (Cruickshank, 1999, cited in Manicom 2005:34)

But "becoming citizens" and "becoming leaders" is a dialectical process: liberal democracy constitutes women as citizens, and women's rights organizations can be absorbed into that project, but women activists seeking entrance into electoral politics can also engage in forms of self-constitution that are not derived, or at least not wholly derived, from that project. Both the particular mode of liberal democracy and the discourses on which women can draw in self-constitution vary tremendously from country to country, and strikingly between Western and African ones. To return to my U.S. comparison: there is little positive discourse of "*powerful* mothers" available to American women politicians from the dominant (white) discourse: a "powerful mother" may still call up a Freudian image of a castrating mother, hardly what a woman candidate wants voters to think about. The "good mother" is nurturing and self-sacrificing, but the "good mother" still tends to carry the traits of the "good wife" as well. In dominant (white) popular political discourse there is still debate about whether a woman can be a "good mother" and work outside the home, much less enter politics, until her children have grown. Despite the movement of large numbers of women, including mothers of young children, into the labor force, the Western white concept of the "good mother" still carries the cultural baggage of the "ideal" bourgeois family, with "mother" in the domestic sphere and "father" in the public economic and political sphere.[2]

Lacking the discourse of powerful mothers who are assumed to be engaged in work to support their children, Western women politicians have rejected the nurturing but dependent wife-mother image and have chosen an androgynous image, recreating themselves as inherently equal to men. The relative success of this strategy is indicated by the absence in U.S. political discourse today of claims that women's "hormonal rages" disqualify them for positions of power—claims quite common twenty years ago. Paradoxically, the success of the androgynous strategy in gaining public acceptance for female political leaders, even a female candidate for President in 2008, has made it attractive to some female politicians to indicate and emphasize their "mother" status as a way to "soften" their images and appeal to voters who are weary of militarism and want more "care"—particularly health care—from government.[3]

In contrast, African women citizens and political leaders can draw on a long historical tradition of powerful mothers, and I would argue that when that tradition is combined with appeals to women's rights based on feminist appropriations of liberal democratic traditions, women can enter male-gendered political spaces as "equal rights powerful mothers"—as citizens, activists and leaders—and potentially transform their societies. This is not an argument about women acting from their material positions as mothers, nor an argument that employs an essentialist construction of "women" as "mothers." It is an argument about political strategy: about what activists can take from the available discourse that has emotive power, and how they can reformulate and deploy that discourse for political effectiveness. We can see this process in action in a small but significant non-post-conflict Southern African state: Botswana.[4]

Women activists in Botswana, as they began to organize in the 1980s, confronted strong resistance to women's entry into the political sphere, and especially to women's leadership. "Politics" and political leadership in Botswana have historically been defined as male and dominated by men. As a Setswana proverb puts it, "A cow cannot lead the herd because she will lead them into a ditch," a particularly striking patriarchal reconstruction of cattle behavior, since heifers can be seen by the side of the road leading herds every day[5] (Emang Basadi 1998: 26). When women have entered the political space of the *kgotla*—the village meeting of adult males—they have been defined as acting for men (as when women acted as regents for male heirs to chiefship); or their discussions of community issues have been construed as "religious," not "political"; or their actions have been lost in male-dominated versions of Tswana history (Griffiths 1997; Holm and Molutsi 1989; Landau 1995; Matemba 2005; Molokomme 1994; Morton and Ramsay 1987; Schapera 1940,1955; Van Allen 2000b). The view that "women did not speak in *kgotla*" is commonly expressed, despite the empirical evidence that some women did; the statement should be taken to reflect the reality that when women spoke in *kgotla*, they either did not speak as "women" but as stand-ins for men, or they were not "speaking" in that their speech was not heard unless repeated by men *for* them, or they were not really speaking in "*kgotla*," but in religious meetings held in the same space as the *real kgotla*—the men's *kgotla*—regardless of the content of those meetings and the women's impact on decisions made in the "real" *kgotla*.

In Botswana today the legacy of "*kgotla* democracy" underlies male-gendered liberal democratic structures and practices, posing significant barriers to women's political activism and leadership. But both Tswana and liberal democratic traditions offer leverage against male political dominance. Liberal democracy's discourse of equal rights can be used by women against the liberal democratic constructions that exclude them. Women's groups in Botswana use claims of rights to expand, reframe, and redirect the meanings of "women," "equality," "citizenship" and "leadership"—drawing on both the liberal democratic values expressed in the Botswana Constitution and on the liberal feminism of international women's rights and human rights discourses. Tswana tradition offers the additional discourse of powerful mothers—imagery and language that can be deployed strategically in struggles for equal rights.

By the early 1980s there was a critical mass of educated, employed women—both professional and working class—including lawyers, university lecturers, journalists and other professionals centered in the capital, Gaborone (Selolwane 2006; Van Allen 2000a). The particular political economy and history of Bechuanaland/Botswana produced this female critical political mass—privileging girls to attend school by sending boys to cattle posts instead of to school, opening jobs to women as the post-diamond development economy expanded—while young men continued to migrate to work in the mines, first in South Africa and then in Botswana (Van Allen 2000a). Women activists had identified marital property laws, in particular, as discriminatory, and produced pamphlets about women's legal rights through the (two-woman) Women's Affairs Unit. But the real catalyst for the women's movement was the passage in 1982 of a Citizenship Amendment Law, which denied women citizens the right to pass on their citizenship to their children if they were married to non-citizens, but allowed male citizens to do so.[6] Provoked into action, a small group of women professionals formed Emang Basadi! (Stand Up, Women!) in 1986 and attempted to lobby the government to change the law, as well as to educate women about their existing rights through conferences, workshops and pamphlets. The intransigence of government radicalized women activists, transforming a request for reform into a movement intent on challenging the male dominance of the whole political and social system (Selolwane 1998, 2006; Van Allen 2000a, 2001). Where would activists be without the intransigence of authorities?

In 1990 Emang Basadi joined forces with regional women lawyers' groups to support a suit brought by lawyer and activist Unity Dow, challenging the Citizenship Amendment Law on both constitutional and international human rights' grounds. Dow's husband was not a Botswana citizen and her daughter had been denied a Botswana passport. In court the government appealed to *customary law*, arguing first that the Constitution was premised upon "the traditional view" that a child born to a married couple "belonged" to the father in all ways, including citizenship and guardianship, and second that the framers of the Constitution had not intended to forbid discrimination on the basis of gender (Molokomme 1994; Dow 1995). Neither of these arguments convinced the courts. Both the High Court and the Court of Appeals upheld Unity Dow's challenge, and the Citizenship Amendment Law was referred back to Parliament in 1992 for revision. High Court Judge Martin Horwitz's decision, upheld on appeal, explicitly argued that since society had changed, women "can no longer be viewed as being chattels of their husbands," and the provision against sex discrimination takes precedence (Dow 1995).

The Dow decision referred to liberal democratic values and the changing status of "women" in striking down the Citizenship Amendment Law, but the case itself was originally posed as "mothers" married to foreigners vs. "fathers" married to foreigners. The court effectively ruled that in this context, "mothers" should have equal status with "fathers," a clear equal rights-based destabilization of both Tswana patriarchal kinship values and of British common law patriarchal values.[7] But there is a subtext here of dueling "traditions." The government and other supporters of the law were upholding a construction of "women" as "wives"—the wife's loyalties were presumed to follow those of her husband, so that if he were a citizen of another state, her loyalties were presumed to follow. She might have the right to vote, but as a "citizen" she was still presumed to be under the authority of her husband—the male head of household— and following patrilineal custom, the children belonged to him. "Women" as "wives" often figure prominently in patriarchal and nationalist political discourses as symbols of the nation who must be controlled and "protected" by the men of the nation against foreign men, and that symbolism has been strongly expressed in public debates about the law. Dow and her supporters, however, drew on a strong counter-tradition of kinship values by constructing "women" as "mothers," powerful mothers who protect and defend their children, and who deserve respect. The decision promised greater control over their own lives for "women" as both "wives" and "mothers," illustrating how a rights discourse and rights claims can effectively challenge the relations of gendered power underlying the law. But the challenge deployed both rights claims and appeals to the powerful aspect of Tswana motherhood validated by kinship values. The Citizenship Amendment Law can be seen as an attempt by government to reassert patriarchal nationalism against changing social and economic conditions and relations, and the Dow decision as a victory not only for equal rights but for powerful mothers with equal rights.

Winning the Citizenship Amendment Case catalyzed the Botswana women's rights movement, led by Emang Basadi. But government continued to stonewall, not actually changing the legislation and even threatening to float a nation-wide referendum on the 1982 amendment, believing that conservative rural voters, women as well as men, would support it. In response Emang Basadi switched to a direct electoral strategy: if men in government were unresponsive to women's issues, they would replace them with women—and not just any women, but women who were "gender-sensitive." Their strategy was (and is) to build women's leadership capacity, recruiting women candidates, training them in workshops and supporting them in elections; and organizing women activists in the political parties. Instead of women acting as a unit of mobilization in support of the party, these activists would be transformed into a force for including women in party leadership and getting women's issues onto party agendas.

Emang Basadi explicitly recognizes that "being female does not necessarily mean that one is gender-sensitive," and includes sensitization to "gender and women's issues" in their training for candidates. (Emang Basadi 1998: 13). Secondly, their focus is on voter education, since women are a clear majority of voters but are often reluctant to vote for women. Voter education programs attempt to convince voters that women have "the capacity to lead," that voters' choices will materially impact on their own and their families' lives, and that they should therefore choose among candidates based on the candidates' political platforms. This is an attempt to challenge "traditional" loyalty to the Botswana Democratic Party—which has been in power since independence—as well as loyalty to chiefs, who cannot constitutionally run for office but can and do have significant influence over rural voters.(Emang Basadi 1998:26-27)

Emang Basadi went on to organize and energize coalitions of women's non-governmental organizations (NGOs) and other women's groups in Botswana, and as these groups have taken on leadership on particular women's issues, Emang Basadi has concentrated on its electoral strategy. Although Emang Basadi has had mixed results in electing women to office, the government did pass a new citizenship law in late 1995 and has moved to re-examine other legislation for discrimination against women. In the 1999 elections, dubbed "The Year of the Woman" by one newspaper, female representation in Parliament doubled and several women were appointed to the Cabinet and to other high-ranking positions. Unity Dow was appointed to the High Court in 1998, joined in 2003 by Athaliah Molokomme, co-organizer and first chair of Emang Basasi, who was then appointed first woman Attorney General in 2005. The 2004 elections, however, were a disappointment for Emang Basadi since, for complex political reasons, fewer women were nominated and elected. Women's representation dropped from 18 percent (8 out of 44) to 9 percent (6 out of 63).[8] But even with a lower percentage of women members, in 2004 Parliament, under pressure from women outside as well as inside the government, revoked the common-law marital power, a major goal of Emang Basadi and other women's groups—and, with support from Emang Basadi, chiefship itself has become open to women (Matemba 2005).

Emang Basadi can be seen as involved in the liberal democratic project of constituting female citizens, of operating part of the "gender industry" and creating "technologies of citizenship" that both enable women's participation and constrain it in particular ways, producing them as gendered citizens "in ways that emphasize gender over other contending social identifications and position them as women (as opposed to racialized or class subjects) in relation to the nation-state" (Manicom, 2005: 34). This author contends that Emang Basadi is also constituting "women" citizens as "mothers"—powerful mothers with equal rights—and that this process not only enhances their entry into politics and increases the likelihood of new legislation and programs that will benefit them as powerful mothers, but also involves the problems identified by Manicom—the privileging of gender over other social identifications. In Botswana, the most significant of these is class—both urban class and rural/urban class interconnections. It was not accidental that in the first women's inter-party caucus march, organized by Emang Basadi, women carried signs emphasizing not only women's solidarity but also their strength as mothers: "Basadi! United We Stand, Divided We Fall!" and "Vote A Woman! Suckle the Nation!"

Motherhood as a model of female power as well as nurturant strength is part of Botswana women's political discourse—sometimes explicit, often running as a subtext—and actual motherhood is not seen as a barrier by either men or women to a woman's standing for office. A candidate *without* children would be more suspect. Male-dominated political discourse itself has historically included nurturing images in praise poems for *dikgosi*—praise poems laud a *kgosi* as the milk-giver or the giver of porridge and meat, or urge him to "carry the nation on your back in a calf-skin sling," as babies are carried by mothers and older siblings (Schapera 1965: 116-118, 162). A good male leader was thus metaphorically *like a mother* as well as *like a father* to his people. It was not actual motherhood and fatherhood that were combined or blurred: actual fathers did not carry children in calf-skin slings, nor did they cook porridge, although as cattle-owners they did provide milk and meat for women to cook. The significance of the metaphorical mothering expected of a good *kgosi* is that it embeds in the political discourse a concept of the "good mother" connected to the exercise of power, a concept that women politicians can activate and manipulate for their own purposes.

Having children is today virtually the defining mark of full adulthood for Batswana women, motherhood having replaced traditional rites of initiation and marriage. It is difficult for a woman in Botswana, as elsewhere in Africa, to be taken seriously as an adult, whatever her educational or financial accomplishments, unless she has had at least one child. Since women in Botswana are expected to contribute significantly to their children's support, wage labor and the remunerative aspect of office-holding are not seen as being in conflict with maternal responsibilities, but as an integral part of the construction of the "good mother." A woman candidate speaking out in public does pose a direct disruption of expected conjugal relations and husbands' authority, but not necessarily of expectations of her parental responsibilities—after all, women running for office usually have maids at home to care for their children and houses. This poses a problem for "women's" solidarity—a point to which we will return below. But it does not pose a problem for women candidates as candidates. Challenges to women candidates as wives who are apparently not under the authority of their husbands express contemporary social tension about changing kinship and gender relations, and about men's perceived and feared loss of control over women. A woman standing for Parliament is not simply a woman outside the home trying to earn money. She is a woman seeking public, political authority and power, including power and authority *over adult men.* That is the point of challenge.

Women's rights campaigns themselves reflect the continuing construction of "woman" as "mother," and the assertion of the nurturing, provisioning, suckling mother as a model of female leadership, both in material goals and in language. Gaitskell and Unterhalter point out that in ANC calls for action, there is a "fusion of women and mothers," and that this "should be read in the context of the vernacular African languages where the word for adult woman and the word for mother are the same" (1989: 72), and the Botswana "Woman's Manifesto" uses the word for "mothers" in its Setswana version (Emang Basadi 1999).[9] The "mother" construction is strikingly illustrated by the symbol chosen by the Women's Affairs Unit: a drawing of the heads and shoulders of three women silhouetted in profile, one carrying a hoe over her shoulder and a baby in a sling on her back, one carrying a load of firewood on her head and one carrying two books, all encircled by the slogan, "*Mosadi ke thari ya sechaba*—"Women carry the nation on their backs," a political (re)appropriation of the use of the mother metaphor already present in the male Tswana praise poem discourse of the *Kgosi* urged to carry the nation on his back. The image of the powerful mother is readily available from Tswana history and culture. In Tswana discourse "mother" is a powerful female role, not a subservient one; a mother is nurturing and will sacrifice her own personal interests for the sake of her child, but she does this from a position of power. A mother has authority not only over children, but over her adult sons as well as her daughters and daughters-in-law, who are expected to treat her with respect and deference.[10] A mother is someone to be taken seriously; a wife is someone who takes orders, serves and acts with deference toward men. A woman politician can be a "good mother" and a "bad wife" at the same time, and she must negotiate her way through party and Parliament by trying to engage her male colleagues from the "mother" role while resisting their attempts to engage her as a "wife" who defers to and takes care of them.

Emang Basadi conveys the existing construction of women as mothers and their practical needs in its policy proposals as well as its use of imagery. The Women's Manifesto devotes considerable attention to women's nurturant roles, emphasizing prenatal care, maternal and child health, child maintenance and child care, with brief attention to reproductive rights, construed in terms of "family planning." Issues related to women as workers also implicitly reflect the cultural construction of motherhood as including the responsibility of supporting one's children as part of caring for them. The woman whose rights and development Emang Basadi seeks to expand is implicitly and explicitly a mother. The assumption that women political leaders, like other women, will bear children is also reflected in the Manifesto. One of the goals expressed in the 1999 version, with its heavy emphasis on moving women into positions of power, is to have daycare centers available for Parliament and other governmental bodies, so that women Members of Parliament and local Councilors can take time to nurse their babies without missing important legislative business. It is assumed that all women, even women legislators, generally over the age of thirty, will continue to have babies, and therefore such babies must be incorporated into the daily life of government. The Manifesto also addresses the problems of women as "wives," as in its demand for the revocation of the marital power—a goal accomplished regarding the marital power in common law in 2004. However, marital power—giving husbands control over wives' property— also directly affects mothers' ability to care for their children. The Manifesto addresses some of the problems of domestic workers, but follows the liberal democratic tendency to construct more privileged women as active citizens and domestic workers as "the most vulnerable," who should be the targets of "help," but without any hint that it is the domestic work and childcare provided by these women—also mothers—that enables other (privileged) mothers to engage in professions and in politics.

To conceptualize, much less advocate, "women" entering politics and political leadership as "powerful mothers with equal rights" means accepting a dual-embodied citizenship and leadership—a recognition of the male *and* female gendered nature of citizenship—perhaps as a move toward some future resolution of gendered, embodied citizenship that moves beyond a dualistic, heteronormic construction, perhaps as a move toward continued gendered and embodied citizenship that could include categories beyond the heteronormic without negating gender. It leaves us, however, with the problem of essentialism: "powerful mother" is as essentialist as "women." How can one retain the power of the "powerful mother" as a political category anymore than one can retain the power of "women" as a political category, without denying the particularities of women and the conflicts and power differentials among "women" and among "mothers"?

Clearly, all mothers are not equal. In the starkest demonstration of that inequality, some mothers must leave their own children in order to work caring for other mothers' children, the paradoxical basis for the way some Botswana women are able to engage in professional work and political activism for women's rights. Many other women, often younger and working in lower paid jobs, send their children to grandmothers in the village, along with remittances that may or may not cover their support. All of this class- and rural/urban-based passing down of responsibility for the care of children creates contradictions among "mothers" and points to problems in the use of "powerful mothers" as a political basis for mobilizing women across class and rural/urban lines. But it also points to the issues that need to be addressed in order to deal with the particularities within the "universal" of powerful mothers. Thinking about women citizens and leaders as "powerful mothers" could open a path to examining the differences and conflicts among actual mothers—which most Botswana, and African, women, after all, are. Such an opening goes beyond adding together the "social characteristics" of women—racialist, class, ethnic, rural/urban—and leads into the social structuring of the gender division of labor and power as it relates to reproduction as well as production. It points our attention at the economy of care as it is allocated by class as well as gender, and could lead to a more progressive women's rights politics.

"Women's" politics can find itself blocked by the attempt to deal with the particularities of "women"—by the differences and conflicts created among women by racialist, class, ethnic, rural/urban and national divisions. These divisions intrude into debate and actions about the gaining of full citizenship by women and provoke confusion among those trying to figure out the praxis of women's citizenship—the blending of theory and practice that can make women's citizenship and political leadership a reality. We seek solutions that retain the power of the universality of citizenship but still recognize the particularity of gender. We seek solutions that retain the power of "women" as a political category but still recognize the particularities among women. Many feminist theorists are trying to resolve these contradictions, wishing to keep the political power of "women" while recognizing diversity within the category. It seems possible that for women in many African countries, some form of "powerful mothers with equal rights," a merging of gender difference with liberal democratic equal rights, may—at least in the present moment—offer a more powerful basis for women's entry into political participation and power than approaches that lead away from difference. This paradigm also poses a risk: the "we are all mothers" link could be used as a path to cross-class alliances, but it could also be misused by privileged women to rally poorer women to vote for them, with no promise of real political reward for that support. This is a political choice, not a predetermined outcome.

Political recognition of differences among women as "mothers" by women activists and leaders—an explicit class-conscious feminist politics—could open possibilities for cross-class understanding and political mobilization. It could provide a basis for moving from the construction of poorer women as "the most vulnerable" women who need to be "helped" to seeing them as worker/mothers whose need is to organize to act for themselves. Explicit political agendas expressing cross-class alliances could begin to address the differential and sometimes conflicting interests of "mothers." Such a strategy could combine appeals to women in their currently construed positions as mothers with the political strategy of constructing women citizens and leaders as powerful mothers with equal rights—a new political vision in which the heifer will (accurately) lead the herd *not* into the ditch, but onto a new, promising (even paved) road.

Notes

[1] By "narrowly biological" I mean pregnancy, childbirth and nursing, which are still constructed differently in different societies, but remain, for the moment, female capacities, often culturally constructed as "responsibilities" or "functions" or "destinies."

[2] The very real conflicts between the demands of childcare and employment are argued as reasons for women to "stay home" with their children, and assume a husband who can support them all. The debate negates the actual situations of the majority of women who have no choice but to seek paid employment, and is easily manipulated in racist directions.

[3] Hillary Clinton in her Presidential bid sometimes cast herself as a "mother," while continuing to emphasize her "toughness" on foreign policy. The vicious sexist attacks on her as "castrating" one minute and "weak" the next indicate the depth of American uneasiness with explicitly powerful women. The most obvious deployment of motherhood in recent U.S. politics has been by Nancy Pelosi (Democrat, California), the first woman Speaker of the House of Representatives, who took her oath of office in 2007 surrounded by children and grandchildren of legislators, including her own grandchildren. Pelosi characterizes her experience as a mother of five as training in organization and efficiency. She moves slightly toward "powerful mother" imagery in saying that as party leader she will use her "mother-of-five voice" when necessary. However, the U.S. press continues to characterize the "mother" appeal only in terms of "softening," whether of particular female candidates or of emphasizing the Democratic Party's alleged image as the "mommy party," the party seen as best able to provide "care" in domestic policy, as opposed to the "daddy party," the Republican Party's alleged competence in providing "toughness" in foreign policy (See Povich 2007; Toner 2007). Whatever the accuracy of the "mommy party/daddy party" characterization, the terms themselves indicate how strongly and "traditionally" gendered U.S. politics remains. The French Socialist Party Presidential nominee Segolene Royal characterized herself as the "mother-protector" of the nation and her opponent as "a survival-of-the-fittest Darwinian male," employing a very "feminine" and sexy image to distinguish herself from "masculine" politicians. This strategy contrasts with the U.S. or British androgyny strategy, but similarly constructs "motherhood" as nurturing and "soft" (Sciolino 2006; Smith 2007). It also failed to gain election for Royal.

[4] Botswana has been a stable multi-party democracy since independence in 1966. Its economic growth rate, based on diamonds discovered after independence, has become one of the highest in the world. The current HIV/AIDS pandemic has put the society and economy under great stress, but shows no signs of undermining political stability. (See, for example, Edge and Lekorwe, 1998; Holm and Molutsi, 1989; Nengwekhulu, 1998; Samatar, 1999; Leith, 2005.)

[5] *"Ga dike di etelela ke manamagadi ele, dika wela ka lemena."* I owe this observation to Lydia Nyati-Ramahobo, who first pointed out to me the heifers leading herds by the roadside.

[6] The law provided for easy access to citizenship by foreign wives, but not foreign husbands, and significantly increased the residency time required to apply for citizenship. It did provide that unmarried women could pass on their citizenship to their children, but this, like the provisions for wives, accorded with Tswana custom, since the child of an unmarried woman would belong to the lineage of the woman's father.

[7] "Patriarchal" is here construed in the narrow sense as meaning "rule by the fathers," a construction of political authority still strong in Botswana, although under contestation by the "sons" as well as by women as wives, mothers and daughters.

[8] These results constitute a reversal rather than progress towards the SADC goal of 30 percent% women by 2005, demonstrating clearly the problems for women of single-member districts ("first past the post") and an absence of quotas. Selolwane (2006) argues that splits among and within opposition parties that virtually guarantee continued dominance by the Botswana Democratic Party (BDP) also make it impossible for women to exert significant leverage on parties. The BDP's overall popular vote majorities have steadily declined, but their majorities in Parliament remain strong. All women elected have been candidates of the dominant Botswana Democratic Party, or appointed by the President. Paradoxically, although the weakness of the opposition reduces the women's movement's leverage, it has sometimes contributed to the election of more (BDP) women. Splits among the opposition parties in 1999 enabled the BDP to take some districts usually held by the Botswana National Front, and a "peace pact" among some of the opposition parties in 2004 reduced that possibility—women candidates are often put in more marginal seats, and both the gains in 1999 and the losses in 2004 reflect that. Margaret Nasha, the most prominent woman parliamentarian and cabinet minister defeated in 2004 (in the Gaborone district she took in 1999) was (re)appointed to Parliament and to the cabinet by President Mogae. She is an outspoken proponent of women's rights and interests.

[9] Printed in Setswana and English back-to-back, as "The Women's Manifesto" and "Dikeletso tsa Bomme mo Botswana." "Basadi," meaning both "women" and "wives," was chosen specifically to echo the national anthem, in which men are urged to stand up for their country and women are urged to stand up beside their men—"emang basadi" urges women to stand up, pointedly leaving out the "beside their men," illustrating the argument of this chapter that existing political and gender discourse offers possibilities for political deployment, but does not determine the deployments chosen by activists.

[10] Schapera observed that when boys left their mothers' houses to go to the cattle posts, they became less amenable to maternal authority (1966 [1940]: 252-3), but deference and respect to mothers continues to be seen as proper behavior

for young men—and the majority of boys now stay in their mothers' or grandmothers' households to attend school.

CHAPTER FOUR
THE ECONOMIC ROOTS OF AFRICAN WOMEN'S POLITICAL PARTICIPATION

Claire Robertson

Dedicated to the Women Traders of Accra and Nairobi

Introduction

Analyses of the Euro-American struggle to achieve women's rights have usually focused on the political, taking an equity approach to explaining why women sought equal rights with men, and focusing on middle-class white women.[1] Thus, the women's suffrage movement often receives most attention, along with arguments about citizenship. Similarly, the argument for women serving in the military is often couched in terms of civil rights and equity issues, pointing out that historically women have been disadvantaged in terms of civil rights often because they have not served in the military, which service has often been a key definer of citizenship rights. Indeed, the U.S. and British suffrage movements are often analyzed specifically in the context of women's war efforts in World War I. This chapter will suggest another approach to explaining how and why women sought and achieved equal rights with men, looking at an alternative explanation for what can be seen as an essential basis for women's achievement of full citizenship rights: economic activism by women, in particular in business. Friedrich Engels said that, "the first condition for the liberation of the wife is to bring the whole female sex back into public industry," which then would require abolition of the monogamous family as "the economic unit of society." He believed that the legal inequality of women and men in marriage was not a cause, "but the effect of the economic oppression of the woman."[2] I would not go so far as to advocate such a monocausal explanation, but we do need to rethink and rescue information about women seeking economic rights. This rethinking, as data about African women are wont to do, problematizes the common distinctions between practical and strategic gender interests a la Molyneux, as well as between the public and the private spheres a la Rosaldo.[3] In this chapter I will examine how in two African contexts involvement in business has, in fact, contributed to women seeking and achieving citizenship rights, and how in an international context the push for women's economic rights goes back hundreds of years before the nineteenth and twentieth century political rights movements began.

Discussion

In July 2002, the world was startled to hear that hundreds of Niger Delta women, aged thirty to ninety, had taken over Nigeria's largest oil export terminal belonging to ChevronTexaco in Escravos, demanding that the company invest in their surrounding communities by providing jobs for their sons and development inputs for their villages such as electricity, piped water, schools and other amenities. Workers were held hostage as women negotiated with the company to achieve their goals. Within the week, women also occupied four pipeline flow stations in an action they described as independent of the Escravos effort. These women were armed only with civil disobedience ethics and the most powerful curse women can place upon men: threatened baring of their genitals to shame their targets by reminding them that they too were sons and bound to obey and defend those who gave them life. The women and ChevronTexaco then signed an agreement intended to implement the women's desired reforms and improvements.[4] The reportage paid no attention to any but the most superficial aspects of this situation, so we are left with many questions: how did these women organize themselves, for instance? A "group" is mentioned but nothing further. Thus, we are left with the impression that the actions, which took place over a considerable area and involved over a thousand women, were spontaneous, which is undoubtedly far from the case.

Thus we find ourselves back in the situation of faulty representations that grossly underestimate the history and actions of African women, especially those involved in trade. In 1929, also in southeastern Nigeria, thousands of Igbo women surrounded the homes of "warrant chiefs," who were the principal instruments of British colonial "indirect" rule, appointed to rule over hitherto chiefless people who had used their lineage structures and oracles to maintain order. This "Women's War" escalated into sometimes bloody confrontations when women's dances and curses turned into casualties as the women were shot. The uprising rendered Igboland ungovernable by the British and forced reorganization of the administration. These demonstrations were labeled spontaneous "riots," but the women had widespread trade contacts and organizations that allowed them to organize effectively. At the same time notable contributions to scholarship were furthered when the government hired several British women to discover (belatedly) what indigenous social and political organizations existed in the area.[5]

But it was not only Igbo women who were involved in such action: across Africa women carried out similar protests against colonialism—in Nairobi, Kenya, with the Harry Thuku demonstration, in Cameroon with Anlu, and in Tanzania with the Pare women, all of whom used similar methods to try to secure their rights against colonialist male incursions abetted by local male collaborators.[6] Many of the participants in these protests came from peoples with long involvement in trade—over hundreds of years—for instance along the West African coast or, dating from the nineteenth century, in the Nairobi area.[7] Their organizational skills, in fact, were honed by trade and trading networks. This essay suggests that involvement in trade necessarily brings women to a situation of having full or at least partial economic rights, and that those economic rights then form a basis for pushing for more political rights, as happened in these demonstrations. Women began with economic grievances and found that remedying them necessitated involvement in political protest.

The more a woman is involved in trade, the more she must have full economic rights. A woman cannot conform to the status of being a legal, or jural, minor if she is involved in trade, since she must constantly make decisions involving controlling her own assets—buying and selling property, taking out loans, etc. So, if the law consigns women to the status of children, involvement in trade means they must contravene the law. The process of raising women's status before the law because of their business activities has taken place in many cultural contexts, including medieval England, where legal exceptions to jural minor status were made for women involved in business.[8] Most African states have now signed on to CEDAW, which international convention recognizes women's legal status as being fully equal to men's (although this is largely unenforced).

This essay looks in particular at the evolution of women's trade in two historical African contexts that I have studied: coastal Accra in Ghana and Nairobi, Kenya—both colonial capitals but very different otherwise. In their differences reside clues as to how women developed rights out of trade. The situation of Ga women in central Accra, an old city in which women have traded at least since the sixteenth century, represents an early example of women's achievement of economic rights, while women traders in Nairobi have been faced with a relatively new situation since Nairobi developed rapidly from its inception in 1899, when it was founded by the British in the process of building the Uganda railroad. Both peoples were subjected to British colonialism, but in quite different incarnations: indirect rule in Gold Coast and settler colonialism in central Kenya, which entailed large-scale expropriation of Kikuyu land in particular, but not exclusively. Both had decentralized polities before the imposition of colonialism in the late nineteenth century, but Accra experienced a long preceding period of steadily increasing European influence, while Nairobi, strategically located at the juncture of several ecological zones but with no prior pattern of urbanization, became a town quite suddenly with the arrival of the British railhead.

Culturally there were also large differences, although both the Ga and the Kikuyu were and are dominantly patrilineal, were and are usually horticulturalists, and originally had communal land rights. However, the Ga practiced what can be called bilocal residence and bilateral inheritance, i.e., sons or daughters residing with the parent of the same sex and inheriting property from them. The Kikuyu still practice virilocality or patrilocality and patrilineal male-dominant inheritance patterns. While the Ga have been located in the area for hundreds of years and became involved in both land- and sea-based trade at least as early as the fifteenth century, when first visited by Europeans, the Kikuyu were Bantu migrants who came to their present location perhaps in the eighteenth century. Their intense involvement in long-distance land-based caravan trade came only in the late nineteenth century, and their highly developed agricultural activities mixed with pastoral influences created an orientation toward the land not characteristic of the Ga. Because of these very different settings, British colonialism had very different impacts on women traders from the two locations.

Ga women's pervasive involvement in trade was first noted by a European observer in 1599, when Pieter de Marees described them as

> very nimble about their businesse, and so earnest therein, that they goe at least five or six miles every day to the places where they have to doe, and are laden like asses; for at their backes they carrie their children, and on their heads they have a heavy burthen of fruit or millia, and so goe laden to the market, and there she buyeth fish to carrie home with her, so that oftentimes they come as heavily laden from the market as they went thither...those women goes seven or eight together, and as they passe along the way they are verie merrie and pleasant, for commonly they sing and make a noise.[9]

Subsequently there are whole series of European descriptions of Ga women traders with long lists of commodities traded by them. By 1911, when the first attempt to count women's occupations was made in the Gold Coast census, it was estimated that over 75 percent of Accra women were involved in trade; in 1948 the estimate was over 88 percent when only the oldest area of Accra settlement, Ussher Town—dominated ethnically by Ga—was counted.[10] When I surveyed Ussher Town in 1971-72 it was evident that all of the women aged forty and over were or had at some time been involved in trade. It was an expectation and a necessity among all but the youngest, better educated women.

What impact has this involvement had upon Ga society and women's rights? First, I believe that the residential system was profoundly affected. Before the twentieth century the tendency was for most men to be fishermen and for the women to sell the fish. Fishing communities are famous for fostering women's autonomy, which has come into English in the term "fish-wife," meaning an unruly and aggressive woman, deriving from fish sellers in London's Billingsgate Market. Because of the long absences of fishermen and the necessity of selling the fish, women in such communities often exercised much authority over themselves and their children. Accra was no exception. Women and men developed residential patterns that maximized their businesses. Women lived with their mothers, sisters and daughters, often in compounds where the oldest woman traced her original residential rights through her father; while men lived with their fathers, brothers and sons in separate patrilineally-related residences. This system fostered trade partnerships among these women and crew solidarity for fishing canoes.[11]

The second impact of Ga women's involvement in trade concerns solidarity. Because people's co-residents were also their business partners in both cases, solidarity by gender was fostered. Same-sex sibling and mother-daughter loyalties were most important for women. Women did not live with their husbands but sent clean laundry and cooked meals to the husband via the children, and visited the husband at his house on a pre-arranged basis. If polygyny was involved, this might have meant wives taking turns cooking for him and visiting him. It also contributed to a high level of affective autonomy, as it were, since conjugal emotional relations were not expected to be as intimate as might be fostered by monogamy. Ussher Town women in the 1970s were clear about expecting marriage to be an economic partnership above all; when men did not help they were readily divorced.[12]

In many African societies polygyny helped to create a high level of economic autonomy for women, since women often were expected to take primary responsibility for feeding their own children. Where polygynous women were technically co-resident with their husbands in a patrilocal or virilocal situation, each wife usually had her own hut that she shared with her children, again taking turns with the other wives cooking and sleeping with the husband. With the Ga, small children stayed with the mother until about age five in the case of boys, when they were supposed to join their fathers. However, by the 1970s, boys were more likely to join their fathers once they were older and capable of earning, leaving much of the economic burden of childrearing with the women for children of both sexes.[13] Thus, a combination of societal factors also emphasized women's economic and social autonomy from husbands, in particular. One consequence was that husbands and wives did not practice communal property, but each kept their resources and property separate. Lineages were zealous to preserve this custom to keep land and other rights from being alienated. A woman belonged to her patrilineage for life, never to her husband's lineage.

The custom of keeping property separately within marriage and maintaining single-sex separate residences then logically meant that women had complete freedom to conduct their businesses as they saw fit. A husband could not claim a wife's earnings or insist that she sell only his fish, for instance. Women routinely kept the details of their businesses from their husbands, lest the husbands reduce the amount of "chop money" they contributed to the household (this contribution was a token of the continuation of the marriage and more often than not token in amount also). He could not force her to loan him money either. My favorite story involves a successful moneylender and priestess (of the indigenous religion), who had married three times and in the 1970s had a husband who was quite a bit younger than herself, the equivalent of a "toy boy." I asked her if she charged interest on her loans; the reply was yes, 60 percent per month. Then I asked her if she had ever loaned her husband money and if so, at what interest. She replied, "Yes, but for him, only 30 percent interest"!

This autonomy came at an increasingly steep price, however. Colonial practices systematically excluded women from getting Western-style formal education equivalent to men's, and hence from white collar jobs. After independence men often felt threatened by women's autonomy, a feeling that translated in the late 1970s into government-orchestrated blame on market women for economic problems, market demolitions, and attacks in which soldiers killed women traders for "profiteering."[14] Less dramatically but perhaps more permanently damaging for more women, pervasive sex segregation made it easier to discriminate against women not only for purposes of persecution but also again in access to Western-type education, and Ghanaian society readily duplicated male-dominant class-based colonial structures. The damage done by colonialism and neocolonialism to women ultimately weakened their political position to the point that they could be attacked with impunity. Nonetheless, the historical involvement of coastal women in trade in Ghana/Gold Coast established their full economic rights to do business as they pleased, and that in turn resulted in, for instance, a relatively low rate of domestic violence against women, although some women did routinely abuse children. Women's economic independence and status as jural majors are both factors that tend to reduce levels of violence against them, since they may break abusive marriages and do not need to stay in them for economic reasons.[15] The fact that most of these particular women did not live in the same residence with their husbands probably also had that effect.

Turning to women traders in Nairobi we see a very different situation. My 1997 study, *Trouble Showed the Way: Women, Men and Trade in the Nairobi Area, 1890-1990* (Bloomington: Indiana University Press) focused primarily on Kikuyu women and secondarily on Akamba women in proportion to their presence in Nairobi area markets as traders in 1987-1988. In contrast to the Accra study, traders—both men and women—were interviewed exclusively in markets, not their homes, but their work histories were gathered to construct a history of petty trade in the Nairobi area. (For both studies extensive archival research was also carried out.) Unlike Accra, Nairobi as a newly founded colonial town grew very rapidly to become almost the size of Accra, requiring exponentially greater efforts to feed its population. We can see that in twentieth century Nairobi a concentrated process requiring hundreds of years to accomplish in Ghana occurred in a relatively short time—that of drawing more and more remote rural areas into growing and exporting dried staples to feed the city.

In the nineteenth century before Nairobi came into being, Kikuyu women were trading and heavily involved in supplying caravans with dried staples, as well as selling at local markets. As Nairobi grew they converted this involvement to supplying food products to Nairobi's African population, in particular. These efforts drew either benign neglect or active opposition from the colonial government, depending on the era and colonialist priorities. Colonial policy also was sporadically informed by a significant level of opposition from influential Kikuyu men, elders and nationalists. These men considered Nairobi to be a corrupting influence on women, whose behavior there they could no longer control despite their best efforts in the form of ethnic associations and African police sent by chiefs to arrest women traders.[16]

Meanwhile, the residential system did not promote women's trade, since the patrilocal or virilocal pattern involved women leaving their natal homes and joining their husbands' families, where they became second-class citizens without inheritance rights. Their inheritance rights in their natal families were also normally truncated at marriage, although there were exceptions for exceptional daughters. Women's primary loyalties were supposed to be to their husbands, although there were important peer-based age-sets created by puberty rites and supposed to generate women's solidarity for life. However, the husband's co-resident female relatives were supposed to help him control his wives. All of this reduced possibilities for women's cooperation in business partnerships, although women's communal work groups that included neighbors and relatives were pervasive. Agriculture, not trade, held pride of place in the societal ideology as women's ideal occupation and women did most of the agricultural labor, usually estimated at about 70 to 80 percent of the work.[17]

Nonetheless, as Nairobi grew many women from surrounding areas went to trade there, many of them forced into trade by loss of use rights in land through divorce or widowhood (women still normally do not have direct ownership rights in land unless they purchase it). As in Accra, women were and are expected to feed themselves and their children, but there is a stronger cultural imperative for men to cover children's expenses. Women's exclusion from land ownership and their prior status as jural minors made control of their earnings (mainly from plantation wage labor and trade) problematic. Especially with colonial impositions of European notions of women as property, local men began to treat bride wealth as the purchase price for women, who became their own private property to be maltreated if they wanted. Thus, as one male trader told me in 1988, "the woman is mine so her earnings are mine."[18]

Women were not passive under this assault, however, and many contravened male strictures not only to go to Nairobi for trade or prostitution, but to prosper at it. At the least, many provided enough wherewithal to feed their families when problems arose. After World War II so many were going that efforts to stem the flow by local men became futile, and after independence in 1963 these efforts were abandoned. The negative associations of women with money, nonetheless, inhibited women from overtly advertising success in trade by purchasing items for themselves and also produced a tendency to mask profits from husbands. Communal property in marriage was practiced only insofar as all property was the man's, creating an effort similar to that in Europe and the U.S. to allow wives to share in marital property. Patrilineages, however, have normally succeeded to the present in claiming the property of their deceased members over and against any spousal rights exerted by women and despite laws giving wives inheritance rights.[19]

It is not surprising, then, that women's trade in Nairobi suffers from difficulties in making partnerships or securing childcare from relatives to allow expansion of a business, in controlling profits independently of men, in passing on businesses to a female relative, in securing adequate capital, and in protecting themselves from a growing level of street violence caused by corruption in the police and desperation on the part of more people. Violence against women has frequently been exercised precisely to keep women from trading; women told me many stories along these lines, including one involving a woman who left home, children and husband to trade in Nairobi, where her husband tracked her down in the market, beat her up and tore up her shoes, a symbolic gesture if there ever was one. The tension caused by women escaping male control in ever larger numbers, confronted by significant numbers of men who subscribe to the notion that these women are their property, has produced a massive explosion of domestic violence against women.[20]

Paradoxically, it is exactly the highly disadvantaged economic position of women that has been especially important in producing strong women's initiatives at every level to improve their situation. Thus, as women seek their economic rights—and many traders by dint of being divorced, separated or widowed have achieved those rights—heightened conflict results. The women are persistent, however, and in many cases have no choice, given the necessity to feed their children, so they keep on coming to Nairobi. Some are well established there and have begun setting up multi-generational businesses in Nairobi, but that is still rare. While traders are increasingly seeking political means to shore up their position and reduce the constant police harassment that diminishes their businesses,[21] other women involved in FIDA (Federation of Women Lawyers Kenya) created enough of a stir about the light punishment meted out to an assistant chief accused of rape that he was sacked (note, not imprisoned), and yet other politically savvy Kenyan women have been very vocal in the push to achieve full political rights in the new constitution (whose review has been indefinitely postponed as of this writing).[22]

A chief push has been the struggle to achieve full property rights for women in the light of massive contravention of the International Covenant on Civil and Political Rights, which Kenya signed. A frequent practice is for a late husband's relatives to evict his widow(s) from their land and homes, sometimes even when they have sons. Many older traders were in Nairobi precisely because of this occurrence. Wambui Waiyaki Otieno's long-running court case disputed this practice when her late husband's lineage tried to seize his body and their property; it was finally settled by a solomonic decision: his lineage received his body for burial in his Luo homeland but she kept the property acquired during the marriage.[23] Daughters usually do not inherit equally with sons on the assumption that they will marry and be provided for by the husband and his family, which frequently does not happen due to widespread destitution—or sometime simple greed. Undocumented customary marriages may not be recognized by the courts for the purpose of establishing a widow's rights. In sum, "men have greater rights than women to own, inherit, acquire, manage, and dispose of property," a recent Human Watch Rights Report on Kenya concluded.[24]

Kenya's current constitution, most recently amended in 1998, outlaws discrimination based on sex, but permits discrimination in personal and customary laws. These laws, in turn, were often codified under colonialism in forms that were prejudicial to women's rights,[25] which were often considerable in precolonial societies. However, an impressionistic rendering of precolonial women's rights among Bantu speakers of eastern and southern Africa indicates that women were more likely to have been male property here than elsewhere. This was definitely not the case in coastal West Africa, where colonialism suppressed women's rights. Meanwhile, it is clear that in Kenya the achievement of women's property rights has top priority among activists, and there is widespread recognition that the lack of same is prejudicial to women achieving political equality. Those who are economically dependent by definition do not have full citizenship rights.

There are indications everywhere that many women will no longer tolerate routinized violence against them, while a few are achieving prominent positions in national politics. Dr. Wangari Maathai has for years led an active women's environmental movement, Greenbelt, that among other things succeeded in preventing a major office building from being erected for President Moi's profit in Nairobi's largest park; she also ran for president and was been beaten up several times by police for her efforts, the sum of which earned her a Nobel Prize. She was head of the Kenya National Council of Women in 1986, in which position she supported Wambui Otieno's fight for her husband's body. Otieno's political career, which began in 1969 with a run for Parliament, continued and more recently contested many Kenyans' notions of proper gender roles. In 2003 she married a man nearly 50 years her junior, a twenty-six year old mason and handyman. Her subsequent entrance into the constitutional convention brought its proceedings to an abrupt temporary halt, while M.P. Bonny Khalwale intoned, "We are discussing African culture and what she did negated the very concept of our culture." Delegate Hubbie Hussein responded, "There are land grabbers, looters, murderers and other criminals among the delegates, but no one has questioned their presence at the conference."[26] Clearly, women's rights in Kenya are still highly contested, while economic necessity fuels political wrangling. Women's emergence into the world of business has been pivotal in raising their awareness generally and contributed to their willingness to become involved in political efforts.

Conclusion

What can we conclude, then, from these two case studies and international perspectives? Perhaps we need to think more seriously about why it is that in both England and the U.S. the first successful mass political efforts to improve women's positions came in the form of pushing for married women's independent rights to property in the nineteenth century. This could be and sometimes has been dismissed as mere elite women's class politics; after all, wealthy women were the ones with property to lose. That is true, but working class women also had much to gain from being able, for instance, to keep their own earnings. Chipping away at jural minor status for women first involved establishing women's economic rights. Within the diverse African cases I have discussed above, it is noteworthy that the same route to political rights seems to be pursued. Part of the explanation may simply reside in the fact that, especially for poor women, the right to earn a living is so crucial that nothing else takes precedence or can fortify them for further struggles. First one must eat. Let us re-examine women's push for economic rights, then, with an open mind and mindfulness of cross-cultural implications.

I have not addressed here the ethics of women in business. One must always query areas in which abuse of power is likely. Just as one must question military activism, as it were, as a beneficial means of achieving women's rights (given the doubtful status of the exercise of legitimized force and killing as a foundational principle for liberatory ethics), so one must also hesitate to enshrine greed and mal-distribution of wealth as conducive to women's rights. In this era when multinational corporations have succeeded in organizing the world economy to profit themselves exclusively, thus increasing poverty tremendously, especially in Africa, it seems inadvisable to advocate involvement in business as a liberatory route for women unless a strong ethic of social responsibility accompanies this push. Happily, in Africa we have studies showing that women tend far more often than men to use their profits for the benefit of others: for their children, primarily, for feeding their families, paying school fees and so on.

We do not have such assurances for the U.S., however, where it seems that women business executives generally share the same corporate culture as men do, which is how they manage to get ahead. As we forge ahead in ever larger numbers into previously male-dominated arenas, how can we insure that we take along an impulse to reform the more unethical and base aspects of the enterprises we enter? It is not just a matter of showing feminist solidarity as we go along and helping other women to get ahead, but of assuring the survival of the world by distributing wealth more equitably, by adopting environmentally sound long-term policies that may mean lower short-term profits, by paying workers more and CEOs less, by honoring union activism, by furthering sound pension and health benefits, and by devoting research and development funds to changing the way we do business so that it is less destructive, not dependent entirely on cheap oil and the cheap (sometimes slave) labor of women and children, for instance, and less hierarchical both in terms of remuneration and decision-making. Some businesses are already on this page, but so far not enough to make a critical difference. Perhaps as women we can make a contribution to bettering both our rights and our world by involvement in business. Let us honor our African foremothers as leading the way by showing us how women's economic rights can be used to achieve female solidarity and exercised for the communal good.

Notes

[1] An unrevised version of this essay was presented at the Radcliffe Conference on Women, Money and Power in October, 2002.

[2] Frederick Engels. *The Origin of the Family, Private Property and the State*, ed. Eleanor Burke Leacock (NY: International Publishers, 1972), pp.136-38.

[3] Maxine Molyneux, "Analysing Women's Movements", in C. Jackson and R. Pearson, eds., *Feminist Visions of Development: Gender Analysis and Policy* (London: Routledge, 1998), pp. 65-88; Michelle Rosaldo and Louise Lamphere, eds., *Woman, Culture and Society* (Stanford: Stanford University Press, 1974).

[4] Nairobi *Daily Nation*, World Section, 13, 15, 16, 17, 19 July, 2002; *Indianapolis Star*, 13 July, 2002, p. A18. It seems significant that *escravos* means "slaves" in Portuguese; the area experienced strong involvement in the slave trade, with thousands exported per year over a long period of time in the eighteenth and nineteenth centuries.

[5] Judith Van Allen, "'Aba Riots' or Igbo 'Women's War'? Ideology, Stratification, and the Invisibility of Women," in *Women in Africa: Studies in Social and Economic Change*, ed. Nancy J. Hafkin and Edna G. Bay (Stanford: Stanford University Press, 1976), pp. 59-85; Margery Perham, *Native Administration in Nigeria* (London: Oxford University Press, 1937); Elizabeth

Isichei, *A History of the Igbo People* (NY: St. Martin's, 1976); Sylvia Leith-Ross, *African Women* (NY: Frederick Praeger, 1965 [1939]); Caroline Ifeka-Moller, "Female Militancy and Colonial Revolt: The Women's War of 1929, Eastern Nigeria," in *Perceiving Women*, ed. Shirley Ardener (London: Malaby, 1975), pp. 127-57; Misty L. Bastian, "'Vultures of the Marketplace': Southeastern Nigerian Women and Discourses of the Ogu Umunwaanyi (Women's War) of 1929" in *Women in African Colonial Histories*, ed. Jean Allman, Susan Geiger and Nakanyike Musisi (Bloomington: Indiana University Press, 2002), pp. 260-81.

[6] Audrey Wipper, "Kikuyu Women and the Harry Thuku Riot: Some Uniformities of Female Militancy," Africa 58, 4 (1988): 300-37; Claire C. Robertson, *Trouble Showed the Way: Women, Men and Trade in the Nairobi Area, 1890-1990* (Bloomington: Indiana University Press, 1997), pp. 35-37; Nancy Dorsey, "Pare Women and the Mbiru Tax Protest in Tanzania, 1943-1947: A Study of Women, Politics and Development," Ohio State University Women's Studies Ph.D. Dissertation (1994); Steven Feierman, *Peasant Intellectuals: Anthropology and History in Tanzania* (Madison: University of Wisconsin Press, 1990). See also Cynthia Brantley, "Mekatalili and the Role of Women in Giriama Resistance," in *Banditry, Rebellion and Social Protest*, ed. Donald Crummey (London: James Currey, 1986), pp. 333-50.

[7] Claire C. Robertson, "Gender and Trade Relations in Central Kenya in the Late Nineteenth Century," *International Journal of African Historical Studies* 30, 1 (1997): 23-47

[8] Barbara Hanawalt, ed. *Women and Work in Pre-industrial Europe* (Bloomington: Indiana University Press, 1986).

[9] Pieter de Marees, "A description and Historical Declaration of the Golden Kingdome of Guinea," in *Hakluytus Posthumus or Purchas His Pilgrimes*, trans. G. A. Dantisc, ed. S. Purchas (NY: AMS Press, Inc., 1965 [1600], VI: 286-87.

[10] Claire C. Robertson, *Sharing the Same Bowl: A Socio-economic History of Women and Class in Accra, Ghana* (Ann Arbor: University of Michigan Press, 1990 [1984]), pp. 76-77.

[11] Ibid, Ch. III.

[12] Ibid, pp. 189-91.

[13] Ibid, Ch. VI.

[14] Robertson, "The Perils of Autonomy," *Gender and History* 3, 1 (Spring, 1991): 91-96; and "The Death of Makola and other Tragedies: Male Strategies against a Female-Dominated System," *Canadian Journal of African Studies* 17, 3 (1983): 674-95.

[15] See David Levinson, *Family Violence in Cross-Cultural Perspective* (Newbury Park, CA: Sage, 1989); Renee Hirschon, ed. *Women and Property, Women as Property* (London: Croom Helm, 1984). Fitnat Adjetey and Gloria Ofori-Boadu, FIDA *Handbook on Domestic Violence in Ghana* (Accra: Friedrich Ebert Foundation, 2000), pp. 6-7, say that over twenty years later, in 1997, all of the cases of physical and sexual assault reported to the Ussher Town Clinic were

women, while in the same year about 15 percent% of 1000 assault cases reported to FIDA involved domestic violence against women (the phrasing of this statistic was particularly unclear).

[16]Robertson, *Trouble,* Ch. III.

[17]Robertson, *Trouble*, Ch. VI.

[18]Ibid.

[19]Ibid, Chs. IV-VI.

[20]UN Habitat/Intermediate Technology Development Group East Africa/ UNDP, "Survivors Speak," unpublished Report (2001), pp. 2-4, stated that 60 % of 195 abused women in a Nairobi sample suffered serious physical abuse, more than a third suffered serious sexual abuse, usually rape, more than half serious economic abuse involving such actions as being prevented from earning an income, being forced to hand over earnings, or non-maintenance by a/n ex-/husband, and more than half being subjected to psychological abuse, including efforts to limit their mobility. Some of the incidents demonstrated calculated sadism, such as the most famous one in which Jackson Kaguai, a bar owner, dissatisfied that his wife of fifteen years, Piah Njoki, had borne him only daughters, organized an attack in which he and his neighbors gouged out her eyes. After his jail term of five years he was released and still dissatisfied that he had lost his considerable coffee farm to her in the compensation settlement, so he managed to repent publicly and convince four churches, his local chief as the government representative, and his sisters to persuade Njoki, successfully, to reconcile with him. An even more famous case involved the mass rape in 1991 of seventy-one boarding-school girls by their male classmates, which resulted in the death of nineteen of them at St. Kizito secondary school north of Nairobi in Meru. The St. Kizito female deputy principal said, "The boys never meant any harm against the girls. They just wanted to rape." The school was closed. Robertson, *Bowl*, p. 221.

[21]Barbara Thomas, *Politics, Participation and Poverty: Development through Self-Help in Kenya* (Boulder: Westview, 1985), p. 180; Robertson, Trouble, p. 270.

[22]Robertson, "Grassroots in Kenya: Women, Genital Mutilation and Collective Action, 1920-1990," *Signs* 21, 3 (Spring, 1996): 615-42; Pamela Chepkemei, "Cry for justice as rapist chief let off lightly," *Daily Nation* 18 July, 2002, p. 4; "Rapist chief on probation sacked as public fury grows," *Daily Nation* 19 July, 2002, p. 4; Mark Agutu, "Women's plea to Ghai team," *Daily Nation* 19 July, 2002, p. 6.

[23]Cora Presley ed., *Mau Mau's Daughter: The Life History of Wambui Otieno* (Boulder, CO: Westview, 1998; Patricia Stamp, "Burying Otieno: The Politics of Gender and Ethnicity in Kenya," *Signs* 16, 4 (1991): 808-45; David William Cohen and E. S. Atieno Odhiambo, eds., *Burying SM: The Politics of Knowledge and the Sociology of Power in Africa* (Portsmouth, NH: Heinemann, 1992).

[24]At http://hrw.org/english/docs/2005/03/16/kenya10330_txt.html

[25] Margaret Jean Hay and Marcia Wright, eds., *African Women and the Law: Historical Perspectives* (Boston: Boston University Papers on Africa Vol. VII, 1982).

[26] Brian Carnell, "Wambui Otieno Mbugua Sets Kenya Abuzz." *Instinct.* http://www.equityfeminism.com/archives/years/2003/000087.html

Part II

Activism, Scholarship, and Gender

CHAPTER FIVE
MOBILIZING FOR CHANGE LOCALLY AND GLOBALLY
African Women as Scholar-Activists in Feminist and Gender Studies

Mary J. Osirim

Over the past two decades, African women scholars have made and continue to make major contributions to gender and feminist studies scholarship in the social sciences. Although feminism is not a term widely embraced by most scholars on the continent, let alone by the general population in the North and the South, some African scholars and social scientists would consider themselves feminists. These scholars have influenced the development of global feminism and have been influenced by the emergence of international feminist movements on the continent and elsewhere. African women scholars in particular, from their locations on the continent and abroad, have been major participants in the development of global feminism and gender studies—through their research, their creation of academic programs in this field, their establishment of feminist journals, and their participation in international conferences and transnational feminist networks—in all of these activities, they have been (and continue to be) important voices for equality and social change. In all these endeavors, these women have largely seen themselves as working beyond the narrow purview of the academy; they have made and continue to make significant contributions to research and outreach in their societies as scholar-activists.

This chapter will explore the contributions of African women social scientists to scholarship in gender and feminist studies, to feminist organizations and transnational feminist networks, and to the development of academic journals and programs. The chapter will focus on the work of African-Anglophone scholars and is centered on the contributions made by African women scholars on the continent. The study also recognizes the transnational nature of the lives of many African (and other) scholars today and thus acknowledges the contributions of African scholars in the

Diaspora. This chapter argues that while women's organizations and associations have a long history on the continent, the new transnational feminist movements and other efforts related to socio-economic development owe much to the major UN Conferences on Women and to the impact of the current globalization phase on African societies—especially their impact on women and children.

Theory-Building and Empirical Work in African Feminist and Gender Studies

Like other feminist perspectives from around the globe, the meaning of African feminism has been a subject of debate in academic circles. One of the foremost pioneers in developing an African feminist perspective was Filomina Steady (1981) in her edited volume, *The Black Woman Cross-Culturally*. Although this volume was published in the U.S. and Steady has worked in the U.S. for decades, she is an African woman scholar who lived and worked in Sierra Leone in her early career and whose definition of African feminism established a foundation from which later works would take their lead.

> African feminism combines racial, sexual, class and cultural dimensions of oppression to produce a more inclusive brand of feminism through which women are viewed first and foremost as human, rather than sexual beings. It can be defined as that ideology which encompasses freedom from oppression based on the political, economic, social and cultural manifestations of racial, cultural, sexual and class biases. It is more inclusive than other forms of feminist ideologies and is largely a product of polarizations and conflicts that represent some of the worst and chronic forms of human suffering...It can be argued that this type of feminism has the potential of emphasizing the totality of human experience, portraying the strength and resilience of the human spirit and resounding with optimism for the total liberation of humanity. African feminism is, in short, humanistic feminism...intrinsically a moral and political statement for human survival and well being (Steady 1981; Reed 2001).

Steady's work, published in 1981, not only marks her as a pioneer in scholarship about and by African women, but also demonstrates that she was a leader in the scholarship on and about women of color. In this regard, she certainly precedes her European-American sisters in the social sciences with respect to some of the early thinking about intersectionality—on the role of race, ethnicity, class and sexuality in the positioning of women of color in society. Steady, however, clearly argues that African feminism is an important ideology for the well-being of

African women, as well as for the continent more generally. On the other hand, she clearly acknowledges the important role that race occupies in many societies, based on her own experiences in the Diaspora and her knowledge of the realities that prevailed within settler colonies on the continent. For Steady, race and racism as opposed to gender occupy the central position in the oppression of black women (and men): "For the Black woman in a racist society, racial factors rather than sexual ones operate more consistently in making her a target for discrimination and marginalization" (Steady 1981, pp.27-28). Within sub-Saharan Africa, this problem of racism would largely apply to such former settler colonies as South Africa, Zimbabwe and Kenya.

One of the foremost feminist scholars on the continent today, Amina Mama, is very proud to carry the feminist label. As Chair of Gender Studies and Director of the African Gender Institute at the University of Cape Town, she has attempted to unite theoretical work in the study of gender relations in African states to a practical understanding of gender mainstreaming in all spheres of life. Her own life embodies the unity of scholarship with activism—she has held positions as an academic at many prestigious institutions around the globe including Oxford and Wellesley, and she has worked as a consultant in several non-governmental organizations and women's associations. She sees feminism as a worldview that links her to a community of scholars and activists around the globe—in the North and the South—from various racial and cultural backgrounds. For her, feminism is a "movement-based term that signals a refusal of oppression, and a commitment to struggling for women's liberation from all forms of oppression—internal, external, psychological, emotional, socio-economic, political and philosophical" (Salo 2003, p.2).

The activist and political praxis emphases have been increasingly central to African scholars' and writers' views of feminism. Patricia McFadden, a feminist social scientist and activist based in Zimbabwe, continues to emphasize that "feminism refers to political praxis that emanates from a very cogent analysis of political, economic and social conditions which shape African women's lives" (Salo 2003, p.3). She maintains that patriarchy in Africa did not appear with the onset of colonialism, but rather that African patriarchy predated the coming of the Europeans—it is, in fact, the oldest patriarchy in the world (McFadden 2003).

Reviewing definitions of African feminism developed by some of the foremost African gender-studies researchers points to some of the major contributions of these works to feminist scholarship more generally. There are many areas in which African feminist paradigms have made major contributions to gender studies scholarship. This chapter will explore four of these areas:

1. The development of a feminist political economy framework;
2. The establishment of the intersectionality paradigm;
3. The role of 'femocracy' in restricting the position of African women; and
4. The linkage of scholarship and activism within the academy and beyond. In these areas, gender studies scholarship in the South and the North has and can continue to benefit.

First, what is the meaning of feminist political economy and how did African gender research contribute to the emergence of a feminist political economy perspective? Feminist political economy is a paradigm within the Neo-Marxist, conflict school in the sociology of development. Scholars working within this perspective assert that both internal factors (such as specific problems in the organization of the state, conflicts resulting from political transitions and/or growing class inequalities) and external factors (such as the long history of colonialism and imperialism, unequal trade and other economic relationships that exist today between/among states in the South, northern hegemonic powers and the international financial institutions) must be considered in charting a nation's prospects for development. Theorists within this tradition draw our attention to how particular nation-states and/or regions become homes to global-assembly line production, other manufacturing and/or service sector activities. Thus, much attention in the feminist political economy literature has focused on the establishment of the *maquiladores* at the U.S./Mexican border and the labor-intensive electronics industries in East Asia, as well as the impact of these activities on development in the region and on gender relations. Feminist political economists are especially concerned with the growing transnational labor flows of care and sex workers and the exploitation of those women who are forced to work against their will as domestic and/or sexual slaves for wealthier men/families. Moreover, these scholars also demonstrate how women and men occupy different positions in the labor market and have differential access to and returns on these activities based on gender. These researchers also recognize that while women's labor market participation rates have recently increased in many nations, most of the increase has been in the low-wage, low-status occupations at the bottom of the socio-economic hierarchy. Feminist political economy scholars, however, also acknowledge that women have resisted and continue to resist oppressive colonial and post-colonial regimes, as well as globalization. For example, as a response to economic crisis and structural adjustment policies (SAPs) in several sub-Saharan African nations such as Nigeria in the 1980s and 90s, women traders have, on occasion, closed markets and limited access to foodstuffs in urban areas. They have also formed alliances with university student groups in response to the imposition of user fees for social services and more specifically with regard to higher tuition charged (Nash and Fernandez-Kelly 1983; Imam 1997; Sassen 1998; Moghadam 1999; Osirim 2003).

Many African gender researchers have worked within a feminist political economy rubric. Although several African scholars and gender studies researchers from the Global South more generally have frequently criticized Euro-American feminism, Amina Mama (1996) acknowledges the importance of capitalism and imperialism in affecting African women's lives, as compared to the problems caused by feminism from abroad. She states, "this does not get away from the main problem, namely white domination of global politics and northern-based white women's relative power to define. ...To put it bluntly, white feminism has never been strong enough to be the enemy—in the way that say, global capitalism can be viewed as an enemy" (Salo 2003, p.4).

In reacting against the Women in Development/Women and Development (WID/WAD) perspectives in development studies which many contemporary African feminists view as too conservative, works by Ayesha Imam, Patricia McFadden, Amina Mama and Charmaine Pereira have made some very important contributions to feminist political economy. For example, Ayesha Imam comments on the contributions of African gender studies scholars to the debates over development paradigms and the resistance of African women to globalization:

> The study of women in general and African women in particular contributed to the breadth and depth of knowledge and theorizing of African realities in a number of diverse ways. It has demonstrated the importance of women not simply as passive breeders but also as economic agents, as active in creating new developments, in resistance to and in collusion with oppression also. It has added fuel to the questioning of assumptions about the beneficial nature of the colonial experience and the development of capitalism and modernization in Africa, by demonstrating that for many women these processes have frequently meant a decrease in economic autonomy, access to resources, status and security (Imam 1997; McFadden 2003, p.6).

In the case of Nigeria, Pereira (2003) notes that Nigerian women's organizations continue to express resistance to multinational oil corporations, to the state and more generally to globalization (Adomako

Ampofo et al 2004). For example, in 2002, women from Delta State, Nigeria demonstrated against Shell and Chevron-Texaco, demanding compensation for environmental degradation and underdevelopment in their region caused by these oil corporations. They protested against the injustices of these companies, who failed to provide significant employment for their kin in these communities. Women human rights activists who gathered outside of the offices of these oil companies were harassed by the police—many were tear gassed and kicked as they sought economic and social justice from the very companies that they viewed as responsible for the extreme poverty of their communities.

A major concern of African gender scholars working within a political economy paradigm is the impact of the current phase of globalization on women's lives. In this regard, African researchers have not only contributed a great deal to the literature, but they have also been far ahead of many of our northern-based scholars in noting that globalization has intensified the burdens of many women, but also provided benefits to other women (Darkwah 2002; Fall 1999; Magubane 2001; Periera 2003). Most African researchers in this area agree that in this phase of globalization, the international financial institutions such as the IMF and the World Bank and their imposed SAPs have led to the growing feminization of the labor market in low-level positions, the growth in sex work, an increase in women's workloads and further feminization of poverty. With the adoption of SAPs in about 40 African nations, governments have retrenched public-sector workers and reduced spending on health care, education, housing and transportation. Thus, African women incurred the re-imposition of tuition for their children's education and user fees in clinics and hospitals. On the other hand, Darkwah (2002) noted that trade liberalization linked to adjustment programs advantaged some Ghanaian women by streamlining their access to imported goods such as clothing. In fact, women who worked in the civil service, such as teachers, noted the increased opportunities presented by transnational trade in this phase of globalization. These women left the civil service and traveled to locations such as Southeast Asia in search of the latest fabrics and clothing, for which there was a market in Ghana. The sale of such items provided these transnational traders with a more substantial income than their prior occupations as teachers, where salaries under economic crisis and adjustment were frequently irregular at best. In Kenya and Uganda, Pheko (1999) observed that trade liberalization increased access to employment for women in non-traditional, export-oriented goods, such as flowers and fruit. Selling these products seemed to offer better income opportunities to women in these nations.

Closely related to their contributions to political economy are the contributions of African feminist scholars to the intersectionality paradigm. As stated above, Steady (1981) was one of the earliest researchers to indicate the myriad of factors that contribute to the oppression of African women (and women of color more generally). She acknowledged the roles of race, ethnicity, class and sexuality in limiting the status and position of African women. In discussing the work of many noted African feminists, Lewis (2002) indicates that these scholars realized the importance of stratification based on the intersectionality of race, class, gender and imperialism in the early 1980s, before the work of noted U.S. feminist sociologists such as Patricia Hill Collins and Margaret Andersen (1992) and Elizabeth Higginbotham (1988) appeared. As indicated above, African women's conceptions of feminism and gender-studies scholarship have been clearly linked to politics, especially to African independence movements and the development of the post-colonial state. Gender studies scholars from the continent clearly consider the role that African women played in struggles against colonialism and imperialism—dating from Nkrumah's call for the mass mobilization of women against British colonialism in Ghana in the 1950s to the liberation war in Zimbabwe in the 1960s and 70s to the struggle for majority rule in South Africa in the second half of the twentieth century. Lewis (2002) notes that the African feminist scholars Bolanle Awe, Maria Nzomo and Patricia McFadden placed imperialism, race, class and increasingly gender at the center of their analyses on women and African development. For example, McFadden (2001) argues that the neo-colonial state sought to retard women's basic human rights through the re-establishment of traditional courts and statuses in the legal systems of Zimbabwe and South Africa. Perhaps one of the best-known cases on re-establishing the importance of customary/ traditional law concerning the status of women in Zimbabwe was the Magaya decision in the late 1990s. At that time, the Supreme Court of Zimbabwe ruled unanimously that Venia Magaya, a 58 year-old seamstress who sued her half-brother for their deceased father's land, was not able to inherit land from her father. Although the Zimbabwean constitution prohibited discrimination on the basis of sex, it exempted customary law from this ruling. In the Magaya case, the Supreme Court clearly considered women unequal to men under African (Zimbabwean) cultural norms/customary law. "Such actions indicate the collusion between men of different classes and races to exclude women from the democratic practices and institutions that women fought so courageously to build" (Adomako Ampofo et al 2004, p.702).

The relationship between political economy and the intersectionality thesis can be seen vividly in the work of Benjamin on gender and work in South Africa. Benjamin (2001) adds race and imperialism/capitalism to the intersecting factors of gender and class in explaining the position of many working class women in the South African labor force today. As a result of South Africa's membership in the World Trade Organization (WTO), thousands of South African women in the textile and clothing industries have lost their jobs. In keeping with the liberal economic agenda of the WTO, South Africa had to lower tariffs to open her doors to imported clothing and textiles. In fact, scholars have noted a significant decline in positions in the formal sector for African women across the continent in the late 1980s into the early 1990s, when an estimated 2.5 million jobs were lost (Adepoju 1994). Such research indicates the consequences of contemporary globalization including the growing feminization of poverty and the significant need for women to organize against an increasingly "masculinist" state.

One of the very significant contributions of African gender studies scholarship to the development of African, and indeed international feminism, lies in the further analysis of gender and the state in sub-Saharan Africa through the concept of "femocracy." Mama (1996) created and defined this term as "a feminine autocracy paralleling and servicing a persistent military dictatorship and advancing a highly conservative brand of gender politics in the name of women and development." Femocracy has certainly been apparent in several African regimes. During the rule of General Babangida as head of state in Nigeria from the mid-80s to the early 90s, Babangida's wife/the administration established programs such as The Better Life Program for Rural Women. This Program was created in part as a response to the increased poverty that poor and low-income women were experiencing under Nigeria's Structural Adjustment Program in the late 80s. In addition to increasing their agricultural output and the number of women's small and micro-enterprises, the Better Life Program was also aimed at the further mobilization and empowerment of women towards assuming more leadership roles in the larger society. This state-sponsored "women's program" did not yield real benefits for the majority of poor women in that nation, but rather served the interests of elite women and reinforced the power of the masculinist state. My own observations of *gari* (ground cassava, a staple in the Nigerian diet, usually accompanying Nigerian soup for a main meal) processing in the city of Enugu in 1992 revealed that much of the credit for establishing, operating and supporting this business was accorded to the governor's wife and her entourage. From my conversations and observations in this and other sites in the area, such as sewing cooperatives, it appeared that few returns from these ventures actually ended up in the hands of local, grassroots women. In the case of Kenya, Nzomo (1993) explored how the post-colonial state failed African women. In the immediate post-independence period in Kenya, women continued to be marginalized in the state as illustrated by their holding less than one percent of the elected seats in Parliament. More importantly, though, Nzomo noted how the patriarchal state ignored or at most compromised women's human rights regarding rape, domestic violence and sexual harassment and continued to treat women as second-class citizens, especially those women from the lower class. The frequency with which such violations occurred and the mild-at-best punishments that were meted out in response to them demonstrates that the male-dominated Kenyan state had not realized the meaning of "democracy." Nzomo (1993) further noted that the women's movement as symbolized by the National Council of Women of Kenya was "muzzled and ineffective." Again, both Mama and Nzomo (1993) recognize the intersectionality of gender, class and to some extent imperialism in such efforts, which clearly limits and most often retards the position and rights of poor women in these regimes while enhancing the status of middle-class women and their relationship to the state.

Uniting Scholarship and Activism

I would argue that gender-studies scholars would find it very difficult, if not impossible, to imagine productive academic lives that did not effectively combine research with activism. Indeed, many African women scholars would regard such a division between scholarship and activism as artificial. Theory-building for African gender-studies scholars is strongly related to their experiences of the world—to their engagement with the real world problems of development, state-formation and gender relations. In this regard, the experiences of many of these Anglophone-African feminists resemble that of their African-American sister scholars who Patricia Hill Collins (1990) defined as being influenced by the merger of theory and action and who draw on their daily actions and experiences in their theoretical work.

Collins' work and that of other feminist scholars of color on both sides of the Atlantic draws our attention to a major question for Africanists and those from the Diaspora and other areas who work in gender studies: what constitutes activism for the scholar? While outreach activity uniting the university with the community in educational and other ventures clearly constitutes activism for scholars, there are other measures of activism for gender-studies scholars. Included among these are the establishment of gender-studies journals that include topics and authors from a range of theoretical and applied backgrounds and the creation of gender-studies programs.

At a more fundamental level, however, gender-studies scholars can be and often are activists in the choices they make as scholars and teachers. This is exemplified first in the very topics they select for research. In general, African gender-studies scholars and their Diasporic sisters tend to select research topics that are more applied in scope, such as those that address questions of development with respect to basic needs for food, clothing, shelter, health care, education and employment. Again, as Collins reminds us, this often enables scholars to draw on experiences of the world in their writings, their theory building and their policy recommendations. Second, the choices these scholars make in what they teach and how they teach it also demonstrate their activism as scholars. Africanist feminist scholars teach not only women's studies, but also most often courses in gender studies that address stratification and power relations based on the intersection of gender, race and class (and increasingly sexuality) in the lives of women (and men) on the continent. In our teaching, we often strive to remove/reduce hierarchies in the classroom and to create an environment more conducive to active learning, such as more discussion-based classes as opposed to lectures. We often strive to unite theory with praxis and choose to teach and engage students in service-learning courses where they can apply the theories and empirical studies they encounter in the classroom to their work in the field (often in communities in which their universities are located). These, as well as other examples, clearly illustrate that African gender-studies scholars, as well as their Diasporic counterparts, engage in scholar-activism at many different levels.

Over the past few decades, African feminist scholars have also been extremely involved in efforts to promote gender studies on the continent. This is an area where I believe Northern feminists can learn some lessons from their African sisters. Building bridges between activism and the academy is a direction adopted not only by gender studies programs and research institutes on the continent, but by leading feminist journals as well. In such journals as *Feminist Africa*, *Agenda* and the previously-published *SAFERE*, it is not unusual to see an article on HIV/AIDS education in Zimbabwe written by an activist in the field, for example, located next to another article written by university researchers on reproductive health in southern Africa. The work of scholar/activists, practitioners and those working in the public policy community, as well as more conventional academics, are welcomed in such journals.

What has been most impressive in many ways is the outreach initiated by many gender-studies programs, women's research centers and networks of women scholars to provide information and instruction about some of the "bread-and-butter" issues in African development and their impact on women and men to those both inside and outside of the academy. While the African Gender Institute, for example, established and operates the Gender Studies Program at the University of Cape Town, it is also engaged in outreach work on gender violence and information technology. The Institute provides training in information technology to local women residents of Cape Town who by and large lack access to further education in the country. On the other hand, the Institute has taken its gender violence program on the road, so to speak, and has educated young women at the University of Botswana about rape, sexual harassment and domestic violence.

The Department of Gender Studies at Makerere University in Kampala, Uganda is also involved in gender training, research and outreach. It is unique on the continent in offering a program in gender studies and development ranging from the bachelor's degree to the doctorate. This Gender Studies Program takes as one of its major aims gender mainstreaming-related training in Ugandan institutions beyond the academy, including government and non-governmental organizations (NGOs). In this regard, it offers a number of short five-week evening courses to managers, trainers and others in Uganda's public and private sectors. Courses are offered in such areas as: Gender and Poverty Reduction, Gender and Social Policy, Gender and Economic Reforms, Gender and Counseling, and Gender and Refugees. Further, this Gender Studies Department has introduced special initiatives to reduce the gender digital divide. The Department offers courses in internet training and computer networking sponsored by Cisco Systems, the United Nations Development Program (UNDP), the United States Agency for International Development (USAID) and others. Women constitute over 70 percent of the enrollment in these classes (http:www.makerere. ac.ug/womenstudies/back ground.html).

African gender studies and its linkages between scholarship and activism have clearly placed work coming from the continent as "cutting edge" in the continued development of a global feminist movement. African feminist scholars and others have made very important contributions to a greater understanding of the experiences of African women, as well as contributions to policy formation to address the many issues they face.

Some Anglophone-African feminists also acknowledge that the work of many scholars in African gender studies is also strongly influenced by the "development industry"—to satisfy the interests and requirements of international donors and non-governmental organizations. Thus, as opposed to choosing those subjects and themes that might be of greatest benefit to their African sisters and to development more generally, some gender scholars pursue an agenda dictated largely by international interests. While this true with some scholars, I would argue that we are increasingly seeing in Anglophone sub-Saharan Africa a generation of women who set their own research agendas. In fact, it is these scholars who increasingly identify themselves as feminist.

African Women Scholars and Transnational Feminist Networks

Transnational feminist movements and networks can be discussed within the context of the social movements' literature, where social movements are defined as "organized group efforts to generate or resist social change" (Smelser 1981, p. 444). Social movements involve some level of deliberative mobilization and planning, but at the same time can operate with loose organizational frameworks and no formalized institutional bases of power, the latter noted by Ferree and Martin (1995) in describing women's movements. Social movements, however, can be very diverse in their purposes, goals and participants and thus can be classified using various criteria. In discussing the environmental movement, Gerlach (1999) describes social movements as "segmentary, polycentric and reticulate" (Moghadam 2005):

> Social movements have many sometimes competing organizations and groups (segmentary); they have multiple and sometimes competing leaders (polycentric); and they are loose networks that link to each other (reticulate). Despite the segmentation, there is a shared opposition and ideology across the movement and its diverse organizations (Gerlach 1999, p. 95; as cited in Moghadam 2005, p. 80).

In her landmark work, *Globalizing Women: Transnational Feminist Networks*, Moghadam (2005) builds on the social movements' and women's movements' literature in defining transnational feminist networks (TFN's) as:

> Structures organized above the national level that unite women from three or more countries around a common agenda, such as women's human rights, reproductive health and rights, violence against women, peace and

antimilitarism, or feminist economics. They are part of the family of political change organizations operating above and across national borders that have been variously described as global civil society organizations, transnational advocacy networks and transnational social movement organizations—and which, along with international nongovernmental organizations, constitute the making of a transnational public sphere (Moghadam 2005, p.4).

While women's organizations and associations have a long history in regions of sub-Saharan Africa, (and the Global South more broadly), the emergence of contemporary TFNs is related to the UN's Decade for Women and the Fourth UN World Conferences on Women—in Mexico City in 1975, in Copenhagen in 1980, in Nairobi in 1985 and in Beijing in 1995—as well as to the current phase of globalization (Desai 2002). With respect to the UN Conferences, not only did they bring particular attention to the problems of poverty and the overall lack of access to resources and human rights that characterized most women's experiences around the globe, but the accompanying NGO Forums for Women also gave voice to the many women's organizations, including some women from grassroots organizations that attended these meetings. In many ways, this was particularly evident at the NGO Forum and the UN Conference on Women in Beijing in 1995, where an estimated 30,000 women were in attendance. Although most of these women were from elite and middle-class backgrounds, some women's groups included poor and low-income women among their participants, and other groups, such as The Zimbabwe Women's Resource Center and Network, assured that both grassroots women's and middle-class women's voices were included in the publication it brought to the forum, *Zimbabwe Women's Voices*. In addition, the UN Conferences on the Environment and Development held in Rio in 1992, the World Conference on Human Rights in 1995, and the International Conference on Population and Development in Cairo in 1994 all drew significant attention to the fact that larger networks of women's organizations were important and necessary if women were to be successful in changing legislation and action around the world regarding women's rights and women's equality. Certainly, organizations that were united across national borders would be far more likely to collectively put pressure on not only governments, but on international financial institutions and multinational capital around the globe. Further, these conferences provided women with an opportunity to learn from each other—to see what worked in various nations with respect to improving economic, social and political conditions for women and to reducing social inequalities.

TFNs were also created in response to the economic crises that hit many nations in the Global South, particularly beginning in the 1980s. Many of these crises were a result of increasing oil prices and decreasing prices for primary products on the world market in this period. In an effort to improve the economic positions of their nations, the majority of southern countries, including forty in Sub-Saharan Africa, adopted structural adjustment programs (SAPs) at the behest of the World Bank and the International Monetary Fund (IMF). As has been demonstrated throughout the continent, and indeed, throughout the Global South, poor women and children disproportionately bore the cost of SAPs. These policies meant major reductions in the size of the state in southern nations, and together with increased unemployment, these policies brought major reductions in government spending on vital social services, such as health care, education, housing and transportation. As a response to these crises and the increasingly negative toll they were taking on poor women and children, many NGOs, state-sponsored and UN-supported programs, such as "Adjustment with a Human Face," were established in African states. These programs were designed to assist women in accessing credit to start small and micro-enterprises and to help them obtain other services, such as assistance in paying their children's tuition in the wake of economic crisis and adjustment. The Better Life Program for Rural Women, mentioned above, was one such program in Nigeria, which although designed to provide training, microcredit and business assistance to poor rural women, actually benefited elite women who were connected to the state (Mama 1996).

The economic crisis besetting many African nations beginning in the mid-1980s was also felt by many African gender studies scholars, who saw a need not only to expand the teaching of women's and gender studies in university curricula, but also to demonstrate the harsh toll that crises and adjustment were taking on women. How might the crises be alleviated and a climate of sustainable gender-sensitive development be undertaken?

While the economic crises and the UN Conferences on Women over the past two decades did lead to the development of transnational feminist movements and networks in Africa and throughout the world, the problems of development and the ways in which women, especially African women, had frequently been left out of the development equation led several African women scholars to begin a network that predated the current crisis. Founded in 1977 (after the declaration of the international women's decade), the Association of African Women for Research and Development (AAWORD) described as one of its central aims the establishment of an agenda for feminism in Africa by facilitating research and activism by African women scholars. AAWORD has certainly been responsible for many academic publications on the continent. In addition, it has combined its scholarship with a more applied focus as noted in its workshops on rural development, reproductive health, the mass media and development assistance (Mama 1996). There is no doubt that much of the impetus and support for beginning women's studies programs and centers throughout the continent came from the work of AAWORD.[12] As economic and political crises ravaged many African states and universities at various times over the past few decades, African transnational networks such as AAWORD kept a vibrant, scholarly culture alive through "reaffirming intellectual traditions that challenged imperial legacies, encouraging trans-disciplinary research and valuing independent publication" (Mama as cited in Tripp 2005, p. 8). This group, like many others on the continent, has been beset by economic and political problems that have sometimes made it difficult for them to have access to the resources that they need to keep abreast of gender studies scholarship on the continent and beyond.

One of the most recent attempts at creating a TFN on the continent with an academic focus is the Gender and Women's Studies for Africa's Transformation Project (GWS Africa). This is a project of the African Gender Institute of the University of Cape Town, South Africa, sponsored by the Ford and Hivos Foundations. This network aims to increase and strengthen teaching and scholarship on African gender studies through workshops combined with online communications. The idea is to bring greater coherence to the community of gender scholars on the continent in an effort to not only increase the academic knowledge base about the issues that confront African women, but also to foster policy advocacy skills that can be used by women to promote gender justice.

During the past five years, the African Gender Institute and GWS have established themselves within the University of Cape Town and developed linkages with national, regional and continental partners, as well as representation at women's international conferences around the world. The Institute has benefited from the technological advances and has developed one of the most advanced information technology centers with a special focus on gender issues in the region. In addition, as discussed above, it provides training in information technology to those who are largely without access to such resources in the larger society. The Institute has not only tried to further the development of gender studies scholarship, especially through its first-rate online journal, but it has also tried to increase Africa's participation in "practical efforts towards gender justice, in educational institutions as well as in the broader policy context" (http://gws africa.org). The GWS Project is a significant addition to and demonstration of African women's scholar-activism, especially considering the challenges that higher education and especially women's and gender-studies faculty and programs continue to experience on the continent.

TFNs Beyond Africa, but Not Beyond the Reach of African Scholar-Activists

One of the most widely known TFNs in which African women scholar-activists have played a major role is Development Alternatives with Women for a New Era (DAWN). From its inception in 1984 on the eve of the UN Conference on Women in Nairobi, DAWN employed a feminist political economy perspective in examining the position of women in the Global South. It rejected the neo-liberal approach to development in favor of a paradigm focusing on women's interpretations and solutions to problems they were encountering, particularly related to economic crises and adjustment in their nations. DAWN was and remains committed to a feminist agenda and to the concerns and struggles of poor women (Moghadam 2005). The organization researched and documented women's responses and alternative visions of the problems they were facing as they promoted efforts towards achieving sustainable development. DAWN also acknowledged the intersectionality paradigm in their efforts—that gender, race and class interact to structure/limit women's positions in the societies of the North and the South.

DAWN has been involved in both research and advocacy to improve the position of women in the Global South, especially the position of poor women. In its major publications, *Development, Crises and Alternative Visions* (Sen and Grown 1987); *Reproductive Rights and Population: Feminist Voices from the South* (1994) and in the film, "Marketisation of Governance: Critical Feminist Perspectives from the South," DAWN has focused on one or more of its major themes in research and advocacy:

1) political economy of globalization; 2) sexual and reproductive health and rights; 3) political restructuring and social transformation; and 4) sustainable livelihoods. As a TFN, DAWN attempts to unite scholarship with activism, as seen in its publications and in its global advocacy work including: "producing and disseminating new analyses, engaging in key global processes and meetings, participating in selected institutional reform initiatives, working in partnership with like-minded feminist and development organizations and networks, and engaging with global civil society and social movements" (http://dawnorg.org).

Another TFN in which African women scholars have played a key role is Women Living Under Muslim Laws (WLUML). Since its inception in 1984, WLUML has been a women's human rights organization that is antifundamentalist and feminist. This organization, which now extends its reach to over 70 countries, works with other groups around the world to monitor the human rights of women living in Muslim countries and those of Muslim women living elsewhere. Included among its monitoring activities are the well-being of non-Muslim women who may have Muslim laws applied to them and their children, women in migrant Muslim communities in the U.S., Europe and around the world, and women born into Muslim communities/families who might not consider themselves Muslim. WLUML has had strong leadership over the years, and although it was first based in France and now in the United Kingdom, African women scholar-activists have played an important role in this TFN. For example, this group has participated in local protests around the arrest and detention of Muslim women under Shari'a Law in Northern Nigeria, as well as provided an impetus for the establishment of such groups as BAOBAB for Women's Human Rights in Nigeria, founded by the scholar-activist, Ayesha Imam. BAOBAB focuses on women's human rights under customary, statutory and religious laws in Nigeria. This organization is concerned with the protection of women's human rights, raising awareness of these rights and strengthening women's organizations that address these rights. Their diligent activities in Nigeria, combined with the efforts of several women's groups worldwide, contributed to the decision of the Shari'a Court of Appeals in Katsina State, Nigeria, to overturn the sentence of death by stoning for Amina Lawal in 2003.

WLUML clearly recognizes the role of intersectionality in the lives of women around the globe. In this regard, it is especially concerned with the rights of marginalized women—those who experience discrimination on the basis of race, religion and sexuality. While WLUML provides assistance to individuals who face oppression on these and other grounds and helps establish and support other international networks concerned with women's human rights, it also produces publications that address the lives, struggles and strategies of women in different Muslim nations. Further, it sponsors networking projects that unite women and women's groups across a range of different cultures within a nation, region or continent.

Conclusion

This chapter illustrates some of the major ways in which African women social scientists as scholar-activists have contributed to the development of feminist and gender-studies scholarship, both on the continent and beyond. African gender-studies scholars based on the continent have provided valuable additions to the discourse on feminism, particularly to the sociological perspectives of feminist political economy and intersectionality. This work also begins to explore the formation of TFNs among these scholar-activists, established in part as a response to globalization and the UN International Conferences on Women. Networks such as AAWORD and GWS-Africa have helped to sustain these women in their research, teaching and activism at a time when many African universities faced a severe depletion of resources and a substantial brain drain due to economic crisis. Further, these gender-studies scholars have demonstrated outstanding organizational skill, foresight and creativity in designing curriculum, programs and institutes that not only benefit students in their classrooms but also extend outside the academy into communities. While African gender studies researchers have been influenced by the UN World Conferences on Women and economic issues related to the current phase of globalization, they have also been leaders in the development of global feminism. African women scholar-activists have been and will continue to be important voices in TFNs outside of the continent. Not only have these scholar-activists participated in the global debates about feminism, human rights, reproductive health and development, but their theory-building and empirical research in these areas has helped to shape/re-shape the field of gender studies. Their participation in TFN's further demonstrates their agency in the face of economic, political and major public health problems. They still have much to contribute to the scholarly discourse and to the emergence of appropriate policies to promote equal rights and sustainable development for the continent.

Note

[1] The first gender studies course in Africa, entitled "Women and Society," was established in 1979 by a group of women's studies activists in the Department of Sociology at Ahmadu Bello University in Zaria, Nigeria.

CHAPTER SIX
THE ANTHROPOLOGICAL COLLABORATOR:
Feminist Scholarship and Activism in Africa
Diana J. Fox

Why was it that virtually all of those being studied were poor people of color from non-Western cultures and virtually all of those doing the studying were white, middle-class men from the United States and Europe? Why did the results of these studies end up in publications that not only were inaccessible to the people who had been studied but made little or no contribution to improving the conditions of their lives? And why was so much emphasis put on the need for objectivity? —Johnetta B. Cole 2001

Introduction

The central objective of this chapter is to reflect on the latest developments in feminist anthropological thought regarding both the production and application of scholarly knowledge about African women. As the above quotation by Johnetta B. Cole implies, these themes have been and remain a source of contestation for anthropologists, as well as for Africanists who hail not only from anthropology but from a broad spectrum of disciplines. As a branch of Cultural Anthropology, U.S.-based feminist anthropology has listened carefully to these critiques, producing some tangible outcomes in the direction of feminist anthropological scholarly pursuits in Africa. Indeed, fieldwork oriented around the improvement of their research subjects' lives, designed in collaboration with those subjects, has become the *modus operandi*. Yet this process of transformation has not been without difficulty, nor is it complete by any means. One particular source of concern that has pervaded the entire discipline since the 1980s is the troublesome dynamic between anthropological practices such as theorizing and people's lived realities.

Black feminist anthropology in particular, although not exclusively, has invoked a deconstruction of the inherent racism in anthropological theorizing and praxis—including, from the perspective of scholar-activism, established practices of hiring and selecting canonical texts. In fact, the quotation from Johnetta Cole, which opens this chapter, is drawn from the Foreword to the recent volume, *Black Feminist Anthropology: Theory, Praxis, Politics and Poetics,* edited by Irma McClaurin and published in 2001. The implication is that Black Feminist Anthropology has carved out its niche in part by defining its scholarship objectives in terms of an action-oriented approach.

This question about the benefits of anthropological knowledge (about Africa) to anthropological subjects has followed from a prior one: To what extent, researchers have asked, do the theoretical frameworks that are meant to translate lived experiences into publishable, scholarly works successfully portray the complexities and contradictions of African women's lives in ways that *they* recognize and which are useful to them? In the 1980s, feminist scholars began to point out that "data" continued to flow out of theoretical constructs reflective of the biases of past eras—colonial interests in cultural evolutionary scales, for example, generating ethnographic portraits that are not only unrecognizable to African women but incapable of being applied in any meaningful/helpful way. In fact, this is stated too benignly. Theories which we know today are false have not only distorted but have subjugated, as for example in the well-known story of Saartijie Baartman. Otherwise known as the Hottentot Venus, Saartijie Baartman was a Khoi Khoi woman who at the age of 20 was transported from Cape Town to Europe in 1810, where on arrival in London and later Paris, she became part of the freak show circuit so popular at the time. As a spectacle, she was representative of the exoticism of Hottentot women's sexual savagery. Saartijie was later subjected to anthropological scrutiny at the Musée de l'Homme in Paris, where following her early death, a cast of her body was made, she was dissected and her brain and case were put on display until 1985 when both were finally put into storage. Yet rather than being an isolated case, although surely the most notorious one, Baartman's victimization was in fact endemic to the anthropological ideas of the time. http://www.theimageofblack.co.uk/2_feature.htm).[1]

In another example of the neglect of African women's realities, Nkiru Nzegwu shares an example of the misuse of African women's testimonies in her article, "Questions of Agency: Development, Donors, and Women of the South" (2002):

> Asked what development means to her, a peasant woman in rural Kenya had this to say: "During the anti-colonial campaigns we were told that development would mean better living conditions. Several years have gone by, and all we see are people coming from the capital to write about us. For me, the hoe and the water pot which served my grandmother still remain

my source of livelihood. When I work on the land and fetch water from the river, I know I can eat. But this development which you talk about has yet to be seen in this village." (Reported by Achola O. Pala 1981, 214, cited in Nzegwu: 1).

This history is the source of great concern for feminist ethnographers who have charged themselves with the task of identifying andro-centric and western-centric biases in early ethnographic accounts. Critique has produced new interpretations based on the conceptual analysis of gender systems, their intersectionality with race and class, and their centrality to the construction of culture (Lewin 2006, Fox, unpublished manuscript).

In particular, the approach known as the personal narrative (or life history) has taken center stage within the subfield of Africanist feminist anthropology as a means of addressing two intersecting points of critique: 1) an exploration of the theoretical, methodological and political underpinnings of feminist inquiry stressing the significance of the subjective voices of women; and 2) the problematization of the historical ambitions of the Africanist enterprise in the U.S. challenging "current assumptions, alliances, and agendas among scholars of Africa" (Martin and West 1999: 113). While these two foci have shaped the direction of feminist ethnography in Africa, each in turn has been influenced by theories of identity—especially feminist standpoint theory—as well as by the broader poststructuralist critique of the Enlightenment project in its challenge to the universalist discourses of the West.

The notion that we all write and speak from specific locations as positioned subjects[2] became the focus of a particular debate in the African Studies Association (ASA) in the 1970s, when the Black Caucus called on the ASA to

> take steps 'toward rendering itself more relevant and competent to deal with the challenging times and conditions of black people in Africa, in the United States, and in the whole black world' in part by recruiting more blacks to the organization...and by giving black scholars a more visible role in the organization (ibid: 98, 99).[3]

One outcome, the Black Caucus hoped, would be the production of Africa-centered scholarship, "a paradigm that places Africans at the center of the knowledge creation process" in order to reconstruct "the African's place in world history" (Keto 1999: 186, 187). In the 1970s and '80s this kind of criticism created a conundrum for feminist ethnographers, whose directive to work toward gender equity depended on ethnographic depictions that accurately portrayed the varied objectives of African women.

Thus the 1980s began a new era in the ethnography of Africa as feminist researchers began to develop new methodologies, among the most prevalent being the collection and analysis of the subjective, diverse voices of women. The personal narrative process was employed to explore how the interaction of societal structures—gender, economic, political, and religious—produced ideologies about relations of power within which practices such as the gendered division of labor, inheritance rights, Female Genital Mutilation (FGM), the socialization of children and the like were followed, negotiated and/or resisted. A corollary objective of these methodologies was to demonstrate that destabilizing notions of scientific objectivity and neutrality actually produced new insights and perspectives that were *more* rather than less accurate in depicting African social realities. Standpoint perspectives were not merely reductive embellishments of broader truths, but constitutive of those truths.

In the late 1990s, the direction once again shifted, moving away from an exclusive focus on the differences reflective of positionality. An interest in commonalities *in relation* to difference emerged—as part of the critique of global sisterhood and as a form of coalition-building across cultures—epitomizing the more recent objectives of transnational feminist discourse.

This brief overview brings us to the present and is the launching point for the remainder of the chapter. The objective is to illustrate the shifting knowledge terrains within the feminist ethnography of African women and the ends to which they have been directed. The study begins by examining the critique of Africanist anthropology, moves to exploring the theoretical and methodological underpinnings of the personal narrative approach that claim to portray African women's truths, and then evaluates the impact of that approach on affecting positive social change for those women who have shared their stories with persistent ethnographers. The final section describes some contemporary examples of applied feminist ethnography which seek to justify the work of the ethnographic enterprise in Africa through an activist orientation around social change.

The Critique of Africanist Anthropology

In the case of global Africa, the challenge becomes one of applying an Africa-centered paradigm, thereby leveling the playing field for the creation of knowledge about the history of people of African descent (Keto 1999: 175).

Much has been written about the history of anthropological fieldwork in Africa. It is a complex, frequently unflattering and ideologically contested past, particularly when measured against contemporary standards within a discipline that has attempted to remake itself through decades of trenchant critique. Colonial anthropology's representation of Africans as Europe's contemporary ancestors reflected a *"pathos of inequality"* that permeated evolutionary discourse and structural-functional frameworks as well as social policy initiatives (Pierterse 1995: 51).[4] Coalescing in the 1980s, however, criticism of anthropological power relationships and ethnographic authority emerged from many corners of the globe, including "a new generation of Western-born anthropologists who had played no role in the colonial regimes [and] felt free to denounce its predecessors" (Gledhill 2004: 4). Critics also included academics from Black and Africana Studies departments, non-Western anthropologists, and former colonial subjects of anthropological fieldwork themselves. Their condemnation provoked anthropology—especially socio-cultural anthropology—into a postmodern critique of its disciplinary "truths" in a period ubiquitously referred to as anthropology's "self-reflexive moment" or "crisis of representation."

Practitioners were inspired to reassess the objectives of the field and to launch explorations into a "new ethnography" which de-centered the authoritative voice of the anthropologist rendering it as one among many (Marcus and Fischer 1986). The outcomes—still underway—have produced more internally rigorous evaluations of the methodologies by which ethnographers develop themes for research, implement those themes, and employ their results through discursive representation or policy initiatives involving various applied projects.

In addition and simultaneously, feminist anthropologists experienced their own self-scrutiny, influenced both by this internal anthropological self-reflexivity and by the standpoint theory strain of feminist thought summarized in the introduction. After exploring the results of this period for feminist ethnography, examining its particular contributions to women's social change in Africa, I will argue that ethnography alone cannot be the end point for feminist anthropology but that instead there must be explicit directives for social change if the subfield is to realize the two interactive directives of feminism—scholarship and activism. In other words, the scholarship itself, while progressive and transformative of prior scholarly enterprises, cannot stand on its own as feminist ethnography's contribution to social movement activism. Instead, anthropologists should work to link academic discourses about gender inequality with African social movement actors involved in socio-cultural change with respect to gender dynamics (Darnovsky, et al. 1995, xviii).

The New Feminist Ethnography

A heightened sensitivity to the politics of representation, fieldwork and research unfolded within feminist anthropology in the 1980s. The critique was in part propelled by self-identified Third World feminists such as Trinh T. Minh-ha (1989) and Chandra T. Mohanty, whose widely influential essay, "Under Western Eyes: Feminist Scholarship and Colonial Discourses," (1983) disparaged the textual strategies harnessed by Western feminists in cross-cultural studies to paint third-world women as monolithically oppressed by patriarchal societies. Such external critiques and the insights that feminist researchers garnered from local people in the course of their fieldwork rendered earlier calls for a global sisterhood based on Western, white, middle-class feminist objectives both culturally and politically ethnocentric.

Galvanized, researchers began to question Western theorizing in general and Western feminist theory specifically, rejecting wholesale both structure/functionalist training (Bryceson 1995: 258) and the persistence of the evolutionary model. They began to theorize gender in ways that challenged previous assumptions of the neutral anthropologist and instead offered a pluralizing feminism that sought the "diversity, multiplicity, and transformative possibilities of women's politics globally" (S. Cole and L. Phillips 1996: 2). As a result, the 1990s saw an outpouring of critical feminist ethnographic scholarship, asserting "a reflexive stance toward one's own social position as a researcher, the frameworks employed and images and discourses deployed" (Montoya, Franzer and Hurtig 2002: 1). The objectives, possibilities, and limitations of feminist ethnography were scrutinized. Feminist anthropologists grappled with tensions between activism and scholarly ambitions and generated new research methodologies based on participatory models and the potentiality of cross-cultural activist alliances. Ethnographers also experimented with writing strategies such as multi-vocality, personal narratives/life histories, and texts multi-authored by anthropologist and research subject(s). In short, feminist anthropology sought to remake itself so that today,

> Feminist anthropology projects can now be characterized by attempts to listen (Myerhoff 1978); to translate (Behar 1993); to give women a voice (Petai 1988); and to provide a forum for the documentation and presentation of the conflicting, contradictory and heterogeneous exploration of women cross-culturally (Personal Narratives Group 1989).

What has been the impact of these developments on feminist ethnography in Africa? What challenges persist, and how might they be addressed?

At this historical juncture, following the significant paradigm shifts in Western feminist theory that have taken place since the 1970s focusing "on questions of subjectivity and identity" (Mohanty 2003: 106), there is a need for relational understanding that moves beyond the problematics of both essentialized difference and universal sisterhood. Feminist ethnography, which also has been engaged with questions of subjectivity and identity, is poised to work toward, in Mohanty's words "ethical and caring dialogues and revolutionary struggles across the divisions, conflicts, and individualist identity formations that interweave feminist communities in the United States." She argues for crafting genealogies of community, home and nation that "envision and enact common political and intellectual projects across these differences" (ibid: 125). The solidarity these produce should embrace "mutality, accountability and the recognition of common interests as the basis for relationships among diverse communities," where "diversity and difference are central values...to be acknowledged and respected, not erased in the building of alliances" (ibid: 7).

Feminist ethnographic practice in Africa since the 1980s has focused on the production of emancipatory knowledges through revised methodologies, theories, and pedagogies. Writing practices continue to challenge "the psychological and cultural furniture" of stereotypes (Pieterse 1992: 12), unpacking and reconfiguring Western popular perceptions of Africans. In part this involves work with North American students, many of whom paint African women as homogeneously oppressed vis-à-vis American women, perceived as homogeneously liberated. More work needs to be done—again quoting Mohanty—"at the level of collective action in groups, networks, and movements constituted around feminist visions of social transformation" (ibid: 4). It is in part through this latter level of praxis that anthropologists can strive to move beyond the persistent conundrums that are endemic to the genre of ethnography.

Feminist Ethnography in Africa: Collaborative Research

> What does empowerment mean to us as black women of Africa and her diaspora? It means social recognition and dignity...it means space to speak, act, and live with joy and responsibility...We want to end our silences and speak our truths as we know them. We wish to have power which positively promotes Life in all its forms; power to remove from our path any thing, person, or structure which threatens to limit our potential for full human growth as the other half of Life's gendered reality... (Molara Ogundipe-Leslie 1994).

Since the 1980s, feminist ethnographers have pursued collaborative relationships in communities across the African continent. Also referred to as participatory research or cooperative research, it is an approach that does not assume sameness between researcher and researched but rather layered relationships where differences and shared values are reflected in project goals and design. Collaboration incorporates collective decision-making about the topics and issues under exploration and involves participation in the process by which "data" become textually codified and communicated.

The 1980s and 1990s generated numerous collaborative case studies— e.g. "Madiume's 1987 study on Igbo women of Eastern Nigeria; Oboler 1985 on Nandi women of Western Kenya; Robertson 1984 on Ga women of Central Accra," Abwunza's on Logoli women of Kenya (cited in Abwunza 1996: 251) and Else Skjonsber's work in Kefa village in the Eastern province of Zambia. Skjonsberg traveled to Zambia, "hoping to solicit the active participation of villagers in mapping and analyzing cultural life" (1996). She says, "I wanted to be certain that it was their everyday life that would prevail rather than my views and biases as a foreign social scientist" (ibid 227). Emphasizing the relationship between ethnographer and the local community, she aimed to establish a dialogue with research *partners* to understand "rather than predict and control social life" through research (ibid: 232). Toward this end, she involved five local assistants with seven to eleven years of schooling rather than her own university-educated student research assistants. She conducted time allocation studies to detail the gendered division of labor, documenting the considerable disparity— produced mainly through women's extensive food processing activities—between men's and women's work burdens.

Skjonsberg also took seriously village members' protestations over her work, incorporating their ideas to improve the design of the project and to take pride in it. At the conclusion of her study, she asserted that through collaboration, researchers can transcend their own cognitive limitations, producing "a meeting point between cultures, intellectual orientations and problem-solving experiences where different and sometimes even contradictory experiences are placed on an equal footing" (ibid, 233-235). She also noted that "even in a seemingly conformist village, individual differences often emerged as more significant than gender differences," and finally, that through the participatory model, "less visible intellectual and social processes have a chance of emerging" (ibid: 235), underscoring the bridge that scholarship builds toward social change. Still, says Deborah Fahy Bryceson, editor of *Women Wielding the Hoe* (1995), "We are only part way toward rethinking powerful propositions of evolutionary and structural theory in light of late twentieth-century dynamics. Until new syntheses may be worked out, the logic of enquiry has to be multiple, experimental and ultimately participatory" (403).

Another form of participatory research contributing to such a rethinking is the personal narrative approach, which, as stated in the introduction, draws from standpoint theory to disrupt longstanding anthropological dichotomies between researcher (read: white male) and researched (read: poor people of color). Personal narratives or life histories as subjective stories rooted in time and place bring anthropology closer to undoing this historical relationship by invoking relational thinking. This involves empathetic understanding, and a careful identification of a matrix of articulated commonalities and variations among collaborators. If such an ideal can be attained, according to anthropologist Sally Cole, "The creation of a self through opposition to an other is blocked, and therefore both the multiplicity of the self and the multiple overlapping and interacting qualities of the other cannot be ignored...offer[ing] the promise of finally undermining the assumption of anthropology that we stand outside" (cited in Behar, p. 359, notes, 2003).

The achievements of such an approach are many, including as historian Claire Robertson notes, "cross-racial, cross-cultural, and cross-class communication" (2000: xxiv). The construction of individual life-histories, such as her work with Berida Ndambuki of Kenya, is perhaps the most amenable to S. Cole's call for relational thinking and for producing transformative, liberatory texts. When the researcher casts herself as a secondary author and as such "does not compromise the material by deleting the controversial, abandoning contradictions, imposing foreign priorities, or grossly mistranslating," as Robertson explains, these texts have a clear value in "expanding the horizons of their readers and challenging their assumptions" (ibid: xxiv). Abwunza agrees, asserting that when such narratives are crafted within ethnography "a conversation between cultures took place." Voices are heard, she contends "because I was there!" (1996: 255).

Yet there remain limitations to this approach, although, as Robertson also notes, these do not negate the many successes of personal narratives. According to Henrietta Moore, personal narratives sidestep the

> political and theoretical complexities of trying to speak *about* women, while avoiding any tendency to speak *for* them. Feminist anthropology, unlike the 'anthropology of women,' has made some progress in this area, because while it acknowledges that 'women are all women together' it also emphasizes that there are fundamental differences between women (Moore, 1988, cited in Abwunza 1992: 35).

The Personal Narratives Group, an interdisciplinary collective of scholars affiliated with the Center for Advanced Feminist Studies at the University of Minnesota, concurs that personal narratives involve both collaboration and discrepancies of power and authority:

> No narrative is pure.... It is the product of complex negotiations between a narrator and the interpreters, and within the individual speakers themselves. Power relations always surround the production and publication of a life history, biography, or autobiography. These hidden hands include, but are not limited to, gender, class, colonialism, ethnicity, religion, politics, economics, and sexuality. In reading or producing such a work, ethics, identities, and ownership come into play in both obvious and subtle ways (Ward 1988: xi).

Sally Cole and Lynn Phillips go so far as to say in their introduction to *Ethnographic Feminisms* (1996) that the feminist project that they outline is perhaps impossible, because:

> The relative political and economic positions of Western feminists and anthropological subjects predetermine and mold the conditions for undertaking collaborative research (p. 4).

And Judith Abwunza comments on her work with Logoli women:

> Simply stated, the tension that exists here is between theorizing women and presenting women. I am forced to engage in benevolent dominance if I analyze, present, analyze. Benevolent because I insist their voices remain. Dominan[t] because I interpret their voices. As Tedlock (1991) has said, we kill the women's voices by our own, we pin them like butterflies to the wall, as we provide the interpretation. In whose interest are these spoken voices heard?

Yet the general consensus is that the scholarship is nonetheless warranted, because the work is undergirded by the political aim "of understanding, revealing and seeking to alleviate women's oppression, wherever it exists" (Cole and Phillips 1996: 4). Abwunza, however, still cautions, "Who do they/I speak for, them or me...The question still hangs: In whose interests are all these spoken voices heard?" (1996: 255).

It is clear that feminist anthropological case studies reveal the ways in which dominance is constructed, reproduced and resisted, challenging the comfortable gaze of the conventional view of Africa. In so doing, they are a form of praxis, contributing to the cultural capital of knowledge exchanged in the university.

Toward Coalitions and Solidarity: African Women's Human Rights

Without discounting the importance of the above contributions of feminist anthropology in documenting and analyzing gendered lives, we cannot ignore the persistence of the difficulties endemic to the ethnographic process in thinking through a viable connection between the scholarship feminist anthropologists produce and an activism that works toward the goals African women define for themselves. Moreover, the process of transferring ethnographic insights to activist organizations and groups is not straightforward, nor is it a guarantee of relevant applicability. Increasingly, for example, a significant number of the goals articulated by African women become re-inscribed into the language and assumptions of Western feminists and human rights campaigners in ways that are potentially detrimental, and risk "being construed as culturally paternalistic and strongly antagonistic, fueling a largely unsought and unsupported battle of the sexes in Africa" (Packer 2003: 165).

Anthropologist Corinne Packer, for example, has examined the way in which a whole range of diverse practices in Africa, including early marriage and pregnancy, dietary taboos, circumcision, scarification, incisions in pregnant women, and some birthing practices, among others, have been construed in the human rights literature as "harmful traditional practices," and thus as examples of violence against women. The Addis Ababa Declaration, adopted by the African Heads of State and Government at their meeting in 1998 in Burkina Faso, makes a series of claims that Packer takes issue with, including the following: "harmful traditional practices only originate from and occur in non-Western countries, especially African and Asian; all harmful practices are principally traditional; all harmful traditional practices represent a form of violence; all harmful traditional practices are directed at women" (ibid: 162).

In outlining the problematic elements associated with these claims, Packer notes that: 1) not all of the included practices are restricted to women, e.g., "the practice of male circumcision among the Xhosa can be, and should be framed as, a violation of a man's human rights to health, freedom from torture and cruel and inhuman treatment, and freedom of belief" (ibid: 164). 2) Moreover, not all of the practices should be considered examples of violence (e.g. dietary taboos such as restrictions on eating eggs during pregnancy that may have originally emerged for good reason and have become integrated into local lore); and 3) not all practices are "traditional" but have been incorporated into cultural complexes at various times in response to different stimuli—such as the recent practice of female genital cutting/mutilation (FGM/FC)[5] among the Zebarma of Sudan (as described later in this chapter), who through contact with another ethnic group practicing FGM/FC have adopted it to encourage their daughters' ability to marry.

In addition to oversimplifying and over-generalizing problems that African women face when these problems are translated into the realm of women's human rights activism, there are additional difficulties in seeking redress for violation of rights. These include structural problems in accessing the judicial system (costs, time, language of the court, distance of courts, attitudes of those administering justice); cultural limitations (women prefer to seek redress through families in a non-confrontational way; law enforcement officers are not sympathetic to women's claims); and psychological impediments to the use of law (developing links between consciousness-raising about rights and feelings of empowerment to report violations, for example) which cannot be overlooked if social science knowledge about African women's lives is going to be usefully translated into meaningful campaigns for change (ibid: 1660). In other words, the generation of knowledge that reflects African women's realities, while an important step, is in fact just a step that can all too easily become undone.

The challenge for feminist ethnographers is to develop ways to work from an African-centered framework for knowledge generation toward the fruitful application of that knowledge into the social, political and cultural terrains where local social movements are themselves emergent or in process. According to Darnovski, "efforts to interpret social reality from the privileged sanctuary of the academy miss the ways in which [social] movement intellectuals and activists are themselves significant contributors to social knowledge" (ibid: xix). At the same time, however, it is important not to overlook the overlap among the multiple institutions pursuing social change, including the academy. Such is the case in Sudan, for example, where feminist anthropologist Ellen Gruenbaum has conducted research on FGM/FC for over two decades. In her efforts to understand the many prongs of the anti-FGM/FC campaign originating in Sudan, she identifies the interconnecting threads of action by leaders promoting change, linking people at Ahfad University for Women with multiple local, national and international organizations. In this case, collaboration involves Gruenbaum's work in researching, writing about, and publicizing these Sudanese feminist activities in Western and international scholarly and activist forums.

Not only does this kind of alliance-building help to dispel Western assumptions that change originates in the West, but it also builds transnational understanding about the ways in which African women take charge of the trajectories of their own transformations. Gruenbaum has taken seriously Egyptian writer and activist Nawal El Saadawi's 1980 proclamation: "So we must deal with female circumcision ourselves. It is our culture, we understand it, when to fight against it and how, because this is the process of liberation" (cited in Gruenbaum 2005: 1)—without excluding herself from a potentially useful role. As we have seen with Packer's critique of the women's international human rights discourse regarding "harmful traditional practices," it is particularly important to understand how this process of liberation is unfolding at the local level. Is the language of human rights, for example, becoming meaningfully appropriated into people's daily realities and "owned?" Gruenbaum's work discussing and analyzing Sudanese efforts provides a potent example of this process. She traveled to a rural village in Sudan where a small NGO, Entishar, was contracting with UNICEF.

> Entishar had started a project that recruited a cohort of women and girls to participate in a women's empowerment project. An unmarried woman school teacher from a family in the village was recruited to lead the project with a couple of assistants. The leaders received training in a city with others from rural areas, to learn the concepts and skills and to inspire them with the importance of their tasks thorough identification with the larger world. A special shelter had been constructed for the meetings of the community cohort, which met for an hour or so about four times a week. The program was to include problem-solving skills, literacy, and development projects identified by the women. The day I visited, the participants were reviewing streamlined versions of the articles of the Convention on the Elimination of All Forms of Discrimination against Women (CEDAW), reciting them from memory by number when called on by the leader (Gruenbaum 2005: 12).

This powerful image conveys collaboration at multiple levels: Local women connecting with an NGO in turn funded by a UN agency; and ultimately, Gruenbaum's publication of the account to illustrate a process of African women's self-directed transformation. Gruenbaum's explicit conclusion following her visit to the Entishar project is that "eventually...[the project] will provide these women with the tools to challenge and eliminate FGC, and along the way, they will probably make progress on mobilizing for improvements in water and sanitation, nutrition, and educational goals for their families" (2005: 12).

The implicit conclusion, however, is that a change in understanding all that surrounds FC/FGM spills far beyond the locales where the procedures take place, out into the global marketplace of ideas, where feminist ethnographers have joined the rigorous efforts to build more complex awareness. There is an important place for the kind of scholarship that feminist anthropologists argue is transformative of public opinion. The sensationalist and over-generalized perceptions of FGM/FC that abound in the U.S., for instance, can be replaced by a more nuanced understanding, one that acknowledges the central role of African women in the FGM/FC abolition movement. There are indeed important roles for the cross-cultural exchange of ideas, opening up opportunities for the articulation and engagement of African feminist perspectives. The work of building theory out of praxis remains critical as well to the ongoing relevance of social science in interpreting and explaining multiple worldviews. All of these efforts also interact with factors barely touched upon here—persistent, global economic inequalities, climates of violence and political unrest, disease, environmental degradation—the world's plagues which continually interrupt, stall and undo so many efforts toward social change yet do not eradicate them. Yet, in acknowledging some of the multiple, overlapping processes that are required to bring about social change, I offer four examples of work that feminist anthropologists are engaged in, in striving toward this goal.

Example 1. The Female Circumcision Controversy[6]

The first example comes from feminist anthropologist Ellen Gruenbaum's work in the Sudan on FGM/FC. Gruenbaum's own efforts, as highlighted above, to work with Sudanese women have been multi-pronged and represent the range of activities embraced by feminist ethnographers. These include writing articles reporting on her collaboration with the FGM/FC abolition movement in Sudan; publishing an ethnography directed at the U.S. college audience to educate them about the realities of FGM/FC; traveling with representatives of UNICEF and CARE, who have adopted platforms for eradication of FGM/FC, reflecting the widespread objectives of the Sudanese abolition movement. She has also interviewed Sudanese women who are leaders in the anti-FGM/FC campaign. Her ethnography, *The Female Circumcision Controversy: an Anthropological Perspective,* represents one among a number of recent efforts to address Western misunderstandings and sensationalism surrounding genital cutting—the effort not to subscribe to a paralyzing moral relativism, but to engender knowledgeable and cross-cultural collaboration in working to diminish the practice (e.g. James and

Robertson 2002; Nnaemeka, 2005). In this section I begin by presenting an overview of the insights depicted in her ethnography, then I discuss how Gruenbaum has aimed to employ ethnographic knowledge toward social change through some of her other efforts in international cooperation.

Gruenbaum has conducted fieldwork in Sudan since 1974. Her ethnography portrays the multiple beliefs, values and norms that shape the varied practices that are collectively referred to as female circumcision (FC) (pp. 3-4). Gruenbaum begins with the controversial discussion about what to call the practice, as it is referred to also as Female Genital Mutilation and Female Genital Cutting. She explains that she is using the term FC—staying true to the anthropological dictum to depict the insider's perspective—because FGM suggests the intent to harm, a view that is not shared by the women who perform the operation in the communities she researches. Here she carves out a distinct place for the feminist anthropological activist who must serve both as an advocate for change, and in so doing represent accurately the perspectives of those she advocates for. Her selection to use FC is highly symbolic of how she has chosen to resolve this dilemma.

The rich, ethnographic texture of her examples draws readers into the lives of the women and men she has encountered in her research, so that readers can no longer talk about FC homogeneously, or in the absence of an empathetic understanding about the complex and contradictory emotions of fear, anxiety, necessity and joy, that permeate family members' decisions to pursue these operations for their little girls.

The book has three recurring themes: (1) what are women's own explanations for why they perform female circumcision on their daughters? (2) What are the cultural norms and values, and the economic and political realities that contribute to the perpetuation of the practice, that offer both possibilities and limitations for change? And (3) How should the answers to questions one and two affect the way cultural outsiders think about the practice and structure their own desire to participate in the process of change?

In researching the impact of economic development on female circumcision, Gruenbaum contests the assumption that such programs can lessen women's financial dependency on men, leading to increased education and access to health care facilities, all of which, theoretically, should contribute to a decline in female circumcision practices. She explores the contradictory impact of the Rahad Irrigation Scheme on two relocated, distinct ethnic communities, the Kenana (who practice infibulation) and the Zebarma (who experience minimal sunna operations). Each group regards itself, through the different circumcision practices, as morally superior. The Zebarma, for instance, maintain religious pride and attachment to Islam, which they believe does not insist on infibulation. The two communities have responded differently to their relocation, living side by side and experiencing changing patterns in the division of labor by gender; the construction of a clinic and a school, and increasing desirability of polygyny for men. The emphasis on polygyny has placed some degree of pressure on the Zebarma to practice infibulation to increase the desirability of their daughters for marriage, while other Zebarma women and girls are resisting infibulation. Economic development is clearly not a panacea, as a critical stance of the anthropology of development has documented. Moreover, it is clear that for Zebarma women, FC is not one of their "traditional" practices, but a relatively recent occurrence, an outcome of the international lending infrastructure.

In approaching the controversies swirling around female circumcision practices, Gruenbaum argues that female circumcision should stop, but will only do so when culturally and economically relevant alternatives are possible. Is her staking out of an opinion paternalistic? A continuation of Western feminist universalist rhetoric? I would argue not, largely because her opinions are couched firmly in detailed cultural knowledge produced through participatory approaches. In addition, her text moves beyond the personal narrative and even statements of opinion, invoking an explicit call for change. Her closing chapters explore channels of involvement for outsiders through linking to a range of existing organizations—both in and outside of Africa—whose missions and values are couched in the participatory framework. Importantly, she renders a forceful caveat, warning of unwelcome and ineffective interference where there is a lack of understanding and respect for cultural differences and the conditions that impact on women's lives and decisions. As such, Gruenbaum employs a notion of partnership with Sudanese women and with African-based organizations that reflects an African-centered definition of the concept, as proffered by Nkiru Nzegwu:

> The term "partner" defines a relationship in which two or more groups of people, who may occupy different sociocultural classes, have chosen to work collaboratively, in a communal effort, to attain a common goal. Central to this idea and relationship is the presumption of equality. Even though their tasks and responsibilities may differ, partners choose to come together for either short- or long-term objectives. Being partners, they cooperatively work toward that common goal. Participants in such ventures or alliances must have mutual respect for each other. Although they may not agree on everything, they must value what each other has to

offer. Without reciprocity in the relationship, without considering and factoring into one's reference scheme the other's opinion, there can be no partnership (2002: 1).

Since the publication of the above ethnography, Gruenbaum has continued conducting research that is oriented around collaboration and the kind of partnering that Nzegwu refers to. In 2003-2004 she returned to Sudan to investigate what has happened in the two years following one community's declaration of intent to discontinue female genital cutting. She also pursued research

> ...in each of five additional rural communities (working with UNICEF and CARE—both are trying to develop better strategies for contributing to the change process for FGM/FC), and interview[ed] feminist leaders involved in the FGM/FC abolition movement. I worked with students/scholars at Ahfad University for Women in Omdurman, Sudan. In my interviews with feminist activists I have looked for collaborative roles. Thus far, it seems my research and writing has been my most important role (I contributed my research report for CARE to a CD-Rom that was compiled for the Interagency Working Group by the Population Reference Bureau, August 2005) against harmful traditional practices. The CD-Rom is entitled *Abandoning Female Genital Mutilation/Cutting: Information From Around the World*, and my report is in the Sudan section. I think additional collaboration is important, but very challenging to undertake! (personal communication, 9/21/06).

Reflecting further on the possibilities for collaboration, Gruenbaum states,

> There are many insightful, hard-working feminists and human rights activists working in Sudan, and they struggle so hard! Working conditions are a challenge, funding is not stable, balancing family life and careers is difficult—as it is anywhere—and there is often political opposition that requires courage to face. Those who are lucky enough to find positions in international organizations (UNICEF, projects of European embassies or missions, international non-governmental organizations, etc.) sometimes have more job security to do their work, but they often face constraints of too much to do, obligations of bureaucratic and diplomatic roles, and other political or public relations constraints.

> International collaboration, it seems to me, would be important in this context. I would like to see us raise funds for fellowships to train women scholars in their home countries with some of the daring programs like the Institute for Women, Gender, and Development Studies at Ahfad University for Women in Sudan. For just a couple of thousand dollars, we could provide funding for a master's degree for a scholar from Sudan who

is far better positioned to do research, teaching, and development work than I can ever be. Yet there is also a role for international collaborators, since we may have better access to publication opportunities, grant funds, or political venues. We should do what we can to maintain our contacts and friendships, using the internet and mobile phones, and we should send books and publications to the libraries and scholars we are in contact with" (personal communication 9/22/06).

As her discussion indicates, Gruenbaum's approach is multi-pronged and multi-layered, involving interactions with students and faculty in a Sudanese academic institution; conducting participant-observation with researchers from CARE and UNICEF; and integrating her suggestions and advice directly so that it doesn't become translated into paternalistic language but is directed toward objectives culled through discussions with Sudanese FGM/FC activists.

Example 2. Beyond the Relativism vs. Universalism of Human Rights Debate: Cross-Disciplinary, Cross-Cultural Dialogues[7]

In this example, I draw primarily upon my work editing a volume of essays entitled *Women's Rights as Human Rights: Activism and Social Change in Africa* (1998). I co-edited the manuscript with Naima Hasci, a Somali social anthropologist and international development worker associated with the World Bank and previously of the United Nations Development Program (UNDP). The project's broad goal was to bring together scholars and activists to think about women's human rights in diverse African situations. It aimed very specifically to link western and African scholars, to engage in the difficult cross-cultural dialog about the relativity or universality of human rights with the focus on African women.

The book project emerged following my journey to Eritrea in 1997 where I had begun to explore what was at the time a hopeful transformation from wartime to constitutional democracy. I had interviewed women and youth from The National Organization of Eritrean Women and The National Organization of Eritrean Youth and Students, as well as members of numerous NGOs including Planned Parenthood International and Grassroots International. In those interviews I asked about the transition that women fighters and commanders would face coming home to communities where their roles and expectations would be dramatically different from those they had experienced during the war with Ethiopia. Because the war had lasted thirty years, many girls recruited to fight did not experience adult womanhood as their non-fighting sisters did in villages and communities throughout the new country. I was interested in how their experiences of leadership over men and work alongside men in a conservative society where a number of ethnic groups were gender-segregated would affect notions of self, their sense of entitlements and rights; and moreover, how they would regard their daughters and sons—many having given birth in the field.

As my interviews revealed the range of opinions about the rate and direction of social change, it became overwhelmingly clear to me that feminist anthropologists who support women's rights as human rights must face the same conundrum that feminist legal scholars have articulated, namely, "how can universal human rights be legitimized in radically different societies without succumbing to either homogenizing universalism or the paralysis of…relativism?" (Cook 1994). Moreover, how is it possible to render human rights' language in culturally meaningful ways, beyond the "rights-speak" that characterizes academic and human rights activism?

On returning home, I pursued these questions by collaborating with a group of scholars and activists to organize a conference held on December 5–6, 1997, at the Massachusetts College of Liberal Arts. The topic was to examine the possibilities for an intersection between cultural specificity and universal principles in women's human rights in Africa. Scholars hailed from cultural anthropology, moral philosophy, social history, political science, and feminist legal studies. Activist participants worked with four primary organizations: Oxfam America, Grassroots International, the United Nations Development Program (UNDP), and the Center for Third World Legal Studies. The collaboration was guided by Oloka-Onyango and Tamale's recommendation for "intra-cultural and cross-cultural dialogue," which recognizes that "the personal is political, but the political is extremely rich and diverse" (Oloka-Onyango and Tamale 1995). Indeed, as Angela Wakhweya, Co-Founder of African Baobab, Inc., noted in her chapter in the book "Women's Health and Human Rights in Uganda: To Be or Not to Be, That is the Question!" the tension that exists within the women's human rights movement internationally is "ultimately healthy and beneficial" because "it galvanizes debate and discussion, disagreement and eventually (hopefully) consensus" (1999: 267).

While the diversity of the conference participants was crucial, the labels which characterized our variations—Westerners / Africans; Western feminists / African feminists; scholars / activists—did so sloppily, subverting existing commonalities for the sake of emphasizing differences, implicitly suggesting the deterministic view that nationality and culture are the dominant factors in human interaction and the primary influences in differences of opinion. Differences certainly existed, but so did commonalities, generated both through shared experiences and through independent development of similar conclusions. Anxieties did surface throughout the project, the result of methodological approaches and intellectual disagreements as well as identity politics. Notions of "ownership" over the discourse, for example, arose, leading to the withdrawal of some of the participants. Nonetheless, the commitment to a shared agenda kept the project together.

One of the first concerns we addressed pertained to the weakness of women's international human rights law. As feminist legal scholar Hilary Charlesworth has demonstrated, the structures supporting women's human rights are more fragile than the mainstream human rights instruments, which do not address gender-specific rights. Charlesworth argues that the international instruments dealing with women have "weaker implementation obligations and procedures; the institutions designed to draft and monitor them are under-resourced and their roles often circumscribed compared to other human rights bodies" (Charlesworth 1994). Women's human rights maintain a marginal status on the general agenda of the human rights movement. This fact in and of itself demonstrates that no matter what differences women have with one another, the marginalization of their human rights affects all women by virtue of their being women.

In addressing this problem, the rather distinct purviews of scholars and activists emerged, although it would be overly simplistic to say that these divisions were rigid along disciplinary lines, and to do so would only reify the labels and their generalized characterizations. Thus, some scholars placed greater weight on the theoretical frameworks adopted to describe and explain the predicament of women's human rights than on on-the-ground experience, while activists generally analyzed the successes or failures of specific women's rights projects designed with the assistance of their organizations. These particular perspectives established the different knowledge terrains of scholarly and activist discourses which Darnovski has noted above, and the importance of maintaining ongoing linkages between the two. What was especially interesting was the way in which the creative process of imagining the construction of the book itself distilled many of the difficulties which exist on a much larger scale in any effort to articulate connections between the academic world and the world of social movements.

For example, it was proposed that the book's essays should be organized into two sections, the first theoretical, the second case studies. Activists protested that this organization would privilege theory over practice, implicitly supporting scholarly knowledge over activist forms. They urged instead a thematic organization which, it was argued, would do away with such dualism. Once we agreed on the framework of the book, a second discussion ensued around the origins of theoretical works used by researchers. A Kenyan scholar argued that the historical tendency of Western scholars to overlook the contributions of African theorists was reflected in the choice of theorists that scholars employed in their discussions. How could we not involve leading African thinkers in a project designed to embrace cultural context in the search for a truly universal human rights? This point led to a commitment on the part of participants to read collectively and incorporate in their chapters articles by African thinkers such as Oloka-Onyango and Mutua. Mutua for instance is principally interested in the nature of the relationship between the individual and society in Africa, which he characterizes as dramatically different from the relationship between the individual and the state in Western societies.

The ubiquitous discussion about the Western hegemony of the international human rights movement was addressed by the African women activists. Many argued that the participation of African women in the international women's rights movement takes place at many levels, among rural womenfolk, at village meetings, in the corridors of academe. This diversity of African women's participation is indicative, according to feminist anthropologist Sumi Colligan, of a shortcoming in the new social movement theory. In her chapter "To Develop Our Listening Capacity to be Sure we Hear Everything: Sorting out Voices on Women's Rights in Morocco," she argued:

> The term "social movement actor" implies that such an actor can clearly be differentiated from other kinds of social actors. Yet . . . "feminist" action in the Third World (and no doubt in the First World as well) assumes many different guises. . . . A narrow definition of social movement can lead to ineffective coalitions and partial solutions (Colligan 1999: 188).

Colligan also noted that an overemphasis on "social location and positioning risks the danger of essentializing consciousness, denying its potential for expansiveness and fluidity" (ibid). This recognition permeated our discussions, as we shared the notion articulated by Alexander and Mohanty that "global processes clearly require global alliances" (cited in Colligan, 188).

Additionally, project participants concurred that historical and local conditions, in overlapping with global processes, necessitate matrices of local/regional/global collaboration and coalitions. This being the case, the debate over the relativity or universality of human rights is one which actually distorts the problem, rather than illuminating the condition of women. The harm in maintaining this bipolar debate, commented Colligan, is that it perpetuates "international hierarchies of power that contribute to the ongoing polarization of the West and the Third World and [limit] ... the definition and scope of struggles perceived to fall within the purview of women's human rights" (idem). These exchanges helped to clarify the intellectual terrain of the book and to identify a common objective: to work toward a theoretical position which recognizes the validity of African women's rights within their respective, concrete, socio-historical settings as human rights with universal import. Hasci's concluding remarks in her chapter on Somali refugees in Kenya summarized the shared view we arrived at the close of the project:

> The issue here is not about maintaining relativism as a dichotomy to universalism, but about integrating, adapting and building on what is universally human and gender-sensitive about a society's cultural and juridical heritage so that it can be genuinely sustained locally, nationally and internationally (Hasci 1999).

Example 3. Open-Access Publishing: The Journal of International Women's Studies

An important venue for collaboration across borders is the emergence of open-access publishing. I would like to comment briefly on the potential of e-publishing as a venue for solidarity building. In 1998, I founded *The Journal of International Women's Studies* (JIWS) as an online, open-access, peer-reviewed journal to provide a forum for scholars, activists, and students to explore the relationship between feminist theory and various forms of organizing globally. I hoped to establish a journal that distilled multiple levels of feminist practice where subscription rates were not an issue, although clearly the digital divide would exclude certain users. As the mission statement says,

> The journal seeks both multidisciplinary and cross-cultural perspectives, and invites submissions in the form of scholarly articles, student papers and literary pieces. Through its diverse collection, the journal aims to create an opportunity for building bridges across the conventional divides of scholarship and activism; "western" and "third world" feminisms; professionals and students; men and women (www.bridgew.edu/jiws/: About the Journal).

In spite of what might be perceived to be the rather conservative title of the journal, "international" being read as fixtures of geopolitical power, and "women's studies" perhaps not embracing GLBTQ theory/praxis, the nature of contributions have spanned the spectrum of feminist discourse. Moreover, the contributions from African scholars and activists have been significant. The Journal has published over thirty articles *by* African scholars and activists and many more *about* African women's political, economic and gender struggles. As well, five members of the board are African women, the majority residing in South Africa, including Caroline Kihato, the editor of the Routledge journal *Development Southern Africa* (DSA), which is based in Johannesburg. When Kihato joined the board of editors, she said the following:

> One of the key interventions I hope to make is to develop a vehicle that gives access to a broad range of voices on the African continent to publish on development issues. Publishing vehicles remain very limited in Africa, and even more so for young African scholars. Through a number of mechanisms such as mentoring, broadening networks, reconstituting the board, and conceptualizing special issues, I hope to build a platform for vibrant scholarly exchanges between people interested in development. We could also create areas of collaboration between JIWS and DSA such as joint special issues on gender and development, and so on.

Here it is significant that the collaboration is being proposed from the other direction—Africa to the U.S.—indicating the mutual flows of feminist transnationalism. Electronic journals which employ the scholarly accoutrements of print journals (blind peer review for example) can be envisioned as a form of academic activism, opening venues for the kind of vibrant debate and exchanges Kihato herself suggests. Here, scholar-activists can articulate the theoretical and practical manifestations of global feminisms, explore radical reformulations of feminist thought, and engage in the scholarly practice of dissent in documenting and rendering visible struggles for change which previously may have remained outside of the global gaze.

Example 4. FORWARD-Germany: FGM through the Eyes of Nigerian Artists

Another realm of collaboration includes the work of NGOs themselves, whose presence has proliferated in multiple forms on the African continent in recent decades. Dominating through global networks Africa's political and economic landscape, these private voluntary organizations aim to address a plethora of causes. Their significant presence has produced scholarly interest in their work among anthropologists, who have produced studies evaluating NGOs' missions, funding sources and patterns of operation.[8] FORWARD-Germany—The Foundation for Women's Health, Research and Development—is one such international NGO focusing on the elimination of gender-based violence against African women and girls, particularly FGM. Dr. Tobe Levin,[9] the President of FORWARD, also serves on the board of the *Journal of International Women's Studies* (see above), illustrating yet another way in which electronic communications can serve as a tool to connect feminist scholar-activists.

Dr. Levin offered a detailed response to my inquiry about the nature of FORWARD's collaboration with African women with respect to FGM:

> Key to work[ing] against FGM is "division of labor." Western women simply can't do certain things, basta! For instance, our former vice-president Dr. Asili Barre-Dirie is Somali. She runs our holistic projects against FGM in Somalia using a gradual approach that firsts asks what the entire community needs (for example, water pumps, repair of fishing nets lost to the tsunami, a building where school children can learn, etc.). Once trust is established, she talks about FGM in private with individual women. Where the mother-tongue is needed, clearly, only someone who speaks it can use it! So what then is the "other role"? Raising funds, of course, and to do that, sensitization campaigns aimed at a Western public need to be devised and staffed. Here I have experienced clear disagreement on acceptable approaches with the division along African/Western lines. For instance, more sensitive to racism than we are, our African members see sensationalism where we miss it. The "barbarity" of FGM might all too easily confirm racist stereotypes of "barbarian" Africans. Working explicitly against this, we try to condemn the genital attacks without condemning the practitioners. Admittedly, that's a challenging high-wire act at times.

> Over the years there have been more than enough high volume complaints about "Western" women's "arrogant interference" (Whenever I read just screeds which is often in U.S. publications, I ask, do they mean me? Interestingly…names are never named, and I had begun wondering years ago precisely who were these officious interlopers? I know Alice Walker has been placed in that category in the U.S.—but not in Europe. However, years ago, Efua Dorkenoo told me to ignore anyone who would discourage activism. She said, no matter what, you're going to be called a racist if you do this work because you will be perceived as a trespasser by just this vocal group who after all speaks for an overwhelming majority of African women who want to continue cutting. Therefore, be bold and choose your allies! Choose to support the 'positive deviants' among African women who are out there asking for your help, and then HELP!" (personal e-mail communiqué, 10/9/2006).

One of the ways that Levin and her branch of FORWARD have aimed to provide exactly this kind of help is through a traveling art exhibit entitled "Through the Eyes of Nigerian Artists: Confronting Female Genital Mutilation." The exhibit portrays "the suffering, sorrow and dignity of Nigerian girls and women attempting to break away from the harmful traditional practice of female genital mutilation (FGM)" (www.FORWARD-Germany.org).[10]

One of the aims of the show is to generate discussion and ideas for projects that address female genital mutilation. The exhibit is the brainchild of Joy Keshi Walker of Nigeria, who is both a Marketing Communication Specialist and campaigner against FGM. She brought together 80 artists to discuss the project and then commissioned them to make the practice the subject of their paintings. The first exhibit was at the Goethe Institute in Lagos in November 1998, after which Joy Keshi Walker traveled to Indianapolis where she showed seven pieces at the University of Indiana for the conference "Women in Africa and the African Diaspora" (WAAD). FORWARD has worked to bring the paintings to over 70 German communities, to Zürich and Behl, Switzerland; Torino, Italy; London; and to Brandeis University in Massachusetts.

In addition, within Nigeria, using art as a medium serves multiple purposes. According to Joy Keshi Walker, "the arts can more easily conquer the barriers of language and cultural diversity in Nigeria, a country of 120 million people, with over 250 languages. Because words can sometimes be offensive or judgmental, in order to avoid emotional stand-offs, a visual medium that transcends ethnic sensitivities was preferred" (ibid). According to FORWARD-Germany, 1998, soon after the exhibition was shown in a number of regions in Nigeria, two states abolished FGM. Today the Nigerian government is working to stop the practice entirely. Moreover, "Joy Keshi Walker believes that the artistic nature of the work ennobles the people and offers a view of cultural dignity without FGM. In other words, while the art is about FGM, it is also about the artists and the possibility of life free from a harmful traditional practice" (ibid). Moreover, I would add that the exhibit contributes to the growing movement to link African art with individual artists, while simultaneously placing that art in its cultural, utilitarian context—a relatively new practice that follows a longer history in the West of isolating Africa creative works from both—artists and use-value, so that they appear in museums transformed into Western notions of "art," housed in both museums of art and ethnology, abstracted from their original concrete meaning, and in fact, rendered *meaningless* in the African context.

While more can be said about the exhibit and the individual artists, this brief example illustrates the web-like threads linking shared ideas, objectives and importantly, to reiterate Levin's words above, "division of labor" in the transformation of those ideas into collaborative practices.

Example 5. Black Feminist Anthropology

Black Feminist Anthropology (BFA), my final example circling back to the starting point of the essay, is a U.S.-based phenomenon, and as such, its emergence is part of the wider critique of American anthropology that took place in the 1980s. Its anti-racism and anti-sexism purviews are explicitly linked to the persistent marginalization of Black anthropologists within the discipline as exemplified, for instance, in the paucity of citations of Black scholars in the academic literature (McClaurin 2001: 3). As a response, BFA echoes the criticisms that the Black Caucus levied against the ASA in the 1970s. BFA's links to anthropology's "self-reflexive moment" of the 1980s is evident in a statement by Irma McClaurin, editor of the 2001 reader *Black Feminist Anthropology: Theory, Politics, Praxis and Poetics*: "despite Postmodern critiques of grand theory, master narratives, and canon formation, the reality is that graduate and undergraduate curricula still largely rely upon canonical works in training students" (ibid: 2). As result BFA is

> ...self-consciously fashioned as an act of knowledge production and sees itself as a form of cultural mediation between the world of Black scholars and the entire Western intellectual tradition, between Black anthropologists and the rest of the discipline, and between Black and white feminists. But more importantly, it is an intervention—a Black feminist anthropological intervention (ibid: 2). As such, BFA combines a scholarship rooted in the intersectionality of gender, race, and class with the political purview of the anthropology of liberation. Coined by Faye V. Harrison, this concept presupposes a link between knowledge production and praxis, and is explored in the volume, through McClaurin's description of the included essays, as a poetics of the diversity of African-American culture and the cultures of the African Diaspora. Such a poetics recognizes that "African-Americans indeed have culture and indigenous forms of theorizing, out of which enduring cultural beliefs and practices have developed in unique and diverse ways in the United States and throughout the African Diaspora" (ibid: 17). The essays serve simultaneously as a launching point for ethnographic exploration, theorizing, and ultimately for many, collaboration with their "ethnographic subjects."

Such is the case for Carolyn Martin Shaw in her essay, "Disciplining the Black Female Body: Learning Feminism in Africa and the United States." She begins with her own coming of age in the 1950s in a segregated Black community in Virginia as a springboard for discussing her development as a scholar-activist within the intellectual and emotional space of "interculturality." Interculturality, Shaw explains, "refers to the intersection of different forms of knowledge and experience, and deployments and effects of power" (2001: 103). When she first went to Kenya in 1971 to study Kikuyu society, this notion played an important role as she noted "individuals caught between competing demands derived from their cultural and social systems" (ibid: 105). Yet, ironically Shaw was at first blind to the significance of Kikuyu gender differences. Her awakening to their importance, by striving to see Kikuyu society from women's perspectives "was as crucial to my becoming a black feminist anthropologist, as were my determination for equal rights for women and my sense of outrage at male domination" (ibid: 105).

As is typical of the anthropological experience of immersion in fieldwork, Shaw's exposure to otherness provided a lens into self. What moves her beyond conventional anthropological insight to the realm of feminism, however, is the fodder that her self-reflexive insights provide for the breakdown of the self/other dichotomy toward the construction of a bridge between herself and the African women she would ultimately work with in political solidarity. Through an auto-ethnographic account, she begins with her early reflections on her own Black female body as the site of intersecting ideologies of race/gender/sexuality, in order to "break down the barriers separating private hurts and social norms" (ibid: 106).

As a child, Shaw says,

> I saw race primarily in terms of the black body and of racism, racism based on the abnegation of the black body—color, form, face and hair... From outside my community, my body was racialized in pernicious ways... Inside the black community, it was again the body that defined me—this time in terms of gender and sexuality (ibid: 103).

Later in life, following her identification as a Black feminist anthropologist, she sees an intersection between her early perceptions of self impacted by the ideology of racism, and the imputation of the authoritarian postcolonial state on African female bodies. She notes the "coercion, violence, and extortion" of the authoritarian male's show of power, as well as the "collusion, compliance and performance" of African women. Yet far from conflating her own and African women's experiences, she explores them relationally, articulating a pathway toward coalition-building and solidarity, by recognizing elements of oneself in the other. Shaw quotes from Historian Achille Mbembe's study of Cameroon, "Provisional Notes on the Postcolony," to illustrate how "the power of the state is dramatized as ecstatic sexual master of women's bodies" even when those bodies are victims of hunger and illness. The quote is so powerful, it is reproduced here:

> In the post-colony bodies have been used to entertain the powerful in ceremonies and official parades. On such occasions some of the bodies have had the marks of famine upon them: flaky scalps, scabies, skin sores. Other bodies have attracted small crowds of flies. But that has not stopped them from breaking out into laughter or peals of joy when the presidential limousines approached. They stamped the ground with their feet, blanketing the air with dust. Wearing the party uniform with the picture of the head of state printed on it, women followed the rhythm of the music and swung their torsos first forward, then back; elsewhere they pulled in, then thrust out their bellies, their undulating movements evoking as usual the slow, prolonged penetration of the penis and its staccato retreat (cited in Shaw: 120).

Shaw's insights into the state's appropriation of the sexualized body as a domain for its display of power, eschewing the real conditions of those bodies, resonated with her own feelings of cultural incompetence as a child: "a whole repertoire of verbal skills and athletic abilities" alluded her, "friends and relatives, adults and children teased me for being awkward and uncoordinated...big for my age," "goose-necked," and with a "'liar's gap' in my teeth" (Shaw: 106, 107). How to survive, let alone excel, within her excoriated body? For years, Shaw notes,

> my personal concern about status and advancement in the university made me shy away from topics that would further marginalize me, topics such as women and children. And my own anger at gender inequality was suppressed so that I could function smoothly at work and at home (ibid: 117).

Coerced and colluding, as with the Cameroonian dancers. Then, in the 1970s her consciousness exploded. Shaw returned to Africa, this time to Zimbabwe in the mid-1980s. There she became politically active, joining an interracial group of feminists from around the world who were protesting the government's "Operation Clean-Up," an effort to rid the capital city of prostitutes and vagrants. Ultimately, her engagement with Zimbabwean women's political struggles was collaborative, in partnership as Nzegwu has defined it above, "a relationship in which two or more groups of people, who may occupy different socio-cultural classes, have chosen to work collaboratively, in a communal effort, to attain a common goal." Shaw's journey underscores not only the challenges of partnership/collaboration with African women for a reflexive feminist anthropology but the responsibilities as well—once the parameters of shared understanding have been broached—to articulate this internal awareness in the social movement spaces of political activism.

In conclusion, the above summary of feminist anthropological alliances with African women suggests but a few of the opportunities for multiple venues for collaboration and solidarity-building that move beyond disciplinary boundaries to engage in feminist transnational, cross-cultural dialog and debate. Individual projects themselves may come to an end. However, their insights and impacts extend beyond their spatial-temporal boundaries both within individuals—in the form of expanded knowledge, understanding and notions of global citizenry—and within the overlapping social spaces we occupy, inspiring ongoing efforts and offering solace in the face of immediate defeat.

Notes

[1] In 2002, Baartman's remains were sent back to South Africa.

[2] It should be noted, however, that philosophers such as Jurgen Habermas who have critiqued post-strucuturalism and post-modernism have also argued that knowledge is always produced in a social context (see for example, D. A. Mosolo, 1994, *African Philosophy in Search of Identity*. Bloomington: Indiana University Press and International African Institute.

[3] Although in the short term the ASA was not successful in having what was known as the Johnson-Cole resolution (authored by Johnetta Cole and Willard Johnson) passed, today the ASA seeks to incorporate a diasporic focus through its annual conferences. Its mission statement remains focused on continental Africa, and the organization is plagued by financial constraints (www.Africanstudies.org).

[4] Joan Vincent has argued that it is "historically inaccurate to regard the discipline simply as a form of colonial ideology" (1990: 2), providing examples of anthropological critiques of the impact of European imperialism. However, as James Gledhill notes, "the critical strands of an anthropological approach to politics were not those that became hegemonic in the discipline" and "most of the profession did display 'willingness to serve'" (1994: 3).

[5] Throughout the remainder of this essay, I use the acronym FGM/FC to refer to the collection of practices that are forms of female circumcision. Following Richa Chauhan (Book Review, *NWSA Journal* 14.2 (2002) 230-233), I use FGM/FC in recognition that "*circumcision* for female genitalia trivializes the damage and scale of the practice. For similar reasons, Nahid Toubia and Anika Rahman, editors of *Female Genital Mutilation,* use FC as well as FGM. They note

that the term FGM remains an 'effective policy and advocacy tool' in the international community."

[6] Segments of this discussion have been drawn from my Review Essay, "Women's Struggles for Equality, Power and Voice in Africa and the Middle East," pp. 347-353) by Diana Fox, in *Journal of Third World Studies*, Fall 2002, Vol. XIX, No. 2. Americus, Georgia.

[7] I have drawn on my article, "Women's Human Rights in Africa: Beyond the Debate of the Universality of Relativity of Human Rights," *African Studies Quarterly*. Vol.2, Issue 3, Nov. 1998.

[8] In his recent manuscript, *Global Shadows: Africa in the Neoliberal World Order* (2006), anthropologist James Ferguson describes a condition which he refers to as "government-by-NGO": "[States] are often effectively governed in a transnational humanitarian or developmental mode, as a hodgepodge of transnational private voluntary organizations carry out the day-to-day work of providing rudimentary governmental and social services, especially in regions of crisis and conflict" (2006: 40). He also illustrates that some NGOs have resorted to sinister strategies in their efforts to achieve ostensibly collaborative missions—as for example in the case of wildlife protection. The environmental NGO, Africa Rainforest and River Conservation (ARRC), based on the Chinko River Basin of the Central African Republic, for instance, made a strange bedfellow of paramilitary tactics. The ARRC, led by its founder, the Wyoming physician Bruce Hayes, has hired mercenaries to attack the Sudanese poachers and to try to form a 400-strong local anti-poaching militia to patrol the Chinko River basin. The NGO's 'director of operations'....sees no conflict between military work and the task of conservation" (ibid: 44). Ferguson also emphasizes that the AARC case is not unique, offering other examples of private security firms working in conjunction with NGOs, particularly in regions where there is significant destitution and the absence of state authority (ibid: 44-46).

[9] Professor of English and Women's Studies at the University of Maryland in Europe and adjunct at the University of Frankfurt.

[10] Readers should note that the term "harmful traditional practices" is employed here, keeping in mind the earlier discussion of the inapplicability of that term to the recent advent of FGM among some ethnic groups due, ironically, to the impact of "modernity" through development projects that impact group dynamics, women's opportunities, marriage, etc.

Part III

Health, Education, and Culture

CHAPTER SEVEN
MATERNAL MORTALITY AND TRANSPORT
Africa's Burden
Margaret Grieco

Introduction: the Intersection of Infrastructural Deficiencies and Gender Disadvantage

Maternal health remains a regional and global scandal, with the odds that a sub-Saharan African woman will die from complications of pregnancy and childbirth during her life at 1 in 16, compared to 1 in 3,800 in the developed world (UN, 2007:2).

For Africa, the transport legacy of colonialism and imperialism has been a deficient transport infrastructure. The extractive demands of empire and colony determined that the development of transport infrastructure take forms suitable to patterns of extraction. The development of roads and railways and the improvement of rivers to move materials from mines to coast for use in manufacturing overseas occurred at the cost of a failure to develop internal transportation infrastructures which would have better connected indigenous peoples to their neighbors and better linked internal economies. These patterns of infrastructure deficiency, and their imperialist derivation, have been well documented (Hilling, 1996; Headrick, 1981). Hilling (1996), for example, provides us with detailed information on transport availability in Africa and compares this with other regions of the world. He discusses this in terms of global discrepancies in transport provision. Africa emerges overall as an area of measured serious under-provision of transport.

Each extractive transport and communication network developed in Africa connected a colony to its respective imperial centre and placed barriers and boundaries in the way of that colony connecting with neighboring African colonies governed by competing European states. The consequence of these imposed boundaries and barriers to normal commercial traffic between neighboring colonies with different European governorships is clear: the transport and communication networks of Africa became unnaturally truncated and fragmented (Headrick, 1981). It is within this legacy that transport provision within Africa has taken place and it is this legacy which continues to contribute towards the continuing and serious under-provision of transport in Africa.

But our purpose here is not to journey further into these larger dynamics of transport infrastructure in Africa but to examine how these dynamics have created additional burdens for African women in the modern period—most particularly, we argue, in respect to the prevalence of maternal mortality within and across Africa (World Health Organization, 2004). A recent WHO document (2004:10) reported that:

> The estimated number of maternal deaths in 2000 for the world was 529,000. These deaths were almost equally divided between Africa (251,000) and Asia (253,000), with about 4 percent (22,000) occurring in Latin America and the Caribbean, and less than one percent (2,500) in the more developed regions of the world. In terms of the maternal mortality ratio, the world figure is estimated to be 400 per 100,000 live births. By region, the MMR [maternal mortality rate] was highest in Africa (830), followed by Asia (330), Oceania (240), Latin America and the Caribbean (190) and the developed countries (20). The country with the highest estimated number of maternal deaths is India (136,000), followed by Nigeria (37,000), Pakistan (26,000), the Democratic Republic of the Congo (24,000), Ethiopia (24,000), the United Republic of Tanzania (21,000), Afghanistan (20,000), Bangladesh (16,000), Angola, China and Kenya (11,000 each) and Indonesia and Uganda (10,000 each). These 13 countries account for 67 percent of all maternal deaths.

However, in terms of the maternal mortality ratio, which reflects the obstetric risk associated with each pregnancy, the list looks rather different. With the sole exception of Afghanistan, the countries with the highest MMRs are in Africa. The highest MMRs of 1,000 or greater, are, in order of magnitude, Sierra Leone (2,000), Afghanistan (1,900), Malawi (1,800), Angola (1,700), Niger (1,600), the United Republic of Tanzania (1,500), Rwanda (1,400), Mali (1,200), Central African Republic, Chad, Guinea-Bissau, Somalia and Zimbabwe (1,100 each) and Burkina Faso, Burundi, Kenya, Mauritania and Mozambique (1,000 each).

Africa is clearly bearing an unacceptable burden in respect to maternal mortality (Abdoulaye, 2006). To provide further and more troubling context, maternal mortality is increasing in Africa while it is decreasing at the global level (Harrison, 1997), and our argument is that deficiencies in Africa's transport legacy and endowment play an important part in this increase.

To start our discussion of maternal mortality and transport, we must begin by noting that there is a general relationship between gender and transport in which women are more poorly resourced in relation to transport and less well served by transport organization than men no matter which locality, region, country or continent we turn our attention to (World Bank, 1999). Furthermore, there is a relationship between mobility, power and well-being (Grieco, 2006): poor access to transport affects health, wealth and autonomy. The differences between male and female travel patterns and the cultural rules and roles associated with these differences are under-charted in the policy environment. The impact of constrained mobility on bargaining also has its impact on what comes to be available as resource and service within local constraints. No better demonstration of these constraints can be found than in Africa's portrait of maternal mortality: constraints on mobility and on the resources for mobility and accessibility have devastating consequences for women's health on the African continent. Lack of transport, or more importantly lack of entitlement to transport, means that the pervasive and uniquely female burden of childbirth becomes a circumstance of crisis and loss of life: the aggregate statistics testify to the consequence of not making provision for this routine need. The obstetric transport barriers experienced in Africa (Krasovec, 2004) require our focused attention: the combination of poor transport structures with the gender-disadvantaged life experience of women is a compound deprivation which requires resolution. The remainder of this chapter explores paths that can be explored and measures that can be taken to ameliorate this present and growing crisis.

Contrary fortunes: rising African maternal mortality in a global context of declining maternal mortality rates

Rising maternal mortality in Africa represents a major failure in terms of meeting the Millennium Development Goals (UN, 2007). It is clear that there is a need for a re-examination of "the politics of priority" in development aid: health or wealth? The gendered character of disparities in health is readily apparent, but many of the heated policy discussions around growth versus poverty reduction as the priority are held without reference to the scale of the crisis in maternal well-being. Maternal mortality is not simply fatal but is often a cruel and harsh lived experience for Africa's women. And yet an evaluation printed in the *Organization for Economic Cooperation and Development (OECD) Observer* (AbouZahr, 2000) of the costs of drastically reducing maternal mortality in Africa indicates that this can be done without the need for significant increases in the wealth of the continent.

Reducing maternal mortality is not necessarily dependent on economic development. It would cost only about $3 a person a year in low-income countries to provide the essential services needed to tackle the problem: that would cover a skilled health worker to assist every delivery, access to essential obstetric care for mothers and their infants when complications arise, and family planning information and services so that unwanted pregnancies and unsafe abortions can be avoided (AbouZahr, 2000:1).

It is a matter of organization—and part of that organization is the provision of transportation and hostel facilities close to hospitals for those in need of, or likely to need, emergency obstetric care. The use of hostels for pregnant women likely to experience obstetric difficulties places these women within timely access to the facilities necessary to avert death. Ironically, maternal mortality—death because of distance from health facilities—is increasing in Africa at the same time that there is a global discourse on the "death of distance."

At present, the mapping of mobility entitlements and accessibility patterns against gender, and the consequences of these patterns, is not adequate within the transport profession and other related policy communities. Identifying the contribution of transport difficulties to maternal mortality is not systematically audited, considered or factored into health and transport planning, yet there is evidence from a host of case studies showing the importance of such difficulties, and evidence in the differential rates of maternal mortality as between rural and urban areas of Africa testify to the importance of this factor. The measurement of maternal mortality and women's health has been under-resourced, with the consequence that current overviews are inadequate and operational and evaluative knowledge on best practice interventions is weak. Nevertheless, there does seem to be a strong corollary between poor transport organization and high levels of maternal mortality. And there is clear ground indicating that improvements in information technology could help reduce rates of maternal mortality: information technology can be used to identify potential difficulties in pregnancy and can be utilized to speed a woman in difficulties through the transport system and the administrative system to treatment. For such technologies to work, however, the cultural environment of a woman has to allow for her traveling to a place of safe delivery. The full set of mobility and empowerment factors needs to be considered and addressed in any campaign to reduce maternal mortality.

Given that the reduction of maternal mortality is a Millennium Development Goal (UN 2007), the current high level African policy discussion has been short on suggestions of how to realize this goal—and the contribution that safe motherhood transport plans could make to this reduction is most definitely under-operationalized within the policy domain.

Mobility perspectives: transport and the better institutional management of African pregnancy

Disciplinary divides have prevented the transport profession's explicit focus on maternal mortality as a measure of transport failure. An inventory or toolkit of transport and associated measures aimed at reducing maternal mortality in Africa could usefully be developed by international agencies such as the World Bank along with other development agencies; however, at present the literature is largely fragmented across specialisms, and a root-and-branch approach to obstetric transport is simply missing within the policy domain despite the specification of maternal health as a Millennium Development Goal.

The understanding that accessibility, mobility and transport are of significance in saving the lives of pregnant women is stressed in many analyses without this having resulted in the routine establishment of the necessary arrangements to protect women in the routine reproductive work of childbirth.

> In addition to contraception, women need access to a broad range of services. *The primary means of preventing maternal deaths is to provide rapid access to emergency obstetrical care, including treatment of hemorrhages, infections, hypertension, and obstructed labor.* It is also important to ensure that a midwife or doctor is present at every delivery.

> In developing countries only about half of deliveries are attended by professional health staff. Skilled attendants must be supported by the right environment. Life-saving interventions—such as antibiotics, surgery, and transportation to medical centers—are unavailable to many women, especially in rural areas. These women may lack the money for health care and transport, or they may simply lack their husbands' permission to seek care (http://www.developmentgoals.org/Maternal_ Health.htm).

In order to appreciate the importance of transport and accessibility interventions in the reduction of maternal mortality, only one statistic is necessary—there is an accessibility time of thirty minutes to services which is crucial for women's health and survival.

> The reason the maternal mortality fell in the U.S. this century was the advent of antibiotics and blood transfusion more than anything else. There is simply no scientific evidence to prove the falling mortality was because birth was moved into the hospital. The evidence does show that *as long as*

there is a system in place to transport women in labor to a facility equipped with antibiotics, blood transfusion and cesarean section capacity within thirty minutes, there should be very little maternal mortality.

Maternal mortality is quite different from perinatal mortality and infant mortality. The latter two are much influenced by socio-economic factors, while maternal mortality is much more directly a function of the quality of the health care available. If midwives (traditional, direct entry, or nurse-midwives) are trained to know the signs of serious complications and have the means of transport, there is no need for a doctor at the site of primary care of pregnant and birthing women who have had no complications. But at the site of the place where the woman is transported, there is need for a doctor who has surgical skills and, ideally, obstetrical skills to manage the complications (Wagner, http://www.geocities.com/Wellesley/5510/wagner.html).

Measuring women's access to maternal health services in Africa using this figure has not yet been undertaken, but there seem to be good planning reasons why it should, and the use of new information communication technologies can make both planning and service delivery more timely. The transport lessons around the reduction of maternal mortality in Africa clearly involve communication and organization issues as well:
- fast information links can save lives
- rendering services locally can reduce the need for mobility
- operating hostels for those at risk can temporarily reduce distance within critical windows of care.

A comprehensive and cohesive accessibility and mobility perspective is clearly called for in order to reduce Africa's burden of maternal mortality. In the absence of such a cohesive and coordinated international plan of action—despite the benchmarking of the MDGs—it is useful to turn to forms of Best Practice in respect to the reduction of maternal mortality which have taken place in Africa.

Local solutions: replicating best African practice on obstetric transport

The specific projects identified here all have explicit transport dimensions which can be replicated elsewhere. Currently, as we have already indicated, there is an institutional vacuum in respect to the transport arrangements required for safe motherhood. The evaluation of the projects identified below and their systematic emulation and replication within a "Safe motherhood transport planning" framework is clearly an activity which can be undertaken within the remit of the development agencies in alignment with meeting the Millennium Development Goals.

Within Malawi, in 2002, the United Nations Population Fund (UNFPA) indicated the presence of a safe motherhood program, though the details given are few:

> A government-backed Safe Motherhood program has reportedly established village committees on safe motherhood, organized transportation plans and provided training to traditional birth attendants so that they can recognize signs of obstructed labor and act efficiently to get a woman to a facility. Telephones and radios have been installed in some health centers to communicate with the referral hospital and request ambulance transport for women in distress. . . . Pervasive gender inequities sometimes prevent women's access to transportation and emergency obstetric care. Decisions about when and where to seek care are usually made by an uncle (or, occasionally, by the husband); without their input, a woman would be unlikely to seek care on her own (http://www.unfpa.org/fistula/docs/eng_malawi.pdf).

This government program combines an early alert system with a modern communication system to speed women to the hospital. Here UNFPA explicitly discusses the transport barriers, both material and cultural, to obstetric care: these barriers are consistent with the rising rate of maternal mortality in Malawi reported by UNFPA on the same Internet information sheet.

An interesting case of local action in respect to the reduction of maternal mortality is to be found in Zegoua, Mali, where local women have themselves formed safe motherhood unions which ensure that the transport of pregnant women to clinics is undertaken.

> The small Malian town of Zegoua—population 22,000—doesn't have a great many "claims to fame." In one respect, however, it has achieved something remarkable. "Since January 2002, there's not been one case of neonatal or maternal mortality in Zegoua or any other nearby village," Yaya Coulibaly, director of the Zegoua Community Health Centre, told a group of local and international journalists recently. The centre caters for nine villages, which are divided into 16 zones. Zegoua is located almost 500 kilometres south of the Malian capital, Bamako, near the country's border with the Ivory Coast. According to Coulibaly, the secret of the area's success in reducing neonatal and maternal mortality lies in the determination of its women to tackle these problems. They have organized themselves into teams for taking charge of their health care. . . . In the event that severe problems develop during a pregnancy, the coordinator of each village team must ensure that the woman concerned is transferred to a

clinic that is equipped to deal with such emergencies (www.comminit. com/en/node/215890).

In a context where Africa is experiencing rising MMRs, this local form of organization appears to be delivering important reductions in MMRs. It seems likely that some part of the explanation lies in the arrangements made by the women's groups around transport costs, but it also seems likely that part of the explanation lies in the formation of support structures by the women to ensure that the entitlement to travel is obtained and enforced. The women's groups are lifting the decision about traveling to obstetric support out of the household domain and into the domain of the community of women. Clearly, a case study of how this has been achieved would be a very useful addition to the literature and to practice in a context where we are seeing rising maternal mortality rates across Africa as a continent.

Other interventions and innovations are also taking place in Mali, though UNFPA reports these as being the outcome of inter-agency collaboration rather than the product of local organization;

> In Mali, interagency collaboration has enabled the country to build and equip seven new community health centers in three regions and a new maternity unit. The government of Mali, with support from various donors, developed a program to bolster its referral system with a rapid-response component. The country has invested in radio communication among referral centers, and has procured vehicles to use for patient transport. District hospitals and local health centers are now linked by a two-way system of radio communication and transportation. A car, equipped with a stretcher, is available to transport women from health centers to district hospitals. Under this system, the time required to transmit an urgent message and transport a patient is reduced from up to a day to just a few hours (http://www.unfpa.org/mothers/case001.htm).

This discussion of the development of rapid-response systems ties into our earlier discussion of the critical window of time involved in the meeting of obstetric emergencies, though as we can readily see the system is not yet meeting the critical time window established elsewhere in the literature. It is, however, clearly a movement in the right direction and one which brings transport and modern communication systems together. But even where the importance of transport is understood and the use of modern communications is undertaken with the result that maternal mortality is reduced, Africa's poor access to transport rapidly reveals itself—"the ambulance sometimes breaks down." This is the report coming out of the RESCUER project in Eastern Uganda's Iganga district, where the combination of local birth attendants, walkie-talkies and transport to obstetric services resulted in a 40 percent reduction in maternal mortality:

> The project has three components: communications, transport and provision of quality health services. The communications system uses VHF radios installed in base stations and health units, in the referral hospital ambulance and the District Medical Officer's vehicle, while the birth attendants have walkie-talkies. The midwives and birth attendants got additional training and now there is better quality care. But transport has been the biggest problem as the ambulance sometimes breaks down.
>
> The initial cost of the project was under $124,000, covering the cost of the radio and monitoring equipment and training for technicians and users. After this phase, running costs decreased. According to Ms. Musoke, the system uses solar energy for electricity. "After the initial expenses, there are the usual maintenance costs, but these are small and easy to bear, which means that even when donors pull out, the project will still be sustainable. Because of its positive results, the RESCUER project is already being replicated in three other districts and there are plans to extend it in phases to 30 more."

The Ugandan case provides us with an example of how dependence on vehicles dedicated to service rural areas can run into problems because of the quality of the roads, the quality of the vehicle and the maintenance of both. The transport legacy of colonialism and imperialism continues to bite hard on the health of women. But there are ways of reducing dependence on dedicated and scarce health vehicles—and the West African experiment with the yellow flag provides an interesting example. The yellow flag system makes use of the existing commercial fleet of vehicles: when a woman is in obstetric crisis a yellow flag is placed by the roadside to summon truck drivers to stop and provide transport assistance:

> Some innovative new schemes are working. [A] BBC producer spoke with Pramila Seneyaki from the International Planned Parenthood Federation, who described an initiative in West Africa which uses a local truck drivers union to provide emergency transport for women. "If there is a woman in difficulty in a village, what we will do is get her family to plant a yellow flag on the main road," she stated. "When you see a yellow flag you know there is a woman in trouble. Somebody will be there to tell you, 'look, my mother is in trouble. If we bring her up to the lorry can you take her the 200 miles?' They [are] delighted to be able to help and we [have] reduced maternal mortality quite significantly because of this initiative."

This yellow flag system receives mention in the British parliamentary publications as operating in Ghana (see www.publications.parliament.uk/pa/cm 199899/cmselect/cmintdev/160/9020207.htm). It is readily seen that the yellow flag system could be improved by the alignment of better communication technologies between trucks and communities with health needs. The use of new information communication technology to harness existing regional vehicle fleets (fleet management) in the better provision of health in Africa seems an unlikely scenario, but given the spread of mobile phone technology it is a scenario worthy of investigation. The provision of dedicated vehicles as opposed to the harnessing of existing spare capacity in regional fleets in a context of low wealth and scarce resources may eventually prove to be the more difficult course.

In Ghana, the Matercare project (www.matercare.org/Midwifery Journal._asp) specifically focused on the operation and evaluation of an Obstetric Transport Service which was based on motorized ambulances (other forms being bicycle, ox-drawn (Zimbabwe) or other animal-traction ambulances, including the human portering of patients). This service will provide the ability to resuscitate and safely transfer mothers with severe childbirth complications from the villages to the district hospital; however, the geographical range of service coverage is clearly less than could be accomplished by the yellow flag system. That such systems work together is critical in developing the fullest form of provision possible.

The cases provided here of Best Practice already taking place in Africa require systematic evaluation, replication and further improvement. The need for better integration of the knowledge which exists scattered over many sites and in the practice of both local and international groups, experts and organization is urgent if maternal mortality in Africa is to be reduced rather than permitted to rise further.

Conclusion—Reducing the Gender Burden, Reducing Maternal Mortality Rates in Africa: Planning the Transport Provision

As we have seen in the course of this chapter, there is now a policy goal of dramatically reducing maternal mortality in Africa and there is a body of evidence which speaks to the scale of the problem, but the literature on concrete measures for bringing about this goal and the operational activities of development agencies in pursuit of this goal are thin on the ground, most particularly in respect to the transport and maternal mortality link.

Within the policy discussion there is a need for:
- more accurate measurement,
- more focused solutions,
- more sensitive social scientific analysis of the relationship between mobility, gender and health.

There is sufficient evidence that transport organization and provision is highly gendered in both the developing and developed context. Gender methodologies have not yet been sufficiently mainstreamed to tackle this existing pattern of inequity. The reduction of maternal mortality in Africa - a Millennium Development Goal - provides an operational ground in which such methodologies are in need of urgent development.

There is evidence that more systematic approaches are beginning to be adopted, but as of yet transport and gender statistics are of a limited character as evidenced by, for example, the World Bank's gender statistics site. The development of a web site which provides consolidated information on the relationship between gender, transport and maternal mortality and carries detailed information on best practices and how to effect them would be a useful addition to the toolkit and process necessary to achieving the Millennium Development Goal of reduced maternal mortality in Africa.

Most importantly, the evidence presented here from Zegoua suggests that the reduction of maternal mortality is most likely if planners and development agencies pay attention to ensuring the participation of women in the process. Simply providing transport for women to obstetric facilities does not ensure their cultural entitlements to access the facilities—the development of participative strategies which empower women to travel through women's group formations may prove to be the critical link in reducing Africa's burden in respect to maternal mortality.

CHAPTER EIGHT
WOMEN IN CHINSAPO, MALAWI
Vulnerability and Risk of HIV/AIDS
Jayati Ghosh and Ezekiel Kalipeni

Introduction

Two decades after their emergence, human immunodeficiency virus (HIV) and acquired immunodeficiency syndrome (AIDS), continue to create havoc worldwide. In sub-Saharan Africa, HIV/AIDS appears to be one of the worst pandemics the region has ever encountered. By the end of 2004 there were an estimated 36 to 43 million people living with HIV/AIDS throughout the world, of which 25.4 million were living in sub-Saharan Africa (UNAIDS, 2004a). The region reports an adult prevalence rate of 7.4 percent, which is considerably higher than the global prevalence rate of 1.1 percent. In 2004, women accounted for 47 percent of HIV-infected cases worldwide, while in sub-Saharan Africa women and girls accounted for 57 percent of all such cases (UNAIDS, 2004a). In light of this crisis, over the years attempts—which include increased political commitment, publicizing information about HIV/AIDS, increased allocations of funding, availability of treatment programs, and prevention efforts (UNAIDS, 2003—have been made to control the pandemic. In spite of all this, the pandemic continues at high prevalence rates, especially in the fifteen to twenty-four-year age group (UNAIDS 2004a). It is further noted that in this age group, women comprise 76 percent of those living with the virus. These statistics indicate that in order to understand the spread of HIV/AIDS it is imperative to address the economic, social, cultural, and political issues that facilitate the spread of the virus and women's infection by it.

Gender Dimensions of HIV/AIDS

Gender inequalities play a role in the spread of HIV as women are both physiologically and socially more vulnerable to HIV infection (Tallis, 1998, 2000). Women often have less access to education, training and

156 Chapter Eight

Figure 8-1. Location of Chinsapo on the Southwestern Periphery of the City of Lilongwe Source: Authors.

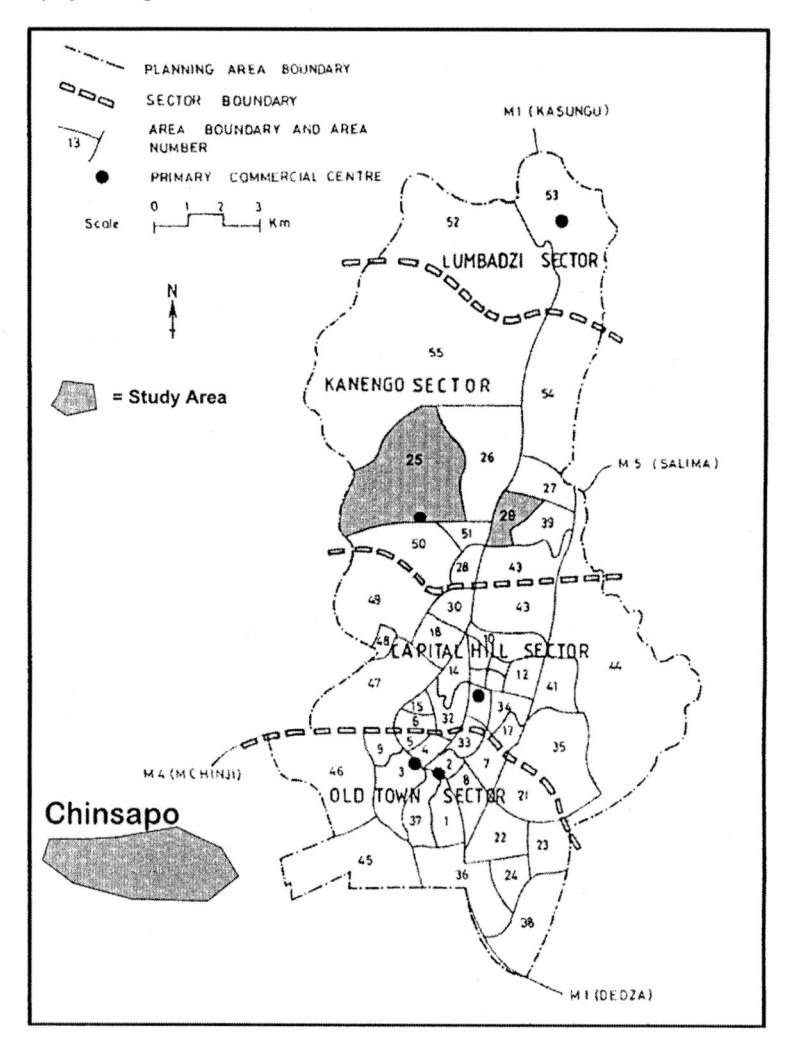

productive resources like land and credit (Weiss et al., 2000). In situations where women live in poverty and have limited resources, sex is often used as a means of survival. If a husband abandons his family or is gone for an extended period of time due to migrant labor, women are left in charge of providing economic stability. Many women have little recourse but to turn to commercial sex work, where condom use is often not an option (Susser and Stein, 2000). If a woman requires that her client use a condom, he may simply visit another commercial sex worker (CSW). The dilemma becomes one of providing for one's family versus protecting oneself from infection (Walden et al., 1999).

Gender inequalities also exist within casual and committed relationships. Males are often dominant within the relationship, making women dependent for their financial support. Husbands who visit commercial sex workers leave their wives at risk by not taking HIV-preventive measures. However, requesting condom use within a marriage implies infidelity, leaving women at risk of abandonment or abuse. Studies in sub-Saharan Africa including Malawi, South Africa, Kenya and Uganda have found that men are in control of condom use (Kishindo, 1995; Maharaj and Cleland, 2004; Buhler and Kohler, 2003; Camlin and Chimbwete, 2003). For many women it is part of their upbringing to view one's husband as dominant regarding sexual relations (Lawson, 1999). Women in long-term relationships claim that boyfriends provide them with financial support and therefore must be respected and trusted (Walden et al., 1999).

Both married women and young girls are at risk of infection when married men seek significantly younger partners. Many men believe that young girls are free of HIV infection because they are sexually inexperienced (Weiss et al., 2000). A similar study in Kenya found that young girls often seek out these relationships to improve their status among peers and to obtain gifts. The girls often live in poverty and their families benefit from the income and gifts they obtain from these relationships. This provides the older men with a position of control, and once again the girls do not request the use of a condom for fear of losing their source of income (Longfield 2004; Longfield et al., 2004).

It is with this background that our theoretical framework for this chapter focuses on poverty, gender inequalities, and regional migration patterns which place individuals, particularly women, in highly vulnerable situations. It should be noted that HIV infection in Malawi is not confined to the poorest of society. There is evidence suggesting that HIV prevalence rates are high among doctors, lawyers, teachers, and other skilled individuals, indicating that HIV rates remain widespread as one moves up the educational and social ladder (Malawi Government and UNDP Malawi, 2002). This may suggest that this group has adopted a life style that makes them vulnerable to HIV. On the other hand, the poverty theoretical framework suggests that the poor lack education and thus have limited marketable skills, poor health, and low labor productivity. As a result they are trapped in poverty. In 2002, 65 percent of the population of Malawi was reported to be living below the poverty line (World Bank, 2003). Rural poverty and lack of sustainable livelihoods compel individuals to migrate to the city, and these migrants ultimately end up in low socio-economic income areas of Lilongwe, creating conditions that facilitate HIV transmission (Government of Malawi, 2003).

In Malawi, migration from rural areas reflects a high incidence of rural poverty and the resultant response to a lack of sustainable economic conditions. According to Englund (2002), many assume migration as a means of improving their economic well-being. Many of these migrants have limited education and training and thus have few marketable skills. Similarly, as one considers rural to urban migration, the vast majority of cases tend to be age- and gender-selective and draw largely from the younger age group. The argument is that migrant populations comprising both men and women, without the traditional social networks of rural society and also living under abject poverty, often find themselves engaging in high-risk situations which in turn render them vulnerable to HIV infection. Furthermore, when poor women head a household they may not be able to provide adequately for their families whether they are working in the formal or informal sectors of the economy. In such circumstances they are forced to engage in commercial sex work to supplement their incomes.

It is also important to note that an individual's vulnerability not only depends on the economic conditions but also on social position. Women in Malawi tend to have limited entitlements, they generally earn low wages, are less than likely to own land, do not receive any government assistance, and do not benefit from international aid programs (Lele, 1990). Furthermore, women in general have less access to education beyond the primary levels, which restricts them in their choices of occupation, formal sector employment, and sustainable wages. The inequality among men and women influences the power structure and hence vulnerability to HIV.

In Malawian society men are viewed as responsible for the family and income generation. On the other hand, women are valued as mothers with limited economic responsibility. Such beliefs are embedded in family, schools, religious and political structures. These messages influence the decisions made by men and women both within and outside of marriages, and regarding sexual exchanges. In addition such assigned roles dictate government policies regarding wage structures and resource allocations. Recent research shows a close relationship between socio-economic status and the spread of HIV/AIDS (Kalipeni, Craddock, & Ghosh, 2004; Oppong & Ghosh, 2004). Urban women who are employed in the formal sector often occupy supporting positions and as a result are subject to sexual exploitation by men. Within marriage they are incapable of protecting themselves, due to their lower status. For rural women, severe poverty and low literacy increases their risk to HIV infection. When many of these women migrate to cities their vulnerability continues, and so HIV/AIDS continues to spread rapidly among the general populace.

Women, HIV/AIDS and Poverty in Malawi

Based on available estimates by the end of 2003 there were 900,000 adults and children in Malawi living with the HIV/AIDS virus (UNAIDS/WHO, 2004). The adult prevalence rate was estimated to be 14 percent, which is higher than the 7.1 percent average rate for sub-Saharan Africa but much lower than that of other countries in southern Africa such as Zimbabwe, Botswana and Lesotho (UNAIDS, 2004a; 2004b). These estimates, however, should be used with caution because samples are often drawn from specific groups such as women going to prenatal clinics in a country where most people do not go to hospitals (Kalipeni, Craddock & Ghosh, 2004). Therefore, officially reported cases should be considered a conservative representation of the actual figures (Kalipeni and Ghosh, forthcoming). The urban prevalence rate is 23 percent, which is considerably higher than the rural prevalence rate of 12.4 percent (UNAIDS/WHO, 2004). The life expectancy has dropped from forty-seven to thirty-nine years because of AIDS (UNAIDS 2004b). Some estimates indicate that it may have already dropped to levels of below thirty years (Haney, 2000; Engender Health, 2002; BBC News, 2002).

In recent years, the HIV/AIDS crisis in Malawi has been made worse by the additional vulnerability from drought and famine. Severe food shortages since 2002 have affected over 5 million people. The shortages exacerbated living conditions for more than 65 percent of the population considered "poor," and for some 14 percent of the adult population infected with HIV/AIDS. Although some international organizations such as USAID and Save the Children Fund report success stories of Malawi in combating the spread of HIV through widespread condom campaigns, HIV continues to wreak havoc in the lives of many Malawians, particularly those in the economically active age range. Although official records indicate the HIV rate to have stabilized at 14 percent, other estimates indicate that the rate might actually be much higher, at about 20 percent, and that it is expected to increase to 24 percent by 2010 (Kalipeni and Zulu, forthcoming).

Furthermore, important national issues such as the worsening food crisis and the plight of HIV/AIDS victims have been sidelined as political instability in Malawi unfolds. Instead of tackling these issues, the government has been distracted and the parliament has lost focus. During the last days of the Muluzi presidency, Western donors froze balance-of-payments support to Malawi over corruption and governance concerns. However, with the new government of Bingu wa Mutharika, donor confidence and aid has been restored. Mutharika, the current president, won the elections in May 2004 under Muluzi's United Democratic Front (UDF) ticket. After taking the reigns of government, Mutharika soon put in place a strong anti-corruption program which displeased Muluzi and his cohorts. They forced Mutharika to resign from the UDF party, plunging Malawi into the current political crisis. This political wrangle has seen the former president (Bakili Muluzi) face a corruption probe from the government's Anti-Corruption Bureau (ACB), and the current incumbent (Bingu wa Mutharika) face impeachment in parliament advanced by Muluzi's political party, the UDF. This is why observers note that the food crisis and the HIV/AIDS epidemic are likely to escalate as a government fighting for its own political survival loses focus.

Since 1990, the UNDP has produced an impressive set of composite indicators of development for each country in the world. These indicators are reported in UNDP's annual publication: the *Human Development Report* as well as on its website http://hdr.undp.org/. The Human Development Index (HDI), the Human Poverty Index (HPI), Gender-Related Development Index (GDI), and the Gender Empowerment Index (GEM) are among the impressive composite measures of development. For each country in the world the Human Development Report offers a rank based on each of these indicators. When we examine these indicators with reference to Malawi, it becomes clear that this country is among the least developed in the world.

According to UNDP 2004, Malawi ranks 165 on the Human Development Index (HDI), which focuses on life expectancy, literacy level, and per capita income. Although the Human Development Index helps us to measure the average progress of a country in human development, it fails to address the various aspects of poverty. A more refined measure that focuses on poverty is the Human Poverty Index (HPI). This composite measure focuses on life expectancy, literacy rates and proportion of people living below a certain level of income. Based on this measure, Malawi ranks 83 among 95 countries (UNDP, 2004). Another specialized measure that looks at gender inequality issues is the Gender-Related Development Index (GDI). This index helps us to understand gender inequalities and their connection to vulnerability, particularly the inequalities that exist between men and women. When this measure is taken into consideration, Malawi ranks 134 out of 144 countries. A similar index on gender issues is the Gender Empowerment Measure (GEM) which takes into account gender inequality in economic and political spheres. Unfortunately this measure was not available for Malawi in the *Human Development Report* due to the lack of data concerning women who are in administrative and managerial positions and professional and technical ranks.

Nevertheless, the poor performance of the country on the above indicators of development testifies to the existence of massive poverty and the high gender disparities in human development. When one carefully examines the position of women in Malawi, one cannot avoid noticing that women in this country increasingly play an important role, especially in the informal sector. In spite of this fact and in spite of the efforts made to improve the status of women, they continue to face discrimination in areas of health, nutrition, access to education, employment, and political participation. Based on our research in Malawi, it was clear to us that women in Malawi continue to be in a disadvantageous position. According to the 2004 report by UNAIDS on Malawi, violence against women, especially wife beating and rape, is widespread in Malawi. Another study points out that a third of Malawi's households are female-headed (Ngwira et al. 2003).

Poverty, according to the World Bank (2003), has many dimensions which include low income, lack of education, environmental degradation, and gender inequality. UNDP (2004) reports that in Malawi between 1990 and 2002, 42 percent of the population lived on less than $1 a day and 75 percent lived on less than $2. The World Bank (2004) reports that nearly 65 percent of the Malawian population lived below the poverty line in the mid-1990s. About 66 percent of the rural population lived below the poverty line while in the urban areas it was reported to be about 55 percent (World Bank 2004).

According to Sen (1999, 87), "poverty must be seen as the deprivation of basic capabilities rather than merely as lowness of income which is the standard criterion of identification of poverty." Sen further argues that poverty is a multifaceted problem and that there are a number of physical, social, and cultural factors, in addition to economic conditions, that can exacerbate the situation. Firstly, as we consider physical conditions, the susceptibility to natural disasters such as droughts can render individuals vulnerable and thus push them towards poverty. Malawi as a country has witnessed severe environmental degradation that has had the potential to displace many from their land, rural homes, and livelihood (Government of Malawi, 2003). This is a big problem in a country where 84 percent of the population lives in rural areas (UNAIDS/WHO, 2004) and 83 percent of economically active people derive their livelihood from agriculture. Women in Malawi are overwhelmingly engaged in the agricultural sector; 97 percent are associated with subsistence farming (Ngwira et al., 2003). This high dependency results in greater shock and vulnerability when lack of rainfall and environmental problems contribute to crop failure and food insecurity, which in some cases compels women to migrate to urban areas as well as to countries such as South Africa in search of jobs.

Secondly, as noted earlier, lack of education and training available to women makes them more vulnerable to poverty and forces them to undertake risky behavior. There is a close association between illiteracy and poverty. Sen (1999) indicates that if family income is not high enough to allocate funds for the education and health care of girls and women, in the long run these women will face multiple problems such as higher mortality, under-nourishment, and medical neglect. Over the years the Malawian government has allocated funding for education, but in spite of that, there is a pronounced gender gap as one continues to look at retention, attendance, and attainment. The drop-out rate is higher for girls and is highest between standard five and standard eight. The reasons for drop-out include higher cost of schooling, demand for girls' labor, puberty-related factors, early marriage, pregnancy and sexual harassment by male teachers and students (Ngwira et al., 2003).

Finally, the social structure also influences an individual's ability to acquire resources and thus improve one's economic situation. This suggests that an individual's location and position in the social structure does determine the ability to acquire and mobilize resources. Since there is a gender gap in access to education (Kalipeni 1997), many girls grow up with limited access to education, which further impedes their capability to earn a living and thus forces them to seek employment in the informal sector. Also, as women are primarily engaged in farming it is assumed that they will not require education or training. On the other hand, men are engaged in production and the service sector, both of which require education and training (Ngwira et al., 2003). With limited education many women continue to work in low-paying jobs such as domestic help, sex workers, sales, and secretarial positions. Their low incomes and lack of alternative avenues make them vulnerable to abuse. This vulnerability makes it difficult on the part of women to report abuse and injustice (Ngwira, et al, 2003).

Methodology

Sample of Women in Chinsapo

During the summer of 2003, constrained by time and resources, we administered a structured questionnaire to 60 women who were randomly selected in Chinsapo residential area in Lilongwe, the capital city of Malawi. We also conducted two focus group interviews with 20 women, 10 women per focus group. Chinsapo is a low-income socio-economic residential area on the outskirts of the city of Lilongwe (see Fig 1). It exhibits both rural and urban characteristics, and its residents predominantly commute into the city center of Lilongwe to work in the informal sector selling crafts and household items by the side of road. Many of the residents in this area are new migrants from rural Malawi (see Englund 2002). We were interested in finding out how women in this area are responding to the HIV/AIDS epidemic, hence the focus on the 60 women and the two focus group interviews that we conducted with an additional group of 20 women.

Chinsapo, as a residential area, is characterized by high population density and poor building standards. The poor and new immigrants prefer to live here because they spend less money on rent, while a few relatively well-to-do families prefer to live here because they can build spacious houses without having to pay high land rents. At the onset this area lacked basic amenities, and houses were built with little regard for access to roads. However, most houses have access to communal water points, which has in turn greatly reduced the disease and death among children (Englund, 2002). As an immigrant society, many of the people who live here are in the twenty to forty-four-year age group. This was confirmed by the distribution of the 80 women in our sample (60 for the structured interviews and 20 for the focus group interviews). The majority of these women (about 76 percent) were in the age group twenty to thirty-four. For a detailed age distribution of the women in the sample see Figure 8-2. As far as the socio-economic condition is concerned, there was little socio-economic variation at least among the women who were sampled.

Consent Protocols

In early 2003 we developed a proposal for this study entitled "HIV/AIDS in Malawi: A Gendered and Vulnerability Perspective." The proposal was submitted to the University of Illinois Institutional Review Board and the Institutional Review Board at Dominican University for

Figure 8-2. Distribution of Women Participants in the Focus Group and Structured Interviews by Age. Source: Authors.

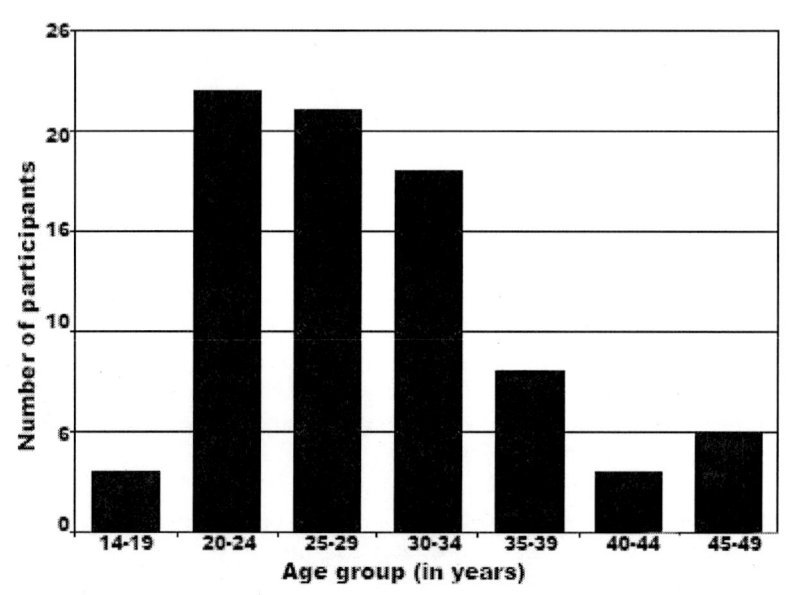

ethical clearance for the research in Malawi since we were going to involve human subjects. The submission of the proposal included consent protocols for both one-on-one interviews and the focus group interviews. For the structured individual interviews, the participant was given the consent form which was in both the local language—Chichewa—and English. All the participants knew how to read and write, at least in Chichewa. The consent forms to the participants emphasized the fact that their participation was entirely voluntary and they did not have to participate if they did not wish to.

The city of Lilongwe is divided into several subdivisions called areas. Some of these areas have number names and others have traditional Malawian names (see Figure 8-1). We were interested in interviewing in five areas, namely, Chinsapo (peri-urban area with many rural characteristics and low income people); areas 25 & 29 (peri-urban areas for low income people); areas 10 & 15 (medium- and high-income residential areas). Each of these areas is further subdivided into several wards with each ward led by a councilor or headman. The study in this chapter only analyzes the interviews we conducted with women in Chinsapo. Permission to hold the structured and focus group interview was also obtained from the councilor or the headman of the ward in which the participants were selected. The focus group interviews were segregated by gender, which was necessitated by the fact that Malawian society is dominated by men. Women do not ordinarily speak freely if men are present; however, when there are only women in the group, they often speak their minds more openly.

Field Work and Study Limitations

During 2003 we carried out fieldwork in this area to examine the perceptions of women about their risks regarding HIV. We hired two female interviewers to conduct interviews in this area with the selected 60 women. The reason for choosing female interviewers to conduct these interviews was that the questions were sensitive and related to private issues, and that women would be more open to discuss these issues with female rather than male interviewers. Indeed, the results of the interviews confirmed our fears. For example, a number of the respondents were not comfortable giving the requested information on their knowledge and practice with regard to AIDS, and whether they had talked with friends about family planning and AIDS. Other women were afraid or shy to give information on extra-marital affairs, due to fear that we might report the information to the husband in spite of the fact that the consent form emphasized confidentiality. Some women refused to offer an interview because, they said, the questionnaire had too many questions and they were afraid their husbands might find them during the lengthy interview (about an hour and half). A few women refused to mention certain words such as condoms because of their religious beliefs, which forbade them to say such words. When a woman objected to being interviewed or to continue the interview after it had started, she was dropped from the sample.

The two female interviewers we hired were familiar with this area as they also lived here and spoke the local language, Chichewa, understood by all the residents in the area. Questions were asked about religion, family background, economic conditions of the individuals, marriage history, family planning and social networks, fertility, sexual partnerships and HIV/AIDS. As noted above, we also conducted two focus group interviews with 20 additional women. Such discussions were informal in nature. We asked about people's perceptions and understanding of HIV, what people thought about prevention of infections, and changing social and cultural practices. Surprisingly, the focus group discussions were a great success as women were more open to discuss issues than in the structured one-on-one interviews. In future studies, we will make sure to carry out more focus group interviews and to slim-line the structured questionnaire. In this light, we wish to acknowledge that the subset sample of 60 women is on the smaller side and therefore may not be a true representation of the general populace in the city of Lilongwe. Nevertheless insights can be gleaned from this sample when coupled with data from focus group interviews.

We used the questionnaire developed by the Malawi Diffusion and Ideational Change Project (MDICP) at the Population Center of the University of Pennsylvania (Watkins, Zulu & Behrman, 2003). The MDICP has conducted similar surveys in rural areas of Kenya and Malawi, which meant the questionnaire had been amply tested in other localities of Malawi. We therefore did not conduct a pilot study, but had we done so, given the reluctance of some women to answer the questions, we might have decided to use a different method to minimize some of the concerns highlighted above.

Results and Discussion of Structured Interviews

Several questions in the structured questionnaire examined issues surrounding vulnerability of women and their perception of risks regarding HIV/AIDS. The descriptive results of these questions are summarized in Tables 8-1 to 8-5 and discussed below.

Gender and Reproductive Issues

On gender issues we asked two central questions: when would it be proper for a wife to leave her husband, and what can a woman without informing her husband. As shown in Table 8-1, the majority of the women (about 53 percent) noted that it was proper to leave the husband if he beats her frequently. This was followed by sexual infidelity (33 percent) and if the woman thought he might be infected with AIDS (about 19 percent). Financial support for her and the children from the husband was not considered to be a reason for leaving the husband nor was the denial by the husband of her right to use family planning. Lilongwe is in the heart of the matrilineal system of descent in which the father is not obligated to support his own children but those of his sisters. Also in a high fertility rate society, begetting children is central to marriage; hence the low percentage scores on these two aspects. When we asked the women whether they could go to the local market or to the local health center without informing their husbands, the majority (over 63 percent) said they could not simply do so without informing the husband. It is clear from these rather low percentages that a woman cannot simply leave a husband, even when he does not provide economic support, is unfaithful, and has AIDS. Furthermore a woman cannot simply do simple things such as going to the local market or a health clinic on her own for fear of being accused of being unfaithful to her husband.

Regarding reproductive rights, we asked women several questions about actions they can take without informing the husband, such as the use of family planning techniques (see Table 8-2). It is clear from this table that the majority of women are dependent on their husbands in terms of deciding whether or not to use contraceptives and regarding decisions on family size. For example 81 percent of the women agreed that there was nothing much they could do to change the mind of their partner when he refuses the use of modern methods of child spacing. Similarly, 58 percent of the women disagreed with the statement that if they wanted to delay the next birth, they would be able to do so. However, it was interesting to note that 54 percent of the women agreed that even if their husbands did not want them to use family planning, if they wanted to, they would go ahead and do so without the husbands' knowledge. This is largely due to the fact that family planning clinics in Malawi and elsewhere in Africa target only women, and the women themselves are the ones who go to the clinics to obtain the techniques which can easily be hidden from their husbands. However, should the husband find out, the consequences could be tragic for the woman.

Knowledge, Attitudes and Worry about AIDS

Tables 8-3 and 8-4 offer the results on questions concerning general knowledge, attitudes, and worry about AIDS and condoms. The results in these two tables are revealing about the general knowledge among women in this area as far as HIV/AIDS is concerned. Over 93 percent of the women had heard a talk at the clinic, hospital or on the radio about how people can protect themselves against AIDS, and 78 percent noted that someone from the health surveillance system had come to their homes to give them information on how to protect themselves from contracting the virus. When asked if they could get AIDS through sex with someone who looks perfectly healthy, 100 percent of the women answered yes.

Knowledge about HIV/AIDS among the women was high, but practice and attitudes were not congruent with this knowledge. As shown in Table 8-3, when asked if it was acceptable to use a condom with a spouse to protect against AIDS, 86 percent of the women said no. When asked if they had ever talked with their husbands about the chances of infection with the virus, only 44 percent of the women said they had. However, 70 percent noted that they suspected their husbands have had sexual relations with other women and that their fellow women have also cheated with men other than their husbands. But when asked if they themselves had engaged in such activities, almost 100 percent of them said no (probably for fear that if they told the truth about themselves, their husbands might know from the interviewers even though we had promised them that these interviews were confidential). It is clear from these results that women, probably due to their vulnerable position, are afraid to raise issues concerning HIV/AIDS with their husbands. While they know that their husbands are cheating, they will not raise a voice concerning AIDS and how to protect themselves from the virus. They simply accept the status quo.

The results in Table 8-4 confirm this sad truth. We asked the respondents to highlight the ways women can become infected with AIDS that they are most worried about. About 70 percent of the women indicated they were worried about getting the virus from their husbands. A few (about 12 percent) were worried about needle injections at hospitals or clinics. Other partners and transfusions were not significant at all as a worry. We further asked the respondents how worried they were that they might be infected with AIDS. Eighty-four percent said they were worried a lot, 9 percent were worried a little, and only 7 percent were not worried. In short the results in these two tables (Tables 8-3 and 8-4) indicate that women have the requisite knowledge about AIDS and the ways people can protect themselves from becoming infected. However, generally women see themselves as helpless and at the mercy of their husbands, boyfriends or other men.

The respondents were further asked to indicate the best ways to protect themselves from contracting HIV/AIDS (see Table 8-5). About 61 percent indicated that advising their partners was one of the best ways of avoiding the virus. This is in contrast to the number of women who had actually spoken to their husbands about HIV (only 44 percent had done so, as shown in Table 8-3). While women do wish to speak to their husbands, they are constrained by their inferior position in society to submit to the dictates of men. By the answers in Table 8-5 it is quite clear that the majority of women do not know the best ways to avoid contracting HIV. Only 38 percent and 40 percent respectively pointed out that using a condom with prostitutes and/or bar girls and avoiding sexual contact with this group would protect a person from getting infected. In spite of their awareness about the disease, they are unable to protect themselves, which increases their vulnerability.

Results and Discussion of Focus Group Interviews

We conducted two focus group interviews with 20 women, 10 women per focus group. The focus group interviews were centered on poverty, position and status of women in society, their income-generating activities, and knowledge and attitudes towards HIV/AIDS. The participants were more open to discuss issues in focus group interviews than in the one-on-one structured interviews. It was clear from these interviews that poverty puts women in very vulnerable positions as far as the spread of HIV/AIDS is concerned.

In response to the questions "What is AIDS"? and "What is HIV?" two of the women offered the following answers:

Respondent 1: "AIDS has always been with us; my grandmother told me that in the past they used to call it *kanyera* or *tsempho* but it was not as bad as these days. Today it is extremely bad, people are dying of simple things such as flu, this AIDS is something else, nobody knows what it is!"

Respondent 2: "You are not answering the question! AIDS is a disease that causes one to get very thin, have lesions on the face, lose hair, and die of TB. Just go to Likuni hospital to see for yourself. I know we all have AIDS and we are going to die of it. See all these little kids running around, they have no parents and they just smoke *chamba* (marijuana)."

There was agreement in both focus group interviews as to the nature of AIDS and its destructive impact on society throughout Malawi. Everybody knew what it was, including a detailed description of its symptoms. A few of the women noted that "AIDS has always been with us," but that somehow it had woken up more recently to wreak havoc on society. When asked if AIDS was curable, many of them said no. A few said they had heard of effective medications called ARVs which when taken might end the symptoms. One woman said she knew a friend who had developed lesions and rashes throughout her body, one of the early symptoms of AIDS. When she began taking the ARVs the lesions disappeared and she gained a lot of weight. We further prodded as to where these medications could be obtained, and the respondent indicated that the woman in question was working for one of the well known hotels in Lilongwe and that she had gotten the medications through a program at her place of work. Knowledge about the disease and its incurability was quite high. We were surprised to hear that some of the women knew that medications could be obtained to end the symptoms, but these medications were restricted to a select few on a pilot basis.

One of the questions dealt with poverty and income-generating activities in the area for men and women. There was total agreement among the women in the focus groups that the area was socio-economically deprived and there were very few opportunities for men and women. The following quotes illustrate this point:

> Respondent 13: "I am sure you have seen for yourself that there is nothing much. The area is poor, there is no water, a few people can afford electricity for lighting, we have to walk a distance to the standing pipe to draw water, there are no schools here for our children to go to, crime and thievery are on the increase...."

> Respondent 15: "Many of our husbands are self-employed, selling second-hand clothing or fixing *kanyenya* (grilled meat) and selling *zibolibori* (curios) at city centre in Lilongwe, or selling goods by the roadside. You see the minibuses passing by, the drivers and conductors are likely to be our husbands in there. The income they bring home is too little to support the whole family. Many of us are lucky to have two meals a day. Just look at the kids running around, they are all malnourished."

> Respondent 19: "Don't forget that those who have school papers work in good positions in the government as messengers or clerks, some even work in banks and they own and drive good cars, but they stay here in Chinsapo."

Many of the women simply spoke about their husbands' and boyfriends employment. When asked about their income-generating activities, the majority indicated that they had no employment. One woman noted that there were some enterprising women going to the lake to buy dried fish and bringing it back to have their children sell by the roadside. Some women were going to surrounding villages to buy peanuts or maize and selling them to others in the area, thereby supplementing their husbands' income. At this point we asked a question on other activities such as women sleeping with men for monetary gain. There was laughter from the women, an indication that this was a common practice as suggested below:

> Respondent 15: "What else can we do! Many of us never went to school, so no jobs for us. When the kids are starving at home and your husband has no income, well one has to do what one has to do to feed the children. So, yes, it happens and I know a few women who do that."

> Respondent 11: "Take the case of Jennifer (not her actual name), she works at Likuni Hospital as an AIDS surveillance clerk and I think she gets

about K3,500 a month (about US$30.00) but she still moves around with other men. Actually it was the husband who started it first, he was moving with this woman. Then she found out that the husband was spending all his money on this woman; she also began moving around with the driver who drives her to various clinics. The husband found out and beat her to death, she was admitted in hospital for two weeks because of the beating. We hear she has now left her husband and moved in with the driver and the driver has left his wife who is now suffering with four small children...."

The above quotes are a sample of the spirited discussions we had with the women who participated in the two focus group interviews. The findings in this study confirm that poverty in low socio-economic income areas puts women at risk of infection from HIV. The vulnerable position of women in society was clearly illustrated in both the structured interviews and in the focus group discussions. The results in our study are similar to the results of other studies being conducted in Malawi. For example, Barden-O'Fallen et al. (2004) found that knowledge of HIV/AIDS does not necessarily translate into perceived risk. As discussed earlier in this study, although we found out that many women knew about AIDS, risky behaviors were quite common due to the circumstances in which women find themselves. In a very interesting study by Kaler (2004), she noted that "while Malawians share many ideas about AIDS, where it comes from and how one contracts it, there is evidently a lack of consensus about whether it is worthwhile to change behavior in order to avoid it." In another recent study, Smith and Watkins (2005), note that in spite of poly-partner sexual activities among men, quite a substantial number of men have began to change their behavior in ways that may reduce the spread of HIV/AIDS, e.g. reducing the number of partners and/or careful partner selection. Nevertheless, the inferior position of women, poverty and other economic circumstances force women to engage in sexual activities that put them at risk of acquiring HIV. Many of the women, even if they are faithful to their husbands, pointed out that they would still get the virus from their unfaithful husbands.

Conclusion

It is quite clear from the analysis in this chapter that the rising epidemic among women in low socio-economic income areas such as Chinsapo is driven in part by the cultural context and poverty which restrict their options. Gender inequality and asymmetrical sexual relations result in the rapid spread of HIV/AIDS among women, as evidenced in the structured interviews and the focus group discussions in our study.

Women are restrained by culture not to leave or divorce their husbands even when the husband does not provide economic support, is unfaithful, and has AIDS. It is only when the man becomes extremely violent that a woman might decide to leave the husband for fear of losing her life. Women can do very little to increase the use of condoms to space or stop having more children or to protect themselves from HIV. As shown in this study, women are very worried about being infected and agree that they will be infected by their husbands because they know their husbands have sexual relationships with other women. Due to economic circumstances some women also engage in sexual relationships with partners other than their husbands to supplement the meager incomes their husbands bring home. This, though, is done without the husband's knowledge or consent. Although awareness of AIDS was very high among the women in the sample, they were unable to protect themselves, which increases their vulnerability to HIV.

Acknowledgments

We are grateful for the financial support received from the Research Board and the Department of Geography at the University of Illinois at Urbana-Champaign, The Compton Foundation Grant (# 03-1162) and Dominican University of California. Without this financial support it would have been extremely difficult to collect high quality data. Many thanks go to the men and women in the areas of our study in the City of Lilongwe for agreeing to participate in the surveys and focus group interviews that resulted in the collection of the data which forms the basis for this chapter. However, the views expressed in this chapter are the responsibility of the authors.

Original version of this chapter was published in Journal of Social Aspects of HIV/AIDS *2(3): 320-332 and reprinted with permission.*

Table 8-1. Questions on gender issues: leaving husband or doing things without husband's knowledge

Action (State whether you agree, disagree, or have no opinion about the following statements).	Agree (%)	Disagree (%)	No Opinion (%)
If your partner does not want to use modern methods of child spacing/ family planning, there is nothing you can do to change his mind.	81.3	16.6	2.1
If you decide that you want to delay the next birth, you will be able to have your way.	35.6	57.8	6.6
If you decide that you want no more children, you will be able to have your way.	44.0	54.1	1.9
Even if your husband does not want you to use family planning, if you want to you will use without his knowledge.	57.3	38.6	4.1

Table 8-2. Questions on gender issues: certain actions that can or cannot be taken by a woman

In your opinion, is it proper for a wife to leave her husband if:	Yes (%)	No (%)	Don't Know (%)
He does not support her and the children financially?	6.5	88.3	5.2
He beats her frequently?	53.2	40.6	6.2
He is sexually unfaithful?	33.3	65.2	1.5
She thinks he might be infected with AIDS?	18.7	75.9	3.4
He does not allow her to use family planning?	11.0	86.4	2.6
Can you do the following without informing your husband: Go to the local market Go to the local health center	33.5 36.3	66.5 63.7	0.0 0.0

Table 8-3. General knowledge and attitudes about AIDS and condoms

Question	Yes (%)	No (%)	Don't Know (%)
Do you think it is acceptable to use a condom with a spouse to protect against AIDS?	12.7	86.3	1.0
Can you get AIDS if you have sex with someone who looks perfectly healthy?	98.8	1.2	0.0
Has your best friend slept with anyone other than her husband in the last 12 months?	70.6	19.1	10.3
Have you ever talked to your husband about the chances that you or he might get infected with AIDS?	44.1	53.8	2.1
Do you suspect or know that your husband has had sexual relations with other women apart from you since you were married?	69.9	27.3	2.8
Have you yourself slept with anyone other than your husband in the last 12 months?	0.1	99.9	0.0
Have you ever heard a talk at the clinic/hospital about how people can protect themselves against AIDS?	94.2	5.8	0.0
Have you ever heard a radio program about how people can protect themselves against AIDS?	93.1	6.9	0.0
Has someone like a Community Based Distribution agent or a Health Surveillance Assistant ever come to your home to give you information about how people can protect themselves against AIDS?	78.2	21.8	0.0

N=60

Table 8-4. Which of the following ways in which women might get infected with the AIDS virus are you most worried about for yourself? And how worried are you that you might catch AIDS?

Way of Getting Infected with the AIDS Virus	% Most Worried About this Way of Getting Infected
Husband	82.1
Other Partner	4.1
Needle Injections	11.8
Transfusions	2.0
Worry That You Might Catch AIDS	
Not Worried at All	6.5
Worried a Little	9.2
Worried a Lot	84.3

N=60

Table 8-5. What do you think is the best way to protect yourself from getting AIDS?

Question: What do you think is the best way to protect yourself from getting AIDS?	Yes (%)	No (%)	Don't Know (%)
Advise spouse to take care	61.2	38.8	0.0
Use condoms with:			
all other partners except spouse	16.1	83.9	0.0
prostitutes / bar girls	38.2	61.8	0.0
people from town	12.2	87.8	0.0
other people you think might be infected	10.7	89.3	0.0
Avoid having sex with:			
any partners except spouse	40.1	59.9	0.0
prostitutes /bar girls	40.3	59.7	0.0
many partners	30.5	69.5	0.0
people from town	35.0	65.0	0.0
other people you think might be infected	29.3	70.7	0.0
Avoid other:			
transfusions/ injections/ sharing razor blades	20.8	79.2	0.0

N=60

CHAPTER NINE
ISLAM AND GIRL'S SCHOOLING IN SUB-SAHARAN AFRICA:
Exploring the Size and Sources of the Gender Gap in Education

Fatou Jah

Introduction

Two important events at the turn of this century have revived interest in the effects of religion on female education. The first is the Millennium Development Summit organized by the United Nations in 2000. At this summit a global commitment to eliminating gender inequality in society, most visibly under the aegis of the United Nations' Millennium Development Goals (MDGs), was adopted by all UN member nations. The second is associated with September 11 events that have reinforced in the public imagination the association of Islam and restrictions on girls' schooling[1] as well as with terrorism (Kadi 2006). Despite these two global events, few studies have specifically examined the role of religion on education in developing countries, especially in Africa (Daun 2000). Previous studies have noted larger gender gaps in education in Muslim countries (Daun 2000; Weeks 1988), but the fundamental reasons for these gaps remain poorly understood. Are these gaps attributable to religion per se or to other developmental or organizational features of Muslim[2] countries? How do the gaps change as these countries grow economically? Would advances in education in these countries be sufficient to foster gains in women's position in society? This chapter seeks to advance empirical understanding of the effects of Islam on girls' schooling in sub-Saharan Africa (SSA). Using data from nineteen sub-Saharan countries, I examine two questions about the net magnitude and reasons for the gender gaps in education in these countries: Specifically:

- How large is the *net* effect of religion on the gender gap, after adjusting for other country correlates that bear on girls' schooling? How large is this net effect (if any) compared to other influences?

- What are the reasons for this inequality in Muslim countries? Do the leading reasons for school dropout differ between Muslim and non-Muslim countries?

To answer these questions, the chapter begins by discussing key conceptual and methodological issues in studying the influences of religion on schooling, and how these issues have been addressed in previous studies. Next it describes the data, measures, and methods used. This is followed by a presentation and discussion of the results. The findings reveal gross differences associated with religion, but these differences wane once socio-economic and national factors are controlled for. At any rate, the net effect of religion is smaller than that of other socio-economic factors. Further, it varies along an east-west gradient, increasing as one moves from South-East to West Africa. The effect of religion also depends on the level of schooling, as it is most visible at the secondary schooling level but absent at the primary level. The final section summarizes the key findings and their policy implications.

Conceptual Background

The gender inequalities in Muslim countries can be analyzed from several perspectives. One can emphasize the impact of Islamic precepts, of cultural norms that predate Islamic times, of colonial experience, or of the religious mix or proportion (and majority status of) Muslims within the society. These conceptual perspectives each provide slightly differing insights into the potential sources of the gender gap.

Cultural traditions and customary laws dating to pre-Islamic times blend with Islamic tenets in ways that can shape the practice of Islam in SSA (Bowman and Anderson 1980; Obermeyer 1994; Weeks 1988). Although these researchers focus primarily on different outcomes (women's participation in education, reproductive health, and the demography of Islamic nations, respectively), some of their findings are instructive as to the influence of religion on gender inequality in schooling.

Beyond the blend of doctrine and local customs and traditions, the practice of Islam in many regions also reflects colonial heritage. Thus Islamic law as it relates to female schooling may mirror legal and civil codes put into place during European colonial rule (Obermeyer 1994; Weeks 1988). Aside from its direct influence on local Islamic jurisprudence, the colonial experiences have influenced the type, language, and quality of education received in the colonies. Through this influence, colonial rule both instituted gender inequalities in colonial education and reinforced existing gender asymmetries. For instance, only a few children—and mainly sons rather than daughters—received European colonial education, whether implemented by Great Britain, France, or Portugal.

Thus, rather than tying the current gender gaps in education to Islam, several African scholars have argued that the gap is primarily the result of patriarchy in contemporary African societies, which was exacerbated by colonialism and reinforced by neo-colonialism (Assie-Lumumba 2000; Brock-Utne 2000). Formal education, then, can be used as a lens to understand how colonialism, as opposed to religion, transformed education in African societies and how this transformation in turn continues to impact female education on the continent. Besides the roles of culture and colonial experience on Islamic practice, it is useful to examine the significance of an individual's religion versus national religion on women's agency within Islamic societies.

Beyond culture and colonial heritage, the majority status of a religion in a country can bear on the effect of this religion. Knodel et al. (1999) find support for this minority status hypothesis in their work on reproduction. More recently, writers on religion and education (Milligan 2006; Tawil 2006) find the majority status thesis to be an important consideration in the schooling of children in other developing regions. A religious group that is a minority at the national level but a majority at the regional level can exert a substantial effect locally. In Tanzania, Muslims are a national minority but a local majority in Zanzibar (DHS 2006). At this local level, any effect of Islamic doctrine on female schooling and, in turn, on women's agency can be distinct from an effect at the national level. Thus, there are variations across time and space in how religion can affect girls' schooling.

Islamic Tradition and Human Rights

Like other religious scripts, interpretations of Islamic texts, primarily the Koran, the *hadith*[3] and the *sunna*,[4] present conflicting messages regarding women's role in society (Obermeyer 1994). Public discussions of the role of women in Muslim societies, therefore, remain contentious, with views polarized around two schools of thought: the liberal and the conservative. Liberals generally uphold the principles of human rights as they relate to female schooling. Further, liberals argue for separation of dogmatic tenets from cultural practices, noting that while some objectionable norms inhere in certain Islamic societies, these features are not intrinsic to Islam. Rather they result from a social system distorted by patriarchy (Obermeyer 1992, 1994). The conservatives, on the other hand, draw upon aspects of the doctrine that imply superiority of men over women. Such aspects are invoked to define the roles of women in society as limiting women's agency and promoting gender inequality (Obermeyer 1994). Thus, Islamic doctrine can and has been used to justify both the subordination (as in the case of Iran regarding limitations on women's reproductive rights) and empowerment (as in Tunisia) of women (Obermeyer 1994).

Although the liberal and conservative perspectives form the dominant views in matters related to female schooling and Islamic interpretations of human rights, some scholars can be viewed as taking an intermediate position. In summarizing his case study of "Pesantren Al-Muayyad," an Islamic boarding institution in Indonesia, to the broader context of religion's place in public life, Pohl (2006, p. 409) asserts that the activities of such institutions generally promote peace, cultural pluralism, respect for human rights and civil society, and accommodate "modernity" and democracy.

Female Education and Women's Position

As with human rights, the discourse on female education and women's position in Muslim-majority countries is framed within two contending perspectives: the secular ("modern") and the Islamic. Proponents of the secular perspective agree with the international development community's notion of education as a core societal objective in its own right as well as a means to economic development (UN 2000; UNICEF 2003; World Bank 2001). Such a notion contends that gains in female education will promote economic growth but also enhance women's position, and ultimately reduce gender inequality in other spheres of life (UN 2000; UNICEF 2003; World Bank 2001). Indeed, scholars (Fortna 2002, Somel 2001 in Herrera 2004) argue that political proponents of the secular view in Muslim societies have used "modern" education as a tool for pushing a host of reforms including *"military, social, political, economic, scientific, and cultural."*

A worldwide expansion of education within the framework of secular ideals has transformed how education is perceived and consequently provided in Muslim societies (Herrera 2004). However, proponents of the non-secular education orientation in and outside Muslim societies view formal or "modern" education, especially female education, as antithetical to Islamic doctrine (Herrera 2004). Such reasons, rather than religion itself, may explain the deficiency in women's education reported in the literature (Basic Education Coalition 2006; King and Mason 2001; Pande et al 2005; UN 2002; UN 2000, 2005; UNICEF 2003) and women's position in Muslim societies.

But a salient question is, "Is gender parity in education synonymous with gender equity in society"? The question has important implications for policies designed to promote equality and equity. Low gender equity in society can prevail where family, educational, and economic institutions operate in ways that reinforce rather than question the bases for gender inequalities both in schooling and in the larger society. Thus from a broad development perspective, closing the gender inequalities in education and its corollary, economic security, may not necessarily improve women's position in the absence of an enabling society (Malhotra and Mather 1997; Pande et al 2005).

Overall, the effects of religion can vary among and across Muslim societies depending upon prevailing socio-economic and national (economic and political) conditions. Generally, an approach that sees Islam not as immutable but as a religion that adapts to its material environment and emerging societal issues is emphasized by recent scholarship (e.g. Fortna 2002 and Somel 2001 in Herrera 2004; Obermeyer 1992).

In sum, each of these perspectives informs an approach that regards Islam as adaptive. Any role that religion may have in explaining the gender gap could thus stem from both the ideological tenants of Islamic tradition and their interplay with other social factors.

Methodological Issues

A central argument throughout this chapter is that large gender gaps in Muslim countries need not imply a religion effect. Other socio-economic or cultural factors can confound the relationship, whether these factors are readily measurable or not. Another important argument has to do with contextual variation. The effect of religion on gender inequality may also depend on the level of schooling. For instance, religious and cultural tenets may hinder female enrollment at the primary level, while other factors, perhaps economic, may operate at the secondary level. Because girls who proceed to secondary education and beyond are highly selected, the religion effect can wane, and other factors (discrimination, pregnancy-related dropouts) may become more important. Alternatively, and considering the contemporary expansion in female schooling, the attainment of primary education may no longer contradict existing religious ideals while female schooling beyond this level may be perceived as unnecessary. The latter perception may stem from a greater emphasis placed on family and motherhood as girls in general reach maturity (Assie-Lumumba 2000), especially in Muslim societies (Csapo 1981). To date, while a handful of studies in SSA have addressed the role of religion in schooling outcomes (e.g. Daun 2000), none has compared the effect of religion at different schooling levels.

Muslim societies are heterogeneous, particularly in terms of their approach to issues of gender. The existing research on the determinants of female schooling in Muslim societies raises questions about patriarchy as a possible explanation for the female educational deprivation in Muslim societies. Low levels of female education are found in both Muslim and non-Muslim societies. Chad, a Central African country with a large Muslim population, has a female schooling record similar to Tanzania's, an East African country with a Muslim minority. Similarly, Muslim societies can experience high schooling enrollments and low gender gaps. According to recent figures (DHS 2006), countries in Central Asia (Kazakhstan, Kyrgyz Republic, and Uzbekistan) which are predominantly Muslim show higher levels of secondary educated females than Brazil and Guatemala (in Latin America and the Caribbean), predominantly non-Muslim countries. The heterogeneity of Muslim countries operates across broad regions too. The gender gap in education is highest in Muslim countries in SSA, and lower (and often negative) in other developing regions such as North Africa and Central Asia, also largely Muslim regions (DHS 2006). Additionally, non-Muslim countries in SSA have lower female school enrollment than Muslim countries in Asia (DHS 2006), further underscoring the heterogeneity of Muslim societies vis-à-vis prevailing socio-economic conditions. Having a Muslim majority does therefore not always translate into wider gender gaps in schooling.

Different sub-regions in sub-Saharan Africa (West, Central, Eastern, and Southern) also condition how religion works as a factor in the religion-female education equation. Geography, interacting with history of Arab trade, has been advanced as a reason for the limited importance accorded girls' education in Muslim societies. Within Africa, countries that have historically been in the Arab trade routes hold the largest Muslim populations (Csapo 1981; Weeks 1988), with females playing an important role in this trade. As a result of this historical trade specialization, women in West Africa reportedly show greater control over their economic resources despite their lower levels of education relative to Central, Eastern, and Southern Africa (DHS 2006), further justifying the methodological significance of geography and other hard-to-measure features.

Researchers are often worried about overlooking unmeasured yet potentially influential factors in analyses of social phenomena (Beise and Voland 2002; DeRose and Kravdal 2005). But few studies on religion and female education have addressed this analytical concern. Unmeasured factors can include students' perceptions of and attitude toward schooling and women's position in the wider society; their educational and life aspirations and ambitions; norms and values that shape parental demand for daughters' education; and group/societal norms regarding women's education. Similarly, the commitment of policy-makers and educational administrators to gender equality in schooling, school quality, and other school elements that reinforce asymmetric gender norms or segregation are hard to measure across countries. Finally, it is difficult to measure how economic institutions, the ultimate benefactor of educational endowments, reward women's education across the divergent occupational sectors in SSA.

Previous Studies

Past studies have examined the effects of religion on formal education, but often these effects are examined incidentally in studies addressing other factors (see Brock and Cammish 1997; Lewin 1993). A small body of demographic literature addresses this question indirectly (Caldwell 1986; Weeks 1988). While some studies attribute the lower female schooling in Muslim relative to non-Muslim countries to religion, others (Weeks 1988) link this poor outcome to local socio-economic conditions. A recent study by Daun (2000) has directly examined the role of religion in female schooling in SSA, noting that both the expansion and decline in education depend more on religious factors than on others.

Previous work is thus sparse and often descriptive. While gross gender gaps have been documented, the size of this gap in a multivariate framework remains poorly documented. There is anecdotal and descriptive evidence on *community* differences in the effect of religion on socio-economic indicators within any particular country. Yet much previous work on religion and schooling fails to consider the conditioning effects of schooling level and the heterogeneity of Muslims across communities and the sub-Saharan African continent, particularly as these relate to local socio-economic and national economic conditions. Similarly, the influence of unmeasured characteristics that can mask the relationship between religion and the gender gap in schooling has received little attention in most studies in SSA. Further, deep insights into the nature of this relationship are difficult to obtain without investigating the association of religion and some of the sources of the gender gap in schooling, including the role of *culture, demographic,* and *economic* conditions. The analyses in this chapter acknowledge the non-homogeneity of Muslim societies and the potential relevance of unmeasured factors in a multivariate perspective.

Data and Measures

Data

The present study employs data from the Demographic and Health Surveys (DHS). The DHS is one of the leading sources of nationally representative and comparable demographic data on developing countries, with much of their strength derived from replication across multiple countries over several periods. Such replication facilitates a comparison of the role of religion on educational outcomes across many countries. Most studies that examine the religion-schooling relationship have relied on data from one or two countries. The rich and comprehensive DHS resource makes it possible to widen the scope of previous analyses, bringing together data from the *same* survey period (roughly between 1994 and 2000) on nineteen countries in SSA. Further, the analyses differentiate between countries from West Africa (Benin 1996, Burkina Faso 1998/99, Cote d'Ivoire 1998/99, Guinea 1999, Mali 1995/96, Niger 1998, Nigeria 1999, and Togo 1998); Central Africa (Cameroon 1998, Central African Republic [CAR] 1994/95, Chad 1996/97, and Gabon 2000); and from East Africa (Kenya 1998, Madagascar 1997, Mozambique 1997, Tanzania 1996, Uganda 1995, Zambia 1996, and Zimbabwe 1994). The use of such comparable data, both in survey timing and design, facilitates more valid comparisons across countries and sub-regions. Thus any differences that emerge from the analyses can more reliably be attributed to variations across these countries and sub-regions and not to timing.

The choice of countries is dictated by several factors: availability of information on reasons for school dropout, religious composition, and country breakdowns into regions/provinces in terms of all the indicators used. Because regional breakdowns of a particular country sometimes differ between survey periods, the third wave of DHS studies (DHS 3) that provides the reasons for dropout from school for all countries surveyed was mostly used.

All the variables, both dependent and independent, are measured at the regional/provincial (hereafter community) level. Thus for every measure, the community percentages aggregated from household data for all the countries were extracted from the Statcompiler of the DHS surveys. The community-level religion (not available from the Statcompiler) was derived from the respective DHS 3 female respondents' file for each country. This design yielded a total of 125 communities from the sampled nineteen countries. For indicators including GNP and female representation in parliament that are available at the national rather than regional level, national averages obtained from the Population Reference Bureau (PRB) database (PRB 2006) were applied to all communities within a country.

Measures

Dependent variables

In line with the paper's research questions, the analyses focus on two main outcomes, the *size* and the *source* of the gender gap. The size of the gender gap is measured as the female-to-male ratio in educational attainment, evaluated at the primary and secondary levels. The source of the gender gap is measured by looking at qualitative differences in boys' and girls' likelihood of dropping out because of a given reason. Among the many possible reasons for the gap, my analyses focus on causes associated with 1) early marriage, 2) disliking school, 3) pregnancy-related dropouts (PRDs), and 4) economic-related dropouts. These four dimensions are expected to reflect "cultural," "values-related," "demographic," and "economic" dimensions of the sources of school dropout.[5] The measures are derived from the responses of females, aged fifteen to twenty-four, on their *stated* reasons for dropping out of school. Relying on stated reasons as opposed to inferences from regressions offers a more direct insight into the causes of dropout. By framing the analyses along these four different dimensions of the qualitative sources of the gender gap, the paper complements previous work insofar at it explores the sources (not just the size) of gender gaps.

Independent variables

The main explanatory variable is religion, measured by the percentage of Muslims (% Muslim) within a community. It is based on the female respondents' religion in the DHS surveys. The choice of female over male respondents' religion is dictated by the design of the DHS surveys, which use women as the primary respondents, with men interviewed only for married women. However, cross-religious marriage is unlikely to be substantial, implying that figures from either gender are expected to be close. Instead of using the raw percentage of Muslims, we used its square root because it gave the most stable estimates. Other variables included factors that reflect socio-economic, compositional and structural characteristics of households, demographic, cultural, and national level variables. The specific variables used depended on the outcomes analyzed as presented in the detailed Tables 9-3 through 9-6 (appendix).

Methods of Analysis

The study used multivariate regression analysis to examine the link between gender gaps and religion. A multivariate analysis makes it possible to control for the influences of multiple measured covariates that can confound the relationship between religion and education outcomes. However, standard regression analyses do not control for unmeasured characteristics of countries or communities (e.g. gender norms and local female leadership) that may have a bearing on the size and source of gender gaps. To this end, the study used a statistical model that controls for the fixed effects of countries and communities as estimated by the GEE (generalized estimating equation) procedure in SAS.

To further understand the factors underlying the differences in gender gaps between Muslim and non-Muslim countries, the study specified a series of nested models. First, we model the influences of religion only, with no control variables added. Then in succeeding steps, we added socio-demographic, household, cultural, and economic controls that can confound the effects of religion. While the study distinguishes between primary and secondary levels in analyzing the size of the gap (Tables 9-3 and 9-4), we did not make this distinction in analyzing its sources (Tables 9-5 and 9-6), because of sparse data.

In modeling the size of the gender gap, we estimated five models in addition to the basic model. The first model (model 1) addresses the effect of regional differences across SSA using West Africa as the reference. Models 2, 3, and 4 reflect the variations in socio-economic, demographic, and national conditions, respectively. Finally, model 5 reflects compositional and structural characteristics of households. Ideally, household effects should be estimated early on in schooling analyses, but analytical reasons warranted their estimation at the very end.[6]

Unlike the detail and stepwise approach taken in the analyses of the size of the gap, the sources of the gap were estimated in three models in addition to the baseline model. Given the chapter's special interest in the influence of regional heterogeneity on schooling, the first model (model 1) considers regional differences. Model 2 excludes the control(s) with several missing cases while model 3 includes them. Although I adjusted for many controls in the analyses, the ones presented in the models are only those that turn out to have a significant effect or where the effects are non significant but have conceptual/analytical salience.[7]

Findings

Table 1 summarizes the gross and net estimates of the effect of religion on the size of the gender gap in primary and secondary schooling. Table 9-2 shows the corresponding estimates from the analyses of the sources of the gap. The gross estimates give the overall effect of religion without adjusting for any correlates while the net estimates give the residual religion effect after adjusting for key correlates.

Table 9-1. Estimates of the effect of Muslim composition (sq. rt. of % Muslims on the female to male ratio; i.e. size of the gender gap, in schooling)

	Primary level		Secondary level	
	Gross % change	Net % change	Gross % change	Net % change
Predictor				
% Muslim (square root)	-1.4 **	-1.2	-2.2 ****	-3.7 #
Regional diversity				
East Africa		13.4 ****		
Central Africa		8.8 #		
West Africa		0.0		
Central Africa vs East Africa		4.2		
Socio-economic characteristics				
Educational attainment		6.4 **		
Family/community wealth		1.7 *		3.1 ****
Mass media				-0.2 ***
Household compositional/structural characteristics				
Family networks		0.2 #		0.5 *
Demographic characteristics				
Family size		3.0 ***		4.7 *
Cultural characteristics				
Cultural emancipation				0.5 ****
National context				
Natural log of GNP				-9.3 *
Natural log of GNP* %Muslim				0.1 *

The symbols: ****, ***, **, *, and # denote significance at < 0.001, 0.001, 0.01, 0.05, and 0.1 levels respectively

Religion and the Size of the Gender Gap

Consistent with theory, the gross effect of religion on female schooling at the primary level is negative and significant, with the odds of Muslim communities approaching gender parity somewhat lower than those of non-Muslim communities. According to this initial estimate, each increase in the root percentage of Muslims results in a small decline of about 1 percent in the female to male ratio in primary schooling (Table 9-1). Stated differently, a (root) percent increase in Muslim composition leads to the widening of the gender gap by about 1 percent. However, with the addition of controls, this effect wanes: while the estimated religion effect continues to be negative, it becomes weaker and non-significant. Subsequent models that control for the effect of socio-demographic, household, and national level influences do not return the effect of religion to significance. See Table 9-3 (appendix) for greater detail.

In sum, adjusting for classic determinants of gender inequality in education is sufficient to account for the gender gap in primary education. Thus, while religion has a gross negative effect on girls' primary schooling, this does not reflect a net effect of religion per se, but the confounding effects of regional, socio-economic, and demographic characteristics of communities.

The same analysis is replicated at the secondary school level and results are also shown in Table 9-1. Similar to observations at the primary level, an overall negative and significant association between religion and female secondary schooling is observed, but with successive inclusions of controls (models 2 through 5), the religion effect is attenuated and loses significance (see Table 9-4 [appendix] for detail). However, in the final and most complex model (model 6), which additionally adjusts for the influence of household compositional and structural characteristics, as well the mass media, the impact of religion gets stronger and regains some of its initial statistical significance. This final estimate indicates that *net* of all the factors controlled for, every (root) percentage increase in the Muslim population results in about 4 percent decline in the female to male enrollment and a subsequent widening of the gap (table 9-1, model 6). Thus, contrary to the findings for lower schooling levels, Islamic religion hinders gender equality at the secondary level, even after adjusting for other socio-demographic and economic correlates associated with gender inequality in schooling. The question, however, is how these religion effects compare with those of other key determinants of girls' schooling.

Religion versus Other Influences

Religion impacts girls' schooling differently at the primary and secondary levels. Its net effect is significant at the secondary but not primary level. Even at the secondary level, where a negative and significant effect on girls' education is observed, religion is *not* the overriding factor in terms of substantive significance (Table 9-1). Some of these factors include regional diversity, socio-economic environment, demographic outlook, and household composition. The importance of these other factors is visible at the primary as well.

Primary level

The study finds an East-West gradient in the gender gap record in primary schooling across the continent. This gradient proves to be a critical factor in schooling depending on the region in question. Girls in Central Africa, and to a greater extent in East Africa (significance level: $p<0.0001$), are more likely to be enrolled in primary school than those in West Africa (table 1). However, and going against the presumed east-west gradient noted, the educational performance of girls in East Africa is not significantly higher than that of girls in Central Africa. Thus, judging from the substantive significance of the estimates, the gradient between contiguous regions is gradual, pointing to the relevance of other factors in primary schooling.

Beyond regional diversity, two socio-economic variables (total educational levels and family/community wealth) turn out to be important relative to religion. Both variables work to foster gender equality in primary schooling. General educational attainment was hypothesized to be important for gender equity because female-to-male education rates are directly related to total enrollment rates, with improvements in the latter affecting enrollment ratios for both genders. The enhancing effect of total educational attainment is therefore unsurprising, but one thing deserves comment. The variable has a consistently large impact throughout, both in terms of substantive significance and magnitude, validating continued national and international efforts at improving girls' schooling at the primary level. With every unit increase in total enrollment, the gender gap is expected to narrow by about 6.4 percent (table 1). Also noteworthy is the finding that girls from wealthier families/communities are more likely to be enrolled in primary schooling. The gender gap in primary schooling is expected to narrow by 1.7 percent with each unit decline in poverty in Muslim communities. This finding is not inconsistent with much of the literature on SSA that notes family economic status to be a factor in schooling (Bowman and Anderson 1980; Csapo 1981; King and Mason 2001; Colclough et al. 1998; Obermeyer 1994; Weeks 1988).

Although a few studies have examined the effects of family size on girls' schooling, (Lloyd and Gage-Brandon 1994), none has explored the effects of community-level fertility. In this study, a large and striking positive effect is found between community family size and the primary schooling of girls. Consistent with older findings (Chernikovsky's 1985;

Gomes 1984) but inconsistent with those from Lloyd and Gage-Brandon's (1994) study, the results here point to a closing of the gender gap at the primary level by 3.3 percent (table 1) as community-level family size increases.

Fosterage, the effect of supportive networks across families, is an important feature of African family systems and its impact on girls' education was examined. *It appears that* an extensive fosterage network is supportive of girls' education and tends to decrease the gap somewhat, by about 0.2 percent (table 1). On the other hand, the direct effect of economic growth and the dependence on economic growth of the religion effect (measured by an interaction term between GNP and percent Muslim) are both unrelated to girls' primary schooling.

Secondary level

The same variables continue to have an effect at the secondary level. Family/community wealth continues to be important in bridging the gap at the secondary level, with the strength of the relationship larger than at the primary level. For each unit increase in the wealth of families and communities, the gender gap is expected to narrow by 3.1 percent (significance: $p < 0.0001$) compared with about 2.0 percent (significance: $p = 0.1$) at the primary level. Similarly, mass media negatively impacts girls' higher education, albeit slightly. As community mass media usage progresses, the likelihood of the gender gap constricting decreases by about 0.2 percent. Although the study did not directly test why, a plausible reason for this negative effect of mass media on girls' schooling may be related to undesirable effects of socio-economic change.

Community-level family size is also influential at the secondary level, with the effect more substantial than was observed at the primary level. Here an additional increase in family size is expected to bridge the secondary school gap by 5 percent as opposed to 3 percent at the primary level.

Similarly, fosterage is strongly associated with a narrowing of the gap, and more so than was found at the primary level. This beneficial effect on the gap is expected given the relative paucity in the distribution of secondary schools. These results for fosterage, while in line with theoretical predictions, are not contradictory to cautionary remarks in the literature on the importance of spatial variations and the limited potential of fosterage in equalizing differentials in schooling at the collective level. This may be especially so when one considers the possible interplay of the dire economic circumstances confronting urban families and the influence of social change on existing inter-family relations and ties (Eloundou-Enyegue and Shapiro 2006).

Intriguingly, improvements in national economies check progress in girls' higher schooling substantially (table 1). As countries advance economically, the gender gap widens by about 9 percent. However, while both religion and economic growth, considered separately, depress girls' secondary education, their interaction has an enhancing effect. As indicated by the interaction of the GNP variable and religion, as national economies improve, Islamic religion *augments* girls' schooling at the secondary level, with the negative effect of religion on girls' secondary schooling decreased by about 1 percent.

Overall, the effects of religion on the size of the gap are modest compared to those of other factors such as region, overall educational levels; community wealth; family size; and fosterage, even at the secondary level where Islam religion has a negative impact on girls' education (at least in terms of substantive significance).

Religion and the Sources of the Gender Gap

Table 9-2 shows the effects of religion on girls' likelihood of dropping out of school through various reasons, including early marriage, dislike of school, PRDs, inability to pay school fees, and the need to earn money.

The gross effect of religion on early marriage is large and positive. However, the association becomes non-significant with the addition of controls for local and national conditions, suggesting the importance of other forces besides religion in affecting dropout through marriage.

Similarly, the gross estimate of the effect of religion on dropping out because of "disliking school" is positive and highly significant. As community populations become predominantly Muslim, the odds of dropping out for this specific reason almost double (increase by about 107 percent). However, in the presence of controls, this relationship becomes non-significant.

Islamic religion does not appear to significantly affect the likelihood of dropping out because of pregnancy, nor does it affect the likelihood of dropping out because of "lack of money or inability to pay tuition" once control is made for all other control variables. However, the results for dropping out for "employment-related reasons" are illuminating. Contrary to the results observed for "lack of tuition money," the initial effect of religion on dropping out for "employment reasons" is negative and non-significant but gains significance with subsequent adjustments for key correlates. The net effect in the final model is positive and statistically significant. With increases in the Muslim composition of communities, the likelihood of girls dropping out to work increases by about 110 percent, suggesting that religion does hinder the education of Muslim girls through early transition to work.

Religion versus Other Factors

Factors *other* than religion are more likely to affect the likelihood of dropping out because of early marriage (table 2). Such factors include advances in female and male secondary education. On average, with every unit of progress in male secondary education, the likelihood of girls dropping out of school for marriage increases by about 78 percent, but progress in female secondary education reduces this likelihood by only about 39 percent. The effect of male educational attainment, while *a priori* surprising, can be explained in economic terms. Higher male educational attainment generally translates into greater economic security and consequently a greater ability to meet the financial obligations of marriage. Another important socio-economic control is household size, which has a large positive impact on dropout for marriage, but the impact is of borderline significance. On the other hand, the fosterage control tends to bridge the gap through marriage. Similarly, family size tends to discourage the likelihood of girls' premature school termination due to marriage. Regarding the cultural environment, high fertility preferences of women between the ages of fifteen and nineteen have a very strong and reinforcing effect on girls' dropout due to marriage, while cultural emancipation, as reflected in community progress in older women's secondary educational attainment, unsurprisingly, has the reverse effect. At the national level, only the women parliamentarian variable is significantly related to female schooling.

Again, as observed for early marriage, *prevailing factors* (regional diversity, socio-economic, cultural, and national)—and not *religion*—are associated with girls' dislike of school (table 2). While no discernible difference between the other regions is evident, girls' disliking school increases the odds of dropping out by 100 percent in Central Africa as compared to East Africa. Regarding socio-economic influences, progress in general schooling enrollments tends to depress this source of dropout by 92 percent. Similarly, economic development and women's political participation are both related to this outcome, with each measurable growth in these estimates resulting in a decline in the odds of girls' dropping out through disliking schooling by 100 percent and 23 percent, respectively. Contrary to predictions, cultural emancipation tends to reinforce the likelihood of dropout through girls disliking of school.

Turning to the likelihood of dropout due to pregnancy, *religion* continues to be unimportant relative to the socio-demographic and national correlates. A percentage rise in girls' primary enrollment is more significant than increases in girls' secondary schooling in predicting the likelihood of dropout because of pregnancy, which increases by about 11 percent with a percentage point increase in primary enrollment. While the link between progress in the educational transition and higher odds of PRDs is expected, the greater risk observed at the lower level—*a priori* intriguing both in terms of the female life course and duration of schooling—can be plausibly explained by 1) secondary school girls' greater selectivity from many of the possible causes of gender inequality, and 2) their possibly wider exposure to reproductive health information. These findings suggest that policy decision makers' general disinclinations toward teen mothers' resumption of schooling in many SSA settings may be unjustified. Additionally, to help offset the observed decline in the presumed beneficial role of religion in stemming PRDs, and in line with Csapo (1981), who call for alternative ways of reaching Muslim girls, the findings signal the need for devising a happy medium between a timely introduction of reproductive health information in schools and Islamic traditions on the continent. Family size and especially later onset of childbearing for women between the ages of twenty-five and twenty-nine years have been observed to substantially reduce the risk of PRDs. However, the estimate for fosterage is strong, positive, and highly significant, suggesting that fostered girls are more likely than non-fostered girls to drop out from pregnancy.[8] While no significant interaction between economic development and religion is visible, societies that are more advanced economically are also more likely to be plagued with PRDs.

The regional, socio-economic, demographic, and national controls are significantly more associated with girls' dropout from tuition-related costs, with their effects visible and very substantial (table 2). The likelihood of the gap widening from tuition-related problems is significant in West Africa compared with East Africa, but no significant difference is observed between West Africa and Central Africa, supporting the possible softening effect of congruity on regional differentials noted earlier. Turning to the remaining controls, progress in overall educational levels, increases in household and family sizes, and economic growth significantly reinforces the likelihood of fee-related dropouts.

Finally, while religion increases the likelihood of dropping out due to work, this effect has *less* substantive significance relative to regional diversity and the interaction of economic development and religion Ttable

9-2). Girls in West Africa are much more likely to end their schooling to seek work than their counterparts in both Central Africa and East Africa, but differences in girls' dropout rates for work between Central and East Africa are again non-significant. Similarly, the interaction of economic growth and religion is unique to this work-related cause of dropout, with the odds of Muslim girls' school dropout for work declining as economies improve. On the other hand, increases in household and family sizes are strongly and positively associated with the likelihood of dropout for work, possibly counteracting their beneficial effects in bridging the size of the gap. This may also serve to explain the differences observed between the initial findings for family size and those of Lloyd and Gage-Brandon (1994).

In sum, religion is not the dominant factor in female schooling in Muslim societies, whether judged in terms of the size of the gap or its qualitative sources. The two exceptions to this statement are at the secondary school level (Figure 9-1) and in the employment-related analyses (Figure 9-2), where religion does widen the gender gap, net of prevailing socio-demographic and economic factors.

Figure 9-1. Gross and net effects of religion on female-male ratio in schooling, SSA

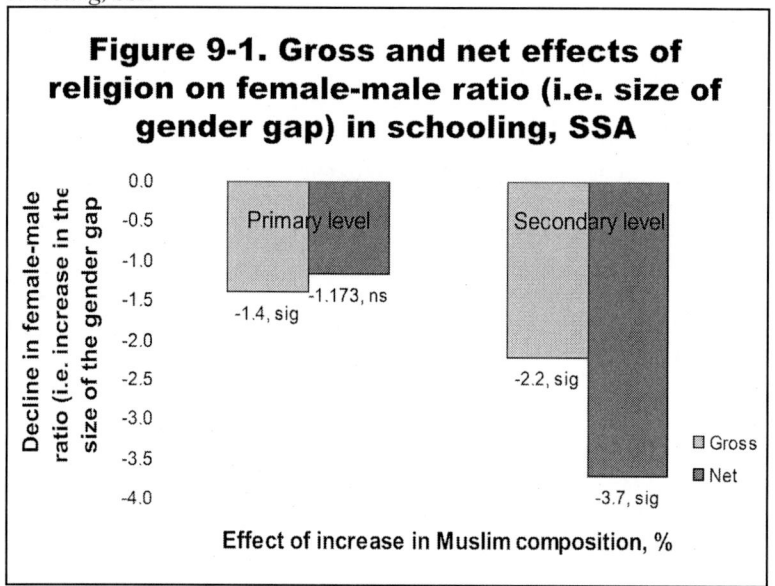

Figure 9-1. Gross and net effects of religion on female-male ratio (i.e. size of gender gap) in schooling, SSA

Primary level: -1.4, sig (Gross); -1.173, ns (Net)
Secondary level: -2.2, sig (Gross); -3.7, sig (Net)

Y-axis: Decline in female-male ratio (i.e. increase in the size of the gender gap)
X-axis: Effect of increase in Muslim composition, %

The letters "ns" and "sig" denote a non-significant/significant effect respectively.

Part of the U.S. government response following September 11, 2001 included promoting young girls' formal education in Afghanistan after the Taliban regime was dismantled. But drawing from the results of this study, the central issue, at least at the primary if not at higher levels, is not per se about being Muslim. Merely getting Muslim girls to school (as the Afghan case demonstrates) without attention to how schooling opportunities interplay with the girls' immediate environment misses important considerations. This study has found regional variations—socio-economic, demographic, and cultural influences—as well national developmental and organizational elements that shape the schooling environment—*not* religion—to be the overriding factors in predicting outcomes for girls in SSA.

Furthermore, explanations of Muslim girls' lower chances of acquiring secondary or higher education as compared to their non-Muslim counterparts have been linked to the notion of Islamic tradition as supportive of early marriage or incompatible with the continued education of girls (see Colclough et al. 1998; Csapo 1981).

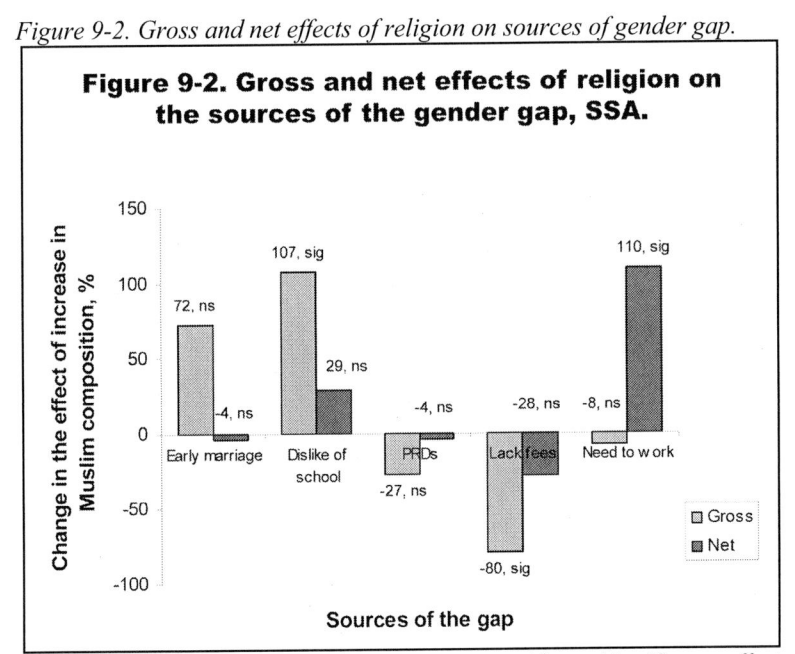

Figure 9-2. Gross and net effects of religion on sources of gender gap.

Figure 9-2. Gross and net effects of religion on the sources of the gender gap, SSA.

[Bar chart showing Change in the effect of increase in Muslim composition, % on y-axis (from -100 to 150) across Sources of the gap on x-axis. Values:
- Early marriage: 72, ns (Gross); -4, ns (Net)
- Dislike of school: 107, sig (Gross); 29, ns (Net)
- PRDs: -4, ns (Gross); -27, ns (Net)
- Lack fees: -28, ns (Gross); -80, sig (Net)
- Need to work: -8, ns (Gross); 110, sig (Net)]

The letters "ns" and "sig" denote a non-significant/significant effect, respectively.

The results gleaned from the detailed analyses of reasons for dropping out are striking. They contradict the presumed theoretical association between religion and the *cultural, values-related, and demographic sources of the gender gap in schooling.* They are therefore inconsistent with the early marriage or the doctrinal incompatibility logic reported in the literature. Being *Muslim* has no bearing on dropping out through early marriage, girls' dislike of school, PRDs, or on tuition-related sources of the gap. These findings, which diverge from the conventional evidence on the association of Islamic religion and female schooling, can be explained partly by social transformations.

Nonetheless, consistent with Weeks (1988) and Colclough (1998), Muslim girls are *more* likely to terminate their schooling to work for pay (Figure 9-2). Further, this effect is particularly strong at the secondary level, where expenses far exceed those incurred at lower levels. This economic dependence, however, varies across regions. It is greater in West Africa (the region with the highest Muslim composition [DHS 2006]) relative to Central and East Africa.

A crucial issue is how these findings speak to the broader question of women's position in society and how it is affected by progress in the education and demographic arena. For instance, the beneficial role of Islamic tradition on PRDs is being eroded by economic progress (Figure 9-2) and may be losing ground to undesirable changes from "modernization." Furthermore, the reinforcing effect of male education on early marriage is greater than the counteractive effect of current advances in female education and cultural emancipation (table 2). The greater likelihood of Muslim girls dropping out of school for marriage as boys' secondary education improves underscores, among other measures, the need to promote a parallel progress in girls' education if any meaningful change in women's agency is to be attained. Additionally, the fertility intentions of younger cohorts may be more important to contemporary schooling outcomes, at least in terms of early marriage and PRDs, than any beneficial group norms or cultural emancipation emanating from progress in older generation of women's education, which is found to be unrelated to PRDs. Lastly, it remains to be tested if and how these findings inhere globally and in SSA in the long range. Evidence from Egypt (Govindasamy and Malhotra 1996) indicates that improved women's education and outside employment may be inimical to their elevated status, raising questions over the economic security and enhanced women's position logic.

Conclusion and Policy Insights

The analyses in this chapter have shed new light on the net effect of Islam on the gender gap in schooling in SSA. First, while Islamic religion has a *net* adverse effect on girls' education, this effect varies by schooling level. It is modest or absent at the primary level but stronger at the secondary level. The primary schooling of girls is therefore not irreconcilable with Islamic tradition, and Muslim girls are as likely as their non-Muslim counterparts to enroll at the primary level. Even at the secondary level where a religion effect is found, this effect is smaller than that of other economic, demographic, and cultural factors. Second, there is substantial heterogeneity across the sub-Saharan region. We find a regional gradient in both the gender gap and the effect of religion on this gap. Muslim girls in West Africa have significantly greater schooling constraints than Muslim girls in Central Africa and East Africa. Third, the effects of religion may also depend on economic development. Further, in looking at the qualitative reasons for dropping out, *economic* reasons (specifically the need to earn money), rather than *cultural, values-related* or *demographic* reasons, are more likely to explain Muslim girls' earlier withdrawal from school.

Finally, disentangling the many nuances that underlie the education of girls in Muslim societies was facilitated by several research design and analytical elements: 1) relying on communities as units of analysis, 2) a multi-variate framework, 3) the use of sophisticated modeling approaches that adequately handle hard-to measure community and country factors, and (4) examining the role of religion on the qualitative sources of the gender gap.

Policy insights

Several policy insights emerge from this study. First, while religion can and does adversely affect gender equality, its importance is *subordinate* to prevailing community characteristics and broader national influences. Second, it is important to differentiate across schooling levels in discussing the effects of religion. Third, policies should be tailored to the individual circumstances of countries, as the effects of religion appear to vary systematically across regions. Fourth, the obstacles to closing the gender gap will be greater in poorer than in wealthier Muslim communities. Fifth, despite the strong and generally undesirable impact of economic development, policies targeting economic development alone are not sufficient in alleviating the economic constraints to Muslim girls' schooling in SSA. Rather, *specificity* in the design of policies that additionally address socio-economic, demographic, and cultural forces is critical to a sustained progress toward gender equality in schooling in the region. Sixth, regarding the broader issue of the potential for improvements in women's position in Muslim societies, the observed positive group norms and the synergies between economic development and religion provide a ray of hope, given an enabling environment, and efforts in facilitating and sustaining these outcomes should be fostered.

Table 9-2. Estimates of the effect of Muslim composition (sq. rt. of % Muslim) on the sources of the female to male ratio (i.e. size of gender gap) in schooling

Predictor	Early marriage Gross % change	Early marriage Net % change	Dislike school Gross % change	Dislike school Net % change	PRDs Gross % change	PRDs Net % change	Lack fees Gross % change	Lack fees Net % change	Earn money Gross % change	Earn money Net % change
% Muslim	72	-4	107 ***	29	-27	-4	-80 ***	-28	-8	110 *
Regional diversity										
East Africa		1307		-94				5.2E+07 #		-90 *
Central Africa		-75		57632				3433		-85 **
West Africa		0		0				0		0
Central Africa vs East Africa		5428		-100 #				1.5E+06		-38
Socio-economic characteristics										
Educational attainment				-92 ****				3303 ****		
Primary education, females		78 *				11 *				
Secondary education, males		-34 #								
Secondary education, females		771 #								
Household size										
Household compositional/structural characteristics										
Family networks		-25 *				31 ***		7198 *		276 *
Demographic characteristics										
Family size		-84 #				-54		1815 *		
Onset of childbearing (25 to 29 years)						-86 ***				
Cultural characteristics										
Cultural emancipation		-6 #		13 *						
Fertility preferences, female youth		6759 ***								
National context										
Natural log of GNP				-100 ***		11542 #		1.3E+09 #		
Natural log of GNP* %Muslim				-23 #						-1.3 **
Female parliamentarians		39 *								

The symbols ****, ***, **, *, and # denote significance at < 0.001, 0.001, 0.01, 0.05, and 0.1 levels respectively

Table 9-3. Estimate of the effect of Muslim composition on the size of the female to male ratio in primary schooling (i.e. gender gap), SSA.

Predictor	Basic Model Beta	Model 1 Beta	Model 2 Beta	Model 3 Beta	Model 4 Beta	Model 5 Beta
% Muslim (sqrt)	-0.014 **	-0.006	0.002	0.0018	-0.011	-0.012
Regional diversity						
East Africa		0.182 **	0.165 ***	0.1656 ***	0.160 ***	0.126 ****
Central Africa		0.148	0.119 **	0.1197 **	0.126 *	0.085 #
West Africa		0.000	0.000	0.000	0.000	0.000
Central Africa vs East Africa		0.034	0.046	0.046	0.034	0.042
Socioeconomic characteristics						
Educational attainment			0.058 **	0.057 **	0.059 ***	0.062 **
Total educ sq			-0.004 #	-0.004 #	-0.004 #	-0.004
Males, aged 10-14			-0.004	-0.004	-0.005	-0.007
Females, aged 10-14			0.009	0.009	0.011	0.010
Family/community wealth			0.024 ****	0.024 ****	0.025 ****	0.017 *
Household size			0.070 **	0.070 **	0.071 **	0.010
Sales & services, females			0.000	0.000	0.000	0.000
Prof & manag work, males						0.001
Mass media						0.001
Household compositional and structural characteristics						
Female hhold heads						0.000
Family networks						0.002 #
Demographic characteristics						
Family size				0.002	0.002	0.029 ***
National context						
Natural log of GNP					-0.005	-0.021
Natural log of GNP* %Muslim					0.000	0.000
Intercept	0.888 ****	0.750 ****	0.249 *	0.236	0.281	0.376 *
N	125	125	125	125	125	105
Likelihood ratio	41.7	49.3	125.6	125.8	127.0	125.3

Models with 125 observations come from 19 countries: Benin, Burkina Faso, CAR, Cameroon,Chad, Cote d'Ivoire, Gabon, Guinea, Kenya, Madagascar, Mali, Mozambique, Nigeria, Niger, Tanzania, Togo, Uganda, Zambia, & Zimbabwe. Model with 105 observations come from 15 countries: CAR, Cameroon, Chad, Gabon, Guinea, Kenya, Mali, Mozambique, Nigeria, Niger, Tanzania, Togo, Uganda, Zambia, and Zimbabwe

Table 9-4. Estimate of the effect of Muslim composition on the size of the female to male ratio in secondary schooling (i.e. gender gap), SSA

Table 9-4. Estimates of the effect of Muslim composition on the size of the female to male ratio in secondary schooling (i.e. gender gap), SSA

Predictor	Basic Model Beta	Model 1 Beta	Model 2 Beta	Model 3 Beta	Model 4 Beta	Model 5 Beta	Model 6 Beta
% Muslim (sqrt)	-0.022 ****	-0.020 **	-0.012	-0.0108	0.001	-0.019	-0.038 #
Regional diversity							
East Africa		0.054	0.0442	0.0559	0.116	0.100	0.059
Central Africa		0.058	0.0563	0.0682	0.077	0.101 *	0.067
West Africa		0.000	0.000	0.000	0.000	0.000	0.000
Central Africa vs East Africa		-0.005	-0.012	-0.012	0.039	-0.002	-0.008
Socioeconomic characteristics							
Educational attainment			0.027	0.029	-0.011	-0.012	-0.017
Males, aged 15-19			0.006	0.004	-0.005	-0.002	-0.002
Females, aged 15-19			0.005	0.004	0.011 #	0.010	0.005
Family/community wealth			0.016	0.018 #	0.010 #	0.012 #	0.031 ****
Household size			0.041	0.039	0.055	0.037	0.031
Sales & services, females			0.001	0.001	0.000	0.000	0.000
Mass media							-0.002 **
Household compositional and structural characteristics							
Female household heads							0.002
Family networks							0.005 *
Demographic characteristics							
Family size				0.024	0.064 ****	0.056 ***	0.046 *
Cultural characteristics							
Cultural emancipation					0.006 ****	0.006 ****	0.005 ****
National context							
Natural log of GNP						-0.054	-0.098 *
Natural log of GNP* %Muslim						0.000	0.001 *
Intercept	0.681 ***	0.636 ***	0.193	0.048	-0.318 **	0.171	0.532
N	125	125	125	125	125	125	111
Likelihood ratio	21.8	22.1	46.0995	47.373	65.88	66.8	58.2704

Models with 125 observations come from 19 countries: Benin, Burkina Faso, CAR, Cameroon,Chad, Cote d'Ivoire, Gabon, Guinea, Kenya, Madagascar, Mali, Mozambique, Niger, Nigeria, Tanzania, Togo, Uganda, Zambia, and Zimbabwe
Model with 111 observations come from 15 countries: CAR, Cameroon, Chad, Gabon, Guinea, Kenya, Mali, Mozambique, Nigeria, Niger, Tanzania, Togo, Uganda, Zambia, and Zimbabwe

Chapter Nine

Table 9-5. Estimates of the effect of Muslim composition on the sources of the female to male ratio in schooling (i.e. gender gap), SSA

	Early marriage				Dislike school			
Predictor	Basic Model Beta	Model 1 Beta	Model 2 Beta	Model 3 Beta	Basic Model Beta	Model 1 Beta	Model 2 Beta	Model 3 Beta
% Muslim	0.542	0.795	-0.096	-0.038	0.729 ***	0.577 ***	0.274	0.257
Regional diversity								
East Africa		4.488	3.935	2.644		-7.842 *	-4.994	-2.839
Central Africa		2.566	0.164	-1.368		-2.837	5.756	6.358
West Africa		0.0	0.0	0.0		0.0	0.0	0.0
Central Africa vs East Africa		1.921	3.771	4.012		-5.005	-10.751 *	-9.198 #
Socioeconomic characteristics								
Educational attainment							-2.019 ****	-2.563 ****
Secondary education, males			0.541 *	0.579 *				
Secondary education, females			-0.436 #	-0.412 #			-0.074	-0.070
Family/community wealth			-0.003	-0.025			0.027	0.081
Household size			1.866	2.164 #				
Sales & services, females			0.018	0.047			-0.035	-0.048
Household compositional and structural characteristics								
Female hhold heads				0.007				0.023
Family networks				-0.286 *				0.098
Demographic characteristics								
Family size			-1.782	-1.848 #				1.864
Onset of childbearing (25 to 29 years)								
Prevalence of teenage motherhood			0.112 #	0.0903 3			-0.100 #	-0.064
Cultural characteristics								
Cultural emancipation			-0.015	-0.057 #			0.112 *	0.126 *
Ideal number of chn (19 to 20)			4.481 ***	4.228 ***			-0.152	-0.807
National context								
Natural log of GNP			-0.226	1.502			-8.772 ***	-8.994 ***
Natural log of GNP* %Muslim			0.003	0.003			0.006	0.007
Female parliamentarians[2]			0.283 #	0.327 *				-0.261 #
Intercept	5.9 ***	2.4	-17.6	-21.4	11.0 ****	15.2 ***	69.7 ***	71.9 ***
N	125	125	125	117	125	125	125	117
Likelihood ratio	-442.4	-438.4	-416.4	-386.2	-469	-456.6	-429.0	-400.7

Models with 125 observations come from 19 countries: Benin, Burkina Faso, CAR, Cameroon,Chad, Cote d'Ivoire, Gabon, Guinea, Kenya, Madagascar, Mali, Mozambique, Nigeria, Niger, Tanzania, Togo, Uganda, Zambia, and Zimbabwe.
Model with 117 observations come from 15 countries: CAR, Cameroon, Chad, Gabon, Guinea, Kenya, Mali, Mozambique, Nigeria, Niger, Tanzania, Togo, Uganda, Zambia, and Zimbabwe

Table 9-6. Estimates of the effect of Muslim composition on the sources of female to male ratio in schooling.

Table 9-6. Estimates of the effect of Muslim composition on the sources of the

Predictor	Basic Model Beta	Model 1 Beta	PRDs Model 2 Beta	Model 3 Beta	Lack Basic Model Beta	Model 1 Beta
% Muslim	-0.32	-0.18	-0.44	-0.04	-1.60 ***	-1.338 **
Regional diversity						
East Africa		2.34 #	-1.55	0.21		16.05 *
Central Africa		11.60 *	3.77	3.53		8.98
West Africa		0.0	0.0	0.0		0.0
Central Africa vs East Africa		-9.27 #		-3.3196		7.08
Educational attainment						
Primary education, females			0.1722 ***	0.104 *		
Secondary education, females						
Socioeconomic characteristics						
Family/community wealth			-0.09	0.1354		
Household size			-0.51	-0.6883		
Sales & services, females			0.05 **	0.033		
Household compositional and structural characteristics						
Female hhold heads				-0.0359		
Family networks				0.273 ***		
Demographic characteristics						
Family size			-0.57	-0.775		
Onset of childbearing (25 to 29 years)			-1.912 ***	-1.9338 ***		
Cultural characteristics						
Cultural emancipation						
National context						
Natural log of GNP			5.32 *	4.757 #		
Natural log of GNP* %Muslim			0.00	-0.004		
Female parliamentarians			0.04	-0.03		
Intercept	8.9 ***	5.3 ***	3.4	7.2	33.1 ****	24.1 ****
N	125	125	125	117	125	125
Likelihood ratio	-412	-392	-362	-338	-517	-516

Models with 125 observations come from 19 countries: Benin, Burkina Faso, CAR, Cameroon, Nigeria, Niger, Tanzania, Togo, Uganda, Zambia, and Zimbabwe
Model with 117 observations come from 15 countries: CAR, Cameroon, Chad, Gabon, Guinea, Zimbabwe

female to male ratio in schooling (i.e. gender gap), SSA

fees		Earn money			
Model 2 Beta	Model 3 Beta	Basic Model Beta	Model 1 Beta	Model 2 Beta	Model 3 Beta
-0.626	-0.333	-0.084	-0.1876 *	-0.098	0.7409 *
11.379	13.163 #		-1.542	-2.026 #	-2.3441 *
1.170	3.565		-1.0509 *	-0.074	-1.8647 **
0.0	0.0	0.0	0.0	0.0	0.0
10.210	9.599		-0.4911	-1.953 #	-0.4794
3.506 ****	3.527 ****			0.103	-0.1562
-0.017	-0.094			0.065	0.0881
0.134	0.031			-0.090	0.1219
3.977 *	4.290 *			1.385 *	1.324 *
-0.080 #	-0.068			0.016	-0.0067
	0.171 #				-0.0025
	-0.030				0.016
2.670 *	2.952 *			0.330	-0.0076
-0.065 #	-0.034			0.003	-0.0092
17.000 #	16.393 #			-0.365	-0.0979
0.000	-0.002				-0.0131 **
0.134	0.114			0.063	0.03
-130.0	-134.7 ***	2.292 ****	3.5979 ****	-1.881	-0.6395
	117	125	125		117
-468	-435	-277	-273	-269	-247

Chad, Cote d'Ivoire, Gabon, Guinea, Kenya, Madagascar, Mali, Mozambique,

Kenya, Mali, Mozambique, Nigeria, Niger, Tanzania, Togo, Uganda, Zambia,

Notes

[1] Evidence of U.S. interest in the education of girls in Muslim societies has crystallized in the opening of schools for girls in Afghanistan (see http://www.state.gov/r/pa/ei/ rls/ 39499.htm) and a detailed USAID study (2003) of education in Muslim countries with the aims of "building a new and freer society" in Afghanistan and "tackling challenges in the Muslim world." Continued interest is provided by the presence of the U.S. First Lady at the launching of the Africa Education Initiative Textbooks Program in Ghana in 2006, where she asserted that President Bush's goal in the African Education Initiative is to get more girls to schools (see also Pohl, 2006 for U.S. interest in Indonesia's Islamic education).

[2] The term "Muslim countries" refers to countries with majority Muslim populations rather than an Islamic country or nation-state. Throughout this chapter, it is used interchangeably with "Muslim" community and society.

[3] The teachings of the Prophet Muhammad.

[4] The biography of the Prophet Muhammad.

[5] Adapting Eloundou-Enyegue and Stokes' (2006) typology in their contextual analysis of the sources of the gender inequality in schooling, the cultural dimension indicates situations where the gender gap is mostly driven by norms that value marriage and motherhood over prolonged female schooling. The values-related dimension describes situations where negative perceptions of girls themselves toward schooling drive the gender gap. These negative perceptions, in turn, can stem from asymmetric gender roles in society or from the limited long-term benefits of formal female education or girls' perception of their long run post-educational opportunities, or they may mirror parental rather than girls' perceptions, especially at lower schooling levels. The demographic dimension refers to the stage in the educational transition where education becomes normative with prolonged schooling predisposing girls to pregnancy- and marriage-related dropouts. Finally, the economic dimension reflects the situation where cultural discrimination against girls has waned, leaving economic considerations in favor of boys as the driving force in gender inequality in low resource settings.

[6] Related to missing data, the household measures and any other variables with similar limitations were estimated last in models 5 and 6 (in the primary and secondary school analyses respectively) and model 3 in the sources analyses because their earlier inclusion would have resulted in loss of cases not only in its estimation but in the estimations of succeeding models as well. However, in general, the estimates that turn out to be significant remain stable across all the models, including model 5, indicating that concerns over missing data did not change the substantive conclusions from the analyses.

[7] As an attempt to ascertain temporal changes, the squared term of the religion variable was estimated in the primary and secondary analyses but dropped from the latter for parsimony because its effect proved to be highly non-significant.

[8] The observed association between fosterage and PRDs is in line with conceptual analyses from the region (Assie-Lumumba 1997). Thus, while this paper finds supportive family networks to have a positive effect on girls' access to both primary and secondary schooling, the reinforcing effects of both family networks and economic development on the incidence of PRDs can prove to be counteractive.

CHAPTER TEN
GENDER EQUITY IN AFRICAN TERTIARY EDUCATION SYSTEMS

A Critical Look at Women's Progress

Philomina Okeke-Ihejirika

Over the past two decades sub-Saharan African leaders, policy makers, social activists, and foreign and local development agencies have consistently lamented women's under-representation in higher education and the professions as a huge stumbling block to social development and nation-building in the twenty-first century. Women's socio-economic mobility, their access to and participation in public decision-making forums, as well as their overall contribution to nation-building, are increasingly linked, at least conceptually, to obtaining tertiary education credentials (UNESCO 1998). Existing scholarship has been consistent in supporting this assertion, citing education—and tertiary education in particular—as a road-map for women's participation in social development (Court 1991). But despite the substantial gains women have made in enrollment, existing evidence still supports the prevalent condition across the continent: gender representation at all levels of sub-Saharan African educational systems continues to skew in favor of males (UNIFEM 2005, UNESCO 2006). Indeed, even the disciplinary segregation along gender lines, which women's increased enrollment has in some ways weakened, still maintains some male preserves and well-ingrained pink collar designations. As the table below shows, much of sub-Saharan Africa reflects this general pattern of gender inequity in overall representation. An even clearer pattern of gross gender inequity emerges when countries such as South Africa and Botswana, with better historically established records, are excluded from the group.[1]

The Potential Gains of Tertiary Education for Women and Society

The attention increasingly being paid to African women's participation in tertiary education, it must be noted, is a relatively new shift. It has only

Table 10-1. Women's Share of Tertiary Enrollment across African Regions (Averaged).[2]

African Region	Year Range	Gross Enrollment Ratio (%)
East Africa	2003-2004	36
Central Africa	1999-2004	25
North Africa	2000-2004	50
Southern Africa	2003-2004	51
West Africa	1999-2004	28

Source: Collated from Table 14: Tertiary Indicators in Tertiary United Nations Statistics Division based on data published by the UNESCO Institute for Statistics, http://www.uis.unesco.org (Accessed June 9, 2006).

been in the past two decades that many stakeholders have begun supporting the argument of advocates that, despite the inequities African societies have consistently thrust upon women, tertiary education credentials hold great potential for women's progress as individuals and as a group. Whether or not women should at present pursue formal training at the primary and secondary levels is no longer a matter of public debate. Lower fertility rates, healthier children, and tertiary economic earnings are only a few of the generally agreed-upon innocuous reasons why women's access to formal education at these levels cannot be compromised (Petrides 1998, Schultz 2002). Arguments for women's access to tertiary education, in contrast, did not garner comparable conviction until the entrance of development organizations into the debate as major sponsors with some degree of economic and political influence. Tertiary education, so we are told, is training over and above what women need for their primary role in the family. In addition, public expenditures on tertiary education cuts into available funding for the lower levels, which command tertiary social returns. Besides, women are not likely to be as gainfully employed as men. All of these reasons add up to lower returns that might not make it worthwhile to provide women with the opportunity to further their education (Psacharopoulos and Woodhall 1985, World Bank 1994).

The case for women's access to tertiary education, eloquently argued by ardent advocates, is increasingly being heard, especially in a contemporary Africa that is eager to show-case representatives of her female population as part of a democratic force characterizing new and pragmatic approaches to social governance. For one thing, advocates point out, the potential benefits to individual women, especially in Africa where gender-related adversities (e.g.: feminization of poverty, maternal and infant mortality) tend to be most pronounced, cannot be overemphasized. Higher education not only holds the potential to lift women above the poverty line, but could also thrust them into enviable economic positions far above their less-educated peers of both genders. Such a comfortable status is likely to afford them the space and means to make decisions about their lives; decisions that would probably otherwise be left in the hands of others. For another, improvements in women's socioeconomic status are likely to impact on the lives of family members. Compared to men, women's closer familial interactions often dictate an equally closer connection between their well-being and those of others around them. Research findings clearly show that compared to men, women's improved economic well-being has a greater positive impact on families, children and society (Anderson Bowman and Anderson 1982, Barrera 1990).

Beyond the personal benefits accruing to individual women, advocates argue, African women's training provides a potential reserve of human expertise that cannot be left untapped if the continent is to build the necessary capacity for a renaissance. Tertiary institutions of learning hold the prospect for capacity building, especially in an era where advances in information technology, as torch bearers, now herald innovations for economic growth and human welfare (Petrides 1998, Dunne and Sayed 2002). The historical disadvantage suffered by African women in formal education and paid work created a man's world—a patriarchal hierarchy that easily excludes women from the potential sites where the possibilities for such innovations could be explored (Petrides 1998, Rao 1991). If the challenge is to create a world that celebrates the diverse visions of its inhabitants and harnesses their talents towards the task of transforming society, then African women cannot stand at the margins, watching men as they march on.

African women's full participation in tertiary education should also be geared towards their recognition as nation builders. As policy makers unanimously recognized and noted in a policy document, "Higher education is traditionally where social and economic leaders, as well as experts in all fields, receive a significant part of their personal and professional training, [and hence]...has special responsibilities for this task which concern men and women on an equal basis (UNESCO 1998:5). Tertiary education in most of postcolonial Africa has been the training ground for new elites who will hold the reigns of public decision-making, control national resources, and shape political and social practices. Although tertiary training does not necessarily guarantee African women a slot, these policy makers admit, it provides them with at least the prerequisites for entrance (Hayward 1997). It is perhaps the major criterion, a foot-in-door, for developing and realizing aspirations of social mobility, professional growth, leadership and social mobilization.

Gender equity in formal training, many scholars agree, also has a direct effect on economic growth. In a recent review of macro-indicators of global trends, Paul Schultz (2002) at the Center for Economic Growth, Yale University, concludes:

> [Regions of the world] which have equalized their educational achievements for men and women in the last several decades have on the average grown faster...East Asia has increased the schooling of women much faster than that of men, closing a historically pronounced gender gap.... Africa...provided schooling mainly to males, although women were heavily engaged in the subsistence and market economies, and therefore should have had as much to gain from schooling as did men (p.12).

Others argue further that in an era of great uncertainly for the continent—a cross-road in time when Africa desperately needs every hand on deck for a much sought-after renaissance—the participation of women should be considered not merely as an equal partnership in which women take their rightful place as leaders along with men, but as a crucial contribution without which renaissance cannot be achieved. There is a growing urgency to make this century an age of renaissance for the continent, a situation which calls for harnessing the expertise of both men and women in order to tackle the challenges ahead. As David Courts, a well-established scholar in the field of tertiary education asserts, "as long as the proportion of women in African universities is less than 50 percent . . . the continent is underutilizing a corresponding proportion of its available human talent" (1991: 343-344). The hard road the continent has traveled over the past few decades provides a written lesson on the need to create a world that celebrates the diverse visions of its inhabitants in the process of Africa's transformation.

As these scholars properly argue, the push for access to and representation in tertiary education must therefore go beyond the challenges of improving the conditions of women's lives across the continent. Africa stands to gain considerably from a female population that is well trained in leadership and decision-making. Existing evidence across the world clearly shows that women, when provided with leadership opportunities, often come out to prove their mettle. Compared to men in similar positions, women who hold public office or senior positions in the civil service often channel more of their efforts towards reshaping existing policies to improve conditions of life for the general population (Kevane 2004: 1-2). Women's participation in social governance has also been found to greatly improve the conduct of public decision-making (World Bank 2001: 12-13). The potential for decision-making forums where women are well integrated as equal partners with men in the deliberation of the challenges faced by the continent in the twenty-first century are endless.

The focus of our analysis, however, is not necessarily on African women's progress at climbing the tertiary educational ladder but on the connections among the following: the conditions under which African women receive tertiary training, the credentials they receive and the possible benefits these credentials fetch in the larger society. We do not set out to prove that gender inequalities exist in Africa's higher education and the places it sends men and women to in the larger society (the civil service, professions, politics, etc.). That is an over-bitten argument in existing literature. Folded around its usual statistical apparel, the argument often tells the same endless story: women's participation is improving, but men are still considerably ahead. In contrast, we hope to extend the debate on women's access and representation beyond numbers. Our main argument is that the overriding emphasis on expanding opportunities for women merely in terms of numbers does not adequately address the problem of gender inequity in Africa's higher education. In other words, confronting gender inequity is not simply a matter of expanding female enrollment at the lower levels and nurturing the investment to fruition at the tertiary level. Any attempts at tackling the problem of gender inequity in higher education should begin *with critical assessments of both the conditions under which African women receive this training and the utility of the credentials received—for women and for society.*

History and Theoretical Background

Much of the scholarship emerging from gender studies in Africa, including the analyses of women's schooling experiences, appears to be embedded in development and feminist debates of the past four decades. Many of the scholars who have reflected on the trend of these debates, notably the WID-WAD-GAD discourse, agree that this type of discourse not only homogenized the diversity of female experiences across the continent but also neglected the peculiarities that define specific social contexts, drew more from women's "biological attributes than from the social character of manhood and womanhood, the production of each of which goes on in the context of the social relations between the two" (Sall, 2000, xii). However, any critical understanding of how African women have fared in the school system, especially at the tertiary level, probably requires a careful reading of this history and theoretical background.

Before the 1970s, the social policies of postcolonial African states largely reflected their aspirations to modernize along Western lines, introducing foreign social institutions, including education, to displace much of what was seen as tradition that held back the engines of development (Isbister, Rist, Cornia and Helleiner). Emerging African states embraced the promises of modernization as a major theoretical prescription for the continent's development. Modernization promised a progressive wave of economic, social and political transformations that would catapult the newly independent states into the global center stage. African intellectuals and policy-makers of the day enthusiastically welcomed the rapid incursion of western institutions of education, commerce, law, and government into their new countries. The establishment of these institutions was seen to have marked the break from a primitive and traditional past and the move toward western modernity. Higher education in particular was seen as the basic machinery for developing much-needed human resources—the stock of human capital for nation-building and industrialization. This proposition was more for men than for women, whose training was not expected to go beyond the social expectations of women's traditional domestic role. But after decades of policy failures, modernization was placed on the back burner of development debates. Meanwhile, the seeds of indigenous and foreign sexism, left to germinate, laid the groundwork for the present hybrid social order (Bujra 1983, Nwuwa, Okeke 2004, Afonja 1990).

Liberal feminists who made their entrance into this discourse in the early 1970s drew largely from the modernization paradigm. They argued for a proper integration of Third World women into the development process, drawing initial attention to the teeming female masses outside the formal sector. By virtue of their crucial role as the major food producers for the continent, African women featured prominently in these debates. As many contributors to the debates argued, the development process, while drawing from women's labor and expertise, nevertheless marginalized women in terms of direct participation and a share of the proceeds from the process (Boserup 1970, Banderage 1984, Kalu 1996). As the debates turned to women's experience of schooling, scholars increasingly highlighted the fact that the strong domestic emphasis common in women's education provided little potential for improving women's socio-economic status.

Feminist scholars called for the expansion of available facilities to raise women's profile in schooling that is tied to paid employment. Women's capacity to embrace the challenges of the modern society, they argued, depended substantially on the economic value of training attained (Smock 1981, Kelly 1989). Although this discourse in general terms boldly advocated for an improvement in the conditions of women's lives, it labeled women as victims of development, shielding more critical discussion of their role as equal partners with men in nation-building. African women's general access to schooling was emphasized, but their role outside the domestic sphere remained vague (Moshi 1998).

Marxist-based analyses, which subsequently conceptualized African women's status in terms of access to and control of productive resources, suggested a more critical reference point to redirect the debate. But again, the main target of this discourse was the female majority outside the formal sector. The female minority among the elite were perceived more as allies to the male ruling class, holding on to vested interests that reinforced class divisions among women. Whether as housewives who were economically dependent on male spouses or as paid workers with an economic asset that might require mortgaging some degree of personal freedom, elite women's vulnerable positions made them weak allies for their less-privileged sisters. A number of western feminist scholars reflected this line of thinking in their re-assessments of African women's education. But even this turn in the debate did not survive the major critique from indigenous scholars who found the entire discourse led by "outsiders" as an uninformed interrogation which homogenized women's experiences, neglecting the diversity across the continent and the peculiarities that define specific social contexts (Amadiume 1987, Okeke 1996, Oyewumi 1997).

As the review of literature in subsequent pages will show, debates on the roots of gender inequity in African education, especially at the tertiary level, remain fairly new and sparse, with only a gradually expanding literature. On a positive note, African women's access to education—and tertiary training in particular—has commanded more attention in the past decade, especially with the entrance of international organizations such as

UNESCO and the World Bank into the debate. Even the basis for redress is increasingly gaining public acceptance and attracting more calls for the expansion of access and representation. But there is even more need for critical appraisals of the particularities of barriers to African women's access to and *use of* tertiary educational credentials. Such assessments would enable policy makers to determine the *substance* of the progress women have made so far and what this progress *has done* for their status and role in society.

Review of Literature on African Women's Educational Experience

As noted earlier, formal education in most of Africa was not instituted with a view to creating a learning environment where both men and women could equally pursue knowledge. In Anglophone West Africa, for instance, formal education below the tertiary level developed with different agendas and, in many cases, separate facilities for boys and girls. Similarly, African institutions of tertiary education, especially universities, were designed by colonial authorities (with pressure from the indigenous male elite) to prepare African men as the future leaders of their countries (Court 1991, UNESCO 1993, Nwauwa 1994). In contrast, African women's education was geared towards their roles as wives and mothers in the emerging elite circles, and therefore, training at the tertiary level was not considered a necessary step (Bujra 1983). The perception of tertiary education as an instrument for African women's social mobility was sown and sharpened only with the advent of the global women's movement in the early 1970s. This movement gave birth to the Women's Decade (1975-1985) sponsored by the United Nations and subsequently unleashed an array of policy measures aimed at improving women's lives, especially in the developing world. In Africa, especially, social debates promoted education as a crucial prerequisite for uplifting the status of women. Over time, these debates increasingly highlighted women's educational attainment as a development issue (Kelly 1991, Sutton 2001). Most scholars and policymakers now share the view that education is a basic precondition for improving women's status and positioning them as equal partners with men in nation-building (World Bank 1998, UNESCO 2004, Kevane 2004).

It is safe to argue that many contributors to the debate perceive women's mere access to and representation across the disciplines within academia as the major underpinning ingredient for achieving gender equity in tertiary education (Wilson 1970, Stanworth 1983, Arnot and

Weiner1987, Briskin 1990). A similar pattern exists in the analyses of gender and education in sub-Saharan Africa, where the inequality in gender participation is globally considered the most pronounced. International reports and statistical updates of the past two decades have persistently denounced sub-Saharan Africa's sharp imbalances in gender representation at all levels (World Bank 1994, 2001, UNESCO 2004). As Dave pointed out earlier, this imbalance constitutes a huge waste to the continent in terms of untapped human resources. Any appreciable progress in women's enrollment across SSA, scholars argue, is further threatened by gender disparities in retention rates at various levels of education. In other words, women's enrollment rates sharply decline when far more girls than boys drop out school for all kinds of reasons including early marriage and lack of parental support (DAE 1994, Hyde 1989, Sutton 2001). Moreover, studies on classroom interaction and the curriculum of specific subjects show that boys are consistently treated as the superior gender. Enrollments in science and the arts at the primary and secondary levels (Kelly and Elliot 1982, Anderson-Levitt, Bloch and Soumare 1998) and major disciplines in higher education indicate solid gender segregations in both the sciences and the male reserves within the arts, such as law and business studies (Smock 1981, Rathgeber 1991, 1998). Furthermore, the impact of social background, especially class, could also worsen the barriers many women face in accessing formal education and moving up the ladder (Biraimah (1987).

In brief terms, three major aspects of the problem have been identified: cultural (the social values conferred on male and female children and the manner in which they shape social roles and opportunities), familial (the reinforcement of gendered cultural values in family decision-making regarding male and female children), and systemic factors (the reinforcement of gendered cultural values in the administration, content, and environment of educational training). While scholars have debated these factors at length, few attempts have been made to capture their multifaceted nature in individual studies. But recent studies show that African scholars in the field are increasingly recognizing just how multifaceted the origins and manifestation of gender inequities are, interacting both within and outside of the immediate school environment. In seeking measures for improvement, Beoku-Betts and other experts (1988) suggest that there is a need to conceptualize the problem in much broader contexts. These scholars have come to recognize that it is important not only to give women access and representation, but also to look at the way these goals are articulated in social thought, mandate and action.

African Higher Education: The Structures of Gender Inequity

In order to be adequately prepared for the challenge of moving the continent into the twenty-first century, African women must fully and meaningfully participate in education, and the utility of credentials received should attract opportunities devoid of any social bias. In this present era of reconstruction and renewal across Africa, we must decide whether women should play an active role in shaping the future or remain in the shadows. Assuming this stance raises the following questions: Why are we sending African women to the universities and other higher educational institutions? What do we expect them to do with the credentials acquired, given the existing hegemonic relations and structures of gender roles as justified by tradition and modernity? For all the fanfare made by African leaders and policy makers about improving women's status through education, how much room would society give and how much political will would the leaders themselves exercise to turn what is largely at present a dream into reality?

Admittedly, African leaders and policy makers, as reflected in all continental policies from the Lagos Plan of Action to the New Partnership for Africa's Development (NEPAD 2001), have responded in various ways to the problem of African women's declining social status. But much of this effort seems to boil down to the yielding of selective spaces of privilege in the larger society (Bauer and Britton 2006). Scholars in the field have also generated a reasonable discourse around gender bias and under-representation in our school systems. But the question remains—to what extent do these responses confront the ideological under-guard and social milieu of conventional training? By ideological under-guard we mean the various ways in which the structure of formal education in Africa—the overt and covert gaps in the curriculum and the process of schooling itself—reflect the existing power relations in society. By social milieu we mean the various ways in which the hegemonic relations of gender in the larger society shape the expectations of society and consequently the students' own aspirations for life after school. We argue that both the ideological under-guard and the social milieu reflect and reinforce the dynamics of social relations in a larger society that subordinates women. Just as in other cultures, there are meanings and values attached to male and female status in African cultures. Gender status not only provides different interpretations of social expectations and personal aspirations for the young but also gives them a good sense of both the boundaries not to cross and the potential penalties for crossing them. Because these meanings and values are deeply embedded in the fabric of tertiary education, they often render null efforts made to improve women's training and exaggerate the benefits of credentials received at any level and in any field. In the end, the substance of training received does not in any way come close to resembling gender equity (Moshi 1998, Okeke 2005).

It is not only the content of male and female educational credentials but also the socially constructed values they carry that could disadvantage women. Unlike their male counterparts, for women these values in many instances short-circuit the boundaries within which they can use their credentials. The socio-cultural expectations embedded in women's lives and roles place pressures, especially on ambitious women, homogenizing the boundaries for every female. Perhaps the fact that women have been socialized to meet certain expectations is a concern, but the larger concern is the fact that our institutions of higher learning provide very little space where men and women could contest the-way-things-are. This state of affairs is evident in the patriarchal structure of administrative and academic hierarchies and the environments they create for learning.

The patriarchal structure of university administration across Africa significantly curtails any latitude women within its ranks could exercise. As with political forums in the larger society, it is unrealistic to expect the few women who find themselves inside the decision-making bodies of these institutions to break through an established order of patriarchal interests to introduce change. As tokenized voices of a subjugated group, their presence is accommodated and their views are, on occasion, listened to—as long as they recognize and accept the limits of their membership. This paternal gesture keeps in place the overwhelming dilemma between cultural demands and professional ambitions these chosen ones must live out in daily life. Moving around in small numbers, watching their backs and what they say, women who get closer to the top present an uncertain profile to younger women. It is uncertain in the sense that as role models they convey all kinds of images: women who managed to persevere and got through despite all challenges; "wizened players" who were able to maneuver their way despite the challenges of a gendered hierarchy; a tiny minority that must operate within the limits of their accommodation, not inclusion. Obviously, a good number of African women have made their mark and many have found ways in spite of obstacles to resist patriarchal demands and pressures tied to their positions. But the fact still remains that for the majority of university women in Africa, university administration is still a male-dominated environment where one's right to speak and act is shrouded in carefully measured paternal privileges. As numerous scholars have argued in the case of women's presence in politics, the question is not representation or numbers per se, but the lack of spaces for critical contestation as part of decision-making bodies. Women enter political spaces where the gendered statuses of members, the issues discussed, and the rules of engagement are seriously embedded in power relations consistently legitimated by the larger society. We cannot say that the-way-things-are leaves exactly the same impressions in the minds of male and female students as to the boundaries of aspiration or the boundaries of potential afforded by their training.

What about the academic ranks? Although disciplinary segregation is still evident, studies carried out over the past two decades clearly show a steady rise in the representation of women as well as a gradual move toward higher levels of administration. The gender ratio, however, conveys the same pattern of patriarchal control. The academic hierarchy not only leaves impressions, as noted above, about a 'normal' situation where those who try to introduce changes must tread carefully, but in reality the organization of labor, the content of academic work, and the rewards of scholarship are in many ways gendered in terms of knowledge that is valued versus knowledge that can only be accommodated as long as it remains in the margins. But marginalizing, for instance, female architects of knowledge and debate on the relations of gender in society could very well block the emergence of those spaces of contestation where young adults could begin their own critical examination of what they have taken for granted. Women's Studies is still a new venture in many parts of Africa—almost a novelty in some areas. It is therefore not surprising that such spaces of contestation are still few and far between. Where they exist, they tend to follow the western historical pattern of marginalization as a project for women in the academy.

With the structure of university administration, academic ranks, and scholarly work characterized in such strong patriarchal terms, the learning environment cannot be the same for men and women. The relations of gender and their impact on the experiences of male and female students, and the choices students make about disciplines and eventual careers, have received considerable attention in the existing literature. Where the literature has failed is in bringing together the relations among these various aspects of university life and their impact on gender equity. What is also left unaddressed is the link between women's university experience and the social expectations they struggle to meet—expectations which could still curtail their ambitions regardless of the discipline they end up in; expectations which work pervasively in tandem with gender relations in the university to keep everyone in his or her place. To argue therefore that the learning process and its prospects thereafter are the same for men and women—even when they find themselves in the same discipline or contemplating similar careers—is to underestimate the potential of power relations in the larger society being seriously embedded in the training experience as well. That our institutions of higher learning are not able to provide critical spaces for rethinking the current state of affairs; that they do not provide enough stimulation in their curricula to encourage students to give critical thought to the decisions they make about marriage, career, and politics, is probably a good indication of the strong grip society has on our institutions of higher learning. The grip explains in part the weak value women's training commands—beyond their participation in paid work. The situation suggests that the real benefits of tertiary training to African women are at present grossly overestimated given its actual current value.

Cutting it in the Larger Society: What does this Training Fetch in Real Terms?

Apparently, more attention has been paid to women's participation in paid work as one potentially resounding benefit of advanced training than to their progress in other equally crucial areas such as public administration, politics, leadership and decision-making. Women's access and representation in formal structures of contemporary society appears largely characterized in very poor and selective terms. Their traditional roles as farmers and traders have been so greatly promoted that it seems to conveniently justify and leave unquestioned their near absence in the formal sector. Ambitious African women must wrestle with indigenous cultural inequities as well as those added as part of the colonial heritage of Africa's modernization history (Afonja 1990, Bujra 1983). The development of the formal sector in the continent, especially the civil service, has grossly and pervasively shaped the opportunities available to African women in paid work and how far the fortunate ones can stretch their ambitions. Beyond the patriarchal barriers that limit African women's progress in the labor force, the gender expectations in the larger society spell out the relations of gender, including the division of labor, in terms that set boundaries on what women can do and how far they can go with these available choices. In specific terms, the expectations of marriage, child-rearing, son preference and maintenance of healthy relations between the nuclear and extended families render the challenge of juggling professional and socio-domestic responsibilities virtually overwhelming. As a primary role with a set of complicated demands (marriage, child bearing, son preference, etc.) embedded within its structure, the latter is placed at loggerheads with the former. Women leave out this dilemma and it becomes part of the daily life women accept with little or no opportunities to contest (Moshi, Okeke 2004). As the pattern is consistently thrust on educated women from one generation to another, one must ask the question—to what extent does their experience and training prepare them for this challenge? To what extent does it equip them with some critical tools for contesting a subjugated status from which they are expected to contribute to their own social mobility and society's progress?

Beyond the weak connections between tertiary education credentials and the challenge of juggling domestic and socioeconomic status, African women's presence in leadership and decision-making also lacks a substantive edge. This connection, many scholars argue, carries the strongest argument for women's training as well as the heaviest critique of its value today in their lives. But unfortunately, the connection is weak. With particular reference to women's presence in public administration, a pervasive trend has developed since the 'lost' decade of the 1980s, a trend that raises important questions not simply about the benefits of educational training to women but even more so about the value of education itself as an asset women could count on for their social mobility. The mid-1980s witnessed the beginning of a growing economic gap between public and private sector workers across Africa. The streamlining of the public service, privatization of public corporations and devaluation of national currencies—part of the severe Structural Adjustments Policy (SAP) packages handed down to African countries by international creditors—left many fewer male preserves. The gross depression in real wages across the length and breath of the formal sector has had far more impact on the civil service as African governments struggle with few resources to provide a reasonable cushion for workers left with little bargaining power to fight back. The brunt of this wage decline in the public sector has been steadily borne far more by women than by men since the former seem to be increasingly ghettoized in the latter (ILO 1989: 3-36). By the end of the 1980s, the public service witnessed a mass exodus of male workers in search of better opportunities elsewhere.

It was suggested in the early stages that the 'brain drain' benefited women, who were left behind to fill the gaps (UNECA 1990:21). But as the 'advantage' stretched into the next decade, its qualified nature became evident. In the first quarter of 1992, for instance, three thousand disgruntled professionals (mostly men) left the public service. These workers "did not rate their chances of advancement in the professional civil service" high enough to stay behind (News Report, *West Africa* 1992,

April 20-26, 683). Many of them opted, instead, for private business ventures. But even with their increasing representation in public service, women are yet to claim their share of the public service work force. The female workforce is increasing, but their representation continues to follow the pattern described above—men still maintain their grip on the few male preserves left. Men hold firmly to the spaces where administrative decision-making commands some currency in the corridors of power. A tiny female minority is often allowed to remain at the top but tokenized; even their political location is carefully guarded to ensure that they either have no voice or that their voices are caged in patriarchal cartilages that offset any potential to contest the status quo. Even with men's significant exodus from the civil service of many African countries over the past two decades, women, who have moved in considerable numbers, are yet to crack the reconstituted remnants of male preserves which house pockets of power held by the old boys clubs (UNECA 1999).

In similar terms, women have been kept outside African formal political forums with intermittent admittances as cheerleaders and token representatives. Indigenous African social formations developed elaborate and effective systems of governing society, especially at the grass roots level—systems that in many cases provided social spaces for women as daughters of extended families, heads of clans, older and revered citizens with ample wisdom to be tapped, leaders who governed in female forums usually inaccessible to men, and guardians who served as go-betweens between humans and the gods in matters of religion, health and social welfare (Mba 1982, Amadiume 1987). While generations of social change and upheaval have destroyed much of this social arrangement, little attempt has been made through women's training to make reconnections, especially in the face of the present governance failure across the continent. This traditional legacy has yet to significantly manifest in contemporary Africa, where women are grossly marginalized in both political forums. Their roles in formal politics are seriously constricted by a set of gender ideologies (hybridized along indigenous and western lines) constructed around their primary roles as wives and mothers (Fatton 1989, Nkiwane 2000). African women have been forced to build their political platforms around their socially acceptable roles in society, cautiously framing their demands to the state to avoid overstepping the boundaries, not as educated citizens well equipped like their male counterparts to handle the challenges of leadership. The historical patterns of African women's participation in political forums clearly show that African leaders have rarely taken the initiative to welcome them as full partners. African governments initially shunned, for the most part, the impact of global feminism on the home front, especially the heated intellectual discourse about African women's declining status. With time, and mostly as a result of pressures from the international community, many governments began to respond to the rise of women's organizations in their countries. From the mid-1970s and increasingly into the 1980s, African governments sought ways to integrate women into formal state machineries and political forums. For instance, during the United Nation's Decade for Women (1975-85), African male leaders unanimously voiced their concern for the well-being of women across the continent and gave official support to the major policy declarations that followed. Over the past three decades, the majority of African countries created state portfolios to address women's issues (over fifty countries in Africa have established state machineries) (Mama 1995). But whatever initiatives followed, these gestures have had little or no salutary effect on African women's plight.

The weak responses to women's concerns in African countries should not come as a surprise to anyone in the field. With regard to the treatment women receive, these governments have devised ingenuous ways of deflecting whatever threats they face within and outside national boundaries. A good number of African countries have deftly worked out a pattern of 'political showcasing'—invalid gestures, empty declarations, and deliberate trivialization of women's efforts at social advancement—all in a bid to present a good testimonial to the world outside.

In their official declarations and commitments, African leaders tend to embellish every word in the book with their desire to confront the 'woman question.' But when it comes to following up this desire with necessary action, they cleverly circumvent those patriarchal continuities and contradictions that pose a barrier to women's progress in contemporary society. Such moves are vividly portrayed in their approach to policy making and implementation. For instance, in 1990, African leaders and United Nations Agencies convened a meeting in Arusha, Tanzania, to address the economic, social and political crises that characterized a decade of Structural Adjustment Programs (SAPs) across Africa. The forum, which was dominated by men, brought together non-government organizations (NGOs), women collectives and youth groups to initiate strategies for mobilizing groups and individuals for Africa's economic recovery through democratic nation-building. Of the twenty-four declarations arrived at by the Arusha delegates, only two specifically addressed the conditions of African women's lives. These declarations stressed, as the excerpts below indicate, African women's crucial role in national development. But, in practical terms, they did not address those forums their strong intent to improve the situation, but are not prepared to tackle the structural and ideological barriers that militate against women's social mobility. More recent policy documents, such as the African Plan for Action (1995) and the New Partnership for Africa's Development in the twenty-first century (NEPAD, 2001), suggest a definite change in direction by African leaders but have yet to be followed through with the necessary directives for action (Lagos Platform for Action 1988, NEPAD 2001).

The wave of democratization that has been sweeping across Africa since the late 1980s seems to have added some momentum to women's mobilization. What appears to be emerging as fairly open political spaces in many African countries is propelling women's groups into public arenas where they can challenge the existing conservative political climate and insert women's political demands (Tripp 2001). But the structure of public governance in Africa remains undeveloped, with women at the margins; a tiny minority tokenized as ornaments showcase the benevolence of inherently patriarchal regimes (Okeke 1988, Mama 1995, Aubrey 2001). The process, a renowned critic argues, is inherently crippled by the "inability of such new 'popular' governments to take full control of the state, to set up structures to mediate and contain opposition and contradictions, and to meet, at the very least, some of the immediate expectations of the electorate," a common scenario that "can set a process of rapid de-legitimization in motion" (Ihonvbere 1995). Following a precedent set before the so-called democratic wave, African women's international profile continues to provide a mirror the states could exploit to polish their image (Amrita Basu, 1995, Okeke 1998, Staudt 1997). As Amina Mama aptly puts it,

> African governments have found it expedient to exploit the gender question so as to receive economic aid in an international climate that has become increasingly sympathetic towards women's demands for equality. The fact is that despite the virtual absence of mass-based women's movements in most African countries, the majority of African states have, for one reason or another, begun to profess a gender politics that is couched in terms of encouraging women's integration into development (1995: 38)

Other critiques of this trend clearly show that many African governments have over the past three decades succeeded in thwarting the efforts of women's organizations in the continent. In many cases, these governments either infiltrate the movements or create their own women's organizations to weaken the feminist surge. Many African states have facets of gender relations in the present social arrangement that stand in the way of women's advancement and full participation in nation-building.

12. In view of the critical contribution made by women to African societies and economies and the extreme subordination and discrimination suffered by women in Africa, it is... [our] consensus... that the attainment of equal rights by women in social, economic and political spheres must become a central feature of a democratic and participatory pattern of development.

14. In view of the vital and central role played by women in family well-being and maintenance, their special commitment to the survival, protection and development of children, as well as survival of society, and their important role in the process of Africa's recovery, ... special emphasis should be put by all the people in terms of eliminating biases ...with respect to the reduction of the burden on women UNECA 1990: 19-20.

These declarations invite a number of questions: How can African women participate as equal partners with men when they are hardly represented (in their own voices) in the forums where the substantive issues of social progress are deliberated upon? How will the burdens they carry be reduced when African women are continually placed in the role of sustainers, holding fort in the shadows and picking up the pieces of social destruction wrought by male ruling classes? The declarations above assert the need to move African women into the center of political mobilization and socioeconomic development in African nations, but not as equal partners with men. African women are recognized only in terms of their contributions as wives, mothers, and food farmers. Their 'crucial' contributions, and the social spaces within which women are expected to make them, are still rigidly tied to their subsistence roles. Narrowly defined, these roles reinforce the rigid social boundaries already drawn for women. Obviously, whatever social specifications these roles may have carried in the indigenous culture cannot be reproduced at present. But their constructions in contemporary terms embody obligations and boundaries that restrict women's entrance into the very public arenas African leaders seek for them. Thus, women's entrance into contemporary public arenas remains selective, with existing openings allowing very limited degrees of access. For example, women enter the open market with greater ease as petty traders rather than as commercial wholesalers. They are welcomed into formal political settings as cheerleaders on the sidelines rather than as contestants with men. Africa's male leaders make empty promises that acknowledge the burdens women carry, but are not prepared to confront the gender relations that affirm this state of affairs. They echo in the right installed their own brands of 'state feminism,' which are merely state-directed processes seemingly designed to advance women's status by integrating them into government machineries and the political system.[3] Obviously, the creation of spaces for women in public governance has neither expanded their sphere of collective action nor exerted much pressure on the state. If anything, state feminism in Africa has suppressed the voices of independent women's organizations outside its political grip. In the majority of cases, African governments are using these state-directed reforms to brush up their human rights image before Western donors, while silencing the progressive elements within the women's movement in their countries.

Even the much hailed increase in women's representation in African parliaments in just over a decade does not significantly deviate from an established pattern. Critical appraisals of how women in the continent are faring in this forum following the democratic fever that gripped the continent from the late 1980s support this assertion. Critical reflections in country case studies, bilateral comparisons and huge continental sweeps by scholars in the field of gender, social activism and politics in Africa raise hopeful as well as disturbing questions about the breadth and depth of women's penetration into Africa's decision-making forums. The analyses of the following connections: women as a socially subjugated constituency representing one-half of the population, their social activism within civil society, and their presence in decision making bodies point to the weak potential of their largely nominal political status (Tripp 2001, Okeke and Franceschet 2002). A close look at how African women are faring in parliament underscores the not-so-encouraging fact that the presence of female bodies in such forums is only one step towards women asserting themselves as equal partners with men in nation-building. In other words, women's nominal increase in such forums has been more 'the result of electoral and institutional engineering' than 'an automatic result of the opening of political spaces and processes' (IPU 2006). African women must therefore continue to wrestle with the challenge of finding and taking their place in the continent's decision-making bodies, and this challenge does not seem to rest in any significant way on their higher educational credentials.

This is not to say that barriers to their participation in shaping what happens in the larger society have completely prevented African women from mobilizing in various forms to project their voices in the corridors of power. Although far removed from the social locations of privilege their male counterparts lay claim to, women have made significant strides in public representation through gradual movements up the civil service ladder, political appointments, entrance into political decision-making forums through electoral quotas, and sheer rubbing of shoulders at the voting station. But those critically conscious of the patriarchal underpinnings of women's lives in Africa see a reflection of their subjugation as a social group in the dismal record of women's participation in public decision-making across the continent. The tentacles of patriarchy have an instinctive hold on every effort African women make to assert their citizenship in society. It defines their group interaction, sphere of action and degree of social support. These tentacles continue to undermine African women's struggle to mobilize beyond the boundaries outside which they would have to confront men, male establishments and strongholds (Chuku 2002, Okeke 2004). African women may be organizing around all kinds of issues but they have yet to question tradition where it holds down their progress. As Nadia Youseff (1995: 287) rightly asserted, "Women's organizations exist in Africa, but most are not the kind through which women can become empowered to use law or to effect changes to secure their rights." Women are left to bear much of the brunt of a social order burdened with archaic systems of gender relations inflexible to the demands of modernization in economic, social and political terms. If they existed, indigenous social spaces of power and authority have suffered the severe stranglehold of modernity, leaving women to seek concessions on very shaky platforms, wrapping their demands in ever so delicate a parcel to avoid stepping on the toes of the powers that be. African women's minimal political representation only underscores the definition of their role in the contemporary society; their place beside men in nation-building. Women's political representation in African reflects the narrow niche carved out for them in a contemporary society where they are expected to harness their efforts towards family subsistence, registering their presence in the public sphere only to the extent that it does not challenge their subordinate status beside men as brothers, fathers, husbands and leaders who hold the fort and chart the path.

The Challenge of Achieving Gender Equity in Africa's Higher Educational Institutions

Along similar lines we must address the following question: why do we push women's education so much when it does not seem to boost their capacity to improve their status, control their destiny or fully participate in directing social progress? If we agree that tertiary education has a place in addressing the barriers that cripple women's full participation in the larger society, an asset they could employ in fighting back, then it is time we begin to confront the conditions of their training as a major factor in deciphering why this asset is not as viable as we would expect.

The challenge of achieving gender equity in African tertiary institutions must begin with gradual steps that would harness the contributions of any available hand or agency. This is not a task that should rest solely on the shoulders of one obvious social group—women. African universities and the larger society have much to gain by including women in the task of producing knowledge. African women's situation does not stand apart from the common pattern characteristic of life in the developing world. But its patriarchal facets display their own peculiar features which give them potency in each cultural domain. In each case, culture appears to have outclassed other factors in marring women's political ambitions and efforts to join the relevant forums. Defined simply as the ways of life of a people, culture could easily shape women's and men's involvement in production, reproduction, resource use and distribution. The defense of such non-egalitarian systems bars those under its oppressive clutches from asking the question: Should tradition serve us or should we serve tradition? It is a similar state of affairs that bars Africa women from questioning (even when they enter the political forums) the underlying patriarchal assumptions which inform cultural practices such as women's usufruct access to land, the treatment of widows, and early marriage. A more decisive question buried within the literature on gender and development in Africa begs to be answered in political terms: is it in society's interest to maintain these practices or is it time for a trade-off between cultural practices and human development priorities such as progress in development, human rights and democracy (UNDP 2004)?

For all the educational credentials African women obtain, it would not do them much good to continue to acquiesce to the status quo in a situation where their present life conditions are clearly traceable to an "insufficient access to resources, a lack of political rights and social options"(Rodenberg 2002:1). At the very core of African women's struggle to be recognized as equal partners with men in nation-building is their denigration, apparent and subtle, in a contemporary society where their potential as productive citizens are exploited rather than nurtured for social progress.

It is not surprising that the dramatic upsurge in the number of African women entering tertiary education has hardly made any significant dent in the existing patterns of gender inequities in contemporary society (e.g.: formal employment, political participation, and public decision-making). This suggests that improvements in gender representation should, at the very least, go hand in hand with a transformation of both the knowledge imparted as well as the social milieu within which learning takes place. It is important that we nurture an environment which encourages men and women to recognize the potential contributions they could make to social change, enables them to share available educational opportunities, and plays a key role in structuring the inherent prospects to benefit individuals and society without any social bias.

Tertiary training cast in this light would not merely prepare men and women to adapt to life in the larger society but would also provide sites for re-examining, contesting and reconfiguring 'the-way-it-is' for the better. It presupposes that we make women agents of change, not simply standing in the shadows, doing charity work, and hoping that their good work will turn the hearts of the powers-that-be, from whom they must curry favor. Changing society, in part, means contestation on certain issues. In many cases, it inevitably means asking questions about the division of labor, the sharing of resources and the already accepted paths for obtaining social justice. As Ayesha Imam (1997) clearly points out to those who challenge the gender biases and other social inequalities inherent in contemporary African societies, the task, among other things, "is also necessarily and simultaneously profoundly a political struggle over power and resources."

African scholars must come to the realization that for change to occur, it must be matched with the zeal to pursue it—by challenging their colleagues and students (male and female alike) to reexamine the status. We must begin to articulate a vision of women's training which equips them with more than coping strategies to protect a status that may be envied by those less privileged, one that instills in our young women the intellectual capacity to rethink their place in society. It is within such an inclusive vision that we can define tertiary education as an asset that offers women the same benefits as men.

Notes

[1] Compared to many other sub-Saharan African Countries, South Africa has established a much longer history of women's education with a stronger participation at the tertiary level.

[2] Although the information provided appears to fit the specifications of existing literature, the data should be treated with some caution since some statistics are more dated than others. The calculations are based on annual statistics of member countries obtained from the UIS website.

[3] Philomina Okeke and Susan Franceschet, "Democratisation and State Feminism: Gender Politics in Africa and Latin America," *Development and*

Change, 3 (2002), 439-33; Kole Shettima, "Engendering Nigeria's Third Republic," *African Studies Review,* 38, 3 (December, 1995), 61-98.

PART IV

LEGAL FRAMEWORK, HUMAN RIGHTS, CONFLICT, AND ECONOMIC EMPOWERMENT

CHAPTER ELEVEN
IMAGINE ALL THE WOMEN
Power, Gender and the Transformative Possibilities of the South African Constitution
Penelope E. Andrews

> It is argued here that a creative jurisprudence of equality coupled with substantive interpretation of the content of 'socio-economic' rights should restore social justice as a premier foundational value of our constitutional democracy side by side, if not interactively with, human dignity, equality, freedom, accountability, responsiveness and openness.[1]

Introduction

This chapter will explore the South African Constitution, and more particularly, the Bill of Rights, as a vehicle for social and economic transformation. By analyzing the provisions relating to gender equality in South Africa's Constitution, as well as decisions of the Constitutional Court, this chapter will examine whether the constitutional rights framework in South Africa contains within it the transformative possibilities[2] that will lead to gender equality in all spheres of South African society, and particularly in the economic sphere. Karl Klare refers to transformative constitutionalism as

> a long-term project of constitutional enactment, interpretation, and enforcement committed (not in isolation, of course, but in a historical context of conducive political developments) to transforming a country's political and social institutions and power relationships in a democratic, participatory, and egalitarian direction."[3]

This chapter's focus on women as a group should not be seen as detracting from the contemporary social reality, where the condition of poverty affects a large number of South Africans of all genders.[4] However, black women continue to be disproportionately represented in all negative indicators, including poverty, rates of unemployment, and occurrence of AIDS. The analysis in this chapter proceeds on the belief that women's access to resources and women's economic empowerment is integrally linked to the legal, political and social conditions that create the possibilities for such access and empowerment. Sandra Liebenberg explains the transformative potential of the South African constitutional framework:

> Unlike many classic liberal constitutions, its primary concern is not to restrain State power, but to facilitate a fundamental change in unjust political, economic and social relations in South Africa.[5]

In line with this theme of transformation, and attempting to provide a comprehensive approach to gender equality, the analysis in this chapter not only references the constitutional text and constitutional jurisprudence that focus on socio-economic rights, but also engages with constitutional text and decisions that articulate a vision of equality, a constitutional proscription of violence against women, and cultural impediments that may thwart the quest for gender equality.

Constitutionalism and Socio-Economic Rights

In South Africa's evolving constitutional democracy, constitutional adjudication is a central component of the basic governance structure. Such a framework, at least symbolically, signifies that the needs and interests of the poor are a matter of national public concern. In addition, such a framework raises the possibility of removing the socio-economic barriers to full citizenship.[6] The inclusion of social and economic rights in the constitution therefore converts the issue of the needs of the poor into the realm of legal entitlement. As the South African scholar Daniel Brand notes:

> First, courts' adjudication of socio-economic rights claims becomes part of the political discourse, even a medium through which this discourse partly plays out. Second, courts also occupy a symbolic, or perhaps more accurately, an exemplary, role with respect to poverty and need discourses—their vocabulary, the conceptual structures they rely on, the rhetorical strategies they employ infiltrate and so influence and shape the political discourses around poverty and need.[7]

Although Karl Klare has cautioned that the "decision" to "accomplish some significant portion" of the law-making process "through adjudication" is one "fraught with institutional consequences,"[8] litigating in the pursuit of socio-economic rights opens up great possibilities for women. For women, especially black women, the Constitution's incorporation of a host of socio-economic rights, and particularly its transformative potential, as outlined above, is an important antidote to the axis of gender subordination: namely, poverty, violence and custom.[9]

This chapter is limited in scope. Although it highlights the powerful symbolic and substantive possibilities of the constitutionalizing of socio-economic rights and rendering such rights fully justiciable, it does not address key economic questions that are central to reducing poverty.[10] In addition, it highlights merely one aspect of the relationship between law and economic development, namely, the possibilities generated by the constitutional enforcement of rights.[11] The prevalence of poverty, as a recurring reality of the majority of Africa's population, including South Africa, continues to be an issue of global concern that has taxed the creativity of a range of scholars.[12]

There is a vast body of literature pointing to the limitations of rights discourse in the face of economic structures that reinforce economic inequality.[13] Legal scholars such as Upendra Baxi and Boa de Sousa Santos have eloquently argued that the language of human rights has in effect replaced the language of economic redistribution and thereby has appropriated other ethical discourses.[14] Indeed, the seductive possibilities generated by litigation for social and economic rights may disproportionately influence communities, especially women, to redirect their attention from non-legal transformative strategies that may produce a deeper and more enduring economic, political and social justice.[15] This debate is a vigorous one within the contemporary human rights community of scholars and advocates, and is also a hackneyed one reminiscent of the earlier civil rights struggle of the United States.[16]

By integrating the questions of women's economic empowerment within the context of violence against women and customs that impede women's equality, I am influenced by the critical voices of legal scholars who insist on a comprehensive intersectional approach to rights. I am in particular referring to the scholarship of Angela Harris and Taunya Banks, who exhort us to eschew essentialism in theorizing women's subordination.[17] In addition, Amanda Gouws has attempted in her work to deconstruct the gendered nature of South African citizenship in its many guises.[18] The approach of the South African Bill of Rights, namely, an expanded notion of equality, distinguishes it from many other constitutional projects, notably that of the United States. In South Africa, constitutional adjudication occurs in a context that recognizes that disadvantage and discrimination are deeply embedded in the political, economic and legal systems, and that the legacy of apartheid and sexism will continue into the foreseeable future.[19] The constitutional text and its interpretation are therefore predicated on a need to derogate purposively from the status quo. As the first President of the Constitutional Court has noted:

> We live in a society in which there are great disparities in wealth. Millions of people are living in deplorable conditions and in great poverty. There is a high level of unemployment, inadequate social security, and many do not have access to clean water or to adequate health services. These conditions already existed when the Constitution was adopted, and a commitment to address them, and to transform our society into one in which there will be human dignity, freedom and equality, lies at the heart of our new constitutional order.[20]

In other words, both text and interpretation are mandated to transform social and economic relations.[21]

Rights Protected in the South African Constitution

The South African Constitution, in particular the Bill of Rights, has been universally heralded as one of the most impressive human rights documents of the twentieth century.[22] Section 1 states very clearly the supremacy of the Constitution, and also states that the new democratic state is founded on values that include "human dignity and the achievement of equality" as well as "non-racialism and non-sexism." The Constitution's generous coverage of a broad range of categories of discrimination, including race, gender, sexual orientation, and national origin, seeks to reassure all South Africans that discrimination in its obvious, as well as intricate variations, will not be tolerated.[23]

Covering both direct and indirect discrimination[24] and recognition of the tenacity of institutionalized discrimination, the Bill of Rights also covers "intersectional discrimination," noting that "no person may unfairly discriminate directly or indirectly against anyone *on one or more grounds.*"[25] Judge Goldstone, in an early gender equality case, noted the complex relationships among the prohibited grounds of discrimination, exhorting against the temptation to force them into neatly self-contained grounds.[26]

This comprehensive definition of equality also embodies a clear commitment to affirmative action, which provides that:

> To promote the achievement of equality, legislative and other measures designed to protect or advance persons, or categories of persons, disadvantaged by unfair discrimination may be taken.[27]

In addition, the Bill of Rights outlaws violence against women in both the public and private sphere,[28] as well as protecting a woman's right to "bodily and psychological integrity," including the "right to make decisions concerning reproduction."[29] The Bill of Rights also protects freedom of expression given that it does not involve advocacy of hatred based on race, ethnicity, gender or religion, and that it does not constitute incitement to cause harm.[30]

But the incorporation of socio-economic rights arguably holds the key to unraveling much of the subordination and disadvantage that disproportionately burden women. Most particularly, these rights that incorporate education,[31] housing,[32] health care, food, water and social security,[33] provide, at least within the formal legal paradigm, a limited access for women to pursue some form of economic empowerment.

The rights of children are comprehensively embraced, especially as they relate to their social and economic well-being. Children are therefore given the right to "basic nutrition, shelter, basic health care services and social services."[34] Children are also protected from "maltreatment, neglect, abuse or degradation"[35] and "exploitative labor practices."[36] These rights are provided on demand, and the provision does not include the limitation found in other socio-economic rights in the Bill of Rights, namely, that the state provide them progressively and "within its available resources."

Although the Constitution is clear about the rights of cultural, religious or linguistic communities to "enjoy their culture, practice their religion and use their language,"[37] they cannot do so if those practices violate the principle of equality. This provides women in those distinct communities significant protections, ensuring that their membership in their discrete communities is not compromised by their being relegated to a second-class status. The Constitution embodies several bodies to promote the rights in the Bill of Rights, including the Human Rights Commission and the Commission for Gender Equality.[38]

The Constitutional Court's Rights Interpretation

Since its establishment in 1995, the Constitutional Court has had occasion to consider the application and interpretation of equality, particularly gender equality, and has for the most part articulated a definition of equality that considers comprehensively the many ways that South African women experience discrimination and disadvantage. The Court has elaborated at length what equality means, and in its several judgments has applied the equality principle in a manner that is mindful of the context in which the discrimination occurs, and the lived reality of the parties under consideration. In addition, the Court has focused on the goal of the Constitution, namely, the achievement of dignity and equality for all South Africans. The Court has therefore embraced a substantive definition of equality, as opposed to a mere formalistic one, in effect focusing on the disparate impact of laws, policies and practices, as opposed to their strict equal treatment of the genders.[39]

One of the first cases on gender equality involved an unmarried father who challenged the provisions of the Child Care Act, which permitted the adoption of children born out of wedlock without the consent of the father.[40] For children born in wedlock, the consent of both parents was required. The father successfully challenged the law and it was declared unconstitutional. In evaluating the Child Care Act, and particularly the gender equality issues raised in this case, the late Justice Mahomed noted:

> In considering appropriate legislative alternatives, parliament should be acutely sensitive to the deep disadvantage experienced by single mothers in our society. Any legislative initiative should not exacerbate that disadvantage.[41]

Adopting a contextual approach, the Court stated that a mother's "biological relationship with the child," nurtured during pregnancy and breastfeeding, is a special one.[42] The Court also noted that the mother gives "succor and support" to a child that is "very direct and not comparable to that of a father."[43] In its analysis, the Court surveyed the several systems of marriage in South Africa, including some that were not formal.[44] Children who were products of such informal unions were rendered illegitimate, therefore disposing of the father's permission for adoption. Such situations of non-recognition placed fathers at an enormous disadvantage *vis a vis* their children with respect to adoption, and were therefore discriminatory. In addition, the Court also considered that the core issue was really the relationship between a father and a child, and that the statute was too broad in its blanket exclusion of the need for an unmarried father's permission for adoption of his child. The Constitutional Court, however, citing the best interest of the child, declined to allow further appeal to set aside the adoption, but instructed Parliament to remedy the situation in a revised statute.

The second case, one in which the Court's analysis provides a lengthy blueprint for the approach to equality in South Africa, has been fairly controversial. In this case the applicant, a convicted prisoner, challenged a Presidential pardon that pardoned certain categories of prisoners, including women in prison, who had children under the age of twelve at the time of South Africa's first election.[45]

Hugo challenged the Presidential pardon on the basis that it violated his constitutional rights to equality and that it discriminated against him on the basis of gender. The Court, in its judgment, went through an elaborate discussion of equality. It then applied the two-pronged test outlined in the Constitution, namely, that if discrimination is alleged and found on any of the particular grounds, such as race, gender, and marital status, that finding creates a presumption of unfairness.[46] The person against whom the allegation of discrimination is made must then rebut the presumption of unfairness by showing the validity of the action. The Court, in its analysis, looked at the Presidential pardon and found it to be unfair; the need for the President to rebut the presumption arose. The Court examined the reasons for the Presidential pardon, including an evaluation of those who would benefit from the pardon. These included children whose mothers or fathers were in prison.

The Court then examined the other group who benefited from the pardon, namely,
women, the most disadvantaged group in South African society. The Court acknowledged that mothers are the primary caregivers of children, but it also recognized that this reinforced a stereotype about women, child-caring, and child-rearing. Despite this, Justice O'Regan noted:

> To determine whether the discrimination is unfair it is necessary to recognize that although the long-term goal of our constitutional order is equal treatment, insisting upon equal treatment in all circumstances of established inequality may well result in the entrenchment of that inequality.[47]

The Court adopted a pragmatic approach and tried to place the issue in the South African context. Observing that women have historically been discriminated against, the Court's approach to equality will likely benefit but it will not perpetuate a disadvantage.

> In this case, mothers have been afforded an advantage on the basis of a proposition that is generally speaking true. There is no doubt that the goal of equality entrenched in our constitution would be better served if the responsibilities of child-rearing were more fairly shared between fathers and mothers. The simple fact is that at present they are not.[48]

Disputing that women are put at a disadvantage when they are perceived as the primary caregivers of children, Justice O'Regan noted further:

> The profound disadvantage lies not in the President's statement, but in the social fact of the role played by mothers in child-rearing and, more

particularly, in the inequality which results from it. There can be no doubt that where reliance upon the generalization results in greater disadvantage for mothers, it would almost without question constitute unfair discrimination.[49]

The dissent forcefully challenged the stereotypes the majority opinion appeared to perpetuate, stating that the Constitution is meant to be transformative. Part of that transformative vision is not to reinforce old stereotypes, but to pursue a vision in which, in this case, fathers are also seen as caregivers of children. The dissent objected strongly to the pragmatic approach that the majority took. Justice Kriegler insisted that where some rebuttal is provided for the presumption of unfairness, such rebuttal must be scrutinized thoroughly and must not be "discharged with relative ease."[50] He took issue with the rationale that women were the primary caregivers of young children, stating this generalization to be

> a root cause of women's inequality in our society. It is both a result and a cause of prejudice: a societal attitude which relegates women to a subservient, occupationally inferior yet unceasingly onerous role. It is a relic and feature of the patriarchy which the Constitution so vehemently condemns.[51]

The majority had considered an alternative, that is, to release fathers of children under the age of twelve, but in assessing this alternative, noted first that there are significantly larger numbers of male prisoners in South Africa than female prisoners, so the numbers of men who would be released would be enormous. Second, the Court recognized the serious problem of crime in South Africa and the public outcry that would follow a large release of male prisoners. The dissenting opinion voiced its alarm at the stereotypes that were reinforced in the majority's judgment.[52] The Hugo decision, although controversial, has been praised in many quarters for specifically contextualizing women's oppression and the discrimination that women suffer in South Africa. But the Court has had difficulty coming to grips with a vision or articulation of equality that some commentators have argued is inconsistent.[53]

The Court has expanded its vision on equality to examine the impact of violence on women's equality. In 2000 the Constitutional Court confronted a challenge to the constitutionality of a provision in the Prevention of Family Violence Act which, it was argued, reversed the onus of proof in domestic violence matters and thus violated the right of an accused person to be presumed innocent.[54] The issue arose out of the conviction of the appellant in the lower court for breaking an interdict issued by the court asking him not to assault his wife or prevent her or other clients from entering or leaving their homes. He was found guilty under the Prevention of Family Violence Act of 1993. He argued that the section under which he was arrested was unconstitutional to the extent that it placed an onus on him to prove no guilt. Justice Sachs, writing for the majority in a unanimous decision, embarked on a thoughtful analysis of the need to deal comprehensively and effectively with the problem of domestic violence. He described the "hidden, repetitive character" of domestic violence, its ubiquity in cutting across class, race, culture and geographic boundaries, and the deleterious consequences for society of its persistence. He characterized domestic violence as a matter of gender equality, noting that because of the gender-specific nature of domestic violence, it mirrored patriarchal domination in a particularly abhorrent manner. In proceeding to analyze the conflicting rights at stake, the Court found that the presumption of innocence had not been disturbed because there were other mechanisms in place to ensure an "accessible, speedy, simple and effective" process.

This judgment follows the *Hugo* and *Fraser* decisions in contextualizing the contemporary reality of South African women. In South Africa widespread violence against women in both the public and private sphere is a cause for great concern. Indeed, some would argue that such violence constitutes a continual violation of women's human rights.[55] Justice Sachs, writing for the majority, forcefully acknowledges the need to eradicate such violence without constraining the constitutional rights of the perpetrators.

Feminist advocates and human rights advocates have argued that private violence, indeed any violence, against women is odious, and that the state ought to deal with this problem aggressively. Although the *Baloyi* decision gives some succor to victims of domestic violence, there is still some dissonance between certain cultural attitudes, fueled by a particular brand of South African masculinity that gives rise to such violence, and the laudable statements of the Court.[56] Closing this gap will require a recognition that the structural and attitudinal impediments to the "right to be free from private violence"[57] as articulated in the Bill of Rights can only be eradicated by a combination of governmental assaults which include education, access to resources, and continued vigilance regarding the extent and persistence of violence. The Constitutional Court, at least, is doing its part, but it needs to be bolstered by other institutional arrangements that will include both legal and extra-legal measures.

It is with respect to the implementation of socio-economic rights that the Constitution holds much promise. The Constitutional Court's decisions regarding the enforcement of socio-economic rights has shown that these rights can bring meaningful relief to the poorest in the country. In 2000 the Constitutional Court had to consider the right to housing as incorporated in Section 26.[58] Although the Court had had occasion to interpret the right to health a few years prior,[59] the *Grootboom* decision was awaited with much anticipation and is widely regarded as an international test case on the enforceability of social and economic rights.[60] The case concerned an application for temporary shelter brought by a group of people, including a number of children, who were without shelter following their brutal eviction from private land on which they were squatting. The conditions under which the community lived were deplorable; they had access to one tap and no sanitation facilities. The Court affirmed that the government had a duty in terms of Section 26 of the Constitution (the right to adequate housing) to adopt reasonable policy, legislative and budgetary measures to provide relief for people who have no access to land, no roof over their heads, and who are living in intolerable conditions. Justice Yacoob, writing for a unanimous court noted:

> I am conscious that it is an extremely difficult task for the state to meet these obligations in the conditions that prevail in our country. This is recognized by the Constitution, which expressly provides that the state is not obliged to go beyond available resources or to realize these rights immediately. I stress however, that despite all these qualifications, these are rights, and the Constitution obliges the state to give effect to them. This is an obligation that courts can, and in appropriate circumstances, must enforce.[61]

The judgment also dealt in detail with the implications of the children's socio-economic rights enshrined in the Bill of Rights.

Although this decision has been widely hailed as setting an important precedent for the enforcement of socio-economic rights at both the local and global level, many commentators have expressed disappointment in the Court's focus on "reasonableness." They instead argue that the Court should have applied the "minimum core approach" as adopted in the interpretation of the International Covenant on Economic, Social and Cultural Rights.[62]

In The Treatment Action case,[63] the appeal to the Constitutional Court was directed at reversing orders made in a high court against the government because of perceived shortcomings in its response to an aspect of the HIV/AIDS challenge. The court found that the government had not reasonably addressed the need to reduce the risk of HIV-positive mothers' transmitting the disease to their babies at birth. More specifically, the finding was that government had acted unreasonably in (a) refusing to make an anti-retroviral drug called *nevirapine* available in the public health sector where the attending doctor considered it medically indicated, and in (b) not setting out a time frame for a national program to prevent mother-to-child transmission of HIV.

In addition to focusing on the positive aspects of socio-economic rights, that is, the obligation of the state to provide certain rights, the Court has also focused on what has been seen as the negative component of socio-economic rights. In a case involving the protection of a tenant against eviction in the process of executing a judgment on debts, the Court held that such a process violated the constitutional right to housing.[64]

In another landmark judgment in 2001,[65] and one which has profound ramifications for development of the common law, the Constitutional Court considered a claim by a woman who had been attacked and seriously injured by a man who was at the time awaiting trial for rape. In spite of a previous conviction for indecent assault and a history of violent behavior towards women, he had been released unconditionally on his own recognizance in the rape matter—despite repeated requests by the victim and other members of the community to keep the assailant in custody. The victim sued the police and prosecution for their negligent failure to take proactive steps to protect her as a potential further victim. A unanimous court stated that the Constitution embodies an objective, normative value system that must shape the common law. The Constitution obliged the state to respect, protect, promote and fulfill the rights in the Bill of Rights, including the right of women to have their safety and security protected. The Constitutional Court found in her favor, namely, that the state officials had a legal duty to take steps to prevent further violent actions by the perpetrator, and referred the matter back to the trial court for determination of further issues in the tort claim. At the later trial the Cape High Court found for the plaintiff and ruled that the state was indeed liable.

In one of the most remarkable judgments of the Constitutional Court, one that has tremendous potential in redressing the structural disadvantages that women experience under customary law, the Court in a detailed and far-reaching judgment struck down the customary African legal principle of primogeniture as it applies to the law of succession, which prevented female children from inheriting when their father died intestate.[66] The applicants in the cases were two minor daughters of the deceased and the sister of an unmarried brother. They had been denied the right to be declared heirs; male relatives instead stood to inherit the property of the deceased. What was particularly significant about the cases was the involvement of the Women's Legal Center, a women's legal advocacy organization in Cape Town that conducted a major campaign around the issues raised by the case.[67]

Possibilities and Limitations of the Constitutional Pursuit of Socio-Economic Rights

An examination of post-apartheid developments reveals that the narrative of the trajectory of gender equality in South African embodies profound contradictions. On the one hand, South Africa ranks as one of the top democracies in the world with respect to women's representation in Parliament, including an impressive number of Ministers, Deputy-Ministers, and parliamentarians. The speaker of Parliament is a woman, and several females hold top ambassadorial posts.[68]

These impressive statistics exist alongside the alarming reality of severe poverty amongst women and children, and the shocking reality of violence against women. Indeed, all research indicators suggest that widespread rape and domestic violence against women has reached epidemic proportions.[69] This apparent contradiction between impressive statistics regarding female involvement in the formal political system—particularly in national governance—on the one hand, and widespread poverty and systemic violence against women on the other, raises troubling questions. This chapter therefore argues that violence against women and its cultural underpinnings are an obstacle to economic development overall, and specifically to the capacity of women to enjoy the benefits promised in the constitutional framework.[70] Moreover, despite solid steps taken by the South African government to improve the plight of women, including the provision of housing and improved access to education and other social and economic benefits, aggressive governmental intervention is imperative in reversing the legacy of apartheid and its disproportionate impact on black women. The gap between the expansive provisions in South Africa's Constitution and the underlying reality of the lives of the majority of South Africa's women raises troubling questions regarding the possibilities of legal change in the face of extra-legal structural impediments to women's equality. At its most basic, this gap raises the question about how a country with such an admirable Constitution and Bill of Rights—with equality at the core—could elude the majority of women its promises and possibilities.[71]

This question is even more perplexing in light of a decade of extraordinary equality jurisprudence generated by the Constitutional Court, as outlined above, in which the judges eschew a formal equality for a more substantive version. The Court has committed itself, if not always successfully, to a transformative vision that centers on women's equality and the right to dignity.[72] In addition, even though the interpretation of socio-economic rights by the Court has for the most part been of limited effect, the Court has provided an overarching framework that allows some possibilities for creative legal advocacy, in conjunction with other non-legal methods of advocacy, to address women's poverty.

The answer to the question, obviously a complex one, may be located in the realm of the particular version of masculinity, a by-product of colonialism and apartheid. This masculinity, embodying indigenous and Western forms of patriarchy, persists despite the constitutional commitment to equality.[73] This dilemma is not peculiar to South Africa, for South Africa is in many ways also a microcosm of other societies, particularly those in the developing world that confront tensions, conflicts and ambiguities in pursuing rights for women. These contradictions also are present in affluent societies, but the reality of pervasive poverty and weak state institutions bedevils the quest for equality in poorer countries. South Africa's ongoing attempts to pursue rights for women therefore are constantly challenged, and often compromised, by this masculinist ethos that constitutional guarantees can only erode so far.

In addition to the conditions of severe economic inequalities and the disturbing patterns of private and public violence against women, as mentioned above, the HIV/AIDS epidemic and its collateral consequences severely impede the quest for women's equality. Many rights are compromised by women's inability to access economic resources. For example, it is extremely difficult for women still caught in a cycle of economic dependency and powerlessness to prevent HIV infection or to gain access to treatment for AIDS. The core issue, really, is how a society is to internalize the formal legal framework that promises gender equality and translate it into a human rights culture.

Conclusion

In the final analysis, the existence of an expansive constitution is only a precondition for legal and other changes. Scholars and advocates have noted that despite laudable efforts by women's groups to incorporate women's rights into the democratic legal framework, including urging the government to pursue a gendered legislative agenda, much work still needs to be done. The constitutional and legal foundations have provided a framework for some possibilities to transform, or at least alter, women's lives for the better.[74] However, the privatized nature of the South African economy and the imperatives of a market-driven agenda may undermine the transformative possibilities of the Constitution. It is widely recognized that women suffer disproportionately from the failure of government to provide adequately for health, education, social welfare services, and the other needs of the population, just like women suffer disproportionately when government cutbacks occur. The South African constitutional paradigm has not provided a vehicle to fundamentally challenge the South African government's economic policies. The Court has merely ensured that government policy takes account of its constitutional mandate. Consequently, the Constitution cannot comprehensively overturn the deep structural inequalities that face women in South Africa today; it may, however, force the powers that be not to ignore these inequalities.

Regarding gender equality, at most, the South African constitutional framework may demonstrate that a comprehensive constitutional and legal framework is necessary. But it also highlights that a constitutional and legal framework must be bolstered by an overarching vision that seeks to transform institutions, laws and practices that subjugate women. In addition, it must be supplanted by a cultural shift across all sectors of society—a shift that takes on board comprehensively the need to eradicate gender inequality in the social, political and economic spheres.

Notes

[1] D. Moseneke, "Transformative Adjudication," *South African Journal of Human Rights* 309, 314 (2002).

[2] Karl Klare, "Legal Culture and Transformative Constitutionalism," *South African Journal of Human Rights* 146 (1998).

[3] Ibid, 150.

[4] See *Sixth Economic and Social Rights Report*, South African Human Rights Commission (2006) at http://www.sahrc.org.za/sahrc_cms/publish/article_215.html.

[5] Sandra Liebenberg, "Needs, Rights and Social Transformation: Adjudicating Social Rights," *Center For Human Rights And Global Justice Working Paper*, Economic And Social Rights Series, Number 8, 2005.

[6] Penelope E. Andrews, "The South African Constitution as a Mechanism for Redressing Poverty," in *Democratic Reform in Africa: Its Impact on Governance & Poverty Alleviation* (Muna Ndulo, ed. 2006) 57.

[7] D. Brand, "The Politics of Need Interpretation and the Adjudication of Socio-Economic Rights Claims in South Africa," in *Theories Of Social And Economic Justice* (A.J. Van der Walt ed. 2005) 17, 24.

[8] Karl Klare, *Legal Culture and Transformative Constitutionalism, supra* note 3 at 147.

[9] I am using the term "custom" very loosely here. It refers to the range of cultural practices and norms that underpin attitudes that embrace notions of female inferiority.

[10] So it does not, for example, engage with the South African government's economic policies, or the manner in which resource allocation is determined by the South African state. For an interesting exploration of these economic issues, see Nicoli Nattrass And Jeremy Seekings, *Class Race and Inequality in South Africa* (2005).

[11] See Penelope E. Andrews, *The South African Constitution as a Vehicle for Redressing Poverty,* supra note 6. See also Murray Wesson, "Grootboom and Beyond: Reassessing Socio-Economic Jurisprudence of the South African Constitutional Court," 20 *South African Journal on Human Rights* 284 (2004).

[12] See, for example, Paul Collier, *The Bottom Billion: Why The Poorest Countries Are Failing And What To Do About It* (2007); Jeffrey D. Sachs, *The End Of Poverty* (2006) And William Easterly, *The White Man's Burden* (2006).

[13] See, for example, Amartya Sen, *Development As Freedom* (1999); Makau wa Mutua, "The Ideology of Human Rights," 36, *Virginia Journal Of International Law* 589 (1996); Philip Alston, "The Myopia of the Handmaidens: International Lawyers and Globalization," 8 *European Journal Of International Law* 435 (1998); and Andy McKay and Polly Vizard, *Human Rights And Poverty Reduction* (March 2005) at http://www.odi.org.uk/publications/\ briefing.html#books.

[14] Upendra Baxi, "Voices of Suffering and the Future of Human Rights," 8 *Transnational Law & Contemporary Problems* 125, 147 (1998); Boaventura De Sousa Santos, *Toward A New Common Sense: Law Science And Politics In The Paradigmatic Transition* 266-67 (1995).

[15] See Bharati Sadasivam, "The Impact of Structural Adjustment on Women: A Governance and Human Rights Agenda," 19 *Human Rights Quarterly* 630 (1997); see also *Economic Justice And Women's Rights,* (Madre), at http://www.madre.org/articles/into/b10/ econjustice.html.

[16] See Thomas E. Jackson, *From Civil Rights To Human Rights* (2006).

[17] See Taunya Lovell Banks, "Toward A Global Critical Feminist Vision: Domestic Work and the Nanny Tax Debate," 3 *Journal of Gender, Race and Justice* 1 (1999); and Angela P. Harris, "Race and Essentialism in Feminist Legal Theory," 42 *Stanford Law Review* 581 (1990).

[18] See *Unlinking Citizenship* (Amanda Gouws ed. 2005).

[19] *Government of South Africa and others v Grootboom and others* 2001 (1) Sa 46 Paragraph 25.

[20] *Soobramoney v Minister of Health, KwaZulu-Natal* 1998 (1) SA 765 (CC) at Paragraph 8.

[21] It is worth noting here that the South African Constitution mandates the South African Human Rights Commission to pursue the enforcement of social and economic rights through education, lobbying and monitoring of human rights. Specifically, Section 184 mandates that the South African Human Rights Commission *promote respect for human rights and a culture of human rights; promote the protection, development and attainment of human rights; and monitor and assess the observance of human rights.* This section also empowers the Commission *to investigate and to report on the assessment of human rights; to educate, carry out research and to redress human rights violations.*

[22] See, for example, Craig Scott and Phillip Alston, "Adjudicating Constitutional Priorities in a Transnational Context: A Comment on Soobramoney's Legacy and Grootboom's Promise," 16 *South African Journal on Human Rights* 206 (2000).

[23] *Constitution of the Republic of South Africa (1996) [Consitution]*. Section 9 (3) provides that: *The state may not unfairly discriminate directly or indirectly against anyone on one or more grounds, including race, gender, sex, pregnancy, marital status, ethnic or social origin, color, sexual orientation, age, disability, religion, conscience, belief, culture, language and birth.*

[24] *Ibid.*

[25] *Ibid.* Section 9 (4) (Emphasis added).

[26] *President of the Republic Of South Africa v Hugo* (1997) (6) BCLR 708 (CC). For a comprehensive discussion on the intersection of race and gender, see Penelope E. Andrews, "Human Rights, Globalization and Critical Race Feminism: Voices from the Margins," 3 *Journal of Gender Race & Justice 373* (2000); see also Adrien Wing & Eunice Carvalho, "Black South African Women: Towards Equal Rights," 8 *Harvard Human Rights Journal 8* (1995).

[27] *Constitution*, supra note 24, Section 9 (2).

[28] *Ibid.* Section 12 (1).

[29] *Ibid.* Section 12 (2).

[30] *Ibid.* Section 16 (2).

[31] Section 29 provides that: Everyone has the right
   (a) to a basic education, including adult basic education; and
   (b) to further education, which the state, through reasonable measures, must make progressively available and accessible. *Ibid.*

[32] Section 26 provides that:
   1. Everyone has the right to have access to adequate housing.
   2. The state must take reasonable legislative and other measures, within its available resources, to achieve the progressive realization of this right. *Ibid.*

[33] Section 27 provides that everyone has the right to have access to:
   (a) health care services, including reproductive health care,
   (b) sufficient food and water, and
   (c) social security, including, if they are unable to support themselves and their dependants, appropriate social assistance. The state must take reasonable legislative and other measures, within its available resources, to achieve the progressive realization of this right. *Ibid.*

[34] *Ibid.* Section 28 (1) (c).

[35] *Ibid.* Section 28 (1) (d).

[36] *Ibid.* Section 28 (1) e). This section also provides that children have the right:
   ... not to be required or permitted to perform work or provide services that are (i) inappropriate for a person of that child's age; or (ii) place at

risk the child's well-being, education, physical or mental health or spiritual, moral or social development. *Ibid.* Section 28 (1) (f).

[37] *Ibid.* Section 31.

[38] *Ibid.* Section 181 (1). This section also includes the Public Protector and The Commission for the Promotion and Protection of the Rights of Cultural, Religious and Linguistic Communities.

[39] As Justice Goldstone noted in *President of the Republic of South Africa v Hugo, supra* note 27:
At heart of the prohibition of unfair discrimination lies a recognition that the purpose of our new constitutional ..... order is the establishment of a society in which all human beings will be accorded equal dignity and respect regardless of their membership of particular groups. *Ibid* at paragraph 41.

[40] *Fraser v The Children's Court, Pretoria North* 1997 (2) BCLR 153 (CC)..

[41] *Ibid.* at Paragraph 44.

[42] *Ibid.* Paragraph 25.

[43] *Ibid.*

[44] To address aspects of this problem, the South African government passed the *Recognition of Customary Marriages Act* in 1998.

[45] *President of the Republic of South Africa v Hugo, supra* note 27.

[46] Constitution, *supra* note 24. Section 9 (5) states: Discrimination . . . is unfair unless it is established that the discrimination is fair.

[47] *President of the Republic of South Africa v Hugo, supra* note 25 at Paragraph 112.

[48] *Ibid* at Paragraph 113.

[49] *Ibid.*

[50] *Ibid.*

[51] *Ibid.*

[52] Justice Kriegler concluded that a small number of women would benefit from the pardon, but the rebuttal and rationale for the rebuttal used by the majority would operate as a "detriment to all South African women who must continue to labour under the social view that their place is in the home." He concluded that the benefit to a few hundred women could not justify the continued stereotyping of women as the primary caregivers. *Ibid.*

[53] Cathi Albertyn and Beth Goldblatt, "Facing the Challenge of Transformation: Difficulties in the Development of an Indigenous Jurisprudence of Equality," 14 *South African Journal on Human Rights* 248 (1998); see also D.M. Davis, "Equality: The Majesty of Legoland Jurisprudence," 116 *South African Law Journal* 398 (1999). It is interesting to note the expectation was that once the Constitutional Court was established, litigants coming before the Court would be the most disadvantaged sector of South African society, in light of the legacy of apartheid. This has not been the case. In the race discrimination area, the major

cases have been brought by white litigants alleging race discrimination, or in one instance, a very wealthy black male. In the gender discrimination area, the litigants have for the most part been either males, or more affluent white females. This is not a problem of the Constitution per se, but rather raises questions about access to justice—a perennial one confronting societies burdened with severe economic inequalities between its citizens. Despite this, however, although the parties seeking relief and protection from the Constitutional Court have come from the ranks of the most disadvantaged in South Africa, one could argue that the Court has confronted the concerns of a large proportion of South Africa's disadvantaged populations, including women.

[54] *S v Baloyi* 2000 (1) BCLR 86 (CC).

[55] See Rhonda Copelon, "Intimate Terror: Understanding Domestic Violence as Torture," in *Human Rights of Women: National and International Perspectives* (Rebecca Cook ed. 1994) 116.

[56] See Penelope E. Andrews, "Learning to Love After Learning to Harm: Post-Conflict Reconstruction, Gender Equality and Cultural Values," 15 *Michigan State Journal of International Law* 41 (2007).

[57] *Supra* note 29.

[58] Section 26 provides as follows: Everyone has the right to have access to adequate housing.
2) The state must take reasonable legislative and other measures, within its available resources, to achieve the progressive realization of this right.
3) No one may be evicted from their home, or have their home demolished, without an order of court made after considering all the relevant circumstances. No legislation may permit arbitrary evictions.

[59] Soobramoney v Minister of Health, supra note 21.

[60] Government of the Republic of South Africa v Grootboom 2000 (11) BCLR 1169.

[61] *Ibid* at paragraph 94.

[62] Marius Pieterse, "Resuscitating Socio-Economic Rights: Constitutional Entitlement to Health Care Service," 22 *South African Journal on Human Rights* 473 (2006)

[63] *Minister of Health and Others v Treatment Action Campaign and Others* 2002 (5) SA 721 (CC).

[64] *Jaftha v Schoeman and Others* 2005 (1) BCLR 78 (CC).

[65] *Carmichele v Minister of Safety and Security and Another* 2001 (4) SA 938 (CC).

[66] *Bhe and Others v Magistrate Khayelitsha and Others*, CCT 49/03; *Shibi v Sithole and Others*, CCT 69/03; *South African Human Rights Commission and Another v President of the Republic of South Africa and Another*, CCT 50/03.

[67] See http://www.wlce.co.za/cus_law_lit.php.

[68] See Mavivi Manzini Mayakayaka, "Political Party-Quotas in South Africa," in *The Implementation of Quotas: African Experiences* (Julie Ballington ed. 2004), available at http://www.idea.int/loader.cfm?url=/commonspot/security/getfile.cfm&pageid=7841.

[69] See Penelope E. Andrews, *Learning to Love After Learning to Harm: Post-Conflict Reconstruction, Gender Equality and Cultural Values,* supra note 55.

[70] *Ibid.*

[71] For a very interesting reflection on the challenges to addressing poverty as a constitutional imperative, see Lucy A. Williams, "Issues and Challenges in Addressing Poverty and Legal Rights: A Comparative United States/South African Analysis," 21 *South African Journal on Human Rights* 436 (2005).

[72] For a critique of the Constitutional Court's equality jurisprudence, see Cathi Albertyn and Beth Goldblatt, *Facing the Challenge of Transformation: Difficulties in the Development of an Indigenous Jurisprudence of Equality, supra* note 42. see also D.M. Davis, *Equality: The Majesty of Legoland Jurisprudence, supra* note 42.

[73] Indeed, Constitutional Court Justice Albie Sachs has referred to patriarchy as the "only truly non-racial institution in South Africa."

[74] The list of laws passed by the South African government to pursue equality for women include the Promotion of Equality and the Prevention of Unfair Discrimination Act, Act 4 of 2000 and the Domestic Violence Act, Act 116 of 1998.

CHAPTER TWELVE
WOMEN AND INHERITANCE
UNDER CUSTOMARY LAW:
The Response of the Courts
Muna Ndulo

Introduction

This chapter considers the predicament of women under customary law with specific reference to rules relating to inheritance. In traditional society, women were not allowed to inherit from the estate of their deceased husbands.[1] There were perhaps sound reasons for this rule based on the structure of traditional society. In modern society this rule can but work injustice and cause hardship. Professor Read has observed that "the customary laws based upon the traditions of rural life and family authority cannot be applied to the conditions of life in modern cities."[2] This is more so when the rule relating to inheritance is derived from the fact that African marriage treated a woman as inferior to the husband in the marriage relationship.[3] This chapter examines the traditional rule, the reasons for the rule, and shows that the premise on which the rule was founded no longer exists. It is contended that in jurisdictions where it survives it does so in part due to the failure of the courts to look at the rule analytically and critically and to see customary law as a dynamic system of law. Insofar as the inability of the courts to examine rules coming before them critically and analytically is concerned, it is contended that this is pervasive in the work of the courts in Africa and is one of the major problems standing in the way of the development of a jurisprudence that advances the rights of women in areas of private law.[4] This also means that many of the gross inadequacies of the law will continue unless rectified by legislation. This applies to both customary and common law principles of law. Africans courts traditionally do not use law to advance public policy. Instead, when confronted with situations which require more than a superficial analysis, the courts exhibit a reflective and stringent reliance on precedent, be it based on customary law or the common law. There are, however, encouraging developments. Courts in more and more jurisdictions are addressing policy issues and eradicating established precedents and advancing equality in society. The change is partly due to the extraordinary success of efforts by women's rights activists throughout the world to end discrimination against women.[5]. This chapter will highlight the cases where the mindset of judges is changing.

Principles of customary law of succession

The pre-colonial law in most African states was essentially customary in character, having its source in the practices and customs of the people.[6] The colonial regimes recognized customary law at the outset.[7] This is particularly true in areas of personal law. In some fields customary law was replaced by western law. Examples of the areas where it was replaced are public law, commercial law and criminal law.[8] Clearly to the colonial regimes, the areas of the law which were especially important were those which in a fundamental way affected their newly acquired wealth (in the form of property) and enabled them to deal with that property free of any restraints imposed by customary law.[9] Customary law was applied as the law between natives and in all native courts. In fact, in most of pre-independence Africa natives were rarely involved in litigation, either original or on appeal (other than criminal proceedings) in courts other than the local courts and courts of that system. In present-day former British Africa, customary law is recognized as applicable in every country,[10] provided such customary law is not repugnant to justice, equity or good conscience and is not incompatible, either in terms or by necessary implication with, any written law in force in the country.[11] Typically customary law is also implied to be recognized by the courts created to administer customary law.[12] For example in Zambia, although the Local Courts Act nowhere expressly recognizes customary law, it provides in section 12(1) that African customary law shall apply to any matter before local courts insofar as such law is not repugnant to natural justice or morality or incompatible with provisions of any written law.

White points out that in traditional society all individuals are members of kinship groups.[13] These are either patrilineal, matrilineal or cognatic descent groups. During his or her lifetime an individual's right to inherit does not lie with one specific relative. Since he or she is a member of an identifiable group, it is within that group as a whole that his succession will be resolved. Secondly, customary law of succession is not solely concerned with the transfer of rights in property, i.e., assets, upon the death of the person to whom these belong.[14] Indeed, in the past extensive individual ownership of property in the form of assets did not exist in many African societies since there was no wealth which could be accumulated outside the ownership of cattle and other domestic animals. Ownership of land was largely communal. Thus the transfer of status and roles traditionally forms an essential component of succession. The term "role" here denotes the social position a person occupies, and status denotes the prestige or rank aspect of his or her position. A person may be both a member of a clan and the head of it. The term "role" relates thus to social behavior in relation to other persons, rights and obligations, expectations of proper behavior and duty fulfillment of others towards one's self. A role may involve rights and obligations concerned with property. Considering first the question of roles, when a person dies some of his or her roles may cease to exist. There may be no successor. Alternatively there may be an automatic successor by reason of a rule or decision of a group. A role might even be divided between two or more successors with a division of rights and duties involved in some instances. Under customary law the question of succession to a dead person's estate is a matter to be resolved by his or her descent group,[15] and it is rare for there to have been any decision on any aspect of this during his or her lifetime. Usually there is no automatic role succession or property inheritance, and there is no automatic heir, at least not in the sense that exists in western law. Himoonga summarizes traditional law in this way: "succession refers to the process of succeeding to the estate, office or status of the deceased person, while inheritance refers to the process of inheriting the property of the deceased. The person selected as successor does not, in the Zambian legal system of succession, as in many other African systems, inherit all the property, although he may have the power to administer the estate and a right to a larger portion of it. Otherwise, the right of inheritance belongs to a much wider group entitled to inherit from the deceased according to the operative system of kinship."[16]

Movable property is a relatively recent economic development in most traditional African societies and does not pre-date colonial society. The exception is cattle ownership among animal-rearing tribes. Under customary law the wife does not inherit a deceased husband's property.[17] Whatever his type of descent, she is never a member of his descent group. Traditionally, a widow might have been provided for by the widow inheritance system;[18] otherwise she would have returned to her own kin to be their responsibility until she remarried. If there are sufficient assets in a deceased estate, a widow of a long-standing marriage who is well liked by her late husband's relatives may reasonably hope to receive something from the estate when it is distributed, but this depends largely upon the fairness of the relatives. It is not an entitlement based on a claim of right as such. This is because under customary law, throughout the marriage the woman remains a part of her kin, maintaining her birth-right identity. She never becomes a part of her husband's clan. The administration of the deceased estate is morally the duty and responsibility of the genealogical successor to the deceased. He should attend to the distribution of the estate, in consultation with other relatives of the descent group of the deceased.[19]

The devolution of property of a person who dies intestate in most African countries can be done under both customary law and the general law.[20] But for the majority of the people it is done under customary law. Under both customary and general law a man may make a will. With the exception of jurisdictions where legislation has intervened and altered customary law, making a will is the only way an African can ensure that his or her property does not fall to the dealings of customary inheritance laws. In no other way can one divest oneself of customary law; even entering into a marriage under the Marriage Act cannot divest the parties of their customary law of intestate succession and inheritance.[21] In short, there is nothing a person can do in his or her life time which is capable of predetermining whether customary or general law shall govern the administration of his or her intestate estate except the making of a will. The result is that the deceased person's relatives are ultimately the only people who will determine how the estate shall be distributed within the context of customary law.

Property acquired by the woman before or during the marriage remains under her control. Whatever property she takes into the marriage belongs to her and her kin, and since she never becomes a part of her husband's clan, the husband consequently acquires no interest in it. The end result of the customary rules is that in the event of death of a husband, the persons most dependent on the deceased, the wife and children, are ordinarily deprived of their husband's or father's assets. This results in tremendous hardship for the wife and children. It also splits the family along the lines of inheritors and disinherited and causes disputes that may transcend generations.[22]

Judicial response to the customary rules: traditional approach

For decades decisions by African courts taking a static view of customary law did not try to mitigate the operation of the discriminatory customary rules that disinherited women and children. The courts consistently denied women the right to participate in the husband's estate on the ground that customary law does not permit such inheritance. In

Munala v. Vengasai,[23] the deceased and his widow were Zimbabwean members of the Karanga tribe; they who had been married in 1961, by Shona law, in Zambia. The widow took out a summons to obtain an order that the deceased's estate be administered by the High Court under the English probate law which applied in Zambia—not under African customary law. The application was opposed by the relatives of the husband. The respondent, a cousin of the deceased, argued that the estate was governed by Shona customary law. Neither party in the proceedings claimed that the deceased had been subject to any African law other than Shona law. The court held that, on the evidence before it, the parties to the marriage had been living in a Shona community and had been married by Shona law, that the deceased had been living among and in the manner of an expatriate Shona, and that it would be catastrophic to hold that persons living in that manner did not retain their customary law, as this would also mean that the customary marriage law would not apply and would bring into doubt the validity of the marriage celebrated under such laws. The court went on to say that since the deceased had not lived in a manner that would have divested him of customary law, it followed that the law to be applied to the administration or distribution of the estate was Shona customary law. Here the court is debating the question not of whether general or customary law applied, but of whether Shona or local (because the Shona are not a Zambian tribe) customary law applied. The court did not even address itself to thee issue of general versus customary law. It took this view with full knowledge that the husband's cousin was bent on disinheriting the widow in favor of the nephew of the deceased. The court could have made an order that the property be administered by the Administrator-General, even though not under English law. This would have ensured that the widow participated in her husband's estate.

On the limited question of who should administer the estate, a different and more progressive approach was adopted in a 1983 Zambian case, *The Estate of Cosmos Pinyolo and in the Matter of the Administrator-General Act*.[24] The court held that the widow and the deceased's children qualified as next of kin; therefore, they rather than the deceased's kin were entitled to decide where the estate should be taken for administration. The courts have not, however, faced squarely the problem of the unsuitability of the customary rule of inheritance to modern conditions and have left the rule intact.[25] When faced with this problem, the courts have not inquired into the nature of the property at issue, the differences between traditional and modern society, the question of the wife's contribution to the building up of the estate, or the question of maintenance of the widow and children after the death of the husband and father. In failing to do this the courts have ignored their responsibility for developing the law according to the needs of society. The courts that stick to the precedent and the strict interpretation of custom forget that respect for the law can only be achieved if the law furthers the needs and conforms to the circumstances of the society immediately subject to it. Their failure to use the law to achieve just social solutions to problems and to reform society effectively thwarts development and advancement in customary law, and consequently also reduces respect for it.

The courts have showed inflexibility and an unwillingness to examine the applicability of legal rules to social conditions before them in other areas of the law. In *Mwiya v. Mwiya*[26] the respondent and the appellant, both Lozi by tribe and married under customary law, were divorced at Mulobezi local court. The appellant appealed to the subordinate court and later to the High Court on the ground *inter alia* that the property bought during the marriage was not shared between the parties. The High Court held that there was no Lozi custom compelling a husband to share property with his wife and refused the appeal. The court did not examine the Lozi rule and its place in modern social conditions. It did not consider things such as the wife's contribution to the matrimonial property.

The post-independence courts' lack of analysis by in the first decades following independence is also evident in the way the courts dealt with English precedents in other areas of the law. Church observes that throughout most of the British colonial courts, the doctrine of precedent commanded stern respect.[27] English decisions were followed exactly, even if strange results were produced. The only major exceptions to the pattern of reflexive reliance on the correctness of English rules and decisions tended to occur in cases dealing with the laws of sedition and civil liberties, in which the courts were harsher than in England.[28] The courts meekly followed what they considered to be the literal mandates of English law, without even attempting to examine whether the results thus produced were particularly appropriate under the circumstances.

This went on despite such observations such as the one made by Lord Denning in *Nyali Ltd. v. AG*:

> The common law cannot be applied in a foreign land without considerable qualification. Just as with an English oak, so with the English common law. You cannot transplant it to the African continent and expect it to retain the tough character it has in England. It will flourish indeed but it needs careful tending. So with the common law. It has many principles of manifest justice and good sense which can be applied with advantage to peoples of every race and color all the world over; but it has also many refinements, subtleties and technicalities which are not suited to other folk.

These off shoots must be cut away. In these far off lands the people must have a law which they understand and which they will respect. The common law cannot fulfill this role except with considerable qualifications. The task of making these qualifications is entrusted to the judges of these lands. It is a great task. I trust that they will not fail therein.[29]

A good illustration of the problem is a Zambian court decision in *Obaid and Quasmi v. The People*.[30] In this case the High Court considered whether a defendant, having been denied bail by one judge, could appeal to another High Court judge. There are no Zambian statutes on that point. The High Court framed the central issue as a question of jurisdiction of the second judge.

The actual ruling of the court is the least troublesome aspect; jurisdiction was denied. But the manner by which the court arrived at its ruling, including the cases and issues it considered, and more importantly, those it ignored, gives cause for concern. Instead of considering the appropriateness of the appeal within the structure of the Zambian judicial system, the court interpreted a Zambian jurisdictional statute to say that such questions before Zambian courts must be resolved in strict accordance with English judicial precedent. In so doing the court ignored the appellant's assertion that bail applications in Britain have been closely regulated by various Acts of Parliament, which is not the case in Zambia. Based on an unimaginative interpretation of its authority under the statute,[31] and ignoring another Zambian statute[32] directly in point with the issue in the case, the *Obaid* court reverted to the posture of a British court in colonial Africa and made its ruling by sole reliance on English case law and commentary.[33] In its opinion the court explicitly disregarded section 123(3) of the Zambian Criminal Procedure Code, (chapter 160 Laws of Zambia) which empowers the High Court to admit any person to bail at any time in response to an appeal from the accused on a contrary ruling. The court avoided this bail statute by simply stating that the statute did not address the precise facts in *Obaid*. Refusing to consider itself bound by the Zambian bail statute, the court was then free, by reliance on the jurisdictional statute, to inextricably tie its rationale authority to British precedent. It then rested its decision on British treaties, Halsbury's Laws of England, and a case decided by the House of Lords, which had interpreted various British statutes,[34] none of which was applicable to the case or even of effect in Zambia.

Although the ultimate conclusion of the court as to appealability may have been correct, the process of reasoning followed in arriving at this result portends continued stagnation of indigenous development of jurisprudence which is responsive to local needs. The court's immediate reference to British authorities without even a nod to its own judicial structure or Zambian public policy is an irresponsible practice that automatically precludes a mode of legal analysis which could advance the law while confining it to the Zambian context. The jurisdictional statute alone was sufficient authority for the court to consider local conditions and advance Zambian jurisprudence. By adopting a more independent rationale, the court would have been free to shape the reasoning of its opinion so that in future cases the result reached would be appropriate in the African context and not simply mimic British precedent. For example, under alternative independent rationale, the court would have been free to consider issues such as whether the appeal should be allowed in certain circumstances relevant in Zambia but non-existent in England. For example, the judiciary in Zambia is under-staffed and over-crowded. As a result criminal cases take a long time before they are resolved. The police and prosecutors tend to be inefficient, resulting in long delays in criminal trials. Prisons are very congested and conditions are bad.

The inapplicability of customary rules of inheritance to modern conditions

Any court which departs from the rigorous application of precedent and a static view of customary law and addresses itself to the social economic basis of the customary rules of inheritance will have no difficulty in finding that customary rules of inheritance can no longer operate in modern society without causing undue hardship. The nature of the society governed by these rules has changed and the rules need modification. A critical analysis of the structure of African society today would lead a court to conclude the same. Pre-colonial African society, in which these rules were developed, was based on an agricultural subsistence economy characterized by self-sufficient joint-family organization.[35] In general a woman's position in traditional society was based on an equitable division of labor. Women were primarily responsible for planting, weeding and harvesting while men performed certain heavy tasks such as clearing the bush and farming. In traditional society individuals were born, grew, married and died without ever leaving the region in which their tribe lived. A sense of community prevailed, from which developed an elaborate customary law system of reciprocal obligations between family members. For example, in most polygamous marriages each wife represented a separate unit of production. Her husband had a responsibility to give her land and equipment with which to farm and provide her with adequate shelter. She in turn was expected to feed herself and her children and, along with her co-wives, to provide food for her husband. African traditions and customary law served the needs of the tribal communities from which they developed, and together the traditional practices and customary rules ensured that all members of the community had access to food, clothing and shelter.[36]

In the modern economy women fend for themselves and help their husbands accumulate property during the course of their marriage. In essence, they have outgrown the status assigned to them in traditional society. Customary law has lagged behind these economic and social changes. As more and more women begin working outside the home, earning money and acquiring property, the gap between their legal status under customary law and their economic status in society widens.[37] The customary law of inheritance developed to suit the needs of a community composed of self-sufficient households practicing subsistence agriculture. Since only a male could be the head of a household in traditional society, the law preserved the unity of the family and ensured its continuity by transferring control of the estate on the death of the patriarch to his senior male descendants. In traditional patriarchal society, women were well cared for by the customary law of succession. As explained earlier, a widow would be placed under the protection of a male relative, who as the new patriarch had an obligation to make sure that she had land from which she could support herself and her children.[38] In most traditional societies "widow inheritance" was practiced to guarantee this outcome. Male primogeniture prevented the partitioning of the estate, thus ensuring that the new headman could meet his obligation to provide land. This system resulted in fair treatment of women only because it was consistent with the structure and function of the joint family in a subsistence economy. It cannot easily be transplanted to modern society.

But as we have seen, the joint family is in a state of decline and African societies are now enmeshed in an exchange economy. Development and industrialization have caused an irreversible breakdown in the traditional African social order. African societies are now highly individualistic, competitive and acquisitive. Unreformed customary rules do not operate to the benefit of women in this type of society. The joint families that remain have lost their self-sufficiency. Modernization, therefore, has had a negative impact on women. It has caused the breakdown of the tribal community and has destroyed the subsistence economy to such an extent that the protection women enjoyed under customary law is rendered useless or at best inadequate. Today widows must support themselves by their own efforts. Application of the traditional concepts of customary law of succession to women in a modern context is unjust and discriminatory.[39] It also ignores the fact that married women work jointly with their husbands to accumulate property during the course of their marriage and should not, therefore, be denied an absolute right in any portion of it. As James and Fimbo observed " . . . all these distinctions between the rights of males and females to inherit have grown out of traditional prejudices which have practically no relevance to modern ways of life. They are unjustifiable discriminations."[40]

Another factor to note is that in traditional society property was basic and simple. The house consisted of a hut built out of wood, grass and mud. A woman did not need to concern herself with such a house as she could easily build another. The household goods consisted of basic farming tools such as hoes and axes. The exception was cattle-owning communities. Gluckman, writing about the Lozi, observed: "With hoes and axes the Lozi cultivated their food, shaped their dug out canoes and paddles, carved pestles and mortars for pounding grain and wooden tools. The Lozi made houses of grass and reeds."[41] In contrast, in today's modern economy one is dealing with property of considerable value. A house on average costs thousands of dollars, is built out of brick and cement and is a permanent fixture. Couples are involved in a variety of investments of considerable value. An increasing number of men and women save money in insurance policies, money market schemes or retirement annuities. All these types of property were unknown in traditional society. It is therefore stretching customary law too far for a court to pretend that it can regulate the inheritance of such a radically different society. It is imperative for a court to critically assess the suitability of any customary law to modern conditions. Failure to do so may result in unjust decisions.

An illustration of the unjust result of the application of the customary approach to inheritance is the Zimbabwe case of Seva & Others v. Dzuda.[42] In this case, through the application of a customary rule favoring sons over daughters and widows, the son inherited the father's immovable property, including the home where his father's wives and his siblings lived. The son then sold the property with the home, and the buyer evicted the deceased's family. The family then sued to try to retain possession of the home by stating that, under customary law, the eldest son is to inherit the property for the purpose of caring for the rest of the family as the patriarch. The court ruled that under Zimbabwean law, the customary heir had the right to inherit the property personally, and not as any sort of trustee. Therefore the son could dispose of the property any way he chose, and the buyer had every right to evict the family. The court did not even mention the obligation of a son who inherited under customary law to take care of the family of the deceased.

Human Rights and Judicial Response to the Primogeniture Rule

Many African constitutions recognize the application of customary law without resolving the conflict between it and human rights provisions. Although some judges have interpreted this situation as permitting the application of customary law provisions that discriminate against women, in the majority of jurisdictions judges are now increasingly asserting the supremacy of human rights norms and declaring inheritance norms that prefer men over women unconstitutional or invalid and inapplicable in modern society. Three cases: *Bhe and Others v. Magistrate, Khayelish, and Others* (Commission for Gender Equality as Amicus Curiae); *Shibi v. Sithole and Others*; and *South African Human Rights Commission and Another v. President of the Republic of South Africa and Another*, were brought to the Constitutional Court at the same time. In *Bhe*, two extramarital minor daughters were ineligible to inherit from the intestate estate of their deceased father. According to section 33 of the Black Administration Act 38 of 1927 and the regulations governing *inter alia* matters of intestate succession in "Black Law and custom," minor children are not entitled to inherit intestate from their deceased father's estate(regulation) 2(e). The estate thus devolved to the deceased's father, who was named sole heir and successor. This provision was challenged in the High Court, where it was ruled unconstitutional. In *Shibi*, the applicant and deceased's sister, Ms. Shibi, was ineligible to become heir of the deceased's intestate estate, notwithstanding the fact that the deceased had neither a civil nor customary law wife, was childless, and did not have surviving parents or grandparents. This was the result of the application of section 23 of the Act, and Regulation 2 (e) in particular, requiring devolution of an African's estate to be made according to custom, and as such one of the deceased's male cousins was named the rightful representative of the estate, with a second male cousin being designated as the sole heir of the deceased's interstate estate. In the High Court, Ms. Shibi was granted a declaratory order pronouncing her as sole heir in her deceased brother's estate. In the *South African Human Rights Commission*, The South African Human Rights Commission and the Women's Legal Centre Trust sought direct access to have section 23 of the Act, or alternatively subsections (1), (2) and (6) of section 23 declared inconsistent with the Constitution of South Africa, in particular section 9 (right to equality), section 10 (right to human dignity) and section 28 (rights of children). The constitutional court declared section 23 and its associated regulations to be discriminatory on the grounds of race, sex and gender, and thus contrary to section 9(3) of the South African constitution. The court further held that the section was also contrary to the right to dignity. Insofar as it precluded minors and extramarital children from inheriting, the regime violated section 28 (Rights of the Child) of the constitution, and was discriminatory on the grounds of sex and birth in terms of section 9(3). The serious violations of these rights was not justifiable in terms of section 36 and therefore was struck down in terms of section 172(1)(a) of the constitution.

In the absence of section 23, the customary law of succession applied to the cases, and in contention was the rule of primogeniture. This rule, in excluding women from inheritance on the grounds of gender, violated section 9(3) of the South African Constitution. It also violated the right of women to human dignity secured by section 10 of the constitution. Furthermore, the rule of primogeniture was held to be discriminatory insofar as it hindered all female children and male extra-marital children from inheriting. Based on the above, in the *Bhe* case, it was held that the minor daughters, Nonkululeko Bhe and Anelisa Bhe, were to be the sole heirs of the deceased's estate. In the *Shibi* case, it was held that Charlotte Shibi, the only sister of the deceased, was to be the sole heir of the estate.

In a Nigerian case, *Augustine Mojekwu v. Caroline Mojekwu*,[43] under the Nnewi custom if a man dies leaving a male issue, the property belongs to the male child. If, however, the deceased had no male issue, his brother will inherit his property. If the male issue who survives the father dies leaving no male issue, the father's brother will inherit the property and on it goes along the lines of males only. In this case the son of the late brother inherited the property of his relation to the exclusion of the daughter of the deceased. The Nigerian Court of Appeals found the Nigerian custom that effectively prevented female family members from inheriting property "repugnant to the principles of natural justice, equity and good sense and a violation of the Convention on the Elimination of All forms of Discrimination Against women.[44] The court held that all human beings are born into a free world and are expected to participate freely without any inhibition on the grounds of gender. Justice Tobi stated: "All human beings—male and female—are born into a free world and are expected to participate freely, without any inhibition on grounds of sex [gender]; and that is constitutional. Any discrimination on grounds of sex, apart from being unconstitutional, is antithesis to a society built on the tenets of democracy which we have freely chosen as a people.... Accordingly, for a custom or customary law to discriminate against a particular sex is to say the least an affront on the Almighty God Himself. Let nobody do such a thing. On my part, I have no difficulty in holding that the 'Oli-ekpe' custom is repugnant to natural justice, equity and good conscience."[45]

In a Kenyan case, *Estate of Andrew Manunzyu Musyoka*[46] *(Deceased)*, the deceased had died intestate. The application was brought by the deceased's daughter, born of his first customary-law marriage. The application was in response to the filing of letters of administration by the deceased's sons and wife, to the effect that they were the beneficiaries of the deceased's estate. The applicant daughter alleged that she was also entitled to inherit from her deceased father's estate. This assertion was met with counter-argument from the respondents saying that application of African customary law stood to exclude her from inheriting. The customary law of the Kamba people is that a female married under African customary law is ineligible to inherit from the estate of her deceased father. The daughter may regain eligibility to inherit, however, if on divorce the "Mbui sya ulee" (goats) are returned by the woman to the husband. The court, finding that no customary marriage had in fact been concluded, held that the applicant was entitled to inherit and that her name was to be added to the filings. The Court held that Kamba customary law was discriminatory insofar as it sought to deny the applicant her inheritance rights on grounds of gender. The law is repugnant to justice and good morals and therefore inapplicable to the case. The court used the Succession Act, which provides that for intestate succession generally, and in Section 3(2) for customary law of succession particularly, section 3(2) provides that where a party to a matter is subject to or affected by African customary law, then the courts are to apply that law so long as it is "not repugnant to justice, morality or inconsistent with any written law . . . according to substantial justice." Finding that Kamba customary law was applicable to the case at hand, the court noted that the customary rule under consideration precludes a married daughter from inheriting from her deceased father's estate. The court, finding that Kamba customary law was discriminatory on the ground of gender, compared this custom to section 40(1) of the Law of Succession Act, which makes gender-neutral provision for intestate succession in the case of polygamous marriages. In terms of section 40(1), the court pronounced on the applicant's eligibility to inherit stating that unless she had opted out of a share of her father's estate, she was entitled to inherit.

Turning to the Constitution, the court noted that section 82(1) of the Constitution provides an exception to the general protection afforded by the section 82(1) non-discrimination provision. The relevant exception, contained in section 82(4)(c) provides that the Constitutional non-discrimination provision does not apply to "the application . . . of customary law." Notwithstanding this Constitutional exception, the Court went on to say that Kenya, as signatory to a number of international conventions and regional agreement including the Universal Declaration of Human Rights,[47] the Covenant on Economic, Social and Cultural Rights,[48] the Covenant on Civil and Political Rights,[49] The Convention on the Elimination of All Forms of Discrimination Against Women (CEDAW), and the African Charter of Human Rights and People's Rights,[50] was under an obligation to observe the doctrines of anti-discrimination contained therein. The court buttressed this point by noting that "international law is applicable in Kenya as part of Kenyan law so long as it is not in conflict with the existing law, even without specific legislation adopting them." Also, accepting as precedent the case of *Marry Rono v. Jane Rono and William Rono*,[51] a Court of Appeal's discriminatory succession case where international law instruments were used, the court endorsed the use of international law in instances of domestic customary law discrimination. The court acknowledged the case of *P & A Cause No. 203/98 Estate of Mutio Ikonyo v. Peter Mutua Ngui*,[52] which is an instance where the customary rule was in fact applied. In that case the court held that the applicant was not entitled to inherit from the deceased's estate as she was a married woman. The judge held that the P & A decision was not binding on the court, and that he disagreed with the P & A holding, especially in light of the Court of Appeal's decision in the *Marry Rono* case. In Tanzania, in *Ibernados Empraim v. Holaria d/o Pastory and Gervazi Keizilege*,[53] the court considered a law where although daughters were entitled to inherit family land, unlike men they could not dispose of the land. The court held this rule to be discriminatory and inconsistent with article 13 (4) of the constitution of Tanzania, which prohibits discrimination against any person.

In Ghana, faced with similar problems, the courts have shown flexibility. Ghanaian courts have, for instance, ruled that the successor's title is subject to the widow's right to the home, her right to all the household goods enjoyed in common with the deceased in the matrimonial home, and the right of the widow and children to maintenance out of the estate. In *Akrofi v. Akrofi*,[54] the plaintiff was the only child of the deceased and sought an order from the court declaring her as the sole successor to her deceased father's estate. This action arose from the fact that the deceased's brother had been appointed heir to the estate. Succession to property in Buem is patrilineal, and male children take preference over female children. However, in the absence of any male children, female children are not precluded from inheriting and are, in the language of the court, within the range of persons entitled to succeed. The court found that no custom excluding women existed and went on to note that if there were a custom under which a person was discriminated against solely on the basis of gender, that custom had out-lived its usefulness and would not at present be in conformity with public policy. The judge, in giving the widow the right to the household goods, said "I must mention that the impact of social and economic changes on this aspect of customary law is to recognize the widow and the children's right to personal matters enjoyed in common with the deceased in the matrimonial home. For it is unreasonable, and therefore, uncustomary, to deprive them of the use and enjoyment of things they have been brought up with and gotten used to."[55]

Unfortunately, in some countries the courts reject this approach and insist that legislation is required to change the offending customary law norms. The Zimbabwe Supreme Court in *Magaya v. Magaya*[56] illustrates this approach. Magaya, the deceased, died intestate. A community court initially made the deceased's eldest child (the female, only child of the deceased's first customary-law wife) the heir of his estate. On appeal, however, this order was set aside, and the second-born son of the deceased's second customary law wife was declared the heir (the first-born son of this second marriage having declined to be declared heir). On further appeal to the Supreme Court, the decision declaring the male child the heir was upheld. The court reasoned that under customary laws of succession males are to be preferred to females as heirs. The court stated that the Constitution of Zimbabwe, while containing anti-discrimination provisions in section 23(1) and (2) does not explicitly prohibit discrimination on grounds of sex or gender. However, even factoring these grounds in by virtue of trite codified international law norms, section 23(3) of the Constitution exempts certain discriminatory behavior. Notably, any law that relates to matters concerning marriage, adoption, divorce, burial, devolution of property on death, or other matters of personal law, and/or the application of African customary law will be exempt from the section 23(1) prohibitions. The court further argued that African customary law is constitutionally sanctioned in terms of section 89 of the constitution, and some would elevate this right to one having been conferred by the Constitution. While acknowledging the importance of gender advancement, the fact that customary law is a long-standing, fundamental and central aspect of African society means that it cannot easily be discarded. Furthermore, the application of customary law is voluntary in the sense that it applies only to those "Africans married under customary law or those who choose to by be bound by it. It reasoned that the matter at hand concerned not only an issue of devolution of property on death, but also concerned an application of African customary law in the context of inheritance and succession of the estate of an Africa who was party to customary law marriages, and therefore the case fell within the sanctuary afforded by section 23(3) of the Zimbabwe constitution. The court concluded that given the complexity of issues arising from the clash between African customary laws on inheritance and succession and non-discrimination provisions, any reform in this area should be left to the legislative machinery. The courts completely ignored the policy arguments applicable to the situation and the fact that Zimbabwe is a party to many human rights conventions which expressly prohibit gender discrimination.

Conclusion

There can neither be any doubt of the unsuitability of customary rules of inheritance to modern conditions nor any doubt of the need for reform. As Justice Ngcobo observed in *Bhe and others,* "having regard to these developments on the continent, the transformation of African communities from rural communities into urban and industrialized communities, and the role that women now play in our society, the exclusion of women from succeeding to the family head can no longer be justified. These developments must be seen against the international instruments that protect women against discrimination, namely: the Convention on the Elimination of All Forms of Discrimination against Women (CEDAW), the African Charter on Human and People's Rights, and the International Covenant on Civil and Political Rights."[57] To this should be added the Protocol on Women's Rights in the African Charter on Human and People's Rights. Changes can come about by legislation or through the courts. As Judge Ngcobo stated in *Bhe and others v. Margistrate, Khayelitsha,*[58] customary law can be developed through legislation to align it to human rights norms. Some countries have enacted legislation which abolished discrimination in inheritance matters. However, changes through legislation have proved slow in coming. This is largely because of opposition from people with vested interest in the status quo. The real hope for speedy reform remains the courts. But for the courts to reform the law they must see law as an instrument of social policy. The courts should stop blindly following what they consider to be the mandates of customary law without even attempting to examine whether the results thus produced are particularly appropriate under the circumstances, or whether the rules they are enforcing advance the social conditions of the people they are designed to serve.

This means that courts should decide these cases after a hard look at society. In other words, the courts should take their responsibility of developing the law seriously. The improved position of women in society can only benefit society. Discrimination against women merely inhibits them from making their contribution towards building a better society. Women are vital to the Zambian economy, and it is important that they are recognized as a major economic force.[59]

Notes

[1] Anderson, JND, *Family Law in Asia and Africa* (1966) 19. There are still strong feelings against inheritance rights for women. Michael Chenge reports how communities in Western Kenya opposed constitutional reforms that proposed equal land inheritance rights for sons and daughters. See Michael Chenge, "Kenya: Back from the Brink," *Journal of Democracy*, Vol. 19, No. 4, October 2008, p. 132.

[2] Read *Family Law in Kenya;* K. M'Baye *Le Droit de la Famille en Africque Noire et a Madagascar* Paris (1968) 251.

[3] Anderson *ibid* 19.

[4] Church, "Common Law in Zambia" (1974) 30, *Zambia Law Journal*. Church argues that *state decisis* was pursued with even more rigor than in England itself, see 29. See also, *Chama v. the People* 1972 ZR 29.

[5] See Donna J. Sullivan, "Women's Human Rights and the 1993 World Conference on Human Rights," 88 *American Journal of International Law*, 152 (1994); World Conference on Human Rights, Jun 14-25, 1993 Vienna Declaration and Program of Action, 18 U.N. Doc. A/CONF. 157/23 (July 12, 1993).

[6] Ndulo "Customary Law and the Zambian Legal System," in *The Individual Under African Law Conference Proceedings,* Swaziland, 1981; Allott, *Essays in African Law* 1960; White *Principles of Customary Civil Law in Zambia,* Government Printer, 1970.

[7] Royal Charter of Incorporation of the British South Africa Company, article 14. This ordinance stated quite clearly that "in the administration of justice to the said peoples or inhabitants, careful regard shall be had to customs and laws of the class or tribe or nation to which the parties respectively belong."

[8] A penal code was passed to be the basis of all criminal law. This is presently Chapter 146 of the Laws of Zambia. In the area of commercial law, for instance, the Sale of Goods Act of England was adopted.

[9] Northern Rhodesia Proclamation No. 1 of the 1913 article 5 reads: "Nothing in this proclamation shall deprive the High Court of the right to observe and enforce the observance, or shall deprive any person of the benefit of any law or custom existing in the territory, such law or custom not being repugnant to natural justice, equity and good government . . ."

[10] Chapter 45 of the Laws of Zambia.

[11] This is what has popularly come to be known as the "repugnancy clause." This has been used in Zambia in *Matengula* v. *R* 5 NRLR 148 and *Ndlovu* v. *R* NRLR 298. These cases are concerned with the custom that arose in the case rather than laying down a principle of general application.

[12] Chapter 54 of the Laws of Zambia.

[13] White *Principles of Customary Civil Law in Zambia* Government printer 1970 133.

[14] *Ibid.*

[15] *Ibid* 135.

[16] C. Himoonga, "The Law of Succession and Inheritance in Zambia and the Proposed Reform," *International Journal of Law and the Family,* Vol. 3 160 at 161, (1989)

[17] *Ibid.* See also Himoonga, *Law and Women in Zambia,* Unpublished 35. In fact customary law on the whole had the thrust that in traditional society the wife and husband did not own property in common even during marriage and could steal from each other. See *R v Mpumpeya* 1956 R&N 240.

[18] This is the practice where a widow is inherited by one of the husband's relatives. This custom, though dying out, was widespread. See White *Supra* 142.

[19] White *supra* 142. In the case of Zambia this has been altered by legislation. See The Zambia Intestate Succession Act, 1989.

[20] The Wills Act of England 1837 applies to Zambia, as do the English Statutes of Distribution 1670, 1677 and 1685. Customary law permits the making of wills. The only problem is one of recording. In traditional society wills were not always respected.

[21] *Coleman v. Shang* 1959 GLR 390. A Ghanaian case argued that a person subject to customary law who marries ordinarily remains subject to customary law in all matters pertaining to the marriage save those specifically excluded by the statute and any other matters which are necessary consequences of the marriage under the ordinance. The situation is hopeless for a party who wishes to divest himself of customary law.

[22] The state of the law leads women to keep separate bank accounts and an inventory of their property prior to marriage. See Kuenyehia, "Employment law and the Nature of Women in Ghana," IPPF *African Regional Workshop* (1978).

[23] 1974 ZLR 91.

[24] High Court case, unreported.

[25] In West Africa at various times the courts have attempted to subvert this rule, e.g., *Bangbase v. Daniel* 1955 AC 107 and *Re Whyte* 18 NLR 70. They have tried to use the repugnancy doctrine and lifestyle of the parties test.

[26] 1974 ZLR 111.

[27] Church "Common Law in Zambia," 1974 *Zambian Law Journal,* generally.

[28] *Ibid.* See also *R v. Am Keyo* 7 EAPLK 14 (1917) on this point; also see Seidman, "The Reception of English Law in Colonial Africa" (1969), 2 *East Africa Law Review* 6.

[29] *Nyali Ltd. v. AG* 1955 1 AII ER 653.

[30] 1977 ZLR 199.

[31] *Ibid*, 123. The court interpreted its jurisdiction under S 10 of the High Court Act, chapter 50 of the Laws of Zambia.

[32] S 123(3) of the Zambian Criminal Procedure Code Chapter 160 of the Laws of Zambia.

[33] The court relied on *Re Kray, Re Smith* 1965 1 All ER 710.

[34] *Ibid* 127. The court also relied on *Re Hastings* (No. 3) 1959 1 All ER 700.

[35] Gluckman, *The Judicial Process Among the Barotse of Northern Rhodesia* 5.

[36] Okoth-Ogendo, "Property Systems and Social Organization in Africa: An Essay on the Relative Position of Women Under African Law," in *The Individual Under African Law Conference Proceedings*, Swaziland 1981.

[37] Simons, *African Women* (1968). See also S. Abrams, *Modernization and the Status of Women in Africa*, unpublished 1984.

[38] White *supra* 5.

[39] The courts could use this as a strong basis for intervention. The constitution unequivocally outlaws discrimination on *ia* grounds of sex, Constitution of Zambia chapter 1 of the *Laws of Zambia* Article 20.

[40] James and Fimbo, *Customary Land Tenure of Tanzania* 209 (1973).

[41] Gluckman *supra* 5.

[42] Seva & Others v. Dzuda, 1991 (2) ZLR 34 (s).

[43] 1997 7 NWLR 283.

[44] Article 5 of CEDAW requires state parties to take appropriate measures: "To modify the social and cultural patterns of conduct of men and women, with a view to achieving the elimination of prejudices and customary and all other practices which are based on the idea of the inferiority or superiority of either of the sexes..." To ensure that family education includes a proper understanding of maternity . . . and the recognition of the common responsibility of men and women in the upbringing and development of their children.."

[45] 1997 7 NWLR 283.

[46] 2005 eKLR

[47] United Nations General Assembly, Dec. 10, 1948. G.A. Res. 217A, 3GAOR, Resolutions (A/810).

[48] 993. U.N. T.S. 3.

[49] 999. U.N.T.S. 171.

[50] OAU Doc. CAB/LEG/67/3 Rev. 5 (1981).

[51] Court of Appeal, 66/02.

[52] Case No. 203/98.

[53] High Court of Civil Appeal, 70/89.

[54] 1965 G.L.R. 13.

[55] In *re Appiah* (Ded); *Yoboah v. Appiah* 473 1975 GLR 1: see also *Amissah-Abadoo v. Abadoo* 1974 GLR 110, and in *re Kofi Antubam* (Decd); *Quaaico v. Fosu* 1965 GLR 138.

[56] 1999 1 ZLR 100 (s)

[57] *Bhe and others*, supra, p.121.

[58] Supra.

[59] Right now although the economic contribution of women in Zambia is the basis on which the male power-structure is built, women are treated unfairly. For instance, women constitute the basic agricultural labor force, but men own and control the land in Zambia. Report of a meeting on women and power. The Group for Equal Rights for Women Vienna 1983.

CHAPTER THIRTEEN
LAND REFORMS, LAND TITLING AND GENDER DILEMMAS IN AFRICA
An Exploration of Issues
Susie Jacobs

African rural women, the majority of whom are poor, are being squeezed in a 'double movement.' On the one hand, they are often unable to access land directly due to the workings of customary law, which usually privileges men. On the other hand, neo-liberal policies of titling and privatization along with the growth of agribusiness are threatening existing, limited access to land. This parallels a global trend toward increased agitation for political rights along with declining living standards (Elson and Gideon, 2004), especially in rural areas (Borras *et al.* 2008).

The issue of women's access to land has increased in importance and now is gaining a higher profile. This chapter concentrates on redistributive land reform processes and the movement to register or title land, women's experiences within these processes, and attempts to forge more gender-equitable policies. The case studies employed are in the main from southern and eastern Africa, with some reference to other areas. The first section of the chapter discusses continued needs for land reform; the second examines some of the provisions and constraints of customary law. The third section turns back to agrarian reform and women's experiences within these processes, while the fourth discusses market-based reforms along with titling and gender implications. The fifth analyses changes in the direction of gender equity, including attempts to 'write-in' equitable provisions to land tenure reforms or alterations. Lastly, the chapter explores some possible ways forward from the conundrums presented.

Need for agrarian reform?

That a need for agrarian reform still exists—particularly in the ex-settler societies of southern Africa but also elsewhere—is not perhaps contentious, given the growth of land-based movements in Africa and worldwide as well as the acknowledgement of such need by the World Bank (2003). Here are a few of the issues relevant to the question of land reform.

First, it is true that what many rural (and urban) people wish for is a secure livelihood, in whatever manner this can be accomplished, rather than agricultural land as such. However, the religious, traditional and affective implications of land, both within African cultures and elsewhere, should not be forgotten (El-Ghonemy, 2001). Neo-liberal policies such as structural adjustment programs and their stringencies, along with curtailment of the role of the state (including the roles of parastatal marking agencies, grain stores, etc.) combined with unequal global trade rules have left many people more impoverished rather than less so (Palmer, 2005:2). These and other processes such as increased migration (Castles and Miller, 2003) and family changes have led to a diversification or fragmentation of rural livelihoods (Ellis, 2000; Francis, 2000) so that agriculture is often of declining importance. This process is perhaps starkest in South Africa, where the history of apartheid and forced removals along with the high rate of urbanization has adversely affected livelihood possibilities.

Whatever people's preferences concerning livelihoods, however (not all wish to farm), many have increased need of land to cultivate. In Zambia, for instance, closure of the copper mines meant a return to farming for many. In many contexts, problems of governance and violent conflicts which devastate natural resources and peoples' livelihoods result in the need to cultivate land for survival.

Along with fragmentation of livelihoods has come a feminization of agriculture. This might mean a preponderance of women and children in rural areas, a growth in the percentage of female-headed households, and women's increased agricultural activity and dependence upon agricultural livelihoods (often at times of declining agricultural profitability). Feminization is in part due to the same processes encouraging fragmentation: male migration to cities or abroad, male absence during conflicts, and increased desertion and divorce (Chant, 1997). While heavy female participation in agriculture is quite common and 'traditional' in most of Africa, in many parts of the world where this is not the case women have nonetheless taken on new roles.

Redistributive land reform is not a panacea in terms of guaranteeing livelihood but is still a vital measure in terms of helping to secure it (Sobhan, 1993). Whether small-scale agriculture is more or less productive than large-scale farming is a hotly-contested issue (see e.g. Griffin, Khan and Ickowitz, 2002; 2004; Byers, 2004), but there exists much evidence that with appropriate supports, small-scale agriculture can be very productive (e.g. Zinyama, 1995). Land reform, relatedly, helps to reduce rural poverty (El-Ghomeny 1990). That agrarian reform is still a 'live' issue for many rural and urban peoples has been emphasized by the recent growth in land and rural-based movements (Moyo and Yeros, 2005), sometimes in conjunction with movements of the urban poor, as in Brazil.

Agarwal (1994) has argued for women's land rights on the basis of equity, welfare and efficiency (see also Deere and Leon, 2001). The first argument is in terms of justice. The slogan 'land to the tiller' has long been emblematic of agrarian movements, and it is well-established that in sub-Saharan Africa women are in most cases the main cultivators, responsible for provisioning their households and feeding the husband, children and often other family members (see. e.g. Bryceson,1995; Davison, ed. 1988). Women as the main cultivators should receive and be able to control land and proceeds from agriculture. A second argument (or arguments) can be made in terms of efficiency, i.e. securing livelihoods and raising production. It is now often acknowledged that constraints facing rural women, such as lack of decision-making power, often affect their capacity to farm to their best abilities and can act as disincentives (Tripp, 2004). McCusker's study of Limpopo, South Africa (2004), for instance, indicates that women's marginalized status in agricultural land reform was one important factor accounting for the relatively unproductive use of land in schemes there.

Relatedly, land reform often results in increased incomes and improved livelihood security for smallholders; in some circumstances, this can increase food security. Whether people's livelihoods improve with land redistribution in practice will depend upon a number of factors such as soil fertility, adequate state and other support, the existence of credit facilities, experience in farming, etc. But certainly, as noted, agrarian reform holds the promise of improved rural living standards; holding or owning agricultural land is the preferred option for many, particularly compared with options such as work on commercial farms, usually for very low pay and in harsh conditions. Given a gender-equitable land reform strategy, this would hold true for women as well as men.

A third argument can be made in terms of family welfare. A number of studies indicate that women's enterprise and incomes are often more explicitly oriented to food security than are men's—perhaps especially in Africa (Carr, 1991), but also elsewhere (Ghimire, 2001). Greater food security is likely to occur because of the cultivation of 'women's [food] crops such as groundnuts and sorghum and also because of women's greater propensity to reinvest in farm activities (Kidder, 1997). This remains the case even in circumstances of livelihood diversification. The World Bank (2003) also cites women's access to land and other resources as crucial to children's nutritional status and education (cited in Ikhdal, 2006: 33). Other evidence indicates that food security does not necessarily increase under male direction of agriculture, even where incomes do. Blumberg (1995) points out that it has not been possible to establish a link between rises in men's incomes and improvements in children's nutritional status in Africa, but such improvements do occur when women's (i.e. mothers') incomes increase.

A fourth argument can be made in terms of economic opportunities that land titles or land holding might permit. Women as farmers face a range of constraints, including lack of control over labor and lack of access to credit and other agricultural supports such as extension advice (Davison, 1988; Momsen, 2004). However, in some cases women have been able to seize opportunities as entrepreneurs either individually or collectively. Spring notes great entrepreneurial activity among African women, including farming (2002).In some Sri Lankan villages, women have banded together to obtain credit and become petty commodity producers of cashew nuts, eliminating middlemen (Momsen, 2004; citing Casinader et al.1987); and a Bugandan study found that by the 1990s, female-headed households were more likely than male-headed ones to purchase land (cited in Tripp, 2004: 14).

A fifth argument is that access to land is likely to increase women's social and economic position within households and communities (e.g. Jacobs, 1984; 1989; 1997; Agarwal, 1994). 'Land rights' may entail broader decision-making powers. As will be seen, it has been uncommon for women to control land, but where they do, indications are that they gain at least a measure of security and power. Interestingly, an unusual—and unusually successful—struggle for women's land rights in Bihar, India, also launched a campaign *against* patrilocal and *for* matrilocal residence, seeing this as crucial to women's interests (see Kelkar and Gala, 1990). For northern Nigeria, Abdullah and Hamza make a strong claim for land rights, which they envisage in terms of independent rights:

> Independent land rights are necessary ... as they would lead to autonomy and the ability to make and take decisions (on fertility, sexuality and incomes) and would enhance [women's] status. In addition, independent land rights would empower women to challenge existing gender inequalities and ultimately would lead to reordering of gender relations (2003: 172).

Customary Law

The operation of customary law throughout most of the continent is an important factor influencing women's access and rights to land. The term 'customary law' was a colonial invention and refers to indigenous African law. Chanock (1989) argued that customary law reflected an informal consensus between colonial administrators, themselves convinced of the inferiority of women, and African lineage elders; and Ranger famously wrote of 'invented traditions' (1983). Alternatively, some see customary law as having greater continuity with pre-colonial practice (Banda, 2005). For some, there exists a tendency to defend 'traditions' attacked by Western colonialism as an anti-racist imperative. However, this ignores the fact that the current practice of 'customary' law is usually detrimental to women.

Banda writes that post-independence, most African states have opted for an 'integrated' model, with primary or lower courts handling customary law claims but reserving provision for appeal to higher courts. Land has a particularly important position within customary law as it is crucial to the unity of a lineage. "Land helps to order relationships between people: living and dead" (Davison, 1988:15). In most sub-Saharan African societies, land was traditionally a communal resource and not subject to 'ownership' by individuals—particularly given the interest of ancestral spirits in their land; however, land in Africa is most often individually worked. In the matrilineal belts of west and east-central Africa, women in some societies have (or had) more rights, but even here land is usually held by and inherited from men, albeit in this case, a maternal uncle. Nevertheless, matrilineality in general is advantageous to women's social position. Women in patrilineal groupings, which form a large majority, are customarily unable to inherit land and other large property as this is held by men on behalf of the lineage. The right to allocate land is usually held by a lineage elder. In some cases a widow might hold land temporarily, usually on behalf of a son, but more frequently the land would be inherited by a brother of her husband.

In most systems of customary law, women (and often younger unmarried men) have the status of legal minors. Particularly within patrilineal systems, marriages are potentially polygynous and it is usually much easier for husbands to divorce wives than for wives to obtain divorce. For instance, in Uganda (even at present) a man has only to accuse his wife of adultery in order to file for divorce (ActionAid, 2006b: 62). In Zimbabwe, a woman's refusal of sex or attempts to use contraception are grounds for divorce, as (among ChiShona speakers) is failure to conceive. The issue of property/land holding, divorce and inheritance is at present much discussed in many African countries given that under customary law, upon the death of a husband, the man's brothers or male members of his lineage may claim rights to land and property. The option of the levirate—whether or not seen as desirable—has today often lapsed. Thus many widows face disinheritance, poverty and/or expulsion.

Under many systems of customary law in Africa, women have, or did have, certain rights. For instance, the right to a certain amount of land allocated by the husband for cultivation of 'women's' and other crops was widespread and was an important source of (partial) security. In the grass fields of Cameroon, for instance, women of the Nso of Bamenda customarily had highly favorable access to land. Goheen (1988) stated that in the '80s, as in the time of Phyllis Kaberry's classic study (*Women of the Grassfields,* 1952), Nso women derived a sense of selfhood from their roles as farmers and were acknowledged to have control over crops. As elsewhere, women cultivated food crops, but cash crops were becoming increasingly important, and men controlled these. Women "owned the crops but not the fields" and customarily did not inherit land (1988: 91). Although in the 1950s wives were allocated Land for personal use and had complete control over this, by the late 1980s this was no longer the case. Arable farmland was less readily available and more used for cash crops. Thus in this case, Nso women had the relatively high status associated with West African gender systems but nevertheless were in a dependent position concerning land and land rights; they cultivated the husband's land, or sometimes later in life a brother's, but they themselves did not own the land (Goheen, 1988). By the beginning of the twenty-first century, with structural adjustment and lower prices for export crops, agricultural incomes had dropped. Since then some women have become more involved in cultivation and processing of export crops (e.g. cocoa, coffee) in order to diversify their incomes and to be freer of male control. Land is becoming more commodified and losing its symbolic/ritual status (Logo and Bikie, 2005).

Even in systems where wives faced more constraints, women tended to have a number of rights. In Zimbabwe and elsewhere a wife had the right to her own *mavoko* income ('of her own hands'), e.g. derived from activities such as beer brewing and craft production. The advent of cash economies and migration in fact operated to give more power to individual husbands and thus reduced women's leverage in calling upon the assistance of wider kin (Pankhurst and Jacobs, 1988). Likewise in Uganda, both cash economies and colonial laws increased the power of individual husbands, reducing women's (partial) tenure security (Businye, 2002).

Customary law has for long been questioned, and is increasingly threatened from a combination of forces such as more egalitarian statutory law and marketization; however it is still of huge importance in most rural contexts. In Zimbabwe, its sway has recently (see Zulu 1999) been strengthened by Supreme Court rulings on women's inheritance rights. In South Africa, national /statutory laws are egalitarian, but in rural areas these may have little effect. In general, the volume edited by Wanyeki (2003) bears striking testimony to the continued strength of customary law and practice across the continent. There does, as indicated, exist variation as well as change. However, law as practiced concerning women's land rights—particularly those of wives—often overrides even religious law, let alone more contemporary statutory law. For instance, Hausa custom in northern Nigeria overrides the provisions of Islamic law and women do not inherit land, even in the reduced shares provided for by Shari'a law, as this provision for inheritance is considered 'unnecessary';[1] female inheritance of land and property, it is said, would lead to 'economic destruction' (Abdullah and Hamza, 2003). Ikhdahl et.al (2006) also note that in some contexts, informal law may be more binding than formal law (2006: xiii).

Gender and Land Reforms

Redistributive agrarian reforms ought to hold the promise of a new system in which some of the constraints of traditional systems can be overcome and other practices can be built upon. Many redistributive land reforms have taken place after social upheavals and revolutions, but others have been enacted 'from above', usually in order to pre-empt rural unrest. Agrarian or land reforms have also taken place in a wide variety of countries and across all continents and may be along collective or 'individual family/ household' lines. Some of the most recent involve 'repeasantization' following decollectivization in eastern Europe and Vietnam. Despite this variation, most redistributive land reform policies along *individual household* lines have discriminated against women, particularly married women; the main (but by no means sole) mechanism of discrimination has been allocation of land or land titles to household heads, usually assumed to be male (Jacobs, 1984; 1989; 1997). Reasons for such policies include that those enacting land reforms made assumptions about the unitary nature of the household and women's roles as 'housewives' within this (Fapohunda, 1987) as well as the structuring of peasant or smallholder households, which rely upon female labor 'at home' and often in the fields and in which wives are usually highly subordinate. Linked to the above are political factors: attempts to shift or reform this household structure by granting women more rights would be likely to meet with serious backlash from male smallholders (Wiergsma, 1988).

Detailed studies of gender and land reforms are relatively rare, but again the results are surprisingly uniform across different cultural contexts and continents (Jacobs, 2009). The following summary is based on a study of twenty-six cases (see Jacobs 1997 for detail on references; additionally, Pankhurst, H 1992; Tadesse, 2003; Goebel, 2005a).

Some aspects of land reform processes have been positive for many women in the sense of increasing their material welfare or influence within households. The most important is perhaps that income levels and food security are often improved through land reform. In some cases, higher income levels also accrue to the wife or wives: this was the case in Zimbabwe (Jacobs, 1989; 2000a also Goebel 1999) in the first wave of land reform (but see below). Despite burdens of heavier work, Tadesse (1982) reported that resettled peasant women were less concerned about hunger after resettlement, and this sentiment is common.

Another 'positive' factor concerns growth of the nuclear family model, or nuclear family 'on-the-ground' arrangements. This is related in part to the fact that land reform often involves relocation and living among unfamiliar people rather than with lineage relatives. Colson (1960) noted that husbands and wives might come to rely upon one another, with increased interdependence. However, less positively, where the nuclear family model is also one of a monogamous family, one or several wives may be left out of agrarian reform arrangements and may have to return home (see also Wanyeki, 2003). However, in my study many wives felt 'freer' away from the husband's patrilineage; many also felt that their influence in the household had increased. Likewise, Judith Stacey (1983) holds that many peasant women preferred the smaller family system under land reform as it undermined the power of the husband's patrilineage, and particularly of the mother-in-law.

In a number of cases, a minority of women-headed households have been allocated land under land reform programs, although this varies. Where this occurs, the woman is usually a widow or divorced woman with children including sons. Unfortunately, negative impacts are more commonly reported in studies of gender and land reform along individual household lines.

> i) Most African studies report that women have lost customary land rights with land reform: this is a function of assigning titles to the husband/head of household, as discussed above. Where this occurs, it means loss of an

important basis of subsistence and autonomy, even though in most cases these rights are informal and may be contingent.

ii) Most reforms greatly increase the burdens of work for beneficiaries. Initial preparatory work (usually completed by men) is arduous, and there is more land to cultivate, more pressure on labor generally and an urge to make a profit, especially where cash cropping is in place. Often, the extra, everyday work burdens fall upon women.

iii) Relatedly, land reforms may increase pressure on women to reproduce children, given the importance of family labor on plots (Palmer, 1985).

iv) It is common to find that provision of services such as shops, clinics, schools, potable water and cattle dips has declined. Women frequently have long distances to travel on foot, especially to fetch fuel and water, and transport difficulties may inhibit marketing of crops. Arduous conditions in new settlements are often linked to poor service provision, and most studies report this.

v) Incomes: despite the fact that women's incomes rose in a few studies, notably in Zimbabwe in the 1980s and early 1990s, most studies report that married women lost control of their 'own' incomes while that of the household head rose. This parallels women's loss of control over land. Women lose income through loss of access to land and loss of economic niches, through relocation, and through the need to travel long distances and loss of personal contacts. At the same time, cash-cropping often becomes available to wives only through male mediation.

vi) Studies in Honduras, Mexico, Libya, the Mwea scheme (Kenya), Zimbabwe and Sri Lanka discuss decision-making. All report loss of decision-making power by wives, due to several factors. These include (again) loss of women's land and an increase in surveillance by the husband—typically, because they are present more constantly, and due to increased emphasis on the 'housewife' role. Despite the countervailing trend to increased (informal) influence of the wife in the nuclear family structure, all of the above factors affect women's bargaining power within households.

In general then, and despite raised household incomes for some, land reforms have disempowered wives through allocating land to the 'household head' and through lack of attention to household and family dynamics. Particularly important is the fact that—as in customary law more generally—most women will lose access to land upon divorce or widowhood.[2] Failure to analyze the complex links between kinship, gender and class relations within the household coupled with the assumption of unitary, cooperative households has been endemic in peasant studies and in their political equivalent, land movements. This tendency has existed not only in the past, when one might argue that second-wave feminist movements had had little impact, but in the present; for instance, the MST (Landless People's Movement) in Brazil, one of the most successful agrarian reform movements to date, is of course not 'historical' but contemporary. Some of its policies have unfortunately discriminated against women (Deere, 2003, Guivart, 2004). Although a number of MST leaders are women, by the mid 1990s under 13 percent of reform beneficiaries in Brazil were female (Deere, 2003). In a welcome congress on agrarian reform—perhaps one of the first global congresses on this issue—held in Valencia, Spain in late 2004 (see www.fmra), only one session was originally allocated for 'gender issues'. In a familiar scenario, several feminists at the FMRA Congress had to agitate for increased 'space' and organized outside the formal conference structures.

Market-based reforms?

If redistributive land reforms have failed (most) rural women, does an answer lie in market-based land reforms and land titling? This is the path which has been promoted by the World Bank since the 1970s and was still evident in the Report of 2003 (WB, 2003). International Financial Institutions (IFIs) have for long been involved in promoting reform of landholding and in designing many such programs. In the 1980s, titling of land was considered to be the appropriate mechanism for privatization and economic liberalization (Toulmin and Quan, 2000:121). Reforms to land tenure were advocated alongside setting up reforms of macro-economic policy (Fortin, 2005: 6) such as structural adjustment, privatization and titling and orientation to export production. Thus, the expansion of export crops, often through agribusiness and farming either on large estates or through contract farming, is a main trend globally, as evident in 'new agricultural countries' such as Chile and Brazil. The World Bank's Land Policies for Growth and Poverty Reduction (2003) sees land as a key asset for the rural and urban poor and emphasizes 'productive' use of land and efficiency viewed in terms of profitability. The Bank's past policy supported subdivision of the commons to establish 'freehold' or private ownership. The 2003 Report recognizes that with regard to Africa, this has proved less than satisfactory. Bruce and Migot-Adhola (1994) argue that individualization has led in Africa to increased land concentration and landlessness. In some conditions, the World Bank's 2003 policy document is prepared to countenance group tenure as providing sufficient security of tenure.

Ikdahl et. al (2005) note that despite this partial backtracking, the market model still serves as an ideal type, informing the whole analysis; this is buttressed discursively. The title of the document gives a guide to the usual (and contentious) neoliberal linkage made between 'growth' and poverty reduction. Manji (2003a; 2003b) critiques two aspects of the Report. The first aspect concerns the World Bank's intention that a land market be developed, including in Africa. Seeing land as an 'asset' indicates not only that it can be alienated but that it can be used for collateral. However, the Report is "curiously silent about the consequences for households defaulting on loans" having used their land as collateral (2003b:105). It is only feasible for formal credit institutions to loan to smallholders if foreclosure is a real possibility, so that land markets and use of land as collateral imply the possibility of loss of land.

In many cases, including in the West, wives may be unaware of husbands' actions with regard to property transactions. Where women have little household power, it is likely that men might use capital gained from land for other ventures such as opening stores, leaving the wives to farm mortgaged land (Manji, 2003b). This observation on the nature of marriage property links with the second critique of the World Bank Report: the Bank's failure to fully disaggregate the notion of a unified 'household' despite intensive feminist critiques over a time span of two generations, in particular, the failure to acknowledge that smallholder farms usually rely on the labor of wives rather than hired labor, and that this is in large part the basis of improved 'efficiency' of small over larger agricultural units (first noted by Kautsky). In its approval of this situation, the World Bank may connive with patriarchal relations in households and communities rather than using its great influence as a counterweight.

However, smallholder/peasant agriculture frequently *does* rely on intensive female labor: this is not an external imposition or discourse. This relation is in fact deepened and exacerbated by land reform, as the previous section indicates. This has happened mainly because of the exclusive assignment of land to one member of the household (the 'head'); however issues go beyond this and to the nature of the smallholder household. We return the question of more equitable means of agrarian reform(s) below. Here, however, I argue, with others, that titling and formalization of land rights is likely to result in further diminution of existing rights of women. Where the socio-economic value of land increases, so may individual men's interest in it, in a context where communal constraints are weak. There is a good deal of difference between a situation in which *all* law is informal or customary (even if codified) and one in which some aspects of property law are regulated by statute (e.g land titling) whereas other aspects (e.g. women's rights to a plot) are left to 'custom'. Titling usually means that the beneficiary of the title gains social and economic power—albeit somewhat less so if the state or a collective continues to hold ultimate land title. Privatization has broken down support mechanisms such as cooperative work and dedicated land resources that help poor households in times of need; women in particular depend upon cooperative mechanisms to access the labor necessary to make land productive (ActionAid, 2006:73). Thus, male elites are often strengthened through privatization.

In these circumstances, some women—especially the more educated or middle-class—will be able to acquire land; however, this will not apply to most of those who lack the necessary resources. This situation parallels the growing splits among women by social class occurring with globalization. A number of commentators have emphasized that *poorer* women tend to lose rights with titling (e.g. Lastarría-Cornhiel, 1997). Hilhorst (2000: 189) writes that land registration is likely to weaken local institutions, providing some security to all community members; the 'African land ethic' (Cross, 1992) traditionally includes concern for subsistence needs of community members. Marcus et. al (1996) maintain that land title registration [in South Africa] would be likely to mean that large numbers of women would lose land, as few poor people can retain their land in a market situation. Recent land grabs in Zambia, for instance, result in part from the opening up of a land market: Zambia Sugar plc is claiming land in south Zambia and seeking to evict 100 families. An interesting twist in this case—and perhaps others—is that chiefs too can become players in the land market rather than guardians of land. (Mpundu, 2006).

A number of women and women's groups have nevertheless called for individualization of titles for women in order to secure land and land access, as women's access to land is chronically threatened under customary law. Famously, Bina Agarwal has called for this (1994; 2003), as have Deere and León (2001). The latter document shows gains for Latin American women from individualization of titles, but in India and Latin America land is already privatized and can be alienated; this is a different context from what exists in much of Africa (Walker, 2003). There exists little consensus in this regard among land advocates, as is evident in some cases cited below.

Initiatives /progress in uniting gender and land claims

Thus a conundrum exists: Titling would go some way towards giving women who held land a measure of economic power and autonomy, particularly if (hypothetically) wives were granted individual titles. A number of authors cited above, for instance, link women's rights with titling. But as the critique of credit markets and potential alienation of land indicates, such a move would at the same time 'free' women to compete in the marketplace, and most who managed to acquire land would be likely to lose it. While both poor men and poor women are likely to lose land and property in competitive/market circumstances, women face a far greater number of constraints: lack of command over labor, childcare, lack of access to credit and inputs, and backlashes against them (see below). On the other hand, as noted, customary law is highly discriminatory against women: widows and divorcees are often left impoverished, and married women's rights—where they still exist—are highly contingent. With a decline in community networks, wives remain dependent upon their husband's goodwill.

However, there has been a degree of recognition of the difficulties faced by rural women in terms of access to land and property, and a number of international and national NGOs (e.g. Oxfam, ActionAid, Uganda Land Alliance) and others have campaigned for women's land rights. So too, sometimes from different perspectives, have international bodies (the United Nations/UNRISD) and local feminist movements, despite a general 'urban' orientation among most women's movements. Although there exists no easy solution, some social and legal changes affecting women's land rights are evident. This section outlines some indicative examples.

Informal/customary rights

First, it should be recognized that customary practice itself is not totally unchanging: customary law is part of society and is affected by overall societal shifts. In Zimbabwe, for instance, the Women and Law in Southern Africa (WLSA) grouping documented changing norms concerning inheritance practices (WLSA, 1994; 1997). Due in part to such change, and in part to civil society and women's campaigns, inheritance laws were enacted in 1997 that were meant to give protection to widows' rights, although these were later overturned by a Supreme Court decision. Another example outlines changes in rural Ugandan parents' attitudes towards inheritance by daughters. This change was due to perceived marriage instability with frequent divorce and separation, leaving daughters vulnerable. A retired woman teacher commented,

> "Broken marriages are several these days, due to poverty, lack of education, heavy drinking and redundancy of many men, leading to the suffering of women. So parents have opted for giving daughters a share of

land so that they do not suffer.... People have realized that, given some opportunities, girls can be equally as useful as boys" (in Bikaako and Ssemkumba: 2003: 265).

Thus, daughters' contribution to parental welfare is increasingly valued.

Land reform—South Africa

In some land reform processes, cognizance has been taken of the need to build in safeguards to women's rights. In South Africa, national legislation equalizes women's position with men's in terms of the law, protects women's employment rights and outlaws domestic violence and sexual crimes. However, implementation of these progressive laws remains weak, even in urban areas (Interview, CGE, 2003). Land reform processes have been notably slow, with only 3.5 percent of agricultural land redistributed by 2005. However, some provision has been made for gender equity; wives are listed as beneficiaries of land titles along with husbands, and female household heads can be allocated land. In Community Property Associations (CPAs)—a type of group ownership—women must be represented on committees: theoretically, they should constitute over 40 percent of committee members.

Although CPAs must comply with the law to receive grant allocations, actual practice does not ensure gender equity, despite the innovatory nature of these bodies. Bob (1999), Pharoah (2001) and Walker (2003) have all explored women's participation in CPA committees within Kwa Zulu Natal Province, where gender norms remain conservative. Pharoah found that women are sometimes elected to committees due to kinship links with men, but also sometimes due to the force of their personalities. Women tend to be elected to posts associated with female roles (secretaries) and find it difficult to speak and to participate due to norms that women should not customarily speak in front of men, or should do so only with deference (Cross and Friedman, 1998; Mogale and Poshoko, 1997). I conducted research in 2002 and 2003 concerning rural women's needs and the place of 'land' and land rights, given overall situations of insecurity faced by most rural women (Jacobs, 2004).[3] Despite difficulties in enacting gender equity 'on the ground,' it was felt that there had been positive spin-offs from the above initiatives, and that some 'spaces' for rural women had opened up.

Land legislation, land titling and gender rights

A number of legislative and policy initiatives which attempt to enact and secure women's land rights have taken place in eastern and southern Africa from the mid-1990s, as explored in the two examples below. Sometimes, these indicate the different 'sides' of the conundrum noted in stark form. Famously, in Uganda a political struggle took place over a clause in the Uganda Land Bill which would have enforced a co-ownership clause. To the surprise of the women's groups who campaigned for this, the clause never appeared in the Act as finally published, due particularly to hostility from the Ministry of Lands, from Parliament and in Cabinet (Kawamara-Mishambi and Ovonji-Odida, 2003: 160). The clause—now known as the 'lost clause'—was seen as threatening to the ownership rights of individual men and of clans.

Tanzania

In Tanzania, the 1999 Land Acts (in force 2001) were the result of complex negotiations between the state, land lobbies and women's groups, constituting a delicate balancing act between statutory and customary law (Ikdahl et. al. 2006:xi). The Land Acts strengthen local customary institutions but seek to erode the influence of discriminatory practices and to strengthen the position of women. For instance, the Village Land Act establishes quotas for women's participation on Village Land Councils. Additionally, spousal consent is needed for disposition of land. A separate 1990 court judgment found that a woman was entitled to sell land she had inherited (op.cit, p. 40). Tsikata gives a detailed account of the splits that occurred in Tanzania over the issues outlined here: the Land Coalition, formed in the late 1990s to ensure a progressive outcome in negotiations over land, soon had to face the fact of serious differences between coalition partners (Tsikata, 2003:164). These occurred over who should control radical titles in land; how discriminatory customary law should be reformed, and the amount of power to be given to the state and to village land management committees. Tensions also occurred over donor funding.

To summarize, the issues outlined here were mirrored in increasingly rancorous differences—differences which are also relevant in other national contexts. The Shivji Commission (on the land question) felt that gender issues were outside its remit and did not consider these except for the issue of succession; its recommendations supported 'evolutionary' change to customary law. Some felt that the Commission (and feminist anthropologists) had overstated the strength of women's land claims in customary law. There are echoes here of the problems that 'peasant studies' has in considering gender issues. The Gender Land Task Force /GLTF showed more concern about joint ownership and registration of spouses' titles than about the concerns of land titling preoccupying the Commission and the Land Forum. The Ministry of Community Development and Women's Affairs commissioned a national study (by Rwebangua), which found that rural women were enthusiastic about land titling, feeling that it would lead to greater security.

Following the Land Acts, the Tanzania Women Lawyers Association (TWLA) held that a number of gains had been made such as the possibility of registration in both spouses' names, equal representation of women on relevant village committees, and the right for a woman to acquire and register land in her own name, as well as gender-neutral language in the Land Acts (2003: 173). Other feminists criticized provisions on customary law as unduly weak. Although discrimination was outlawed, the onus was placed upon individuals to challenge such discrimination, and such action by a wife is likely to be seen as hostile.

The Land Commission alleged that women's groups were used by the state to divide civil society ranks (an old charge against feminists) as their demands did not oppose the free market paradigm (Tsikata, 2003:174). It was argued that equality with men was necessary but not sufficient to create equitable land access, since both genders faced the prospect of landlessness with titling (2003:176). However, women lawyers leading the GTLF argued that 'evolution' would take too long, and that in any case there was no guarantee of change.

After the Land Acts, Ikdahl et.al note the slow pace of implementation: for instance, husbands often sell homes and land without the wife's consent (Ikdahl et al. 2006: 39), but nevertheless the legislation can at least serve as an example of good practice in statutory terms. However, Ikdahl et.al also note that the main aim of legislation was to strengthen the land market, and in this drive, gender concerns have been sidelined. Although NGOs attempt to spread information about women's rights, most women remain unaware of these, and Ikdahl et.al hold that gender initiatives have declined in visibility.

Mozambique

Mozambique has arguably the most smallholder-friendly land law in Africa (Palmer, 2005). Palmer comments that following the end of the long and violent civil war, in 1992, external agencies such as USAID advocated privatization of land, as had occurred in Uganda. Although Mozambique had a history of directive top-down governance and although the situation post-conflict was highly confused with many people displaced, competing claims, etc., the consultation concerning land was remarkably open and was followed by a radical campaign to raise public awareness: the *Campanha Terra*, in which around 15,000 volunteers worked imaginatively, using many types of media. The Land Law gives communities rights over land on the basis of occupancy; the communities have the right to delimit and to register their lands, including fallow and reserve land (Palmer, 2005; citing Hanlon, 2002). The Land Law affirms that land use titles can be given to men and women and attempts to give women more decision-making power in land matters (ActionAid, 2006: 56). Another piece of legislation, the Family Law (2004) also has great relevance for women's land rights: women (and men's) rights to land through inheritance and after divorce are addressed in the Family Law, and it is stipulated that women can inherit land. Other key issues relate to the codification of different forms of marriage and the principles of equity between the genders in property, as in other matters (Ikdahl etal. 2006: xii).

Due to a number of factors, women have strong use-rights in Mozambique, perhaps especially in the north. Customary practices vary widely in Mozambique, along with patrilineal patterns; some groups in the north are matrilineal and Islam is practiced more commonly in the south. However, Bonate's study (2003) in Nampula Province found that customary law was of far more importance than religious or other factors in determining land rights, particularly as the state had little control over rural populations during the civil war. However, as elsewhere, women's informal rights have their limits. One Mozambiqan woman commented to a researcher,

> When women are working, the men approve that the women have their own pieces of land, but when it comes to harvest time, the men say: "You are my own, and so whatever you are harvesting is also my own" (Norfolk, 2004: cited in ActionAid, 2006: 58).

The sentiments expressed in this statement are likely to be of much relevance in other national contexts.

The continued effects of displacement, sexual abuse during wartime and other effects of conflict upon women have been serious, and there is a need to emphasize land rights in order to build some stability into women's lives (Waterhouse, 1998). Ikdahl et al. (2006) note that the debates on land and gender and family law have been carried out rather separately. Urgent land debates concern how to deal with emerging land markets, and land-grabbing by the wealthy and other interests. The same authors estimate that Mozambican law comes closest (in their comparative

African study) to meeting the stipulations of a Human Rights-Based Approach in granting women property rights, and it does so in the context of collective property rights. Nevertheless, there is a lack of knowledge about how the multiple contemporary laws in Mozambique have impacted locally upon rural women. Action Aid (2006) notes that many women are still unaware of their rights, even after a concerted popular information campaign; this is due in part to low educational levels as well as widespread poverty and the continued effects of conflict.

This section has emphasized the efforts made to incorporate gender-friendly stipulations concerning property, land titles and land rights in several cases. However, it is clear that these have met with a range of constraints. Aside from failure to implement, as in Uganda, many rural women are unable to utilize statutory law where it does exist. As is now well-documented, this is due to a combination of lack of knowledge about new laws; lack of resources to attend court (sometimes, even local courts); lack of education and confidence, meaning that it is difficult to present a case; and lack of confidence in male-dominated legal settings. Another set of factors concerns the weakness of local and national states: even in situations in which a case is brought to court and a favorable judgment reached, this still requires implementation, implying a strong institutional infrastructure and accountability (Banda, 2005).

Lastly, a major factor concerns backlashes against women, particularly violent backlashes (Jacobs, 2000b). This is mentioned in passing in some cases, e.g. Rugadya et. al 2004 and the Action Aid document. However, this factor is deserving of more extended analysis. Women bringing legal cases are often subject to threats and violence as well as risking their marriages (Banda, 2005). Momsen observes that increased power or gains by women may result in a backlash, taking the form of desertion and/or violence (2003:240).

It is perhaps evident from the above cases that effecting an egalitarian agrarian or land tenure reform is not a straightforward matter. It should be recalled that rights are not only 'economic' or legal but concern personal security in that women's assertion of rights or claims may result in violence against them. Given the impediments that many women face in terms of attaining basic rights, the best chances of achieving this would seem to lie in a confluence of factors. An ideal scenario would include a broadly democratic polity that sees 'democracy' as inclusive of economic as well as political/social rights; in societies where agriculture is an important means of livelihood, the scenario would include a polity committed to redistribution of land, transparent political processes, and vigorous civil society, including one in which women's movements are active. Such an 'ideal type' of course, is not often met, but nevertheless is worth putting forward as a goal. It has proved, and continues to prove, difficult for women to have their needs or demands for land met in most circumstances; a real and broad-based commitment to achieving gender equity appears to be necessary given that much gender discrimination is rooted in everyday (especially family) life and gender-biased social and legal norms.

Zimbabwe

Some accounts correctly setting out the justice of a case for land reform fail to mention other aspects of Zimbabwe's fast-track resettlement or wider politics (Thomas, 2003). In its 'fast-track' land resettlement (following on a well-organized and ordered resettlement in the 1980s that offered some benefits for women) the Government 'resettled' over 200,000 people by late 2003 (Masiiwa, 2004). In 2004, the share of land held by white commercial farmers had been reduced from over 30 percent down to 3 percent (Goebel, 2005a: 47), and land confiscations and redistribution continue. Attention has focused on land confiscations; in my view, the failure of land reform has resulted mainly from other factors. The 'fast-track' resettlement program has been marred by extreme violence, not only against white farmers but also against African farm workers: the latter should be important beneficiaries of any land reform but have instead been marginalized and victimized (Sachikonye, 2003). The process has been marked by its main intent: to increase state power rather than to benefit smallholders. Such processes have been paralleled by other violent 'Operations' such as the recent *Murambatsvina* (Operation 'Clean Up the Filth'), which destroyed the homes of up to one million people in urban and peri-urban areas, and Operation *Taguta/Sisuthi* (ironically, 'eat well') in Matabeleland; the latter, under the rubric of strengthening militarization of maize planting, has destroyed irrigation facilities and vegetable gardens (Solidarity Peace Trust, 2006). Thus land reform has been part of a process that has resulted in economic disaster. Agricultural productivity has dropped seriously due to a lack of support for resettled farmers, chaos due to violence and intimidation, and lack of inputs such as fuel (Jacobs, 2003; Human Rights Watch, 2002). Kinsey observed in 2006 that almost no cultivation was occurring (Kinsey, 2006) in areas he visited.

It is now commonly acknowledged that the economy is in 'meltdown', with the IMF estimating that 40 percent of economic capacity (possibly an underestimate) has been lost in the past seven years (Josh, 2005). A very recent WHO report estimates Zimbabwean life expectancy as possibly the lowest in the world, at thirty-seven years for men and thirty-four years for women (down from sixty years in the early 1980s). As the incidence of HIV/AIDS has declined recently, the main reason appears to be malnutrition and the economic crisis (BBC, 2006). It is estimated that there was need for food aid for 4.3 million people in a population of over 12 million people in 2006 [*Independent Review,* 2005:18).

There is virtually no data—and no systematic data at all—concerning recipients of land, although it is often acknowledged that the process has been confused, less than transparent and often corrupt (IRIN, 2003). Although some women have gained land in this process, many rapes of 'political opponents' and other women are reported (Itano, 2003; Goebel, 2005b), and the atmosphere of extreme violence and intimidation is not one normally conducive to gender rights. Aside from the consequences for Zimbabwe and the whole region, this situation threatens to 'besmirch' the reputation of redistributive land reform for many years to come. It is to be hoped that the land (and gendered land) struggles of people in the region will overcome any legacy of this counter-example.

Thoughts about ways forward on gender and land

Different positions are evident in the 'woman and land' question. A number of NGOs critical of titling and privatization support the rights of local communities to hold land and to govern land tenure arrangements. They may at the same time champion women's rights and attempt to ameliorate the most discriminatory aspects of customary law. The argument is that liberalization and titling threaten to undermine the livelihood basis—or at least its agrarian aspect—of local communities. The hope expressed is that civil society and particularly women's groups will be able to alter customary law in a more gender-friendly direction. Tripp writes that in Zambia, the Women for Change in Zambia fight for women's rights by seeking to preserve customary tenure but also encourage traditional authorities to pursue pro-woman policies (2004:3).

In contrast, most women's and feminist organizations, as Tripp (2004), Whitehead and Tsikata (2003) note, emphasize the importance of changing statutory law to secure women's rights, which may imply titling, registration and privatization. Tripp writes that many African women have mounted new movements to eradicate customary land tenure practices and to fight for individual rights of women (2004: 2). In the disputes over women's rights and types of land tenure in Tanzania (above), it seems clear that some feminists did not take on board the wider issues facing the 'community' or smallholders, while the Land Commission found it to treat gender issues as serious concerns. Tsikata writes that statutory law must be brought 'closer to people' as one claim of customary law is that of proximity.

A related issue here concerns the ability of many men to "navigate between customary and statutory law as they see fit" (ActionAid, 2006: 65), while most women's lives are regulated through customary law. Thus Tripp's observation (2004) that individualized land rights are not simply the preoccupation of an elite class of women, but also of poorer/rural women, seems apposite. I agree that this is not simply an 'elite' or middle-class orientation—but noting this does not answer the question posed by issues of privatization and titling.

There exists no easy 'way out' of the dilemmas posed here, which are replicated in a number of settings throughout Africa. Diane Elson's comment is useful, however: fulfillment of human rights is a complex process unfolding over time, not a single legislative act (Elson, 2002: 80). Elson also writes of the importance of accountability: to have an entitlement implies access to an accountable process; if a person's access to a resource is at the arbitrary discretion of a public official, or dependent upon patronage or the goodwill of a husband, then access to the resource is not of right (Elson, 2002: 102-3). Thus entitlements imply *accountability,* although this could refer to a local community as well as a national government. Many legislative changes founder on a lack of accountability and are never effectively enforced.

Ikdahl etal. (2006) argue for a human rights-based approach (HRBA) in order to enforce both women's and group rights to land. Similarly, Elson and Gideon (2004) argue that the International Covenant on Economic, Social and Cultural Rights (ICESCR, coming into force in 1976) has much potential in curtailing current encroachments upon economic rights. Feminists have focused on the ICESCR as an arena for activism, both in terms of improving the Covenant as a normative framework and in using it to 'name and shame' errant governments. Lawyers Day and Brodsky have pointed out why the ICESCR is of interest to feminists. Firstly, its subject matter is practical, material conditions and as such is of great interest to most women—including poorer rural women. Secondly—and echoing an important theme of this chapter—for women a division between rights to economic security and to personal liberty is purely artificial; this is clear, for instance, in the case of violent abuse. Thirdly, the ICESCR precludes equalization 'downwards' (as in the current 'race to the bottom' often cited as a consequence of deregulation). Thus the ICESCR provides a better basis than the CEDAW against erosion of living standards. The weakness of ICESCR (and similar instruments), the authors argue, is in a world where economic power is increasingly concentrated; its strength is deploying a discourse of rights including economic rights.

Although legally-based campaigns have great strengths, they can have an unduly individualistic orientation. Nevertheless, as Razavi (2006) argues, changes in statutory law are worthwhile, not necessarily because they always result in change 'on the ground' but because they provide an aim. And it is conceivable that the strategies mentioned may provide bases for group as well as (not instead of) individual rights. In this respect, as in others, there exists little substitute for social mobilization to secure rights.

There is a need to keep considering whether there is a way out of the impasse between individualization/gender rights vs. collective rights/customary law entailing gender discrimination. Here I cite an example from Cameroon: some women are acquiring land despite customary stipulations against this, and are forming *tontine* or mutual aid groups in order to cultivate large farms; their incomes have risen in this manner (Logo and Bikie, 2005: 59). Here women have used their agency to benefit themselves but have followed a cooperative path. Such solutions point in a helpful direction. Alternatively, feminists may have to opt for hopeful but imperfect 'ways forward' in thinking of more gender-equitable land rights in Africa and elsewhere. Many rural men see their social power—and indeed the stability of 'society'—as tied up with land rights: thus, this remains a contentious and emotive topic.

Notes

[1] Abdullah and Hamza also note that establishment of *shari'a* law would also mean that women became secluded and so could not themselves farm (2003).

[2] In Zimbabwean Resettlement Areas before the current 'fast-track 'land reform, customary law did not apply, or not formally. Land was administered by a Resettlement Office (RO) as well as by Village Development Committees. A number of ROs used their influence to alter land tenure arrangements in favor of women, e.g. allowing widows to remain on land after a husband's death (Jacobs, 2000a; Goebel, 1999).

[3] I conducted a total of 51 interviews: these were held in six locations in South Africa: Pretoria (Tshwane); Johannesburg; Cape Town, Stellenbosch; Durban and Pietermaritzburg.

CHAPTER FOURTEEN
EMPOWERING WOMEN IN THE AFRICAN ENTREPRENEURIAL LANDSCAPE

Micro-entrepreneurs to Business Globalists in the Formal and Informal Sectors

Anita Spring

Introduction: The Range of Women Entrepreneurs in Africa

This chapter maps out the African entrepreneurial landscape and constructs models that consider the informal and formal sectors and their characteristics. With increased emphasis on the micro- and small-scale levels, and with the majority of women at these levels, this study queries whether the dichotomy is simply convenient and heuristic or valid intrinsically because of certain characteristics. It also focuses on whether or not entrepreneurs can move within and between sectors in Africa, and whether scale limits women's agency and empowerment. At the formal-sector level is the question of the "missing middle" in Africa, and what inhibits woman-owned, small- and medium-size formal sector companies from being upwardly mobile. In other words, why are there fewer "rags to riches stories" in African countries than in developed countries? Can there be movement within the informal sector from micro to small enterprises, and from small enterprises to large ones, as well as movement in the formal sector from small to medium, and medium to large businesses? And finally, what of the small but growing cadre of women who are top-of-the-heap mainstream formal-sector business owners—already empowered—who may both confound researchers/donors and provide role models for success within their societies?

This chapter considers the characteristics of women's business participation and the scale of their enterprises. The components of the entrepreneurial landscape include: demographic characteristics of the entrepreneurs (e.g., education, business training, employment history, and marital and family status); types of enterprises or firms in terms of sector and scale; sources of start-up capital (including microfinance and microcredit at the smallest levels); product sources and marketing channels; and network and association memberships. These help delineate some of the features that facilitate or limit movement within and between the sectors. The range of women entrepreneurs considered here is from traditional micro-enterprises to owners of large-scale companies, some of whom are emerging global business-persons; most likely this paradigm also applies to male entrepreneurs.

African entrepreneurial activities are traditionally engendered in terms of access, control, and remuneration. More men than women are in the more lucrative enterprises, especially in the formal sector, as owners and managers of large firms and small industries, while many women tend to be in the smallest, informal sector of micro-enterprises. Both genders share the middle ground of higher-profit informal sector activities. Men and women traders and wholesalers may specialize in different commodities altogether and employ different strategies. But African women entrepreneurs are not a homogeneous group. Traditionally, middle- and upper-class women often succeed in both the formal and informal sectors, while poor women are limited to informal sector vending with limited sales and do not progress because they lack education, networks, and capital.

African women entrepreneurs most typically studied by social science researchers are marketers and owners of small-scale businesses. The problems that these women face include: lack of start-up funds (e.g., having to raise their own capital, begging start-up funds from spouses and relatives, and lacking access to bank loans) and buying and selling difficulties (e.g., poor market conditions, regulations and harassment from authorities; transport problems; product spoilage, etc.). Many are local market women who are ignored in formal arenas. Their entrepreneurial activities are often linked to or are extensions of their domestic realm, and they are involved in selling prepared foods, agricultural products, crafts, clothing, cosmetics, and small household furnishings. They may conceal profits from their husbands and cross borders surreptitiously to sell outside their countries. Orisim (1998), among others, reports that they have limited profits and are highly affected by structural adjustment problems. Various authors in Spring and McDade (1998) noted that the large numbers of women involved in marketing agricultural commodities in most African countries also feed and provision their households, communities, and large cities. Traditional patriarchal gender ideology often prevents adequate recognition of women's contributions (Spring 2000).

There are many other categories of women entrepreneurs on the continent (Spring 2002). Women are bulk wholesalers and large traders who import and export such commodities as textiles, crafts, household goods, appliances and electronics. Some use the Internet and global communication methods (fax, cell phones, web sites). Another emerging part of the entrepreneurial landscape includes e-commerce. Many traditional large-scale traders are in the informal sector but may appear to have or actually have ties to the formal sector in terms of obtaining bank loans and having a company name. They move products through urban and rural areas but contribute little to building their country's infrastructure and GDP.

Then there are businesswomen in the formal sector who head small-, medium- and large-scale industries and companies producing manufactured items and services, and selling products made in their countries and elsewhere; these may be categorized in terms of revenues and number of employees. Similar to their male counterparts, women conduct a range of types of businesses: where there is little to total financial transparency; where family members versus credentialed workers are hired; where there are patronage links or no links at all to government; where operation of multiple businesses minimizes risks or the entrepreneur concentrates on just one business. Some use "old-boys/girls" networks while others prefer new associations and business networks. For start-up capital, some rely on family, while others obtain standard bank loans (Kuada 2006). Finally, there is an emerging category of entrepreneurs who are apolitical and anti-patronage, who practice financial transparency and accountability, and who use global business methods. They called themselves the "New Generation of African Entrepreneurs" (NGAEs) and are the subject of a multi-country study that Barbara McDade and I did from 2000 to 2006 (Spring 2002, 2006b; McDade and Spring 2005).

This chapter considers notions of women's involvement in the informal and formal sectors, and what that means in terms of women's agency and empowerment. The components of the entrepreneurial landscape described here are: 1) the informal sector of micro-entrepreneurs, home-based industries, and large-scale traders; 2) the "formalized informal" sector of microcredit, microfinance, and e-commerce; 3) the formal-sector small industries, medium-scale firms, and large companies, and 4) the formal sector medium to large businesses by emerging globalists. The next section explains the models in terms of the variables mentioned above. The main thrust is to consider the diversity of women's activities and factors that may account for their success or stagnation.

The Formal and Informal Sectors in Africa

Informal and formal can be seen as "dual economies" of African countries. There is no conclusive definition of the informal sector, although the term has been in existence since the 1970s. Schneider (2001:743) wrote that initially "[the term 'informal sector'] was rooted in a government perspective of order," although it was the formal sector with its political interests and bureaucracy and corruption that was mysterious for people without power, while the informal sector was more accessible to them. In *African Entrepreneurship: Theory and Reality,* Spring and McDade (1998) argued that the informal referred to unregistered, unregulated, and untaxed businesses, including service enterprises, production activities, and street vending, while the formal sector included taxed, registered and regulated businesses. Looking back on the dichotomy, Hart (2001:157), an original founder of the term 'informal sector,' wrote that the informal economy "was nothing less than the self-organized energies of people biding their time to escape from the strictures of state rule." The informal and formal sectors as used here should not be confused with "Second Economy" and "First Economy" rubrics used in the literature. MacCaffey (1998) uses "Second Economy" to refer to entrepreneurial activities in the Democratic Republic of the Congo in the absence of government. Hansen and Vaa (2002) use the same term to refer to home-based industries in urban areas. South Africa's President Mbeki uses "Second Economy" to refer to the underclass of the unemployed (mostly uneducated Africans), compared to the "First Economy" of employed affluent citizens of all races.

In Africa, the unregistered, unregulated businesses include service enterprises (e.g., hairdressing, commercial transportation, auto repairing, etc.), fabrications (e.g., furniture, metal equipment manufacturing, etc.), street vending (e.g., produce, food, clothing, medicines, etc.), and the like. Charmes (1999) estimates that the informal sector contributes 20 to 40 percent of total GDP in African countries, and 40 to 60 percent of non-agricultural GDP. Historically, African governments mostly concerned themselves with the formal sector; donor agencies supported the informal; and social scientists studied the informal market sector.

The distinctions of what is formal and what is informal are not clear-cut. There are multiple reasons and situations that make the distinctions and boundaries fuzzy. There are consequences for censuses and enumeration, taxation, and calculations of national indicators, on the one hand, and confusion for lending organizations, inter-regional and international commerce, state programmatic efforts, and so forth, on the other. In addition, when governments regulate, enumerate, and tax, or donor projects provide finance and training, what was informal suddenly takes on characteristics of the formal sector. Three examples show how these lines can blur: municipal 'sites and services" for market women; microcredit and micro-savings programs for micro-entrepreneurs, and e-commerce websites used by unregistered non-tax-paying entrepreneurs (the latter is considered in a later section).

First, in recent decades, municipalities set up "sites and services" for market women whom they enumerated and from whom they collected market fees/taxes. Some governments were initially bothered by informal enterprises, especially market and street vendors—the bulk of whom are women—and sometimes harassed, forcibly removed them, or confiscated their wares. In the 1990s, perspectives changed in places like Zambia, Zimbabwe and Kenya, and municipalities began to capacitate the informal sector by providing market locales, stalls, storage, etc. (Hansen and Vaa 2002). In South Africa from the post-apartheid period to the present, major cities such as Durban and Johannesburg vacillated between capacitating such market areas and working with vendor associations, on the one hand, and "cleaning up the streets by removing large number of vendors and their goods, on the other (Valodia et al. 2006). Sometimes reclassification from informal to formal became a matter of expediency by municipal governments that registered these businesses primarily to tax them. Using this conception, most informal entrepreneurs, except the illegal ones, would be in the formal sector, although many are still at the micro-level in size.

Second, microcredit and micro-savings institutions "formalize" micro-entrepreneurs by program requirements such as registration, enumeration, training, and financial transactions. The thrust by donors and NGOs to advance microcredit and microfinance schemes, previously dismissed by the banking systems as too cumbersome, requires registration and accounting of participants. With 2005 designated as the "International Year of Microcredit," donor and NGO projects rigorously embraced microfinance/microcredit (www.yearofmicrocredit.org). As well, some national banks and government microfinance institutions also began extending services to include micro-savings and microcredit. The new rhetoric is that the poor are now clients rather than beneficiaries; they have purchasing power and can even increase the formal banking sector's wealth (Prahalad 2004). Hence, it is difficult to know whether these enterprises still comprise the informal sector, or if they would more accurately be called the *"formalized informal sector"* (Spring n.d.).

Third, because of structural adjustment programs, formal-sector workers (more men than women) have been "retrenched" from their jobs and seek income in the informal sector. As well, formal-sector firms seeking lower prices and more flexible credit may turn to suppliers in the informal sector. People and firms with less income might shift their purchases from the formal to the informal sector, "where negotiations about prices and credit are more flexible" (Grawert and Konig 2001:701). For women in particular, there has been increased competition from retrenched male labor and an increase in cross-border activities in certain places (Osirim 1998). Forward and backward linkages between the sectors are widespread, and capital diverted from formal-sector businesses/salaries are used to purchase supplies from informal enterprises. Machinery, cloth, and agricultural inputs manufactured in the formal sector are used and traded in the informal, while spare parts from cross-border trade and craft/cloth items from the informal sector wind up in small retail stores.

A main question here is what types of evidence exists concerning movement *between* the sectors and *within* the sectors in terms of scale. The work by Ngau and Keino (1996) on Kenyan women entrepreneurs in Nairobi markets indicates that they have diverse social backgrounds that shape their types of enterprises. Daniels and others argue that ease of entry is related to high- and low-profit enterprises that are worlds apart even in the informal sector category. Data from Zimbabwe show women in relation to men being involved in only 37 percent of high-profit enterprises versus their involvement in 83 percent of low-profit ones (1994, 1998).

This chapter delineates the various categories of women entrepreneurs, since there has been a tendency to see African women mostly as micro- and small-scale entrepreneurs. Sometimes donors and researchers have "lumped" African women entrepreneurs together. To give an example from my interviews, some formal-sector women business-persons (members of the NGAEs discussed below), noted that donors and some scholars "lump" them together with micro-entrepreneurs in the informal sector. An owner of a medium-sized formal-sector business in Uganda told me she declined the invitation of a bilateral donor agency to join a weekly forum with traditional female micro-entrepreneurs. She felt that the advice and assistance required to take her business to the "next level" would not be found in groups interested in obtaining loans of around US$100. She and other medium and large company owners said they sympathized with micro- and small-scale entrepreneurs in the informal sector, but noted that their business-enhancement needs fell into a gap in lending practices. They needed medium-sized loans (US$50,000 to $1 million) to expand their businesses. These were often difficult to find, being too large for donors and too small for major banks that loaned to large (often multilateral) corporations.

The Entrepreneurial Landscape in Africa

Entrepreneurship is a major catalyst for economic growth in both industrialized and developing countries. Entrepreneurs establish new businesses that create employment and provide services and products to increase the wealth of their local and national economies. Gender influences the entrepreneurial landscape. Micro-entrepreneurs, technically, consist of one to five employees and are mostly in the informal sector (Daniels et al. 1995; Kibera 1999; Jalloh and Falola 2002). Some have defined small-scale as having fewer than five (or sometimes nine) employees, medium as having ten to twenty-nine employees, and large as having 50-400 employees (Spring and McDade 1998; Kuada 2006). In the 1990s, only 2 percent of all African businesses had ten or more employees (Spring and McDade 1998; Manu 1999:110).

Snyder argues that "entrepreneurs create wealth where there was none" (2000:1). She considered women entrepreneurs in Uganda who establish and operate successful businesses that cover the entire spectrum of the entrepreneurial landscape, from micro informal to large formal sector. These women use entrepreneurial activities to empower themselves, and include market women (who sell everything from water to curtains), manufacturers of custom leather shoes, owners of private clinics and supermarkets, tourism industry operatives, and hoteliers. The entrepreneurial landscape in Africa is a composite of business enterprises that include micro-enterprises providing marginal employment for one individual to large multinational corporations employing hundreds of people. Classification of businesses by size (number of employees, sales, or revenues) varies among countries (Spring and McDade 1998). The following sections provide a synopsis of the entrepreneurial landscape in Africa. (The concern here is with the typology; only some studies are mentioned; the section on Models below has others.) Also included are home-based industries, microcredit/finance, and e-commerce, since less has been written on them and they are the new "hot" topics.

Micro-entrepreneurs in the informal sector

Much has been written about the majority of women in African countries who are engaged in micro-enterprises in the informal sector Prominent among micro-entrepreneurs are the agriculturalists and traders who provision their rural areas, as well as towns and cities all over Africa. The literature on them is substantial (e.g., MacGaffey 1987; Clark 1994, 1998; Horn 1994, 1998; Arould 1995; House-Midamba and Ekechi 1995; Orisim 1998; Robertson 1997; Aspaas 1998; Spring and McDade 1998; Jalloh 1999; Snyder 2000; Jalloh and Falola 2002; Spring 2000, 2002; Mandel 2003) and also includes other references mentioned below. A study of 50,000 such businesses in Southern and Eastern Africa during the period 1990-98 showed that 48 percent were owned by women (Mead 1999). In addition to the urban, there are also rural, non-agricultural micro- and small enterprises (e.g., making craft products, roof tiles, furniture, metal tools, etc.), but their density, size, and growth rate are lower than in urban areas.

Home-Based Industries—informal and sometimes formal

Home-based enterprises (HBEs) in large cities in Africa are "a particular type of enterprise situated at the very frontier between the formal and the informal city" (Kamete 2002:120). HBEs take place around the housing unit and differ from those in localized areas designated for small-scale urban informal economic activities. Some are similar to *jua kali* or "in the hot sun industries" and include metalworking, carpentry, auto-repair, etc., mostly done by men. Some are micro in scale, while others are similar to small industries and retail shops. The goods and services they produce are cheaper and outside the legal formal sector. Kamete's (2002) study of the spatial and operational features of the small informal sector in Harare (Table 1) shows that HBE sites in residential areas "bring goods and services closer to the people" and are affordable (ibid 129). Transactions are a mixture of cash and kind. HBEs also have business locations that tend to be recognizable over time. Although HBEs existed during colonialism, urban planners are currently factoring them into the urban business matrix, and a small percentage may pay taxes on occasion. The flexibility of household space in the urban areas help women, including those employed in the formal sector who have extra time to engage in enterprises from the home (Kazimbaya-Senkwe 2002).

Microcredit and Microfinance (formalizing the informal)

Are the growing number of women (and men) at the micro-level really empowered by microcredit and micro-savings, and can they "enhance their enterprises" by these new services? The literature is equivocal on the women participants in these savings and credit programs. On one hand, there are individual success stories of women who use their funds wisely and progress. Ackerly (1995) used "accounting knowledge" as an indicator of women's empowerment. Women who knew the costs of funded projects, sales revenues, and profits were "judged" to be empowered. Most studies glorify the positive effects of microcredit. Kabeer (2001) concludes that access to credit has a positive impact on women's empowerment. I also argue in *Women Farmers and Commercial Ventures* (Spring 2000) and *Agricultural Development and Gender Issues in Malawi* (Spring 1995) that credit for agricultural inputs has a decided effect on enhanced enterprise scale, food security, and household empowerment.

On the other hand, Okurut, Banga and Mukungu (2004) show that village bank credit schemes do not have significant impacts on physical asset accumulation and expenditure. The poorest women are in a debt cycle, while women who have larger loans and serve as bank committee members re-loan funds at higher interest rates to poorer women. Results vary in terms of gender empowerment, depending on whether or not women have managerial control over funds as compared to only project participation without control and full authority. The data from Ethiopia (Rakesh, Tamiru and Singh 2006) show women repay too quickly, thereby depriving themselves of capital to use for health care and education, as well as for enterprise expansion.

The IMF concludes that microfinance complements the banking sector; it mobilizes deposits and enables women to obtain loans. MicroSave's (www.MicroSave.org) example shows that women use a variety of financial mechanism simultaneously: Informal Rotating Savings and Credit Associations (ROSCAs), Accumulating Savings and Credit Associations (ASCAs), and formal loans (Aryeetey and Steel 1994). MicroSave terms it "the Diversified Informal." In one MicroSave example (Table 2), a rural Kenyan woman has capital in both the informal and formal sectors. She belongs to two ROSCAs, one ASCA, and an informal funeral insurance group, and in addition has some cash savings and a cow. She has also recently obtained a formal micro-loan from a microfinance institution that technically is in the formal sector (Wright 2005).

E-commerce

In Africa as elsewhere, the internet is used for many business endeavors such as customer and marketing research and intelligence (e.g., product comparison, sourcing, and marketing); business transactions (sales and purchases); networking, formal websites (e.g., for information; firm and product PR, and sales); and e-commerce shops and merchants.[1]

Many so-called e-commerce sites based in Africa are not shops but rather information and publicity sites on entrepreneurs and businesses. It should be noted that many sites that sell African craft and furnishings products are not based on the continent, but are owned by Africans and others residing in the UK, Europe and North America. Because few Africans have credit cards or can set up Paypal accounts, except in South Africa, there are a few e-shops that can accept online payments or ship reliably. Formal-sector firms have websites to show products and prices. Website designers and server host sites are plentiful in countries like Ghana, Kenya, and South Africa; they have global standards and their services are competitive (Spring 2006a).

Rhodes (2003) comments that African e-shops have difficulty in handling large orders for artisan products in a timely fashion. Her case study of South Africa, where poor rural women were organized and developed an e-commerce strategy, shows the weaknesses of such groups attempting to do e-commerce successfully, even though the area in which the group is located received a telecenter adequate for e-commerce in 1998. She concludes that most women's groups can produce quality products but the volume varies and they lack marketing research, as well as management, financial accounting, packing and shipping skills.

E-shopAfrica, based in Accra, is a success case of overcoming these problems (www.eshopafrica.com). The site aims "to prove that e-commerce can work for small businesses in Africa" (products have been featured in *The Economist* and *Fortune Small Business Magazine*).[2] The site sells household and art products produced by women's groups and individual artisans from Ghana, Burkina Faso, and Zimbabwe. Women-owners include a Sudanese manager who has lived in Ghana for twenty years, a Canadian product procurer who has lived in Ghana for a decade, and a Ghanaian office manager. By contrast, www.africancraft.com is an example of a website initiated in the U.S. to help African craftspeople sell goods. Other sites like www.ethiogift.com cater to the African expatriate clients in the U.S.; this site offers Moma Konjit's chocolate cake and/or flowers, liquor and live sheep to be sent to relatives in Addis Ababa for special occasions—but paid in the U.S. with credit cards!

Female medium- and large-scale importers/exporters use the Internet, as do NGAE women owners (see below) to obtain market intelligence. NGAE women keep in contact with other network members and use websites for company PR. A study by Hinson and Buatsi (2005) on internet use by Ghana's corporate sector (small and medium formal sector businesses), found there was high use of websites for market research, some use for PR, and little use for payments (for products or raw materials). Finally, most African national governments and export associations have websites on export products and business linkages (e.g., www.ethioexport.org and www.ghana-exporter.org). These medium and large formal-sector companies may be listed on these sites as well, but do not carry out e-commerce.

Medium-scale African firms

Most African economies have a large small-scale sector and a small large-scale sector with a relatively insignificant medium-scale sector (Olomi 1999)—a structure described as the "missing middle" (Esbin 1994; Ferrand 1996; Kiribiti 1999). However, though small, the medium-scale sector is viable and emerging. Marsden (1990:5) showed a wide range of medium-scale firms in six countries (Botswana, Cote d"Ivoire, Ghana, Kenya, Malawi, and Tanzania), and concluded that "the middle is not missing"; but he did not account for gender. Women have played a limited role as owners and managers in the formal sector (Agbaw 2000). Even in the modern formal sector, African women entrepreneurs feel obstructed by the "gender divide" that prevails in most African countries (Hagos 2000). In addition to what are described as "traditional African attitudes" that inhibit women in the formal business sector, African women are outside of "old boys' networks" such as social clubs where businessmen congregate. Snyder (2000) identifies a growing segment of Ugandan women owners of middle-level businesses. Some have formed business associations and assert that they are seizing the challenge that the current government's private sector-friendly policies have afforded. However, Snyder also concludes that despite women's activism and its positive impacts, the situation for the majority of African women shows continuing gender disparities across all socio-economic and political indicators of development (ibid: 29).

By contrast, in some countries the small–medium part sector is changing rapidly, as educated women are involved in both traditional sectors (e.g., textiles, agro-processing and fishing, retail establishments), and non-traditional ones (ICT and computer services, tourism, PR and consultancy firms, real estate, construction). They are more often aided by family capital, but some obtain bank and program loans. In Ghana, some women entrepreneurs are aided by international agencies capacitating the medium-scale sector. Kuada (2006) provides examples of women utilizing private-sector development programs such as the Danish International Development Association, African Project Development Facility (a UN affiliate), and the Commonwealth Development Council for business feasibility studies, investments, and foreign partners. He also documents gender differences in the way resources are leveraged, with women having more difficulties than men accessing bank loans, but compensating by using social capital to leverage business resources.

Business Partners Ltd, South Africa's "Leading Investment Company for Small and Medium Enterprises" (SMEs) invests in formal enterprises with investment financing of between R150,000 and R15 million (http://www.businesspartners. co.za/). It sponsors an annual Business Women of the Year competition to give visibility to its female recipients whose ventures include a chain of appliance retail stores, tourism, and petrol service stations. One of its funds focuses on female entrepreneurs, and during 2004-2005, R154 million was invested in 159 businesses owned and run by women. Data from other funds show 370 women-led medium and large businesses were capitalized with funding of R150 to R300 million (R7.4 = US$1.00).

Large companies in Africa

The number of African businesses that employ hundreds of people and earn annual revenues in the millions of dollars is small, but they are found continent-wide. These businesses conform to regulations, exhibit high levels of human and financial capital, pay taxes, and are integrated into the structures of the formal economy (Bowditch 1999; Kerr 1999; Goedhuys and Sleuwaegen 2000). From independence to the mid-1980s, most large nationally-owned private enterprises were in manufacturing, construction materials, and transportation (Schulpen and Gibbon 2001). They were also found in the sub-sectors of beverages, clothing, furniture, printing, rubber, leather working, plastics, soaps and toiletries, and pharmaceuticals. However, "national" ownership may mean ownership by ethnic minorities such as Asians, Syrians/ Lebanese, and Europeans residing in Africa. Ramachandran and Shah (1999) show that indigenous Africans own few large industrial firms (e.g., Kenya has only 3.6 percent ownership compared to Zimbabwe, which has more than 30 percent).

Fick (2002) profiles a number of individuals who own large-scale businesses continent-wide, including a woman hotel owner in Madagascar and a designer-manufacturer in Ethiopia. His 2006 book profiles women owners of mining, construction, investment, and health care companies in South Africa. McDade and Spring (2005) discuss the networks and business characteristics of a network of medium- and large-scale business owners. Women who owned large-scale businesses were interviewed throughout the continent, including those who owned a commercial supermarket in Ethiopia; food processing plants in Zimbabwe and Malawi;

wood furniture factory in Ghana; shoe factory in Eritrea; leather factory in Ethiopia, textile/clothing factories in Ghana, Mauritius, and Swaziland; a vegetable and cut-flower export operation in Kenya, construction materials factories in Ethiopia and South Africa, and so forth. As well, I met with the owners of an investment company in South Africa (the first women and black-owned company on the Johannesburg Stock Exchange (JSE) and a woman-owned company that changed the JSE to electronic trading (Spring, field notes 2000, 2006).

An emerging segment: medium to large-scale company globalists in Africa

An emerging segment, who called themselves the "new generation of African entrepreneurs" (NGAEs), were constituted into a pan-African, three-regional, thirty-one-country network between 1993 and 2003 to advocate and change the entrepreneurial landscape (Africa Enterprise Network [AEN] Conference Report 2000; Courcelle and de Lattre 1996; Enterprise Network Newsletters 1993-2000; Orsini 1999, 2001; Orsini et al. 1996; SAEN 1999; WAEN 1993; Wohlmuth and Wauschkunh 2001). Barbara McDade and I carried out research on this group (McDade and Spring 2005; Spring 2002; Spring forthcoming) based on fieldwork between 2000 and 2003 in Botswana, Ethiopia, Ghana, Kenya, South Africa, and Uganda (Table 3). I continued fieldwork between 2003-2006 in Ethiopia, Senegal, South Africa, and Tanzania. The networks disbanded in 2003-04, but the entrepreneurs continue to manage their medium- to large-scale firms.

Women comprise 23 percent of the total network members of about 550 for the thirty-one chapters, with each network kept purposefully small to maintain trust and financial transparency.[3] Women network members vary from 40 percent of forty-five members in Ghana to none among Ethiopia's seven members. The national chairs of several country networks are women (e.g. Botswana, Kenya, and South Africa). Many have formal sector business experience before starting their own firms. Women are in all business sectors, including non-traditional businesses such as construction, IT, transportation, and manufacturing; most said that their gender was not a problem for doing business or to their status in the network. All were in formal-sector businesses. Women members noted that females in business face different issues in society, such as childcare responsibilities and restrictions in access to credit and land ownership. They seek mechanisms to address these topics. Some act as spokespersons for women's issues in their countries, have sponsored training courses for women entrepreneurs (from micro- to medium-scale businesses), and have hired female managers. Others have assisted market women and traders with bookkeeping skills (Spring 2002). However, their primary focus, like that of their male counterparts, is on innovating and expanding their own businesses. A few women confide that they appreciate being able to interact with other female network members, since there are not many women who have similar business experiences.

The NGAE networks were constituted with USAID and OECD funding. After donor funding ended, these business-people continued with their own formal-sector businesses and contacts. They differ from other business-people because of their emphasis on financial transparency, being apolitical, using merit rather than kinship and ethnicity in hiring practices, adhering to ethical business practices, advocating for the private sector with governments, and having global perspectives. Members succeeded in influencing business conditions when they implemented cross-national joint business ventures; created a professional sub-network; gained official observer status at the regional economic organizations (Economic Community of West African States [ECOWAS], Common Market for Eastern and Southern Africa [COMESA], and Southern African Development Community [SADC]); signed memoranda of understanding with multilateral agencies (World Bank and Ecobank); formed venture capital funds; and changed government regulations (McDade and Spring 2005; Spring 2002, 2006b). Table 9-3 details the countries, members interviewed (in relation to national network membership), business position, and how businesses were acquired (self, through family or by taking over state-owned enterprises [SOEs]). The data on this group form the end-point in the model's continuum of the formal sector, as discussed below.

Models of the Entrepreneurial Landscape

Movement between sectors

Despite the support from donor agencies and non-governmental agencies (NGOs) for over thirty years, the expected growth and transition of most informal-sector micro to small into medium or large-scale enterprises has not occurred (K'obonyo 1999; Spring 2002). The question relating to agency and empowerment is whether or not women, as well as men, can increase business prowess and move within and between sectors. This model is given in Figure 14-1, which summarizes data from primary and secondary research including the NGAE study. It models the informal sector (micro-entrepreneurs to large traders); the formal sector (small industries and retail shops, small and medium-sized companies, and large manufacturing firms); and the NGAEs, (business globalists who function as the other end-point of the continuum). There is some fluidity within and between sectors. However, many reasons limit upward movement within and between the heuristic spectrum categories. These include: (1) lack of ability to expand due to lack of capital, management skills, formal education, and formal-sector business experience; (2) inability to source necessary materials and find profitable markets; (3) government regulations on business transactions that are "rent-seeking" (i.e., bribes and scams) or simply hinder; (4) inability to widen the extent of the business and compete outside local areas due to the lack of networks, fiscal transparency, more global experience, etc.; and (5) the political landscape in many countries that may put limits on private enterprise (e.g., regulations that preclude private sectors' endeavors and state-owned enterprises that preclude competition).

In terms of movement between small- and large-scale informal trading businesses, there are women who have made such moves, but they are rare. Esther Occlu, former head of the Ghanaian Association of Professional Business, is a well-known example. Starting in the 1960s when her grandmother gave her some "small change" with which she bought oranges and made marmalade, her entrepreneurial activities grew into ownership of food and textile factories (first informally and then in the formal sector), as documented in the film *Fear Woman* (UN Television, 1974) and personal communication (July 2000). But usually, family connections and capital are necessary for movement to higher levels. The new route is to have a college degree (bachelors and/or MBAs), especially for those without family backgrounds in business.

Demographic Profiles

Figure 14-2 is a heuristic guide concerning some demographic characteristics of women entrepreneurs—educational levels, formal-sector work experience, marital status, and husband's financial contribution—in the formal and informal sectors. Women micro-entrepreneurs may have no education to some primary education (Clark 1994; Robertson 1995, 1997, 1998; Spring 2000, 2002); conventional large-scale entrepreneurs may have primary to secondary to some college, and some are assisted in doing e-commerce by their educated children (Spring's interviews with Ethiopian and Uganda traders; Coquery-Vidrovitch 1997). By contrast, small and medium business owners, such as members of the Uganda Women Entrepreneurs Ltd. (UWEAL) and Ghanaian Association of

Women Entrepreneurs (GAWE) have mostly completed secondary school, with some having gone on to college and a few having completed degrees (Spring's field notes 2000, 2001, 2006). Conventional large-scale businesses owned by Africans are mostly in the manufacturing and agricultural sectors (Spring and McDade 1998; McDade and Spring 2005). Some of the women owners in Uganda (Synder 2000), Kenya (Spring's fieldnotes 2001), and Ethiopia (Spring's fieldnotes 2000) have college degrees. By contrast, most of the NGAEs have bachelor degrees, some have MAs and MBAs, and a few have Ph.D.s (Spring's fieldnotes 2000, 2001; Spring 2002; McDade and Spring 2005).

It is possible but not likely that micro-entrepreneurs could have employment in the formal sector, but almost by definition, this is uncommon. Large-scale traders usually have not been salaried workers, except for the new phenomenon of retrenched workers (Trip 199X). Coquery-Vidrovitch (1997) notes that some West African women passed down such businesses for hundreds of years to their offspring, but in the past generation, their offspring are well-educated and prefer to become formal-sector professionals. Owners of small to large businesses have several pathways; they may have been salaried workers who left to start their own companies, or more commonly, they are women who take over family businesses. By contrast, 85 percent of the NGAEs interviewed started their businesses, while 11 percent took over SOEs (Table 3; McDade and Spring 2005). Most had salaried positions in formal sector companies in their own countries, as well as in the US, the UK, and Europe before starting their companies; a few started companies after college graduation. Some were CEOs and Chief Operating Officers (COOs) of the companies they worked for. Among the NGAEs, some spouses own businesses together, but they more often have their own businesses; in some cases, both spouses were network members. A few NGAEs were business partners with other family members (e.g., daughter and father, mother and son, and siblings).

Considering women's financial relations with their husbands, in some parts of Africa, village and peri-urban women expect to receive money from their husbands to open micro or small enterprises for market sales in surplus products, cooked foods, and textiles. Yoruba and Igbo women in Nigeria (Falola 1995; House-Midamba and Ekecki 1995) and some Ghanaian women (Clark 1993; 1998) were traditionally in this arena. In other places, this capacitation by husbands was not automatic but sometimes occurred, and both married and female head-of-household women were market traders (Robertson 1995, 1998; House-Midamba 1995; Horn 1994, 1998). In some cases, women were supposed to turn over profits to their husbands, but many often hid the money (Spring 2000). By contrast, salaried women workers had a variety of arrangements, from holding separate purses (Khasiani 1995) to separate responsibilities for household and children to having joint-bank-accounts (Spring 2002). Data from elsewhere also support the notion that when women earn their own income, their husbands reduce their household allowances (Spring 2000). However, this reduction in basic household funds does not occur for formal-sector company owners who are wealthier and come from affluent family backgrounds.

Types of Enterprises and Firms (excluding e-commerce)

Figure 14-3 provides summaries of the types of enterprises. Small-scale traders and marketers sell agricultural produce, cooked food, beer, crafts, herbs/medicines, and cloth. In West Africa, some specialize in palm and kola nuts, salt, fish, and shea butter, while in Central and East Africa, the products are grains, tubers, vegetables, and fruits. In certain locales such as Lagos, women specialized in herbals and household utensils in the past, but this has now become "male" territory (Coquery-Vidrovitch 1997:99). Traders of any size who buy from the rural areas and sell in peri-urban and urban areas often provide forward and backward linkages between these areas in terms of moving agricultural and craft products in one direction (towards the city) and manufactured items (agricultural tools and inputs, cloth, and household utensils) in the other (towards the country-side) (Clark 2000; Spring and Trager 1989). In urban areas, informal vendors use both informal and formal sector-wholesale markets for produce.

In most places, there is a gender division of labor. Women trade produce, food, cloth, crafts, and pottery, while men trade metal and wood products. Commodities that require capital and direct connections to international markets are usually male-controlled; items having to do with daily subsistence and local markets are usually female-controlled because of women's limited cash resources. For large-scale traders, there are exceptions, such as women in the Democratic Republic of Congo (DRC) who sell gold, diamonds, and appliances (MacGaffey 1998) and women in Ethiopia who sell appliances and electronics purchased in Dubai.

Some large-scale women traders in West Africa are involved in extensive networks; some operate internationally dealing both in wholesale and cash-and-carry in salt, fish, palm and kola nuts, shea butter, cloth, and gold (Coquery-Vidrovitch 1997). In the Horn of Africa, such women move manufactured products from Dubai, and in East Africa, women move crafts made in Kenya, Uganda, and Tanzania between these countries (Spring's fieldnotes 2001). Generally the large-scale vendors are involved in the cloth trade and household goods. Once food production and distribution becomes industrialized in the formal sector, bakeries, groceries, and restaurants at the small and medium scale are owned by women, while only a few women are large manufacturers of baked goods and packaged food and beverages. A few women own supermarkets. The NGAE women and men are heavily involved in the service sector (tourism, computers, information technology, public relations and consultancy companies) and high-value agricultural exports such as vanilla bean (Uganda) and roses (Ethiopia, Kenya, Zambia). Occasionally, businesses have successful growth and expansion, e.g., in retail from one to multiple stores and chains (food markets, electonics/applicance stores) and in transport companies (from several trucks and buses to fleets).

Microcredit and Microfinance and 'Sites and Services'—Formalized–Informal

Figure 14-4 contrasts traditional micro-entrepreneurs with those who obtain microcredit and microfinance, as well as those who are a part of municipal/government "sites and services" programs. Once women are involved in formal credit and savings programs they are exposed to enumeration, registration, and fees. Interest rates may vary from 10 to 40 percent. Ironically, informal traders doing as much as a million dollars or more a year are not registered and do not pay taxes (Coquery-Vidrovitch 1997; author's fieldnotes for Ethiopia, Uganda, Kenya).

E-commerce: Global domain or informal and formal e-shops

Figures 14-5 models a range of E-commerce usage. All usages are carried out on the global stage of the internet, yet the scale varies from an individual craftsperson/artist, to cooperative groups, to African e-shops located in Africa. The use of e-commerce by formal-sector businesses is small and mostly used for publicity and product specifications rather than for business transactions (Hinson and Buatsi 2005; Spring's study of 100 top companies in Ghana 2006; Spring 2006a).

Start-up Capital

Figure 14-6 models the sources of capital, probably the single largest factor in the continuum (education/training may be second). ROSCAs and ASCAs work among micro- and small-scale entrepreneurs as a means of helping them accumulate sums they could not hope to have in ordinary daily or monthly revenues. Donor loans and projects are usually directed at micro-entrepreneurs in the informal realm. With formal loans and savings programs and the involvement of financial institutions, these clients are now in the formalized-informal sector.

Formal sector businesses require significant capital. Small to medium firms are often unable to borrow and resort to bank overdrafts, which they use as supplier credit-finessing receipts and payments in order to survive (Fafchamps 1998). There are also new programs funded by donors to target this sector. For example, USAID's GEMINI project targeted small formal-sector industries for training and loans. USAID/OECD targeted the NGAEs to capacitate their networks only. Many major multilateral and bilateral agencies have funding programs for small and mid-size firm development (Kuada 2006), as do private-sector investment companies such as Business Partners Ltd., but these reach only a small percent of businesses. While all levels can use their own and family money and can inherit family businesses, the model also shows that NGAEs usually start their own firms and overcome the problems of limited capital markets by using previous salaries for start-ups and obtaining bank credit successfully.

Sourcing and Markets

Figure 14-7 models the differences and similarities between sectors and levels, the sources of raw materials, and the markets that are targeted. It is obvious that micro-entrepreneurs use mostly local resources and their sales are in local markets, while globalists can source regionally and internationally and sell in such markets. There are African e-commerce shops on the World Wide Web/ Internet, but with limited clientele. The most successful international formal-sector companies also have successful national businesses. Large-scale informal sector traders are global in their purchases of (inexpensive) manufactured goods for local, informal-sector distribution. They perform a valuable service of bringing products to local people, but do not contribute to GDP in terms of manufacturing and using local raw materials.

Networks and Associations

Figure 14-8 models the kinds of business enterprise networks and associations to which entrepreneurs belong. The types and services they provide for members are diagnostic of business levels and may prove helpful for programs that affect entrepreneurs. "One size does not fit all," and one type of network or organization cannot accommodate all entrepreneurial levels. Small-scale traders often are members of local organizations of market women. Women exporters have formed associations in some countries such as Ethiopia, Eritrea, Ghana and Kenya. Small to large formal-sector businesswomen belong to national women's organizations (e.g., Ghanaian Association of Women Entrepreneurs [GAWE] and the African Federation of Women Entrepreneurs [AFWE]).[4] As well, there are women members and women subsections of most national and city-specific chambers of commerce.[5]

The NGAEs as a pan-African professional network are categorically different from other formal sector firms due to their global perspective and emphasis on fiscal transparency. Few have membership in chambers of commerce that they view as too inclusive (includes all levels and business practices) and not helpful to their businesses. They strive for small networks of like-minded people whom they can trust (McDade and Spring 2005). The NGAE women belong to the country and regional networks, as well as to professional organizations related to their businesses and professions (e.g., manufacturers' association for factory owners and architectural associations for architects).[6]

Conclusion

The informal-formal distinction is useful to disentangle the entrepreneurial landscape, and there is some fluidity between sectors. Dual economies are a reality of the African landscape, but the boundaries are "fuzzy." Movement upwards is possible but depends on a variety of factors: the entrepreneurial levels a woman starts from, her educational and employment experience, her business skills, her capital sources, etc. Some people have the "gift" of being savvy entrepreneurs. Circumstances of the entrepreneur and her family may improve. Her network and fortune may change because of innovation, new products, and training. Many women gain new agency through their active participation in networks and associations. But the results do not all lead to empowerment. Those who have good outcomes in the formal sector (especially those with high educational levels and good incomes) can be classified as "empowered." Similarly, micro-entrepreneurial women who gain loans/credit/training (either on their own or as part of microfinance programs) and prosper as a result are empowered. But natural disasters, weather conditions affecting agriculture production and marketing, world commodity prices, family situations, etc., enter the equation and affect the results. In terms of the general categories, there are limitations.

For example, there is some movement backwards from formal to informal sector for failed businesses and retrenched workers, and formal-sector companies finding suppliers and workers in the informal sector.

However, movement between categories may not be as substantial as desired for the large number of women at the bottom to gain much empowerment because they lack the entry requirements of capital, education, networks, etc. to move to the next level. Within the informal sector, movement from micro- and small-scale to large-scale exists but is rare and depends on capital and networks rather than on innovation and new products. Here is where the new microfinance projects may make a difference for some women, although the data from microsaving and microcredit are mixed. A four-country study of Benin, Ghana, Guinea, and Tanzania found that women benefited a great deal from microfinance (savings), but credit outreach was limited, and donors and NGOs were more successful than government programs (Basu, Blavy and Yulek 2004). Evaluative studies of the new wave of microfinance activities in terms of empowerment and agency are forthcoming. The use of new communication technologies such as the Internet may or may not be a distinguishing characteristic of empowerment depending on whether the woman is an Internet e-shop owner or simply an artisan selling craft products.

Traders and importers/exporters who move large quantities of product that they did not manufacture often have substantial operations in terms of capital; data from Ethiopia and Ghana show they may have as much income as entire formal-sector firms. However, these traders use informal business methods such as avoiding registration and taxes, thereby separating themselves from formal-sector businesses. They have little interest in moving to the formal sector, as their empowerment as "big women" in the traditional or conventional society is through wealth and property ownership.

Within the formal sector (small to medium to large firms) there is some movement, but women owners are limited by access to capital, networks, market intelligence, product innovation and niches. The data on the global NGAEs show that these women differ from the traditional formal-sector women owners based on new types of businesses, networks, and access to capital. They also use global business methods (i.e., financial transparency and advocacy for the private sector). Women who own or manage formal-sector enterprises often do so based on formal education and formal-sector employment backgrounds; they are usually considered as mainstream business-people and not as a separate category of "women entrepreneurs." As such, they have agency to operate their businesses, and are as "empowered" as male colleagues.

In sum, the entrepreneurial landscape of participation and remuneration and the outcomes for women in terms of agency and empowerment is a complicated and changing one. Researchers and intervention planners should not confuse small- and large-scale entrepreneurs and informal and formal sector activities, enterprises, businesses, industries, firms, and corporations. Increasing women's decision-making and financial empowerment depends on knowing the landscape in terms of constraints and opportunities.

Notes

A briefer version of this chapter was published in the *Journal of African Business,* Vol.10, No. 2, 2009.

[1] E-commerce as defined as "business transactions where buyers and sellers connect electronically to enhance business efficiency through lowering transactions costs" (Rhodes 2003:158). E-commerce business models are predicated on lowering entry barriers, reducing transactions costs, and giving customers improved access to information. In some cases there is customer-oriented pricing (e.g., auctions and bidding), and there are minimal regulatory actions from public authorities.

[2] The site states that it pays higher rates than people can get at local markets, and that items "help to improve the lives of these rural women." Women craft specialists include the Maata N Tudu Association of rural women in Bolgatanga, Northern Ghana who supply baskets; an Accra-based designer with a bead manufacturing business, women from Somanya, Ghana who supply powder and painted glass beads and jewelry; the Tendiwe Handicraft Cooperative in Zimbabwe that supplies table baskets; the Sowutum Mothers Association (single women) from Accra who supply table cloths, napkins and bags; Village Artisanal de Ouagadougou (Burkina Faso) who weave wide loom cloth, etc. Men craft specialists produce beads, brass statutes, masks, sculptures, T-shirts, drums, and decorated chests and coffins.

[3] The sample has disproportionately more women (33%), since we endeavoured to interview women to learn of their business experiences.

[4] AFWE sponsored three international trade fairs and investment forums (in Ghana, Ethiopia, and the United States), and received funding from bilateral and multilateral organizations such as Norway/NORAD and UNIFEM, respectively, perhaps indicative that there were informal (larger-scale in this case), as well as private sector entrepreneurs involved.

[5] GAWE and AFWE are specifically women's organizations. Founded by Lucia Quachey in 1990, members initially were concerned with women's issues such as divorce and female genital mutilation. The group subsequently took up women's economic issues. Quachey said, "We stopped talking about equality and rights, and just focused on making money" (personnel communication and 1999).

She remarked "women were not being invited to anything important or considered an economic force. Women just come in handy [to be present or to speak] on women's issues." Subsequently, GAWE and AFWE organized proposals and received funding from donors.

[6] Members regularly traveled to meetings within their country, as well as to regional and international meetings. WAEN, EAEN, and SAEN operated using global standards and the principles of management capabilities (Orsini 1999 2001; Spring 2002; McDade and Spring 2005; Spring and McDade forthcoming). They focus on regional networks, trade and investment, as well as on improving the business climate in their own countries. Some of the achievements of the enterprise networks included: (1) cross-national joint ventures; (2) creation of a professional West African subnetwork on accountancy lead by a female owner of one of the largest firms; (3) official observer status at ECOWAS and COMESA; (4) memoranda of understanding with the World Bank and Ecobank; (5) regional and national investment funds (members assemble their own funds to attract investment, and network members act as advisors); and (6) South-South capacity building (Orsini 1999, 2001).

Table 14-1. Spatial and Operational Features of the Small Informal Sector in Harare

TYPE	LOCATIONAL FEATURES	COMMON ACTIVITIES
Home-based industries (HBEs)	In and around the housing unit	Sell foodstuffs, small household goods, repairs, services
Home industries	Designated sites within residential areas	Manufacturing, repairs. welding. trading, hair dressing, services
Street vending	Along busy streets, on pavements, at intersections	Sell confectionery, cigarettes, vegetables, fruits, books, clothing
Shop-front vending	Near or at entrances of busy supermarkets	Sell plastic bags, confectionery, vegetables, fruits, books
Bus-stop vending	At public transport termini	Sell confectionery, cosmetics, cigarettes, vegetables, fruits, books, clothing items
People's markets	Designated area—bus-stops and shopping centers in middle and high-income areas	Make and sell crafts, sale of confectionery, cigarettes, vegetables, fruits, books, clothing items
Flea markets	Designated sites—central business district and suburban shopping centers	Sell mixed consumer goods
Roadside stalls	Busy distributors or national roads leading out of the city	Sell curios, building materials and accessories, crafts. maize, fruits, vegetables
Designated vending sites	On site within the central business district identified by planners	Sell confectionery, cigarettes, vegetables, fruits, books, clothing items

Source: adapted from Kamete (2002:122)

Table 14-2: Informal and Formal Financial Activities for a Kenyan Woman

Diversified and Informal

ROSCA 1
4 members – daily contribution of $0.29. Each month around $35.00 is paid out to members in turn.
    Use: School fees for grandchildren
 	
ROSCA 2
4 members – weekly contribution of $2.90. Each week $11.60 is paid out to members in turn.
    Use: Re-stocking business
    Small market-stall selling basic commodities: salt, rice, biscuits, soap etc.
 	
ASCA
40 members save $1.03 a week; can borrow from the fund. Liquidated annually in December.
    Use: Celebrating Christmas (savings) and emergencies (loan)
 	
Informal Funeral Insurance Fund:
100 members contribute $11.40 per month – covers immediate family
    Use: Risk pooling for "repatriation" to village
 	
Emergency cash
In the home: $3-$5
    Use: Emergencies requiring immediate cash
 	
Cow
Back in the village: looked after by brother
    Use: Provision for old age/social capital maintenance

Formal Loan
Working capital loan Loan for $356 from Faulu Microfinance Institution   Use: Building a small room to rent out (to provide stable income for old age) Source: Wright 2003

Table 14-3. NGAE Members Interviewed by Business Position and Business Acquisition

Country	Members Interviewed[a] N=57	National Network Membership	Business Position Owner	Business Position Manager	Business Acquisition Self	Business Acquisition Family	Business Acquisition SOE*
Botswana	6	14	6		6		
Ethiopia	3	7	2	1	1		1
Ghana	13	44	13		9	3	1
Kenya	11	11	11		10	1	
Mali[b]	2	17	1	1	1		
Senegal	5	18	5		5		
South Africa	6	9	5	1	5		
Uganda	8	10	8		6	2	
Zambia[c]	1	10	1		1		
Zimbabwe[c]	2	8	2		2		
Total	57		54	3	46	6	2
Percent			95%	5%	85%t	11%	4%

[a] Tanzanian members interviewed by Spring not included
[b] Interviewed by Delores Koenig
[c] Interviewed by Spring in Ethiopia; the other interviews were in the country specified

Source: McDade and Spring 2005

Figure 14-1. Movement within and between sectors by size/type of business

Figure 14-1 Movement Within and Between Sectors by Size/Type of Business Enterprise

Informal Sector		Formal Sector	
Micro→→→→→→Large Enterprises/Traders**	Small→→Medium→→Large Firms/Companies		NGAE Medium and Large Firms
Movement possible to formal sector but rare →→→→→→→	Movement upward and downward, dependent on capital, education, networks, etc. →→→→→→→		Movement upwards and downward, dependent on capital →→→→→→→ ←←←←←←
	Retrenched salaried workers may move to informal sector ←←←←←←		
Movement possible but rare. Lack education, networks, and desire to pay taxes or be registered →→→→→→→	Stay in sector		
			Movement possible but need to be financially transparent, highly transparent, highly education, and a-political →→→→→→→
	Movement possible but most do not want to go back to informal sector or lower levels of business →→→→→→→		

* Agricultural and artisan producers to traders moving products

Source: Spring

Figure 14-2. Some Demographic Characteristics: Education, Work Experience, Marital Status and Contribution

	Informal Sector		Formal Sector		
	Micro →→→→→→→Large	Small→→→Medium→→Large			NGAEs
Education	None or little	Primary to secondary to some college	Secondary Some primary, some college	Secondary and college	BAs, MAs, PhDs
Formal Work Experience	None	None to retrenched workers	None, retrenched workers, some salaried in the formal	Salaried, formal	Salaried, formal, CEOs, COOs,
Marital Status	Married and female head of household				Married, some divorced legally
Husband's contribution	None to some	Income may reduce husband's contribution (varies)		Share financial responsibilities (varies)	May be business partners

Informal sector entrepreneurs may have primary education and higher. Some now use the Internet for sales often assisted by their educated children

Source: Spring

Figure 14-3. Types of Enterprises/Firms

Figure 14-3. Types of Enterprises/Firms (excludes E-commerce)

Informal Sector	Formal Sector		
Micro→→→→→→Large Enterprises	Small→→→→→Medium→→→→Large Firms/companies		NGAEs Firms/Companies
• Farm surplus • Prepared foods • Crafts • Herbals • Household goods • Hair-dressing	• Ag. produce and grains • Textiles • Food products • Transport • Furniture • Household goods • Electronics and appliances	• Manufacturing of clothing • Furniture • Bakeries • Retail shops • Clinics, healthcare	• Manufacturing of textiles, clothing, agro-processing • Retail shops • Transport firms • Clinics, healthcare • Construction and materials	• Manufacturing of textiles, clothing, agropro-cessing, industrial products • Super-markets • Transport firms • Retail shops chains • Construction and materials	• High value agricultural exports • Tourism • Computers • Real Estate • Public Relations • Manufacturing • Information Technology • Manufactured products • TV/Radio

Source: Spring

Figure 14-4. Formalized-Informal Sector: Microcredit/finance, Sites and Services

Informal Sector	Formalized-Informal Sector		Informal
Traditional Micros* Individual Family Self starter Female heads Small quantities Low profits Low volume Seasonal Illiterate Numerate?	Micro credit/finance Project driven Donors Individuals Women's groups Specific commodities Monitored Taught skills Literacy?? Numeracy??	Sites and services Government markets Market improvements Registration Enumerated Taxation/fees Literacy?? Numeracy Market associations	Wholesalers** Family histories Kinship and market networks High volume High profits/income Literacy?? Numeracy Bank accounts?
Movement possible and encouraged by donors and projects Encouraged by governments			

Source: Spring

Figure 14-5. E-Commerce Categories, Use of Internet, Family, Shipping

Formalized Informal		Formal (world domain, unregulated)	Formal	
Individual	*Coop of producers*	*E-shop*	*Local Companies E-merchant Store*	*National Companies Informative Website*
Internet	Internet, project office	Internet, possible office to collect and pack	Business locations	Business locations Brands
Crafts, art, textiles	Crafts, art, textiles	Crafts, art, textiles, services, products	Services, products (e.g., cell phones, flowers, foods)	Services, manufactured products
Family members assist in website	Donors, projects, web designers	Webmaster	Hire experts	Hire experts
Wire transfers	Credit cards	Paypal, credit cards	Advertisement, sign ups	Wholesale orders Customer PR Market channels
International customers and deliveries	International customers and deliveries	International customers and deliveries	In-country delivery. Could cater to African expatriates	National, regional, international
Movement to Entrepreneurial website				

Figure 14-6. Sources of Start-up Capital by Informal and Formal Sector

	Informal Sector		Formal Sector			
	Micro→Large		Small→	Medium→	Large	NGAEs
Own	x	x	x	x	x	x
Family money	x	x	x	x	x	
ROSCAs, and ARCAS informal institutions	x		x			
Microcredit	x					
Microfinance	x	x	x			
Inherited businesses	(x)	x	x	x	x	
Donor loans	x		x			
Retirement funds		x	x			
Previous salaries		x	x	x	x	x
Diversified investments		x	x	x	x	
Bank credit		(x)		(x)	x	x
Bank overdrafts		x	x	x	x	

Source: Spring

Figure14-7 Sourcing and Markets by Informal and Formal Sector

	Informal Sector		Formal Sector			
	Micro →Large		Small→	Medium→	Large	NGAEs
Local sources	x	(x)	(x)			
Local markets	x	x				
National sources			x	x	x	
National markets		x	x	x	x	x
Regional sources		x		x	x	
Regional markets		x		x	x	x
International sources		x			x	x
International markets					x	x
World Wide Web		x	x	(x)	(x)	(x)

Source: Spring

Figure 14-8. Membership in Networks and Associations by Informal and Formal Sector

	Informal Sector		Formal Sector			
	Micro→Large Enterprises		Small→Medium→Large Firms			NGAEs Firms
Local Organizations	x	x	x			
Chambers of Commerce			x	x	x	
Manufacturer's Associations				x	x	
Employers" Federations				(x)*	x	(x)*
Professional Associations				x	x	x
Regional & International Associations					(x)*	x

Source: Spring

CHAPTER FIFTEEN
ARMED CONFLICT, DISPLACEMENT, GENDER-BASED VIOLENCE IN AFRICA AND *ANOMIE*

The Case of Darfur

Kabahenda Nyakabwa

War/Armed Conflict and Displacement

This chapter pleads for an alternative explanation for understanding the prevalence of gender-based violence against women in the form of mass rape in times of armed conflict/war and displacement. It is proposed that this crime against women and humanity, including other forms of horrific sexual atrocities perpetrated against women, is possible because of *anomie* or the total breakdown of social order and social norms in the "cultural structure" which occurs during times of armed conflict and other major crises. Cultural structure is defined as "that organized set of normative values governing behavior which is common to members of a designated society or group" (Merton 1964, 12) *and which prevents human beings from acting in ways that are not socially and morally acceptable.*[1]

The fragmentation of state power, irredentism, insurgencies and counter-insurgency operations, political instability, political discontent, ethnic-based political violence, lack of good governance and human rights violations in various post-independent African countries, including Angola, Burundi, Côte d'Ivoire, the Central African Republic, Eritrea, Ethiopia, the Democratic Republic of the Congo, Liberia, Mozambique, Rwanda, Sierra Leone, Somalia, and Sudan and Uganda have resulted in millions of refugees and internally displaced persons.

Refugees and Internally Displaced Persons

A refugee is a person who, "owing to well-founded fear of being persecuted for reasons of race, religion, nationality, membership of a particular social group or political opinion, is outside the country of his/her nationality and is unable, or owing to such fear, is unwilling to avail himself/herself of the protection of that country" (UNHCR 1951). On the other hand,

> internally displaced persons (IDPs) are persons or groups of persons who have been forced or obliged to flee or to leave their homes or places of habitual residence, in particular as a result of or in order to avoid the effects of armed conflict, situations of generalized violence, violations of human rights or natural or human-made disasters, and who have not crossed an internationally recognized State border (OCHA 1998).

This distinction is significant because refugees enjoy the protection of the United Nations High Commissioner for Refugees (UNHCR) whereas IDPs are left to the mercy of their governments. Since they remain within the borders of their national territories, the primary responsibility for the protection, welfare and security needs of IDP and IDW falls within the jurisdiction of their governments. However, some African governments, like that of the Islamic Republic of Sudan, have apparently transformed "the responsibility to protect" into a mandate to hire and arm militias who obstruct international efforts to reach the IDP, commit extrajudicial executions, torture, abductions, mass rapes of IDW and destruction of villages and property (OHCHR 25 Jan. 2005).

The issue of IDP is currently one of the more pressing humanitarian, human rights and political and security issues facing countries like the Democratic Republic of the Congo, Sudan and the Congo "which together accounted for over 9 million internally displaced persons" (Internal Displacement Centre 2006).

Sudan has approximately 2.0 million IDP, and over 200,000 people have sought refuge in neighboring Chad (Oxfam 29 Aug. 2006; *New York Times* 26 Feb. 2006), while more than 300,000 have died since the outbreak of the conflict in early 2004 (*The Economist* (April 15th - 21st 2006). In most UN reports, it is claimed that women and children constitute more than 75 percent of refugees and IDPs. Thus, a significant number of people affected by the Darfur crisis are women and children.

The Darfur Crisis

The western region of Darfur is located in northwestern Sudan, bordering Chad to the West, Libya to the northwest, and the Central African Republic to the southwest. It is comprised of three states, North, South and West Darfur. Darfur is home to approximately 6 million people comprising between 36 and 90 ethnic groups (Ylönen, 2005, 124; ICG 23 Mar. 2004). The population is divided between two predominant ethnic groups: the non-Arab group or "Zurga" (black), including the *Fur*, the *Masaleit* (also spelled 'Masaalit'), the *Zaghawa*, and the Arab group, mainly the *Baggara*.

In comparison to other regions, Darfur has suffered from political marginalization and lack of economic opportunities. These two factors, together with the government's exploitation of ethnic cleavages between the Arab and African populations, explain the recent conflict in the Darfur region (Ylönen, 2005, 124; ICG 23 Mar. 2004; HRW Apr. 2004).

The conflict opposes fighters of the Sudan Liberation Movement/Army and Justice Equality Movement (SLM/A & JEM) and the government of Sudan. The (SLM/A) claims to have a national agenda with the main objective of creating a united democratic Sudan based on equality, the devolution of power, cultural and political pluralism and prosperity for all Sudanese (Ylönen, 2005, 124; ICG 23 Mar. 2004).

In April 2003 the two rebel groups launched a surprise attack on El Fashir, the capital of North Darfur. They destroyed several government Antonov aircraft and helicopters and looted fuel and arms depots. In a counter-insurgency operation, the government unleashed members the *Janjaweed* militias on Darfur. Numerous accounts attribute the suffering of the people and particularly the women of Darfur to the activities of the *janjaweed* militias and government forces (Refugees International 2005; Amnesty International 2004; MSF-Netherlands 2005; OHCHR Jan. 2005; ICG 23 Mar. 2004; HRW Apr. 2004).

Armed Conflict & Sexual and Gender-Based Violence

The definition of sexual and gender-based violence "encompasses a wider variety of abuses that includes sexual threats, exploitation, humiliation, assaults, molestation, domestic violence, incest, involuntary prostitution (sexual bartering), torture, insertion of objects into genital openings and attempted rape or actual rape (IPPF n.d.). For the purposes of this chapter, however, the term SGBV will be used to refer to the mass rape of women because it is the most common form of SGBV reported in times of armed conflict, internal displacement and in refugee camps (Refugees International 2005; Amnesty International 2004; MSF-Netherlands 2005; OHCHR Jan. 2005; Lumeya 2004; Fitzgerald 1998; Turshen and Twagiramariya 1998; Human Rights Watch 1996, 1993).

The mass rape of Muslim Women in Bosnia in 1992 (Stilgmayer 1994; Neier 1998), Somali women in Dadaab camps of Kenya (HRW 1993, Fitzgerald 1998); the rape and forced pregnancy of Tutsi women during the 1994 genocide of Rwanda (HRW 1996; Twagiramariya and Turshen 1998, 101-117; *The New York Times Magazine* 15 Sept. 2002); the massive rape of women in the Democratic Republic of the Congo (HRW 2005; OCHA 2004), and lately the violation of women's bodily integrity in Sudan (OHCRH Jan. 2005; MSF-Netherlands 2005, Lumley 2004) have all attracted substantial international outrage and alerted the world to what happens to women during times of armed conflict. Sexual atrocities in the context of armed conflict and war are different from what happens in peace times. This does not minimize the gravity and trauma of the phenomenon, but the gender-based violence that takes place in peace times occurs in the privacy of the home, university campuses or other closed environments. It usually involves two individuals who may or may not be strangers to each others. If proven, it is prosecutable.

The violence and aggression that occur within the context of armed conflict, in flight or refugee or displaced people's camps is different in the sense that it occurs on a massive scale. It is indiscriminate; it targets women and children regardless of their age; and it also targets men, albeit on a very small scale (HRW 2005; Lentin 1997; Neier 1998: Zarkov 2001). The perpetrators include the military, camp guards, members of rebel militias, male child soldiers often forcibly recruited, women, erstwhile friends and neighbors, state security agents, emasculated refugees and internally displaced males, and lately peacekeepers (Refugees International 2005; Apr. 2006).

The women of Darfur have been victims of this indignity since the beginning of the conflict in 2003. Medécins Sans Frontier (MSF) Netherlands reports the following:

In West Darfur alone, between October 2004 and 15 February 2005, MSF health clinics treated 297 rape victims, 99 percent of whom were women. The ages of the victims vary between 12 and 45 years old with an average age of 27.... More than half of the rapes were reported within 30 days. Almost 90 percent said that the rape occurred outside a populated village.

Almost a third (28 percent) of the victims reported that they were raped more than one time, either by single or multiple assailants. In more than half of the cases, physical violence was inflicted beyond sexual violence; women are beaten with sticks, whips or axes. Further, some of the raped women were visibly pregnant at the time of the assault, sometimes up to eight months. In one case, the rape provoked miscarriage... In most instances, the assailants are men carrying guns; sometimes wearing military uniforms (MSF-Netherlands, 8 Mar. 2005).

The mass rape of women in Sudan has not abated to date. Grono and Prendergast report that:

> The horrific humanitarian situation in Darfur is getting worse. There are more clashes now than a year ago, the number of rapes has steadily climbed and humanitarian workers are being attacked. The Darfur Peace Agreement, signed in May, is on the verge of collapse, and more than two million people continue to languish in refugee camps (International Herald Tribune 28 Aug. 2006).

Explanatory Constructs

Academics, feminists and practitioners have attempted to explain this phenomenon from various perspectives: According to the political economy perspective,

> armies use rape systematically to strip women of their economic and political assets. Women's assets reside in the first instance in their productive and reproductive labor power and in the second instance in their possession and access to valuable assets such as land and livestock (Turshen 2001, 44-68).

Feminists have tended to attribute this problem to the "structural inequality of power" that exists between men and women in society, the "construction of masculinity" [and] "the idolization of masculinity," the destruction of the "adversary's culture," social constructionism and misogyny (Seifert 1992; Sideris 2001, 142-158; Zarkov 2001; Moser 2001, 30-51; Skjelsbaek 2001, 211-237).

These explanations have increased our understanding of this complex and hideous phenomenon. Nonetheless, there is a body of literature that shows women's complicity, agency and leadership as perpetrators and beneficiaries within the processes and structures that perpetuate violence (Africa Rights 1995; Turshen 1998; Jacobs 2000, 218-237; Jacobson, Jacobs and Marchbank 2000,11-14; El-Bushra 2000, 66-86; Mukta 2000, 164-177; Turshen 1998, 13; Hague 1997; Pankhurst 2003, 158-177; Goldblatt & Meintjes 1998, 43; Ibanez, 2001,128).

During the genocide of Rwanda, the former minister for family and women's affairs, Pauline Nyiramasuhuko, ordered the rape of Tutsi women (New York Times Magazine 15 Sept. 2002, 83-89, 116, 125, 130-132) and is currently facing charges of genocide and rape before the International Criminal Tribunal for Rwanda (ICTR) in Arusha, Tanzania. She is the first woman in the world to ever face charges of crimes against humanity.

In addition, Human Rights Watch has documented the rape of males in the Democratic Republic of the Congo (2005, 20-23). During the wars in the former Yugoslavia, men were subjected to brutal and systematic violence, including rape and assault by foreign objects, castration and the severing of the testicle, while both prisoners and guards occasionally subjected themselves to this violence (Hague 1997; Zarkov 2001, 71). According to Neier,

> sexual abuse in the Bosnian conflict was primarily, but not exclusively, directed against women. As in other wars, some male prisoners were also sexually abused and humiliated by their captors....The United Nations War Crimes Commission also reported one case in which a Bosnian prisoner's penis was cut off; another in which a prisoner was given electric shocks to his scrotum; and a third in which guards forced a father and a son to perform a sex act with each other (1998, 175).

Moreover, when a child-soldier is abducted and forcibly recruited in a fighting faction, and when this child is forced to sexually violate his sister or mother in public, is this act a demonstration of unequal gender relations? Why do UN peacekeepers who have no political or economic stake in the conflict participate in these violations? (Refugees International 2005).

These two examples illustrate the need for alternative explanations for the sexual terror that we witness in times of armed conflict. Indeed, researchers now caution against "the binary stereotype of active males/passive females" (Turshen 1998, 1) while Jacobson, Jacobs and Marchbank question the notion of a "one size fits all" model of masculine aggression and female victimhood (2000, 12). The implication is that sexual violence during armed conflict is a social issue in need of an integrated theory.

This chapter proposes that mass rape is possible in times of armed conflict and displacement because of the confusion and total breakdown of legal and local protective mechanisms and traditional social and moral norms or *anomie*.

Anomie

All societies have written and unwritten rules that govern or regulate individuals' behavior. This means that society exercises a moralizing influence on individuals' actions and behaviors. In times of armed conflict, political upheaval or acute social crisis, society's regulating forces, both social and political, break down. In this state of "deregulation" or anomie (Thompson 2000, 108-115), hell breaks loose.

Anomie is a French word which originated from the Greek word *anomia,* meaning an absence of restraint or guidance for individual behavior and attitudes (Munch 1974, 243-261). As a sociological concept, "anomie" was first used by the French sociologist Emile Durkheim in his *Division of Labour in Society* and later in *Suicide* (1951) to explain the incidence of suicide during times of industrial crises in western societies.[2] His research showed that

> every disturbance of equilibrium [in the collective order], even though it achieves greater comfort and a heightening of general vitality, is an impulse to voluntary death. Whenever serious readjustments take place in social order, whether or not due to a sudden growth or to an unexpected catastrophe, men are more inclined to self-destruction (1951, 246).

For Nielsen, *anomie*

> reveals the fragility of social integration and asks us to examine the sources and manifestations of social dislocation and the collapse of moral order... [It] involves precisely those madnesses, excesses, and imbalances which possess societies under given circumstances"(1996, 397 & 400).

According to de Grazia, *anomie* signifies "the disintegrated state of a society that possesses no body of common values or morals which effectively govern conduct" (1948, xii-ix). Marshall Clinard adds that "the stability of any society depends greatly on the functioning of its institutions and on their ability, through formal and informal means, to maintain social control" (1963, 8). Thus, states of *anomie* engender the kind of deviant behavior or conduct that departs significantly from social norms or "standardized ways of acting, or expectations governing limits of variations in behavior" (ibid. 9).

The manner in which women are violated perverts social norms and threatens familial, social and cultural cohesion and is a manifestation of anomie. For example, in *The Rape of Nanking,* Iris Chang describes the state of "anomie" during the Sino-Japanese war in which approximately 20,000 to 80,000 women were raped:

> many soldiers went beyond rape to disembowel women, slice off their breasts, nail them alive to walls. Fathers were forced to rape their daughters and sons their mothers as other family members watched... Not only did live burials, castration, the carving of organs and the roasting of people become routine, but more diabolical tortures were practiced, such as hanging people by their tongues on iron hooks or burying people to their

waists and watching them torn apart by German shepherds."... (Chang 1977, quoted in *New York Times* 14 December 1997).

In *Sarajevo: A War Journal*, Zlatko Dizdarevic succinctly illustrates what *anomie* is about:

> We are witnessing the abolition of all recognized human values...Madness seems to be contagious, while the normal, humane, intelligent, and rational behavior doesn't pass muster... Here the gates of hell have opened, and out of darkness have emerged monsters—worse than monsters—capable of raping six-year-old girls, of burning people alive, of destroying age-old monuments (1993, 7, 155 & 173).

In Sudan, MSF reported that

> The assaults are particularly brutal, and several victims account that family members (husbands, children, mothers, etc.) or friends got severely beaten while witnessing or trying to intervene during the assault (8 Mar. 2005).

Although Durkheim and other social scientists have used this concept to explain suicide and other various forms of deviant behavior in Western societies (Merton 1957), the concept has relevance for understanding the kind of gender-based violence perpetrated against women we witness in times of armed conflict.

Effects of SGBV on Women's Lives

Armed conflict and displacement impact women in both negative and positive ways. On the negative side, the number of women heads of households, including girls, elderly women, widows and single mothers in the context of displacement far exceeds that of men (Norwegian Council for Refugees 2005; Turner 2000, 8-9). Young single women often turn to multiple partners for survival or for sexual gratification or to satisfy their maternal instincts. But African societies are implacable when it comes to women whose behavior is perceived as "immoral." Such women are perceived as bringing shame and dishonor on their families and communities, which in turn stigmatize and ostracize them even when they may not have entered into these relationships voluntarily (El-Bushira 2000, 5, Human Right Watch 1996; Nyakabwa & Lavoie 1993). In most instances, the rape of a married woman leads to family violence and ultimately to family breakdown because men tend to blame women who find themselves in these situations. Thus, the violated woman will become a social outcast for the rest of her life (Amnesty International 2004;

Twagiramariya and Turshen 1998, 104; Lumeya 2004; Nyakabwa & Lavoie 1993).

The violation of women's body integrity in contexts of internal displacement has terrible ramifications for women's health (Turshen 1998, 17-19; Codou 2001, 19-34; Twagiramariya and Turshen 1998, 110-111). The risk of HIV infections, ignorance of modes of transmission, lack of reproductive health services in IDP camps and the potential explosion of AIDS in these situations has wreaked havoc on the lives of women and their children. For example, during the genocide of Rwanda, "seventy percent of women raped were infected with the AIDS virus" (*New York Times Magazine* 15 Sept. 2002, 83-89, 116, 125, 130-132).

A UNICEF study based on the testimonies of IDP revealed that "assaults on the people of Darfur, western Sudan, have resulted not only in physical injuries, but in a range of psychological traumas, including suicidal impulses and nightmares" for the affected women as well as their husbands and relatives (UN News Service 9 Sept. 2005). On that account, IDP camps become breeding grounds for mental illness and emotional disturbances with grave health, social and economic implications for IDP's successful reintegration into their communities when they return.

Taking into consideration the fact that in several African countries, family, clan and tribal honor and continuity are deeply associated with a woman's sexual organs and reproductive health, the prevention of SGBV in refugee settings becomes urgent. An assault on the body of a woman belonging to an enemy clan or tribe may be considered the "best way" to degrade and dehumanize the "conquered" clan or tribe (Castel 1992, 38-56). During the genocide of Rwanda, for example, sexual violence was perpetrated against Tutsi women "as a means of dehumanizing and subjugating all Tutsi" (Human Rights Watch 1996). The implications of SGBV for women's human rights, reproductive health, and their enjoyment of life are long term.

Since a woman's reproductive capacity ensures the continuity of the family, the clan and the tribe, the total destruction of her reproductive organs and thereby, her capacity to reproduce, constitutes a form of genocide or social murder for the woman and social suicide for her tribe. At the same time, infertility, unwanted pregnancies and the bearing of enemy children poses a social hazard for the sexually assaulted woman because she and her child risk becoming social rejects (Human Rights Watch 2000, 92; Twagiramariya and Turshen 1998, 104-105; Nyakabwa and Lavoie 1993).

Consequently, the majority of women choose to suffer in silence for fear that the perpetrator, when punished, will come back to inflict more harm on her already damaged body (Sideris 2001, 144-157). SGBV has long term effects on women's reintegration into their societies (Cliffe 1991, 15-33) and their eventual participation in the economies of their countries (Carillo 1992).

Prolonged displacement is another gender concern for women. Traumatized by several months or years of displacement, women often return to communities only to find that they have been arbitrarily and unlawfully deprived of their homes and properties. In some African countries, women do not have a right to inherit land and property, and the majority lack the means to seek effective legal redress. This situation plunges them and their children into poverty and may compel them to return to a situation of displacement, thus permanently uprooting them from their societies and from family and kin.

Armed Conflict and Women's "Empowerment"

In the aftermath of armed conflict, women find new roles as heads of households and decision-makers (Absharaf 2006 71-73; El Bushira 2003; ICG 28 June 2006, 3-4; Turshen 1998, 20-21). Positive outcomes include changes in the gender division of labor, women's inclusion in peace-building initiatives, the proliferation of self-help and self-reliance organizations, increased decision-making in the private sphere of marriage and sexual relations, political participation and representation in national parliaments, and increasing demands for more legal, property and land rights in countries like Uganda, Somalia, Rwanda and Sudan (Abusharaf 2006, 60-73; ICG 26 Aug. 2006; El Bushra 2000, 69-75; Turshen 1998, 2021; Turshen and Twagiramariya 1998, 114).

The notion that armed conflict endangers women's lives but also "empowers" them calls for a more critical analysis. In terms of political participation, we need to distinguish between three types of "empowerment": empowerment by right; empowerment by co-optation, and empowerment through adversity. Empowerment by right would give 50-50 representation in national parliaments based on women's natural equality with men. This type of "empowerment" has yet to be achieved even in more progressive western societies such as Sweden. Empowerment by co-optation is a situation whereby a government allocates parliamentary seats to women in order to advance its own agendas and appease donors, but when the same women begin to assert themselves, they become political outcasts—as the rise and fall of Winnie Banyima within the NRM government in Uganda succinctly demonstrates.

In empowerment through adversity, women accede to high positions in government and other sectors of the economy because of the decimation of their male companions during armed conflict. The 2003 election in Rwanda elevated the percentage of women in government to 48.8 per cent, "the top of Inter-Parliamentary Union's World ranking of women in national parliaments" (*The World of Parliaments* Dec. 2003).

Even though the Rwandese women campaigned in their own right, it would be enlightening to find out whether this kind of "empowerment" was a result of Rwanda being a progressive African country or a quantum leap somewhat correlated with the genocide. Finally, whether accession to positions of authority and leadership through calamity is the kind of "empowerment" African women want is a question worthy of further exploration.

Ostensibly the gains made by African women in conflict-ridden countries like Uganda and Rwanda are a manifestation of positive social changes, but whether these kinds of "empowerment" will translate into long term fundamental changes in the monolithic patriarchal structures is an issue that is becoming controversial among researchers studying women, gender and development. As *The World of Parliaments* observed, "it will be interesting to see what the entry of so many women into Parliament will do for politics in Rwanda. Whether this change at the decision-making level will usher in changes in the more traditional societal expectations of women remains to be seen" (Dec. 2003).

El-Bushra notes that

> the ideological underpinnings of gender relations have barely been touched at all and may even have become further reinforced through conflict.... The expectation of development practitioners that conflict provides opportunities for radical improvement of the position of women needs some rethinking" (2003, 264).

Jacobs warns against the assumption that women's "empowerment" is necessarily a positive outcome of armed conflict because "there is no analytical reason to view women's actions as operating in a direction which will strengthen links among women as a gender group" (Jacobs, 2000, 232). Furthermore, we should not we assume that all women in all countries affected by armed conflict are "empowered" equitably. More research should be undertaken in order to determine to what extent issues of class, ethnicity, region, religion, political participation and ties [kinship and political] to governments ante-conflict and to rebel movements that take over the reins of the state in the aftermath of conflict come into play to determine women's opportunities and misfortunes.

As far as Sudan is concerned, the ICG states that

the role of Sudanese women varies by region. Though women contribute prominently to peace building through civil society, they were largely excluded from both the North-South and Darfur peace negotiations... Neither the 2005 Comprehensive Peace Agreement nor the May 2006 Darfur Peace Agreement provide guarantees for women's participation in the implementation processes. Women are under-represented at national and local levels, and even [in] stated commitments to their participation in formal government structures (26 Aug. 2006).

"Empowerment" notwithstanding, the legacy of war, armed conflict and displacement for the majority of African women includes widowhood, mental, emotional and reproductive distress, dispossession, loss of social status, female-headed households, single parenting, loneliness, ostracism, social isolation and feminization of poverty, which in some cases drives women into prostitution and polygamy. All these are social problems with negative consequences for women's quality of life and for the development of their respective countries.

Hope at the End of the Tunnel

One of the most formidable challenges facing women victims of widespread rape, their families, feminists and humanitarian workers has been the culture of impunity and the total lack of channels of redress. This situation is changing and there is hope at the end of the tunnel. Following the discovery that UN peacekeepers had committed acts of sexual violence against the women they were employed to protect, the "United Nations has increased its measures to handle the problem of sexual exploitation and abuse in its peacekeeping mission" (Refugees International 6 Apr. 2006). The statute of Rome recognized rape as a crime against humanity and created the International Criminal Court (ICC) in July 2002 to adjudicate cases of crimes against humanity. For the first time in history, seven soldiers serving in the national army of the DRC were "sentenced to life in prison for crimes against humanity," including the massive rape of about 119 women in the northwestern province of Equateur in 2003 (HRW Mar. 2005). In addition

> The court also ordered the Congolese government, which it said was "jointly responsible," to compensate the victims of the soldiers. It directed that a family of a rape victim who died following the attack be paid US $10,000, $5,000 for rape survivors and other victims; and damages and interest of $200 to $500 to families whom the soldiers robbed IRIN 14 Apr.2006).

As an official of the United Nations Mission in the Democratic Republic of Congo (MONUC) stated, the court's "decision is a significant step which will help advance the fight against impunity, particularly against sexual violence" (HRW, Jan. 2006). It is a landmark ruling which promises to bring about social change by challenging existing power and gender relations in Africa.

Summary and Conclusion

In the past decade or so, feminists, researchers, women's organizations and human rights organizations have increased our awareness of the nature, extent and severity of the problem of SGBV in times of armed conflict. The recognition that men are equally targeted, though in smaller numbers, indicates that "the binary stereotype of active males/passive females" (Turshen 1998, 1) is no longer sufficient to explain the perverted forms of sexual aggression that takes place in times of armed conflict.

This chapter has pleaded for an alternative model which transcends issues of gender, race, ethnicity and geography. It suggests that a "pathological state of disequilibrium" (Thompson 2000, 18) or *anomie* characterized by a total breakdown of a society's legal, moral and cultural norms and values may be sufficient to explain this phenomenon wherever there is war, armed conflict or serious crisis, including during the displacement caused by Hurricane Katrina in New Orleans, Louisiana, USA in the summer of 2005 (Cook Lauer 13 Sept. 2005).

Durkheim warned that

> Whenever serious readjustments take place in social order, whether or not due to a sudden growth or to an unexpected catastrophe, men are more inclined to self-destruction (1951, 246).

Allegedly there are cases where rapes have led to actual suicides or victims' contemplation of suicide (UN News Service 9 Sept. 2005; Twagiramariya & Turshen 1998, 110). Furthermore, the destruction of women's wombs through gang rapes and the use of objects which destroy their capacity to procreate, and the spread of HIV/AIDS through sexual violence are forms of "self-destruction" or social suicide to the extent both the perpetrators and the victims will eventually die. Thus, *anomie* as an alternative explanation for what happens in times of armed conflict is a concept worthy of further exploration.

Finally, if the international community is serious about ending the suffering of the people of Darfur, it should search for definitive solutions, including the prosecution of its perpetrators, a total ban on small arms trade as well as targeting Sudan's "sources of illicit income" because "it is the cash flows from these off-budget entities that enable the regime to buy the loyalty of tribal leaders, and through them the *janjaweed* militias, and pay the salaries and equipment of its foot soldiers" (Grono and Prendergast 22 Aug. 2006).

This is the only way to end the *anomie* that has wreaked havoc on the lives of women in the Darfur region.

Notes

[1] The emphasis is this author's.

[2] The different types of suicides that Durkheim outlines will not be explained because they are beyond the scope of this paper.

BIBLIOGRAPHY

Abdoulaye, D. 2006. "Maternal Mortality In Africa," *The Internet Journal of Health* 5:1.

Abdullah, Hussaina and Hamza, Ibrahim. 2003. "Women and Land in northern Nigeria: the need for independent ownership rights." In Wanyeki, L. Muthoni (ed.), *Women and Land in Africa,* London: Zed.

Abou Zahr, C. 2000. "Maternal mortality: helping mothers live. The reduction of maternal mortality ratios by three-quarters between 1990 and 2015 as an international development goal." *Organization of Economic Cooperation & Development Observer* No. 223, December.

Abreu, Alcinda. 2004a. 'Enhancing Women's Participation in Electoral Processes in Post-Conflict Countries: Experiences from Mozambique.' United Nations Office of the Special Adviser on Gender Issues and Advancement of Women (OSAGI). EGM/ELEC/2004/EP.4.

_____. 2004b. 'Political Party Quotas in Mozambique: The Experience of the Frelimo Party.' In Ballington, ed. *The Implementation of Quotas: African Experiences.*

Abusharaf, R.M. 2006. "Competing Masculinities: Probing political disputes as acts of violence against women." *Human Rights Review* (January-March), 59-73.

Abwunza, Judith M. "Conversation between culture's outrageous voices? Issues of voice and text in feminist anthroplogy." In S. Cole and L. Phillips, eds. *Ethnographic Feminisms: Essays in Anthropology* (pp. 127-153). Ottowa: Carleton University Press.

Ackerly, B. 1995. "Testing the tools of development: Credit programmes, loan involvement and women's empowerment." *IDS Bulletin,* Vol. 26, No. 3, pp.56-68.

ActionAid. 2006. Cultivating Women's Rights for Access to Land: www.oxfam.org.uk/ what_we_do/issues/livelihoods/landrights/downloads

Adepoju, Aderanti. 1994. "The Demographic Profile: Sustained High Mortality and Fertility and Migration for Employment." In Adepoju and Oppong, (eds.), *Gender, Work and Population in Sub-Saharan Africa.* Portsmouth, NH: Heinemann.

Adomako Ampofo, Akosua, Josephine Beoku-Betts, Wairimu Njambi and Mary Osirim. 2004. "Women's and Gender Studies in English-Speaking Sub-Saharan Africa: A Review of Research in the Social Sciences." *Gender and Society,* Vol. 18, No. 6.

AEN Conference Report. 2000. Engaging African entrepreneurs: Enterprise Networks' first pan-African Conference. Addis Ababa, Ethiopia. OECD Working Paper, VIII: 98.

Afonja, S. 1990. "Changing Patterns of Gender Stratification in West Africa," in I. Tinker(ed.) *Persistent Inequalities: Women and World Development,* 198-209. Oxford: Oxford University Press.

Africa Rights. 1995. *Not so Innocent: When Women Become Killers.* London: Africa Rights.

African Studies Review 49:2. September 2006 Special Issue: Autochthony and the Crisis of Citizenship.

Agarwal, Bina. 1994. *A Field of One's Own: Women and Land Rights in South Asia.* Cambridge: Cambridge University Press.

_____. 2003. "Gender and Land Rights Revisited: Exploring new prospects via the state, family and market." *Journal of Agrarian Studies,* vol. 3: 1-2.

Agbaw, M. 2000. "'Buying Futures:' the upsurge of female entrepreneurship." Leiden: Universiteit Leiden: Research School of Asian, African and Amerindian Studies.

Agence France Presse [Kinshasa], 23 June 2006. "DR Congo soldiers get life imprisonment for 'crimes against humanity.'"

Akeroyd, A. 1997. "Sociocultural aspects of AIDS in Africa: occupational and gender issues." In G. Bond; J. Kreniske; I. Susser, and J. Vincent (Ed.), *AIDS in Africa and the Caribbean.* Boulder, CO: Westview Press.

Albanese, Patrizia. 2006. *Mothers of the Nation.* Toronto: University of Toronto Press.

Amadiume, Ifi. 1997. *Male Daughters and Female Husbands: Gender and Class in an African Society,* London: Zed Books

Amnesty International. 1995. *It's About Time! Human Rights are Women's Rights.* New York: Amnesty International.

_____. 2004. *Sudan: Darfur: Rape a Weapon of War: Sexual violence and its Consequence.* http://web.amnesty.org/library/index/engafr540762004

Amrita Basu (ed.) 1995. *The Challenge of Local Feminisms: Women's Movements in Global Perspective,* Boulder: Westview Press

Andersen, Margaret and Patricia Hill Collins, eds. 1992. *Race, Class and Gender: an Anthology.* Belmont, CA: Wadsworth Publishing Co.

Anderson-Levitt K., M. Bloch and A. Soumare A. 1998. "Inside Classrooms in Guinea: Girls' Experiences," in M. Block, J. Beoku-Betts and R. Tabachnick (eds.) *Women and*

Antrobus, Peggy. 2004. *The Global Women's Movement: Origins, Issues and Strategies.* Zed Books.

Arnould, E. 1995. "West African marketing channels." In J. Sherry ed., *Contemporary Marketing and Consumer Behaviour: An Anthropological Sourcebook.* Thousand Oaks, CA: Sage Publications. pp. 109-161.

Aryeetey, E. and William S. 1994. "Informal Savings Collectors in Ghana: Can They Intermediate?" *Finance and Development* 31:1, March, pp. 36-37.

Asoka Banderage. 1984. "Women in Development: Liberalism, Marxism and Marxist feminism," *Development and Change* 15: 495-515.

Aspaas, H. 1998. "Heading households and heading businesses: rural Kenyan women in the informal sector." *Professional Geographer,* 502 192-204.

Assié-lumumba, N. T. 2000. "Educational and Economic Reforms, Gender Equity, and Access to Schooling in Africa, *IJCS* 2000/05/01 Prn:3/05/2000; 9:56 F:IJCS329.tex; TEV/LK p. 1 (33-118) Koninklijke Brill NV, Leiden.

_____. 1997. "Educating Africa's girls and women: A Conceptual and Historical Analysis of Gender Inequality." In *Engendering African Social Sciences,* edited by A. Imam, A. Mama, and F. Sow. Dakar, Senegal: CODESRIA Book Series.

Assiter, Alison. 1999. Citizenship Revisited. In N. Yuval and P. Werbner (eds.). *Women, Citizenship and Difference.* London and New York: Zed Books.

Aubrey, Lisa. 2001. "Gender, Development, and Democratization in Africa," *Journal of Asian and African Studies,* 36, 1: 87-111.

AWID International Forum on Women's Rights and Development. 2005. "Opening Plenary: What have we changed and how?" Rochelle Jones, 27 October; and "Final Plenary: How does change happen? A Wrap-up," Kathambi Kinoti, 30 October. www.AWID. org.

Ballington, Julie, ed. 2004b. 'The Implementation of Quotas: African Experiences.' Quota Report Series No. 3. Stockholm: International Idea.

_____. 2004a. 'Conclusion: Women's Political Participation and Quotas in Africa.' In Ballington, ed. *The Implementation of Quotas: African Experiences.*

Banda, Fareda. 2005. *Women, Law and Human Rights: an African Perspective.* Oxford: Hart.

Barden-O'Fallon, J. L., J. deGraft-Johnson, T. Bisika, S. Sulzbach, A. Benson, & A.O. Tsui. 2004. "Factors associated with HIV/AIDS knowledge and risk perception in rural Malawi." *AIDS and Behavior* 8(2), 131-140.

Bauer, Gretchen and Scott Taylor. 2005. *Politics in Southern Africa.* Boulder, CO: Lynne Reiner.

Bauer, Gretchen, and Hannah E. Britton, eds. 2006b. *Women in African Parliaments.* Boulder: Lynne Rienner Publishers.

_____. 2006a. 'Women in African Parliaments: A Continental Shift?' In Bauer and Britton, eds. *Women in African Parliaments.* Boulder: Lynne Rienner Publishers.

Bauer, Gretchen. 2006. 'Namibia: Losing Ground without Mandatory Quotas.' In Bauer and Britton, eds. *Women in African Parliaments.* Boulder: Lynne Rienner Publishers.

_____. 2008. "Reserved Seats and Women MPs in Uganda: Affirmative Action for the National Women's Movement or the National Resistance Movement?" In Manon Tremblay, ed. *Women and Legislative Representation: Electoral Systems, Political Parties, and Sex Quotas.* Palgrave Macmillan.

BBC News. 2002. Life expectancy still falling in Africa. Monday, 11 February, 2002. Full text: http://news.bbc.co.uk/2/hi/africa/1814609.stm

BBC. 2006. "Zimbabweans have 'shortest lives.' BBC Online: http://news.bbc.co.uk/2/hi/ africa/4890508.stm

Becker, Heike. 1995. *Namibian Women's Movement 1980 to 1992: From Anti-colonial Resistance to Reconstruction.* Frankfurt: IKO.

Behar, Ruth. 1993. *Translated Woman: Crossing the Border with Esperanza's Story.* Boston: Beacon Press.

Beise, J. and E. Voland. 2002. "A Multilevel Event History Analysis of the Effects of Grandmothers on Child Mortality in a Historical German Population (Krummhörn, Ostfriesland, 1720-1874)." MPIDR Working Paper 2002-023.

Benjamin, Saranel. 2001. "Masculinisation of the State and the Feminization of Poverty."*Agenda,* Volume 48.

Bernstein, Henry and Campbell, Bonnie. 1985. *Contradictions of Accumulation in Africa,* London: Sage.

Bikaako, Winnie and Ssemkumba, John. 2003. "Gender, land and rights: contemporary contestations in Law, Policy and Practice in Uganda." In Wanyeki, L. Muthoni (ed.), *Women and Land in Africa.* London: Zed/Cape Town, D. Philip.

Biraimah, K. 1987. "Class, Gender and Life Chances: A Nigerian University Case Study." *Comparative Education Review,* 31:570-582.

Bloch, Marianne, Josephine A. Beoku-Betts, and Robert B. Tabachnick (eds.). 1998. *Women and Education in Sub-Saharan Africa: Power, Opportunities and Constraints.* Boulder: Lynne Rienner.

Blumberg, Rae L. 1995. *Engendering Wealth and Well-being: Empowerment for Global Change.* Boulder: Westview.

Bob, Urmilla. 1999. "African Rural Women and Land Reform in South Africa: case studies from the Midlands Region of KwaZulu Natal." Ph.D Thesis, W. Virginia University.

Bonate, Lizzat. 2003. "Women's Land Rights in Mozambique." In Wanyeki, L. Muthoni (ed.), *Women and Land in Africa.* London: Zed/Cape Town, D. Philip.

Boserup, E. 1970. *Women's Role in Development,* New York: St. Martin's Press.

Bowditch, N. 1999. *The Last Emerging Market: From Asian Tigers to African Lions.* Westport, CT: Praeger.

Bowman, M.J. and C.A. Anderson. 1980. "The Participation of Women in Education in the Third World." *Comparative Education Review* 24(2):13-32.

Briskin, L. 1990. "Gender in the Classroom." CORE: Newsletter of the Centre for the Support of Teaching, York, 1/1.

Britton, Hannah. 2005. *Women in the South African Parliament: From Resistance to Governance.* Champaign: University of Illinois Press.

_____. 2005. *Women in the South African Parliament: From Resistance to Governance.* Urbana and Chicago: University of Chicago Press.

_____. 2006. 'South Africa: Mainstreaming Gender in a New Democracy.' In Bauer and Britton, eds. *Women in African Parliaments.*

Brock, C. and N. Cammish. 1997. "Factors Affecting Female Participation in Education in Seven Developing Countries." Education Research Paper No. 09, Universities of Oxford and Hull, (Second Edition).

Brock-Utne, B. 2000. *Whose Education for All? The Recolonization of the African Mind.* Falmer Press, New York.

Bruce, J, and Migot-Adhola, S. 1994. *Searching for Land Security in Africa.* Washington: World Bank.

Bryceson, Deborah Fahy, ed. 1995. *Women Wielding the Hoe: Lessons from Rural Africa for Feminist Theory and Development Practice.* Oxford: Berg Publishers.

Bühler, C., & Kohler, H.-P. 2003. Talking about AIDS: the influence of communication networks on individual risk perceptions of HIV/AIDS infection and favored protective behaviors in South Nyanza District, Kenya." Demographic Research. Full text at www. demographic_research.org.

Bujra, J., & Baylies, C. 1999. Solidarity and stress: gender and local mobilization in Tanzania and Zambia. In P. Aggleton, P. Davies, & G. Hart, (Ed.), *Families and communities responding to AIDS* (pp. 35-52). London: UCL Press.

Bujra, Janet M. 1983. "Class, Gender and Capitalist Transformation in Africa," *African Development* 8, July, p.17-42.

Business Partners, Ltd. http://www.businesspartners.co.za/

Businge, Harriett. 2002. "Customary land tenure reform in Uganda: Lessons for South Africa." Paper at PLAAS/Programme for Land and Agrarian Studies.

Butler, Judith. 1990. *Gender Trouble: Feminism and the Subversion of Identity.* New York: Routledge.

Byres, Terry. 2004. "On Neo-classical neo-Populism 25 years on: Déjà-vu and déjà – passé." *Journal of Agrarian Change* 4:1-2.

Caldwell, J. C., P. Caldwell, & P. Quiggin. 1989. "The social context of AIDS in sub-Saharan Africa." *Population and Development Review* 15(2), 185-234.

Caldwell, J.C. 1986. "Routes to Low Mortality in Poor countries," *Population and Development Review* 12:171–220.

Camlin, C. S., & C.E. Chimbwete. 2003. "Does knowing someone with AIDS affect condom use? An analysis from South Africa." *AIDS Education and Prevention* 15(3), 231-244.

Carillo, R.. 1992. *Battered Dreams: Violence against Women as an Obstacle to Development.* New York: United Nations Development Fund for Women.

Carothers, Thomas. 2003. 'Promoting the Rule of Law Abroad: The Problem of Knowledge.' The Rule of Law Series, Democracy and Rule of Law Project, Carnegie Endowment for International Peace, No. 34. 2003)

Carr, Marilyn. 1991. *Women and Food Security: the African Experience.* London: Intermediate Technology.

Castel, J.R.. 1992. "Rape, Sexual Assault and the Meaning of Persecution." *International Journal of Refugee Law.* Vol. 4. No. 1, 38-56.

Castles, Stephen and Miller, Mark. 2003. *The Age of Migration.* London: Palgrave Macmillan.

Centre for Development and Population Activities, CEDPA: www.cedpa.org

Chang, I. 1997. *The Rape of Nanking: The Forgotten Holocaust of World War II*, quoted In Orville Schell New York Times, 14 December, "Bearing Witness." *http://query. nytimes.com/gst/fullpage.html?res=940DE5D6123DF937A25751CA961958260&s ec=&pagewanted=print>*)

Chanock, Martin. 1989. "Neither Customary nor Legal: African Customary Law in an Era of Family Law Reform." *International Journal of Law and Family,* 72:3.

Chant, Sylvia. 1997. *Woman-Headed Households*. Houndmills: Macmillan.

Charlesworth, Hilary. 1994. "What are 'Women's International Human Rights'?" in Cook, Rebecca J., *Human Rights of Women: National and International Perspectives*. University of Pennsylvania Press.

Charmes, J. 1999. "Micro-enterprises in West Africa," in King, K. and McGrath, S., eds., *Enterprise in Africa: Between Poverty and Growth*. London: Intermediate Technology Publications.

Chemonics International, Inc.: www.chemonics.com

Chernichovsky, D. 1985. "Socioeconomic and Demographic Aspects of School Enrolment and Attendance in Rural Botswana." *Economic Development and Cultural Change* 33:319–32.

Chirwa, W. 1998. Aliens and AIDS in southern Africa: the Malawi-South Africa debate. *African Affairs* 97, 53-79.

Chuku, Gloria. 2002. "Women and Nationalist Movements." In Falola, Toyin ed. *Africa (Volume 4): The End of Colonial Rule: Nationalism and Decolonisation.* 109-131, Durham: Carolina Academic Press.

Clark, Carolyn. 1980. Land and Food, Women and Power in Nineteenth Century Kikuyu. *Africa: Journal of the International African Institute,* 1980;50(4):357-370.

Clark, G. 1994. *Onions Are My Husband*. Chicago: University of Chicago Press.

Clark, G. 2000. "Small scale traders' key role in stabilizing and diversifying Ghana's rural communities and livelihoods." In A. Spring, ed., *Women Farmers and Commercial Ventures: Increasing Food Security in Developing Countries*. Boulder: Lynne Rienner Publishers. pp. 253-270.

Cliffe, J.. 1991. "The War on Women in Mozambique: Health Consequences of South African Destabilization, Economic Crisis, and Structural Adjustment." In Meredeth Turshen (ed.), *Women and Health in Africa*. Trenton: New Jersey: Africa World Press.

Clinard, M.B.. 1963. *Sociology of Deviant Behaviour,* rev. ed., New York: Hold, Rinehart and Winston.

Codou, B. 2001. "Women in Conflict: Their Gains and Their Losses," In Meintjes, S. Anu Pillay and Meredeth Turshen (eds.), *The Aftermath: Women in Post-Conflict Trans-formation*. London: Zed Books.

Colclough, C.P. Rose and M. Tembon. 1998. "Gender Inequalities in Primary Schooling: The Roles of Poverty and Adverse Cultural Practice." IDS Working Paper 78 IDS III. Website: http://www.ids.ac.uk/ids/publicat.

Cole, Johnetta. 2001. "Foreword" pp. ix-xi. *In Black Feminist Anthropology: Theory, Praxis, Politics and Poetics.* Ed. Irma McClaurin. New Brunswick: Rutgers University Press.

Cole, Sally and Lynn Phillips, (eds.). 1995. *Ethnographic Feminisms: Essays in Anthropology.* Ottowa: Carelton University Press.

Colligan Sumi. 1999. "'To Develop Our Listening Capacity, To Be Sure that We Hear Everything': Sorting Out Voices on Women's Rights in Morocco," in Diana J. Fox and Naima Hasci, eds., *The Challenges of Women's Activism and Human Rights in Africa.* Edwin Mellen Press.

Collins, Patricia Hill. 1990. *Black Feminist Thought: Knowledge, Consciousness and The Politics of Empowerment.* New York: Routledge, Chapman and Hall.

Colson, Elizabeth. 1960. *The Social Organisation of the Gwembe Tonga: Vol. I The Human Consequences of Resettlement.* Lusaka: University of Zambia.

Cook Lauer, N. September 2005. "Rape Reporting Procedure Missing After Hurricane." http://www.womensenews.org/article.cfm/dyn/aid/2448

Cook, Rebecca J. 1994. "Women's International Human Rights Law: The Way Forward," in Cook, Rebecca J., *Human Rights of Women: National and International Perspectives.* University of Pennsylvania Press.

Coquery-Vidrovitch, C. 1997. *African Women: A Modern History.* Boulder: Westview Press.

Cornia, G and G. Helleiner, G. (eds.) 1994. *From Adjustment to Development in Africa: Conflict, Controversy, Convergence, Consensus?* London: Macmillan Press.

Courcelle, M, and de Lattre, A. 1996. "The enterprise impulse in West Africa," *OECD Observer,* 203: 32-34

Cross, Catherine and Friedman, Michelle. 1997. "Women and land: marginality and the left-hand power." In Meer, S (ed.), *Women, Land and Authority.* Oxford: Oxfam:17-34.

Cross, Catherine. 1992. "An Alternate Legality: the Property Rights Question in relation to South African Land Reform" *S. African J. on Human Rights,* 305-331.

Cruickshank, B. 1999. *The Will to Power: Democratic Citizens and Other Subjects.* Ithaca, NY: Cornell University Press.

Csapo, M. 1981. "Religious, Social and Economic Factors Hindering the Education of Girls in Northern Nigeria." *Comparative Education* 17(3):311-319.

DAE (Donors to African Education). 1994. *A Statistical Profile of Education Sub-Saharan African in the 1980s.* Paris: UNESCO

Dahlerup, Drude, and Lenita Freidenvall. 2005. 'Quotas as a "Fast Track" to Equal Representation for Women: Why Scandinavia is No Longer the Model.' *International Feminist Journal of Politics.* 7(1): 26-48.

Dahlerup, Drude, ed. 2006. *Women in Politics: Electoral Quotas, Equality and Democracy.* London: Routledge.

Dahlerup, Drude. 2004. "Quotas are Changing the History of Women." In Ballington, ed. *The Implementation of Quotas: African Experiences.*

Daniels, L, Mead, D., and Musinga, M. 1995. Employment and income in micro- and small enterprises in Kenya: Results of a 1995 survey. GEMINI Research Paper 26. Nairobi: K-REP.

Daniels, L. 1994. "Changes in the small-scale enterprise sector from 1991-1993: Results of a nationwide survey in Zimbabwe." GEMINI Technical Report No. 71. Bethesda, MD: Development Alternatives.

_____. 1998. "What drives the small-scale enterprise sector in Zimbabwe: Surplus labor or market demand?" In A. Spring and B. McDade, eds., *African Entrepreneurship: Theory and Reality.* Gainesville and Tallahassee: University Press of Florida. pp. 51-68.

Darkwah, Akosua. 2002. "Trading Goes Global: Market Women in an Era of Globalization." *Asian Women,* Volume 18.

Darnovsky, Marcy et al. (eds.). 1995. *Cultural Politics and Social Movements.* Philadelphia: Temple University Press.

Daun, H. 2000. "Primary Education in Sub-Saharan Africa—A Moral Issue, an Economic Matter, or Both?" *Comparative Education* 36(1):37-53.

David, Court. 1991. "The development of University Education in Sub-Saharan Africa," In Altbach, Philip (ed.), *International Higher Education: An Encyclopedia, Volume 1,* (p.329-347), New York: Garland Publishing.

Davison, Jean. 1988. "Land and Women's Agricultural Production: the Context." In Davison (ed.), *Women, Agriculture and Land: the African Experience.* Boulder: Westview.

De Grazia, S. 1948. *The Political Community: A Study of Anomie,* Chicago: The University of Chicago Press, xii-ix.

Deere, Carmen Diana and Leon, Magdalena. 2001. *Empowering Women: Land and Property Rights in Latin America.* Pittsburgh: Pittsburgh University Press.

Deere, Carmen Diana. 2003. "Women's land rights and social movements in the Brazilian agrarian reform." *Journal of Agrarian Change,* vol. 3 nos. 1-2.

DeRose, L.F. and O. Kravdal. 2005. "The Effects of Educational Reversals on First Births in sub-Saharan Africa: A Dynamic Multi-level Perspective." Paper Delivered at the Population Association of America Annual Meeting, Philadelphia, Pennsylvania.

Desai, Manisha. 2002. "Transnational Solidarity: Women's Agency, Structural Adjustment and Globalization," in Naples and Desai, (eds.), *Women's Activism and Globalization: Linking Local Struggles and Transnational Politics.* New York: Routledge.

Development Alternatives with Women for a New Era (DAWN). www.dawnorg. Org.

DHS 2006. Demographic and Health Surveys StatCompiler. 2006. ORC, Macro. Accessed February 2006. Available on line at http://www.measuredhs.com.

Disney, Jennifer Leigh. 2006. 'Mozambique: Empowering Women Through Family Law.' In Bauer and Britton, eds. *Women in African Parliaments.*

Dizdarevic, Z.. 1993. *Sarajevo: A war journal,* New York: Fromm International.

Donald A. Nielsen. 1996. "Pericles and the Plague: Civil religion, anomie and injustice in Thucydides," *Sociology of Religion:* 57 (4), 397 & 400.

Dow, Unity (ed.). 1995. *The Citizenship Case: The Attorney General of the Republic of Botswana vs. Unity Dow: Court Documents, Judgments, Cases and Materials.* Gaborone, Botswana: Lentswe La Lesedi.

Durkheim, Emile. 1951. *Suicide: A Study in Sociology.* Translated by John A. Spauling and George Simpson. New York: Free Press.

EAEN. 1998. Profiles, in *EAEN Newsletter* 2:2, October.

EAEN. 1999. "New generation entrepreneurs address regional cooperation in East Africa." *EAEN Newsletter*, 2 February 1.

EAEN. 2000. "New generation entrepreneurs address regional cooperation in East Africa," *EAEN Newsletter,* 2: 5 March.

Edge, Wayne A. and M.H. Lekorwe (eds.). 1998. *Botswana: Politics and Society.* Pretoria, South Africa: J.L. van Schaik.

Education in Sub-Saharan Africa: Power, Opportunities and Constraints, 99-130. Boulder: Lynne Rienner.

El-Bushra, J. 2000a. "Transforming conflict: some thoughts on a gendered understanding of conflict dynamics." In S. Jacobs, R. Jacobson, and J. Marchbank (Eds.), *States of Conflict: Gender, Violence and Resistance.* London & New York: Zed Books, 66-85.

_____. 2000b. "Gender and Forced Migration:" Editorial. *Forced Migration Review* 9 December: 4-7.

_____. 2003. "Fused in combat: gender relations and armed conflict." *Development in Practice*, Vol. 13, nos. 2 & 3, 252-265.

Electronic commerce in Africa: The African Development Forum 99. www.uncea.org/adf99/adf99ecommerce.htm

El-Ghonemy, M. Riad. 1990. *The Political Economy of Rural Poverty: the Case for Land Reform.* London: Macmillan.

El-Ghonemy, M. Riad. 2001. "The political economy of market-based land reform." In Ghimire (ed.), *Land Reform and Peasant Livelihoods.* London: ITDG.

Ellis, Frank. 2000. *Rural Livelihoods and Diversity in Developing Countries.* Oxford: Oxford University Press.

Eloundou-Enyegue, P. M, and S. C. Stokes. 2004. "Teen Fertility and Gender Inequality in Education: A Contextual Hypothesis." *Demographic Research* 11(11):305-334.

Eloundou-Enyegue, P.M, and L.B. Williams. 2006. "Family Size and Schooling in Sub-Saharan African Settings: A Reexamination." *Demography* 43(1): 25-52.

Eloundou-Enyegue, P.M. 2004. "Pregnancy-Related Dropouts and Gender Inequality in Education: A life Table Approach and Application to Cameroon." *Demography* 41:509-528.

Eloundou-Enyegue, P.M. and D. Shapiro. 2005. "Confiage d'Enfants et Nivellement des Inégalités Scolaires." [Fosterage and Reduction of Schooling Inequality]. *Cahiers Québécois de Démographie.*

Elson, Diane and Gideon, Jasmine. 2004. "Organising for Women's Economic and Social Rights: how useful is the International Covenant on Economic, Social and Cultural Rights?" In Jacobs, S. (ed.), Special issue: 'Women's Organisations and Networks in a Globalising Era': *Journal of Interdisciplinary Gender Studies.* Australia: 8: 1-2:

Elson, Diane. 2002. "Gender Justice, Human Rights and Neo-liberal economic policies." In Maxine Molyneux and Shahra Ravazi (eds.), *Gender Justice, Development and Rights.* Oxford: Oxford University Press: 78-114.

Emang Basadi Women's Association. 1999. *The Women's Manifesto: A Summary of Botswana Women's Issues and Demands.* Gaborone, Botswana: Lentswe La Lesedi.

_____. 1998. *Emang Basadi's Political Education Project: A Strategy that Works.* Gaborone, Botswana: Lentswe La Lesedi.

EngenderHealth. 2002. Country by country: Malawi. Full text http://www.engenderhealth. org/ia/cbc/malawi.html)

Englund, H. 2002. "The village in the city, the city in the village: migrants in Lilongwe." *Journal of Southern African Studies* 28(1), 137-154.

Esbin, H. 1994. *The marketing and promotion of Jua Kali by government and institutional partners.* Geneva: ILO.

Fall, Yassine. 1999. "Globalization, its Institutions and African Women's Resistance," in fall edited, *Africa: Gender, Globalization and Resistance.* Dakar: AAWORD Book Series.

Falola, T. 1995. "Gender, business, and space control: Yoruba market women and power." In B. House-Midamba and F. Ekechi. eds., *African Market Women and Economic Power.* Westport CT: Greenwood Press. pp. 23-40.

Fan, H.Y., R.F. Conner, & L.P. Villarreeal. 2004. *AIDS science and society.* Sudbury, MA: Jones and Bartlett Publishers.

Fapohunda, Eleanor. 1987. "The Nuclear Household Model in Nigeria." *Development and Change,* 18 (2): 281-91.

Fatton, R. 1989. "Gender, Class and the State in Africa." In *Women and the State in Africa,* (47-66) Ed. J. L. Parpart and K. Staudt, London: Lynne Rienner.

Ferrand, D. 1996. "A study of the missing middle in Kenya." IDS Working Paper 515. Nairobi: Institute of Development Studies.

Ferree, Myra Marx and Patricia Yancey Martin, (eds.) 1995. *Feminist Organi-zations: Harvest of the New Women's Movement.* Philadelphia: Temple University Press.

Fick, D. 2002. *Entrepreneurship in Africa: A Study of Successes.* Westport, CT: Quorum Books.

Fick, D. 2006. *Africa: Continent of Economic Opportunities.* Johannesburg: STE Publications.

Filmer, D. and L. Pritchett. 2001. "Estimating Wealth Effects Without Expenditure Data—or Tears: An Application to Educational Enrollments in States of India." *Demography* 38:115–32.

Fortin, Elizabeth. 2005. "Reforming Land Rights: the World Bank and the Globalisation of Agriculture." *Social and Legal Studies*: 14 (2).

Fortna, B.C. 2002 in Herrera 2004. *Imperial Classroom: Islam, the State, and Education in the Late Ottoman Empire.* Oxford: Oxford University Press.

Fox, Diana. "Arriving and Departing…and Arriving Again." In *Cultural DNA? Gender at the Root of Everyday Life in Rural Jamaica.* Manuscript in progress.

Francis, Elizabeth. 2000. *Making a Living: Rural Livelihoods in Africa.* London: Routledge.

Friedman, Lawrence and Stewart Macaulay. 1970. 'Legal Culture and Social Development,' (Law and Culture), *Law and the Behavioral Sciences.*

Friedman, Marilyn (ed.). 2005. *Women and Citizenship.* Oxford and New York: Oxford University Press.

Gaitskell, Deborah and Elaine Unterhalter. 1989. "Mothers of the Nation: A Comparative Analysis of Nation, Race and Motherhood in Afrikaner Nationalism and the African National Congress." In F. Anthias and N. Yuval-Davis (eds.) *Women-Nation-State.* Basingstoke: Macmillan.

Geisler, Gisela. 2004. *Women and the Remaking of Politics in Southern Africa: Negotiating Autonomy, Incorporation and Representation.* Sweden: Nordiska Afrikainstitutet.

Gerlach, Luther. 1999. "Social Movements as Segmentary, Polycentric and Reticulate," in Freeman and Johnson, (eds.), *Waves of Protest: Social Movements since the Sixties.* Lanham, MD.: Rowman and Littlefield.

Ghimire, Krishna (ed). 2001) Land Reform and Peasant Livelihoods, London, ITDG

Gledhill, John. 2000. *Power and its Disguises: Anthropological Perspectives on Politics.* Second Edition. London: Pluto Press.

Goebel, Allison. 1999. "Here it is our land, the two of us": women, men and land in a Zimbabwean resettlement area." *Journal of Contemporary African Studies,* 17: 75-96.

Goebel, Allison. 2005a. *Gender and Land Reform: the Zimbabwean Experience.* Montreal: McGill-Queens University Press.

Goebel, Allison. 2005b. "Zimbabwe's 'Fast-Track' Land Reform: What about Women?" *Gender, Place and Culture* vol. 12, no. 2: 145-72.

Goedhuys, M. and Sleuwaegen, L. 2000. "Entrepreneurship and growth of entrepreneurial firms in Côte d"Ivoire," *Journal of Development Studies,* 363: 123-142.

Goetz, Ann Marie and Shireen Hassim. 2003. *No Shortcuts to Power.* London and New York: Zed Press.

Goetz, Anne Marie and Shireen Hassim. 2003. 'Introduction: Women in Power in Uganda and South Africa.' In Anne Marie Goetz and Shireen Hassim, eds. *No Shortcuts to Power: African Women and Politics and Policy Making.* London: Zed Books and Cape Town: David Philip.

Goetz, Anne Marie. 2003. 'The Problem with Patronage: Constraints on Women's Political Effectiveness in Uganda.' In Anne Marie Goetz and Shireen Hassim, eds. *No Shortcuts to Power: African Women and Politics and Policy Making.* London: Zed Books and Cape Town: David Philip.

Goheen, Miriam. 1988. "Land and the Household Economy: Women of the Grassfields Today." In Davison (ed.), *Women, Agriculture and Land,* Boulder: Westview.

Goldblatt and Meintjes. 1998. "South African Women Demand the Truth." In Meredeth Turshen and Clotilde Twagiramariya, *Gender and Conflict in Africa.* London & New York: Zed Books (27-61).

Gomes, M. 1984. "Family Size and Educational Attainment in Kenya." *Population and Development Review* 10:647–60.

Gouws, Amanda (ed.). 2005a. "Shaping Women's Citizenship: Contesting the Boundaries of State and Discourse," in A. Gouws (ed.), *(Un)thinking Citizenship: Feminist Debates in Contemporary South Africa.* Burlington, VT: Ashgate.

_____. 2005. (Un)thinking Citizenship: Feminist Debates in Contemporary South Africa. Burlington, VT: Ashgate.

Government of Malawi. 2003. The annual review of the Malawi poverty reduction strategy 2002/2003. Lilongwe: Government of Malawi. Full text at http://www.sarpn.org.za/ documents/d0000375/p356_Malawi_PRS.pdf.

Govindasamy, P. and A. Malhotra. 1996. "Women's Position and Family Planning in Egypt." *Studies in Family Planning* 27(6):328-340.

Grawert, R. and Konig, A. "African women in the globalising economy." In K. Wohlmuth, H. Bass, et al. eds., *Africa's Reintegration into the World Economy.* Hamburg: LIT Verlag. pp. 697-704.

Grieco, M. 2006. "Gender, transport and social empowerment: Investigating the consequences of the interaction between gender and constrained mobility." In Ernst, W. and Bohle, U. (Eds) *Naturbilder und Lebensgrundlage: Konstruktionen von Geschlecht.* Pp 53-64. Lit Verlag, Hamburg.

Griffin, Keith, Kahn, A.R. and Ickowitz, Amy. 2002. "Poverty and the Distribution of Land" *J. Agrarian Change,* vol. 2 (3).

Grono, N. & Prendergast, J. 22 August 2006. "To Halt Sudan's Atrocities, Follow the Money." International Herald Tribune. http://www.crisisgroup.org/home/index.cfm?id= 4352&l=1

Gruenbaum, Ellen.. "Feminist Activism for the Abolition of FGM/FC in Sudan." *Journal of Middle East Women's Studies,* Vol. 1, No. 2, Spring 2005: 89-111.

_____. Gruenbaum, Ellen. 2001. *The Female Circumcision Controversy: An Anthro-pological Perspective.* Philadelphia: University of Pennsylvania Press.

Guivant, Julia. 2003. "Agrarian Change, Gender and Land Rights: a Brazilian Case Study." UNRISD, Geneva, Social Policy and Development Paper no. 14.

Hagos, G. 2000. "Gender Divide Stifles Women Entrepreneurs." Pan African News Agency. http://allafrica.com.

Hague, E. 1997. "Rape, Power and Masculinity: The Construction of Gender and National Identity in the War in Bosnia-Herzegovina." In Lentin, R. (Ed.), *Gender and Catastrophe.* London & New York: Zed Books.

Haney, D. Q. 2000. AIDS expected to cut life expectancy to 30 in parts of Africa. Full text: http://www.ardmoreite.com/stories/071100/new_aids.shtml

Hanlon, Joseph. 2002. "The Land Debate in Mozambique: will Foreign Investors, the Urban Elite, Advanced Peasants or Family Farmers drive Rural development?" (Cited in Palmer, 2005.) www.oxfam.org.uk/what_we_do/issues/livelihoods

Hansen, K. and Vaa, M. 2002. *Reconsidering Informality: Perspectives from Urban Africa.* Uppsala: Nordiska Afrikainstitutet.

Harrison, K.A. "Maternal Mortality in Nigeria: The Real Issues," *African Journal of Reproductive Health / La Revue Africaine de la Santé Reproductive*, Vol. 1 No. 1 (March, 1997), pp. 7-13 doi:10.2307/3583270.

Hart, K. 2001. *Money in an Unequal World.* New York: Texere.

Hasci, Naima. 1999. "Out of the Frying Pan into the Fire: Somali Refugee Women's Rights in Kenya," In Diana J. Fox and Naima Hasci, eds., *The Challenges of Women's Activism and Human Rights in Africa.* Lewiston, NY: Edwin Mellen Press.

Hassim, Shireen, and Sheila Meintjes. 2005. Overview Paper prepared for Expert Group Meeting on Democratic Governance in Africa: Strategies for Greater Participation of Women. Arusha, Tanzania. 6-8 December.

Hassim, Shireen. 2006. *Women's Organizations and Democracy in South Africa: Contesting Authority.* Madison, WI: University of Wisconsin Press.

_____. 2005. "Nationalism Displaced: Citizenship Discourses in the Transition," in A. Gouws (ed.), *(Un)thinking Citizenship: Feminist Debates in Contemporary South Africa.* Burlington, VT: Ashgate.

Headrick, D.R. 1981. *The tools of empire-technology and European imperialism in the nineteenth century.* Oxford University Press.

Herrera, L. 2004. "Education, Islam, and Modernity: Beyond Westernization and Centralization." *Comparative Education Review* 48(3):318-326.

Higginbotham, Elizabeth and Lynn Weber Cannon. 1988. *Rethinking Mobility: Towards a Race and Gender Inclusive Theory.* Memphis: Center for Research on Women, Memphis State University.

Hilhorst, Thea. 2001. "Women's Land Rights: current developments in sub-Saharan Africa." In Toulmin and Quan (eds.), *Evolving Land Rights:* London, IIED.

Hilling, D. 1996. Transport and developing countries. Routledge: London.

Hinson, R. and Buatsi, S. 2005. "Non-Traditional Exporters and the Internet in Ghana: Current use and internationalization issues." Paper presented at International Academy of African Business Development Conference: Dar es Salaam, Tanzania, April.

Hobson, Barbara, Jane Lewis and Birte Siim (eds.). 2002. *Contested Concepts in Gender and Social Politics.* Northampton, MA: Edward Elgar.

Holm, John and Patrick Molutsi (eds.). 1989. *Democracy in Botswana.* Gaborone, Botswana and Athens, OH: Botswana Society and Ohio University Press.

Horn, N. 1994, *Cultivating Customers: Market Women in Harare, Zimbabwe.* Boulder: Lynne Rienner Publishers.

Horn, N. 1998. "Overcoming challenges: Women microentrepreneurs in Harare, Zimbabwe." In A. Spring and B. McDade, eds., *African Entrepreneurship: Theory and Reality.* Gainesville and Tallahassee: University Press of Florida. pp. 128-146.

House-Midamba, B. and Ekechi, F. eds. 1995. *African Market Women and Economic Power.* Westport, CT: Greenwood Press.

Human Rights Watch. March 2005. Vol. 17, No. 1 (A). *Seeking Justice: The Prosecution of Sexual Violence in the Congo War.*

_____. 1993. *Seeking Refuge, Finding Terror: The Widespread Rape of Somali Women Refugees in North Eastern Kenya.*

_____. April 2004. Vol. 16, No. 5(A). *Darfur in Flames: Atrocities in Western Sudan.* http://www.hrw.org/reports/2004/sudan0404

_____. 2002. Fast-Tract land Reform in Zimbabwe; vol. 14, no. 1(A), March. http://www.hrw.org/reports/2002/zimbabwe

_____. 2006. "Impunity in the Great Lakes Region." Statement by Human Rights Watch prepared for the "Arria Formula" Meeting January 24, 2006. http://hrw. org/english/docs/2006/01/24/congo12758.htm

Human Rights Watch/Women's Rights Project. 1996. *Shattered Lives: Sexual Violence during the Rwandan Genocide and its Aftermath.* New York: Human Rights Watch.

Hyde , K.A.L. 1989. "Improving Women's Education in Sub-Saharan African: A Review of Literature." Washington DC. Education and Employment Division, Population and Human Resources Department, World Bank.

Ibanez, A. C. 2001. "El Salvador War and Untold Stories: Women Guerrillas," 128. In Caroline O.N. Moser and Fiona Clark (eds.), *Victims, Perpetrators or Actors? Gender, Armed Conflict and Political Violence.* London & New York: Zed Books.

IFPRI. 2002. "The High Price of Gender Inequality: IFPRI Perspectives, vol. 24. http://www.ifpri/org.reports/02spring/02springc.htm

Ikdahl, Ingunn, Hellum, Anne; Kaarhus, Randi, Benjaminsen, Tor A. and Kameri-Mbote, Patricia. 2006. "Human Rights, formalisation and women's land rights in southern and eastern Africa," *Studies in Women's Law* no. 57, University of Oslo.

ILO. 1989. World Labour Report, International Labour Organization, Geneva: ILO.

Imam Ayesha. 1997. Introduction. Imam Ayesha, Mama, Amina and Sow Fatou (eds.) *Engendering African Social Sciences* (eds.) Daka, Senegal: CODESRI)

Imam, Ayesha, Amina Mama and Fatou Sou. 1997. *Engendering African Social Sciences.* Dakar: CODESRIA.

Independent Review of Land Issues (Shaun Williams) 2005. Vol. II, no. 1, Southern Africa, December. www.oxfam.org.uk/what_we_do/issues/livelihoods/landrights/ downloads/ ind_ land_newsletter

Internal Displacement Monitoring Centre (IDCM). 2006. "Internal Displacement Global Overview of Trends & developments in 2006." http://www.internal-displacement.org

International Crisis Group (ICG). 28 June 2006. *Beyond Victimhood: Women's Peacebuilding in Sudan, Congo and Uganda.* Africa Report. No. 112. http://www.crisisgroup.org/home/index.cfm?id=4185&l=1>)

_____. 23 March 2004, ICG Africa Report No. 76, *Darfur Rising: Sudan's New Crisis*. www.crisisgroup.org

International Planned Parenthood Federation (IPPF). n.d. *Reproductive Health in Refugee Situations: An Interagency Field Manual*: An Inter-agency Manual. http://www.ippf.org/resource/refugeehealth/manual/foreword.htm

International Year of MicroCredit: www.yearofmicrocredit.org

Inter-Parliamentary Union (IPU). 2006. "The Participation of Women and Men in Decision- Making: The Parliamentary Dimension." Expert Group Meeting on "Equal Participation of Women and Men in Decision-Making Processes, with Particular Emphasis on Political Participation and Leadership," 24-27 October 2005. Addis Ababa, Ethiopia: Bauer and Britton.

Inter-Parliamentary Union. 2006. 'Women in Parliament in 2005: The Year in Perspective.' Web site.

IRIN News. 2003. "Zimbabwe: Land reform beneficiaries under scrutiny" 24 February. www.irinnews.org/report.asp?ReportID=32476

IRIN News. 2004. "Zimbabwe: Calls for review of inheritance laws." http://inirnews.org/prit.asp?ReportID=43985

Isbister, J. 1993. *Promises not Kept: The Betrayal of Social Change in the Third World*, West Hartford: Kumarian Press.

Itano, Nicole. 2003. "Sex Assault now a political act in Zimbabwe." Women's enews, 9 May http://www.womensenews.org./article.cfm/dyn/aid/

Jacobs, Susie. 2000. "Globalisation, States and 'Women's Agency: Possibilities and Pitfalls," 218-237. In Susie Jacobs, Ruth Jacobson and Jennifer Marchbank, *States of Conflict: Gender, Violence and Resistance*. London. New York: Zed Books.

_____. 1984. "Women and Land Resettlement in Zimbabwe." *Review of African Political Economy* no. 27/28: 33-50.

_____. 1989. "Gender Relations and Land Resettlement in Zimbabwe," Ph.D. thesis, Institute of Development Studies, Univ. of Sussex, Falmer, Brighton.

_____. 1995. "Changing Gender Relations in Zimbabwe: Experiences of Individual Family Resettlement Schemes" in Elson, Diane (ed.), *Male Bias in the Development Process*, Manchester: Manchester University Press, 2nd edition.

_____. 1997. "Land to the Tiller? Gender Relations and Land Reforms: Society in Transition." *J. of S. African Sociology* 1: 1-4: 82-100.

_____. 1998. "The Gendered Politics of Land Reform: Three Comparative Studies." In Randall, V. and Waylen, G (eds.), *Gender, Politics and the State*. London: Routledge.

_____. 2000a. "Zimbabwe: why land reform is a gender issue." *Sociological Review Online*: 5, 2.

_____. 2000b. "Globalisation, States and Women's Agency: possibilities and pitfalls." In Jacobs, S. Jacobson, R and Marchbank, J. (eds.), *States of Conflict: Gender, Violence and Resistance,* London: Zed.

_____. 2002. "Land Reform: still a goal worth pursuing for rural women? *Journal of International Development*, 14: 887-898.

_____. 2003. "Democracy, Class and Gender in Land Reforms: a Zimbabwean Example." In Bell, Michael M. etal. (eds.), *Walking Towards Justice: Democratization in Rural Life*. JAI/Elsevier, Oxford and Amsterdam: 203-229.

_____. 2004. "Livelihoods, Security and Needs: Gender Relations and Land Reform in South Africa." *Journal of International Women's Studies,* 6:1, November. www.bridgew.edu/soas/jiws/

_____. 2009. *Gender and Agrarian Reforms* (Routledge International Studies of Women and Place).

Jacobson, R., Jacobs, S. and Marchbank, J.. 2000. "Introduction: States of Conflict." In Susie Jacobs, Ruth Jacobson and Jennifer Marchbank, *States of Conflict: Gender, Violence and Resistance*. London. New York: Zed Books

Jaggar, Alison M. 2005). "Arenas of Citizenship: Civil Society, the State, and the Global Order." In M. Friedman (ed.) *Women and Citizenship*. Oxford and New York: Oxford University Press.

Jalloh, A. 1999. *African Entrepreneurship: Muslim Fula Merchants in Sierra Leone*. Columbus: Ohio University Centre for International Studies.

Jalloh, A. and Falola, T. eds. 2002. *Black Business and Economic Power*. Rochester, NY: University of Rochester Press.

James, Stanlie M. and Claire Robertson, Eds. 2005. *Genital Cutting and Trans-national Sisterhood: Disputing U.S. Polemics*. University of Illinois Press.

Jetter, Alexis, Annelise Orleck. 1997a. "'The River Has Been Crossed': Wangari Maathai and the Mothers of the Green Belt Movement—An Interview with Wangari Maathai." In Jetter et. al. *The Politics of Motherhood,* Hanover and London: University Press of New England.

Jetter, Alexis, Annelise Orleck and Diana Taylor (eds.). 1997. *The Politics of Motherhood,* Hanover and London: University Press of New England.

Joseph, Suad. 2005. "The Kin Contract and Citizenship in the Middle East." In M. Friedman (ed.) *Women and Citizenship*. Oxford and New York: Oxford University Press.

Josh, Jitendra. 2005. "IMF reveals scale of Zimbabwe's crisis." *Mail and Guardian,* 5 October.

Journal of International Women's Studies, www.bridgew.edu/jiws/

Julius Ihonvbere. 1995. "From Movement to Government: The Movement for Multi-Party Democracy and the Crisis of Democratic Consolidation in Zambia," *Canadian Journal of African Studies,* 29 1, 2.

K'obonyo, P. 1999. "Flexible Specialization and small enterprise development in Kenya: Issues and problems." In L. Kinunda-Rutashobya and Olomi, D., eds, *African entrepreneurship and small business development*. Dar es Salaam: DUP Ltd.

Kabeer, N. 2001. "Conflicts over credit: Re-evaluating the empowerment of potential loans to women in rural Bangladesh." *World Development* Vol. 29, No. 1, pp. 63-84.

Kadi, W. 2006. "Guest Editorial on Special Issues on Islam and Education: Myths and Truths." *Comparative Education Review* 50 (3):311-324.

Kaler, M. 2004. "AIDS-talk in everyday life: the presence of HIV/AIDS in men's informal conversation in southern Malawi." *Social Science & Medicine* 59(2), 285-299.

Kalipeni, E. 1997. "Gender and regional differences in schooling between boys and girls in Malawi." *East African Geographical Review* 19(1), 14-32.

Kalipeni, E. and L. Zulu. Forthcoming. "Using GIS to model and forecast HIV/AIDS rates in Africa, 1986-2010." *Professional Geographer*.

Kalipeni, E., & J. Ghosh. Forthcoming. "Concern and practice among men about HIV/AIDS in low socioeconomic income areas of Lilongwe, Malawi." *Social Science and Medicine* (in press).

Kalipeni, E., S. Craddock, & J. Ghosh. 2004. "Mapping the AIDS epidemic in eastern and southern Africa: a critical overview." In Kalipeni, E., S. Craddock, J.R. Oppong, & J. Ghosh (Ed.), *HIV and AIDS in Africa: beyond epidemiology* (pp. 58-69). Malden, MA: Blackwell Publishing.

Kamete, A. 2002. "Home industries and the formal city in Harare." In K. Hansen and M. Vaa. eds., *Reconsidering Informality: Perspectives from Urban Africa*. Uppsala: Nordiska Afrikainstitutet. pp. 120-137.

Kanakuze, Judith. 2004. 'The Challenge of Implementation and Enforcement in Rwanda.' In Ballington, ed. *The Implementation of Quotas: African Experiences*.

Kaplan, Temma. 1982. "Female Consciousness and Collective Action: The Case of Barcelona." *Signs,* 7:3 Summer, pp. 545-566.

Kawamara-Mishambi, Sheila and Ovonji-Odida, Irene. 2003. "The 'Lost Clause': the Campaign to Advance Women's Property Rights in the Uganda Land Act". 1998), in Goetz, Anne-Marie and Hassim, Shirin (eds.), *No Shortcuts to Power*. London/Cape Town: Zed and David Philip.

Kazimbaya-Senkwe, B. 2002. "Home based enterprises in a period of economic restructuring in Zambia." In K. Hansen and M. Vaa., eds., *Reconsidering Informality: Perspectives from Urban Africa*. Uppsala: Nordiska Afrikainstitutet. pp. 99-118.

Kelkar, G. and Gala, C. 1990. "The Bodghaya Land Struggle" in A.Sen (ed.), *A Space in the Struggle*. Delhi: Kali for Women.

Kelly, Grace. 1991a. "Women and Higher Education." In Altbach, Philip. (ed.) *International Higher Education: An Encyclopedia*. Volume 1, (p. 297-323) New York: Garaland Publishing.

Kelly, J.P. and Elliot, C.M. (eds.) 1982. *Women's Education in the Third World: Comparative Perspectives* (p.11-39). Albany: State University of New York Press.

Kerr, B. 1999. "The Role and potential of technical and vocational education in formal education systems in Africa." In K. King and S. McGrath. eds., *Enterprise in Africa: Between Poverty and Growth*. London: Intermediate Technology Publications.

Keto, C. Tsehloane. 1999. "The Challenge of the Africa-Centered Paradigm in the Construction of African Historical Knowledge." pg. 175-187. In *Out of One, Many Africas: Reconstructing the Study and Meaning of Africa.* Eds. William Martin and Michael West. Urbana and Chicago: University of Illinois Press.

Kevane, Michael. 2004. *Women and Development in Africa: How Gender Works.* Boulder: Lynne Rienner.

Khasiani, S. 1995. *Migration, Women's Status and Poverty in Kenya.* Nairobi: Fasipress.

Kibera, F. 1999. "Female entrepreneurship in small scale enterprises in Kenya." In Kinunda-Rutashobya, L and Olomi, D., eds., *African entrepreneurship and small business development.* Dar es Salaam: DUP Ltd.

Kibiriti, P. 1999. "Entrepreneurship in East Africa," *EAEN Newsletter* 23: 2.

Kidder, Thea. 1997. "Micro-finance and women: how to improve food security? Links, *Oxfam/UKI Newsletter*: October.

King, E. and A. Mason. 2001. "Engendering Development through Gender Equality in Rights, Resources, and Voice." *World Bank Policy Research Report.* Oxford: Oxford University Press.

Kinsey, Bill. 1999. "Land reform, growth and equity: emerging evidence from Zimbabwe's resettlement areas." *J. Southern African Studies,* 25 (2) June.

Kinsey, Bill. 2006. "Land Issues. 1. Fast Track down the Furrow." In *Britain-Zimbabwe Society Newsletter,* Issues 06/1, pp 1-3.

Kishindo, P. 1995. "Sexual behavior in the face of risk: the case of bar girls in Malawi's major cities." *Health Transition Review* 5 (Suppl.), 153-160.

Knodel, J., R.S. Gray, P. Sriwatcharin, and S. Peracca. 1999. "Religion and Reproduction: Muslims in Buddhist Thailand." *Population Studies* 53:149–164.

Krasovec, K. 2004. "Auxiliary technologies related to transport and communi-cation for obstetric emergencies." *International Journal of Gynecology & Obstetrics,* Volume 85, Pages S14-S23.

Kritz, M.M. and D.T. Gurak. 1989. "Women's Status, Education and Family Formation in Sub-Saharan Africa." *International Family Planning Perspectives* 15:100-105.

Krook, Mona Lena. 2005. 'Quota Laws for Women in Politics: A New Type of State Feminism?' Paper presented at the European Consortium for Political Research, Granada, Spain, April 14-19.

Kuada, J. 2006. "Gender, social networks and entrepreneurship in Ghana." *Journal of African Business* special issue on gender. Spring, A. and Rutashobya, L., eds.

Kuenyehia, Akua. 1992. 'Legal Literacy and Law Enforcement Agencies in Ghana,' in *Legal Literacy: A Tool for Women's Empowerment,* Eds. Margaret Schuler and SakuntalaKadirgamar-Rajasingham, UNIFEM, pp. 301-312.

Landau, Paul. 1995. *The Realm of the Word.* Portsmouth: Heinemann.

Lastarría-Cornheil, Susana. 1997. "Impact of privatization on gender and property rights in Africa." *World Development* 25 (8): 1317-1333.

Lawson, A.L.G. 1999. "Women and AIDS in Africa: sociocultural dimensions of the HIV/AIDS epidemic." *International Social Science Journal* 51(3), 391-401.

LeBeau, Debie, and Edith Dima. 2005. 'Multiparty Democracy and Elections in Namibia.' EISA Research Report No. 13. Johannesburg: European Institute for Sustainable Development in Agriculture.

Leith, J. Clark. 2005. *Why Botswana Prospered.* Montreal and Kingston: McGill-Queen's University Press.

Lele, U. 1990. "Structural adjustment, agricultural development and the poor: some lessons from the Malawian experience." *World Development* 18(9), 1207-1219.

Lentin, R. (ed.). *Gender and Catastrophe.* London: Zed Books.

Lessie Jo Frazier, Janise Hurtig, Rosario Montoya del Solar. 2002. *Gender's Place: Feminist Anthropologies of Latin America.* Palgrave Macmillan.

Lewin, Ellen. 2006. "Introduction" pp. 1-39. In *Feminist Anthropology: A Reader.* Ellen Lewin, Ed. Blackwell Publishing.

Lewin, K.M. 1993. "Education and Development: The Issues and the Evidence." Education Research Paper No. 06. Center for International Education, University of Sussex (Reprinted July 1997).

Lewis, Desiree. 2002. "Review Essay: African Feminist Studies: 1980-2002." *Gender and Women's Studies Africa.*

Lister, Ruth. 1997. *Citizenship: Feminist Perspectives.* New York: New York University Press.

Lloyd, C.B. and A. Gage-Brandon. 1994. "High Fertility and Children's Schooling in Ghana: Sex Differences in Parental Contributions and Educational Outcomes." *Population Studies* 48:293–306.

Logo, Patrice and Bikie, Elise-Henriette. 2003. "Women and Land in Cameroon" in Wanyeki, L. Muthoni Wanyeki (ed.), *Women and Land in Africa,* London: Zed.

Longfield, K. 2004. "Rich fools, spare tires and boyfriends: partner categories, relationship dynamics and Ivorian women's risk for STIs and HIV." *Cultural Health and Sexuality* 6(6), 483-500.

Longfield, K., A. Glick, M. Waithaka & J. Berman, J. 2004. "Relationships between older men and younger women: implications for STIs/HIV in Kenya." *Studies in Family Planning* 35(2), 125-134.

Longman, Timothy. 2006. 'Rwanda: Achieving Equality or Serving an Authoritarian State?' In Bauer and Britton, eds. *Women in African Parliaments.*

Lumeya, F. 2004. "Rape, Islam and Darfur's women refugees and war displaced." http://www.refugeesinternational.org/content/article/detail/ 3215?

MacGaffey, J. 1987. *Entrepreneurs and Parasites.* Cambridge: Cambridge University Press.

Magubane, Zine. 2001. "Globalization and the South African Woman: A Historical Overview," in *Visions of Gender Theories and Social Development in Africa: Harnessing Knowledge for Social Justice and Equality.* Dakar: AAWORD Book Series.

Maharaj, P., and J. Cleland. 2004. "Condom use within marital and cohabiting partnerships in KwaZulu-Natal, South Africa." *Studies in Family Planning* 35(2), 116-124.

Mahlouf Obermeyer, C. 1992. "Reproductive Choice in Islam: "Islam, Women and Politics." *Population and Development Review* 18(1):33–57.

Mahlouf Obermeyer, C. 1994. "Reproductive Choice in Islam: Gender and State in Iran and Tunisia." *Studies in Family Planning* 25:41–51.

Makerere University Gender Studies Program. www.makkerere.ac.ug/women studies/background/html.

Malawi Government & UNDP Malawi. 2002. "The impact of HIV/AIDS on human resources in the Malawi public sector." Lilongwe: Malawi Government and UNDP Malawi.

Malhotra A. and M. Mather. 1997. "Do Schooling and Work Empower Women in Developing Countries? Gender and Domestic Decisions in Sri Lanka." *Sociological Forum* 12: No. 4.

Mama, Amina. 1995. "Feminism or Femocracy? State Feminism and Democratization in Nigeria," *African Development,* 20 (1): 37-58.

Mama, Amina. 1996. "Women's Studies and Studies of Women in Africa during the 1990s." Working paper Series. Dakar: CODESRIA.

Mandel, J. 2003. "Negotiating expectations in the field: Gatekeepers, research fatigue and cultural biases." *Singapore Journal of Tropical Geography,* 242 198-210.

Manicom, Linzi. 2005. "Constituting 'Women' as Citizens: Ambiguities in the Making of Gendered Political Subjects in Post-apartheid South Africa," in A. Gouws (ed.), *(Un)thinking Citizenship: Feminist Debates in Contemporary South Africa.* Burlington, VT: Ashgate.

Manji, Ambreena. 2003a. "Remortgaging Women's Lives: the World Bank's Land Agenda in Africa." *Feminist Legal Studies* 11: 139-63.

Manji, Ambreena. 2003b. "Capital, Labour and land relations in Africa: a gender analysis of the World Bank's Policy Research Report on Land Institutions and Land Policy." *Third World Quarterly,* 24 (1): 97-114.

Manu, G. 1999. "Enterprise development in Africa: Strategies for impact and growth." In K. King and S. McGrath, *Enterprise in Africa: Between Poverty and Growth.* London: Intermediate Technology Publications.

Marcus, George E. and Michael M. J. Fischer. 1986. *Anthropology as Cultural Critique.* Chicago and London: University of Chicago Press.

Marcus, Tessa, Eales, K, Wildschut, A. 1996) Down to Earth: Land Demand in the new South Africa, Indicator Press, Durban, University of Natal

Marsden, K. 1990. "African Entrepreneurs: Pioneers of Development." Discussion Paper No. 9, Washington, DC: The World Bank.

Martin, William G. and Michael O. West. 1999. "The Africanist Enterprise, U.S.A." In *Out of One, Many Africas: Reconstructing the Study and Meaning of Africa.* Eds. William Martin and Michael West. Urbana and Chicago: University of Illinois Press.

Masiiwa, Medicine. 2004. "Land Reform Programme in Zimbabwe: Disparity between Policy Design and Implementation." May, Institute of Development Studies, Harare.

Matemba, Yonah Hisbon. 2005. "A Chief Called 'Woman': Historical Perspectives on the Changing Face of Bogosi (Chieftainship) in Botswana, 1834-2004." *Jenda: A Journal of Culture and African Women Studies:* 7. www.jendajournal.com/issue7/matemba.html

Matembe, Miria. 2006. 'Participating in Vain: The Betrayal of Women's Rights in Uganda.' Paper presented to the Reagan-Fascell Democracy Fellows, Washington, DC, 16 May.

Matland, Richard. 2006. 'Electoral Quotas: Frequency and Effectiveness.' In Dahlerup, ed. *Women, Quotas and Politics.*

Mba, N. E. 1982. "Nigerian Women Mobilised: Women's Political Activities in Southern Nigeria: 1900–1965." *Research Series,* No. 48. Institute of African Studies: Berkeley, University of California.

Mba, Nina. 1982. *Nigerian Women Mobilized.* Berkeley, CA: Institute for International Studies.

McClaurin, Irma. 2001. "Introduction: Forging a Theory, Politics, Praxis, and Poetics of Black Feminist Anthropology." In *Black Feminist Anthropology: Theory, Politics, Praxis, and Poetics.* Ed. Irma McClaurin. New Brunswick, NJ: Rutgers University Press.

McCusker, Brent. 2004) "Land Use and Cover Change as an Indicator of Transformation on Recently Redistributed Farms in Limpopo Province, South Africa" Human Ecology, vol. 32, no. 1, Feb

McDade, B. and Spring, A. 2005. The "New Generation of African Entrepreneurs": Changing the environment for business development and economic growth. *Entrepreneurship and Regional Development* (1-26).

McFadden, Patricia. 2003. "Sexual Pleasure as Feminist Choice." *Feminist Africa,* Volume 2.

_____. 1999. Preface. In McFadden, Patricia (ed.), *Reflections on Gender Issues in Africa.* Harare, Zimbabwe: Sapes Books.

_____. 2001. *Patriarchy: Political Power, Sexuality and Globalization.* Port Louis, Mauritius: Ledikasyon Pu Travayer.

Mead, D. 1999. "MSEs tackle both poverty and growth but in differing proportions." In K. King and S. McGrath, *Enterprise in Africa: Between Poverty and Growth.* London: Intermediate Technology Publications.

Meagher, Robert and D. Silverstein.1988. 'Law and Social Change,' in *Law and Social Change: Indo-American Reflections,* N.M. Tripathi Pvt Ltd., Bombay.

Meena, Ruth. 2004. 'The Politics of Quotas in Tanzania.' In Ballington, ed. *The Implementation of Quotas: African Experiences.*

Merton, R.K. 1964. Quoted in Marshal B. Clinard, *Anomie and Deviant Behaviour: A Discussion and Critique.* New York: Free Press.

Mihh-ha, Trinh T. 1989. *Woman, Native, Other.* Bloomington: Indiana University Press,

Modern Law Review. 2006. Workshop on Gender and land rights: Univ. of Keele, Keele, Staffordshire, January.

Moghadam, Valentine. 1999. "Gender and the Global Economy," in Ferree, Lorber and Hess, eds., *Revisioning Gender.* Thousand Oaks, CA: Sage.

Moghadam, Valentine. 2005. *Globalizing Women: Transnational Feminist Networks.* Baltimore: Johns Hopkins University Press.

Mohanty, Chandra T. _____. *Feminism without Borders: Decolonizing Theory, Practicing Solidarity.* Durham, North Carolina: Duke University Press, 2003.

Mohanty, Chandra T. 1991. "Under Western Eyes: Feminist Scholarship and Colonial Discourse," In *Third World Women and the Politics of Feminism.* Mohanty, Chandra Talpade, Ann Russo, and Lourdes Torres, eds. Indianapolis: Indiana University Press.

Molara Ogundipe-Leslie. 1994. *Re-Creating Ourselves: African Women & Critical Transformations.* Africa World Press.

Molokomme, Athaliah. 1994. "Customary Law in Botswana: Past, Present and Future," in *Botswana in the 21st Century.* Gaborone, Botswana: Botswana Society.

Molyneux, Maxine and Shahra Razavi (eds.). 2002. *Gender Justice, Development, and Rights,* Oxford and New York: Oxford University Press.

Momsen, Janet. 2003. *Gender and Development,* London: Routledge.

Moore, Henrietta L. 1988. *Feminism and Anthropology.* Minneapolis: University of Minnesota Press.

Moore, Sally Falk. 1978. 'Law and Social Change: The Semi-Autonomous Social Field as an Appropriate Subject of Study,' *Law as Process,* Routledge & Kegan, Paul.

Morna, Colleen Lowe, ed. 2004b. *Ringing up the Changes: Gender in Southern African Politics.* Johannesburg: Gender Links.

Morna, Colleen Lowe. 2004a. 'Beyond Numbers: Quotas in Practice.' In Ballington, ed. *The Implementation of Quotas: African Experiences.*

Moser, C. N. 2001. "The Gendered Continuum of Violence and Conflict: An Operational Framework," 30-51. In Caroline O.N. Moser and Fiona Clark, *Victims, Perpetrators or Actors? Gender, Armed Conflict and Political Violence.* London and New York: Zed Books.

Moshi, Liobi. 1998. Foreword. Bloch, Beoku-Betts and Tabachnick, (eds.), *Women and Education in Sub-Saharan Africa.* Boulder: Lynne Rienner.

Motala, S. 2002. "Organizing in the Informal Economy: A Case Study of Street Trading in South Africa." Seed Working Paper No. 36. Geneva: International Labor Office.

Moussa, H. 1993. *Storm and Sanctuary: The Journey of Ethiopian and Eritrean Women Refugees.* Toronto: Artemis Enterprises.

Moyo, Sam and Yeros, Paris (eds.) 2005. *Reclaiming the Land,* London: Zed.

Mpundu, Mildred. 2006. "We know no other home than this: land disputes in Zambia." Panos, London. http://www.panos.org.uk/newsfeatures/featuredetails.asp?id=1241

MSF-Netherlands. 8 March 2005. "The Crushing Burden of Rape: Sexual Violence in Darfur." www.doctorswithoutborders.org/publications/reports/2005/sudan03.pdf

Muhumuza, Rodney. 2006. 'Women Legislators Come of Age.' *The Monitor* (Kampala).

Mukta, P. 2000. "Gender, Community, Nation: The Myth of Innocence," 163-179. In Susie Jacobs, Ruth Jacobson and Jennifer Marchbank, *States of Conflict: Gender, Violence and Resistance.* London: Zed Books.

Munch, P. A. June 1974. "Anarchy and *Anomie* in an Atomistic Community," *Man* 9, 243-261.

Mutukwa, Gladys, 'Home-grown rights instruments: Supporting the Protocol on the Rights of Women in Africa,' AWID/WHR website,. 2005-06-30)

Mwagiru, Makumi. 1998. "Women's Land and Property Rights in Three Eastern African Countries." www.oxfam.org.uk/http://what_we_do/issues/liveilhoods/landrights/down loads

Myakayaka-Manzini, Mavivi. 2004. 'Political Party Quotas in South Africa.' In Ballington, ed. *The Implementation of Quotas: African Experiences.*

Nash, June and Patricia Fernandez-Kelly, eds. 1983. *Women, Men and the International Division of Labor.* Albany: SUNY Press.

National Democratic Institute, "Increasing Women's Political Participation" (a pamphlet).

_____. www.NDI.org.

Ndambuki and Claire Robertson. 2000. *We Only Come Here to Struggle: Stories from Berida's Life.* Bloomington: University of Indiana Press.

Neier, A. 1998. *War Crimes: Brutality, Genocide, Terror, and the Struggle for Justice.* London: Times Books.

Nengwekhulu, R. 1998. "Human Rights, Development and the Rule of the Law in Post-Colonial Botswana." In W.A. Edge and M.H. Lekorwe. *Botswana: Politics and Society.* Pretoria, South Africa: J.L. van Schaik.

NEPAD. 2001) New Partnership for African Development (NEPAD), launched at the African Union Meeting. Abuja: Nigeria, October.

Ngau, P.M. and Keino, C.I. 1996. "Women's Social Background and Entrepreneurship in Nairobi," in D. McCormick and P. ove Pederson (eds.), *Small Enterprises, Flexibiliby and Networking in an African Context.* Nairobi: Longhorn.

Ngwira, N., G. Kamchedzera, & L. Semu. 2003. Malawi strategic country gender assessment (SCGA). http://siteresources.worldbank.org/EXTAFRREGTOPGENDER/Resources/MalawiSCGA.pdf)

Nkiwane, T.. 2000) "Gender, Citizenship, and Constitutionalism in Zimbabwe: The Fight against Amendment 14." *Citizenship Studies* 4, 3: 325–38.

Nwauwa, Appollos. 1994. *Imperialism, Academe, and Nationalism: Britain and University Education for Africans, 1860-1960.* London: F. Cass.

Nzegwu, Nkiru. 2002. "Questions of Agency: Development, Donors, and Women of the South." In *Jenda: A Journal of Culture and African Women's Studies* 2(1).

Nzomo, Maria. 1993. "Engendering Democratization in Kenya: A Political Perspective," in Mukabi-Kabira, Adhiambo-Oduol and Nzomo eds., *Democratic Change in Africa: Women's Perspective.* Nairobi: AAWORD.

O'Barr, Jean. 1975-76. "Pare Women: A Case of Political Involvement." *Rural Africana,* 29:121-134.

OAU. 1980. *Lagos Plan of Action for the Economic Development of Africa, 1980-2000.* Organization for African Unity. Lagos: Nigeria, April. http://www.uneca.org/itca/ariportal/docs/lagos_plan.pdf

Obioma Nnaemeka. 2005. *Female Circumcision and the Politics of Knowledge: African Women in Imperialist Discourses.* Greenwood Publishing Group.

OCHA (United Nations Office for the Coordination of Humanitarian Affairs). 1998. *Guiding principles on internal displacement, New York.* http://www.relief web.int/ocha_ol/pub/idp_gp/idp.html>.

OHCHR (Office of the High Commissioner for Human Rights). 25 January 2005. "Report of the International Commission of Inquiry on Darfur to the United Nations Secretary-General. Pursuant to Security Council Resolution 1564 of 18 September 2004." www.ohchr.org/english/darfur.htm

Okeke, P.E. 2005. "Higher Education for Africa's Women: Prospects and Challenges," in Abdi Ali A. and Cleghorn, Ailie (eds.), *Issues in African Education: Sociological Perspectives.* New York: Palgrave and Macmillan.

Okeke, P.E. and S. Franceschet. 2002. "Democratisation and 'State Feminism': A Comparison of Gender Politics in Africa and Latin America." *Development and Change* 439-33(3): 446.

Okeke, P.E. "The First Lady Syndrome: The (En)Gendering of Bureaucratic Corruption in Nigeria." *Council for the Development of Social Science Research in Africa Bulletin,* 3, 4 (CODESRIA, 1988): 16–19.

Okeke-Ihejirika, P.E. 2004. *Negotiating Power and Privilege: Igbo Career Women in Contemporary Nigeria.* Athens: Ohio University Press.

Okonjo, Kamene. 1976. "The Dual Sex Political System in Operation." In N. Hafkin and E. Bay (eds.). *Women in Africa.* Stanford, CA: Stanford University Press.

Okurut, F., Banga, M, and Mukungu A. 2004. *Microfinance and poverty reduction in Uganda: Achievements and challenges.* Kampala: Economic Policy Research Centre.

Oloka-Onyango, J. and Sylvia Tamale. 1995. "'The Personal is Political'," or Why Women's Rights are Indeed Human Rights: An African Perspective on International Feminism," *Human Rights Quarterly,* Vol. 17: 691-731.

Olomi, D. 1999. "Scope and role of research on entrepreneurship and small business development." In K. King and S. McGrath. *Enterprise in Africa: Between Poverty and Growth.* London: Intermediate Technology Publications.

Oppong, J.R & E. Kalipeni, E. 2004. "Perceptions and misperceptions of AIDS in Africa." In Kalipeni, E., S. Craddock, J.R. Oppong, & J. Ghosh (Eds.), *HIV and AIDS in Africa: beyond epidemiology* (pp. 47-57). Malden, MA: Blackwell Publishing.

Oppong, J.R. & J. Ghosh. 2004. "Concluding remarks: beyond epidemiology." In E. Kalipeni, S. Craddock, J. R. Oppong, & J. Ghosh (Ed.), *HIV and AIDS in Africa: beyond epidemiology* (pp. 323-326).Oxford: Blackwell Publishing.

Orleck, Annelise. 1997. "Tradition Unbound: Radical Mothers in International Perspective," in Jetter, et. al. (eds.). *The Politics of Motherhood.* Hanover and London: University Press of New England.

Orsini, D. 1999. "The enterprise network initiative: a new generation of African entrepreneurs emerges." Paper presented at USA-Africa Trade and Investment Symposium. Orlando, Florida.

Orsini, D. 2001. Case study of East African Enterprise Network, Southern African Enterprise Network, West African Enterprise Network, Organization for Economic Cooperation and Development OECD DCD 200010/ANN5.

Orsini, D., Courcelle, M., and Brinkerhoff, D. 1996. "Increasing private sector capacity for policy dialogue: the West African Enterprise Network." *World Development* 24:9:1453-1466.

Osirim, Mary J.. 1998. "Negotiating identities during adjustment programs: Women microentrepreneurs in urban Zimbabwe." In A. Spring and B. McDade, eds., *African Entrepreneurship: Theory and Reality.* Gainesville and Tallahassee: University Press of Florida. pp. 277-297.

_____. 2003. "Carrying the Burdens of Adjustment and Globalization: Women and Microenterprise Development in Urban Zimbabwe." *International Sociology,* Volume 18, Number 3.

Packer, Corinne. 2003. "African Women, Traditions, and Human Rights: A Critical Analysis of Contemporary 'Universal Discourses and Approaches.'" Pp. 159-181. In *Human Rights and Diversity: Area Studies Revisited.* Eds. David P. Forsythe and Patrice C. McMahon. Lincoln: University of Nebraska Press.

Palmer, Ingrid. 1985. *Women's Roles and Gender Differences in Development: the NEMOW Case.* Hartford, Conn; Kumarian Press.

Palmer, Robin. 2005. "Critical Reflections on the role of an international NGO seeing to work globally on land rights, with specific focus on Oxfam's experiences in southern Africa." http://www.oxfam.org.uk/.what_we_do/issues/liveilhoods/landrights/downloads

Pande, R., A. Malhotra, and C. Grown. 2005. "Impact of Investments in Female Education on Gender Equality." Paper prepared for presentation at the XXV IUSSP International Population Conference, Tours, France. International Center for Research on Women.

Pankhurst, Donna and Jacobs, Susie. 1988. "Land Tenure, Gender Relations and Agricultural Production: the Case of Zimbabwe's Peasantry." In J. Davison (ed.), *Women, Land and Agriculture,* Boulder: Westview.

Pankhurst, Helen. 1992. *Gender, Development and Identity: an Ethiopian Study.* London: Zed.

Panorama: British Broadcasting Company/BBC. 2004, 29 February.

Pateman, Carole. 1988. *The Sexual Contract.* Stanford, CA: Stanford University Press.

Pereira, Charmaine. 2003. "Configuring 'Global,' 'National,' and 'Local' in Governance Agendas in Nigeria." *Social Research,* Volume 69, Number 3.

Personal Narratives Group. 1989. *Interpreting Women's Lives: Feminist Theory and Personal Narratives.* P. 263. Bloomington: Indiana University Press.

Petrides, Lisa. 2001. "Higher Education and Professional Preparation." In Stromquist, Nelly (ed.), *Women in the Third World: an Encyclopedia of Contemporary Issues,* p. 408-417. London: Taylor and Francis.

Pharoah, Robyn. 2001? n.d. "Social Capital and Women's Participation in Three Land Reform Trusts: a case of mixed blessings." MA Thesis, Durban, Univ. of Natal.

Pheko, Mohau. 1999. "Privatization, Trade Liberalization and Women's Socio-economic Rights: Exploring Policy Alternatives," in Fall, ed., *Africa: Gender, Globalization and Resistance.* Dakar: AAWORD Book Series.

Pieterse, Jan Nederveen. 1992. *White on Black: Images of Africa and Blacks in Western Popular Culture.* New Haven: Yale University Press.

Pohl, F. 2006. "Islamic Education and Civil Society: Reflections on the Pesantren Tradition in Contemporary Indonesia." *Comparative Education Review* 50 (3):389-409.

Position of women in Malawi. http://womenandaids.unaids.org/documents/factsheet malawi.pdf)

Poverty indicators HDI (http://hdr.undp.org/statistics/data/cty/cty_f_MWI.html)

Powley, Elisabeth. 2004. 'Strengthening Governance: The Role of Women in Rwanda's Transition.' Report from the Office of the Special Advisor on Gender Issues and Advancement of Women (OSAGI). New York: United Nations.

Prahalad. C. K. 2004. *The Fortune at the Bottom of the Pyramid: Eradicating Poverty through Profits.* Philadelphia: Wharton School Publishing.

PRB 2006. Population Reference Bureau. Accessed February 2006. http://www.prb.org.

Presley, Cora Ann. 1986. "Labor Unrest among Kijuyu women in Colonial Kenya." In C. Robertson and I. Berger (eds.). *Women and Class in Africa.* New York: Africana.

Quachey, L. 1999. "The Impact of women in Africa's economy." Presentation at the US-Africa Trade & Investment Symposium Orlando, Florida. 9 Aug.

Raftopoulos, Brian, Jensen, Stig and Hammar, Amanda. 2004. Zimbabwe's Unfinished Business, Harare: Weaver Press.

Rakesh, B., Tamiru, T and Singh, G. 2006. Microfinance and sustained economic improvement: A study on women small-scale entrepreneurs in Addis Ababa." *Journal of African Business,* special issue on gender, Spring, A. and Rutashobya, L. eds.

Ramachandran, V. and Shah, M. K. 1999. "Minority entrepreneurs and firm performance in Sub-Saharan Africa." *Journal of Development Studies,* 362: 71-87.

Ranger, Terence. 1983. "The Invention of Tradition in Colonial Africa." In E. Hobsbawm and T. Ranger, *The Invention of Tradition,* Cambridge: Cambridge Univ. Press.

Rathgeber, Eva. 1991. "Women and Higher Education in Africa: Access and Choices." In Kelly, G. and Slaughter, S. (eds.), *Women's Higher Education in Comparative Perspectives.* Kluwer Academic Publishers.

Rathgeber, Eva. 1998. "Women's Participation in Science and Technology," in Nelly Stromquist, ed., *Women in the Third World: An Encyclopedia of Contemporary Issues*, p. 427-435. London: Garland Publishing.

Ravazi, Shahra (ed). 2002. *Shifting Burdens: Gender and Agrarian change under Neoliberalism.* New Haven: Kumarian Press.

Ravazi, Shahra. 2006. "Land Tenure Reform and Gender Equity" UNRISD Briefing 4.

Refugees International. 7 April 2006. "Statement on the Allegations of Sexual Abuse and Exploitation by African Union Peacekeepers," http://refugees international.org/content/article/detail/8341

_____. 18 October 2005. *Must Boys be Boys: Ending Sexual Exploitation & Abuse in UN Peacekeeping Missions.* http://www.refugeesinternational.org/content/ publication/detail/6976.)

Rhodes, J. 2003. "Can E-commerce enable marketing in an African rural women's community based development organization?" *Informing Science Journal*, Vol.6, pp. 157-172.

Rimbaud, A. "Hottentot Venus: the Story." The Image of Black: Discovering the Hidden History. www.theimageofblack.co.uk/2_feature.htm

Ritzenthaler, Robert. 1960. "Anlu: A Women's Uprising in British Cameroons." *African Studies Review* 19(3).

Robertson, C. 1995. "Comparative advantage: Women in trade in Accra, Ghana and Nairobi, Kenya." In B. House-Midamba and F. Ekechi, eds. *African Market Women and Economic Power.* Westport CT: Greenwood Press. pp. 99-120.

Robertson, C. 1997. *Trouble Showed the Way: Women, Men and Trade in the Nairobi Area, 1890-1990.* Bloomington: Indiana University Press.

_____. 1998. "Women entrepreneurs? Trade and the gender division of labor in Nairobi." In A. Spring and B. McDade, eds., *African Entrepreneurship: Theory and Reality.* Gainesville and Tallahassee: University Press of Florida. pp. 109-127.

Ruddick, Sara. 1980. Maternal Thinking. *Feminist Studies* 6(2).

Rugadya, Margaret, Obaikol, E and Kamusiime, Herbert. 2004. *Gender and the Land Reform Process in Uganda,* Associates for Development, Land Research Series No. 2. Margaret Rugadya, Esther Obaikol, and Herbert Kamusiime). August. www.oxfam. org.uk/.what_we_do/issues/liveilhoods/landrights/downloads

Rushing, W. A. 1995. *The AIDS epidemic: social dimensions of an infectious disease.* Boulder, Colorado: Westview Press.

Sachikonye, Lloyd. 2003. "The situation of commercial farmers after land reform in Zimbabwe," Report to Farm Community Trust of Zimbabwe.

SAEN website. 2002. http://www.saen.info/saen/frameset.htm

SAEN. 1999. "Building a southern African regional market: issues for the private sector." Final Report on SAEN First Regional Conference Mauritius: The Mauritius Enterprise Network.

Sall, Ebrima. (ed.) 2000. *Women in Academia.* Dakar, Senegal: CODESRIA.

Salo, Elaine. 2003. "African Women's Voices: Talking About Feminism in Africa." Women's World. http://www.wworld.org

Salon Media Group. 2005. "Whatever the price, I had to tell the truth." News story, Ed Vulliamy, Oct. 6. http://www.salon.com/news/feature/2005/10/05/saudi_woman/print

Samatar, Abdi Ismail. 1999. *An African Miracle: State and Class Leadership and Colonial Legacy in Botswana Development.* Portsmouth, NH: Heinemann.

Sassen, Saskia. 1998. *Globalization and its Discontents.* London: The New Press.

Schapera, Isaac. 1965. *Praise-Poems of Tswana Chiefs,* Oxford University Press, London.

_____. 1966 [1940]. *Married Life in an African Tribe.* Evanston, IL: Northwestern University Press.

Schneider, G. 2001. "Women's economy between subsistence and market production in Harare, Zimbabwe." In B. Wohlmuth, E. Hans-Heinrich, A. Grawert, R. Gutowski, A. Kappel,. A. Konig and M. Wauschkuhn, eds., *Africa's Integration into the World Economy.* Hamburg: LIT Verlag. pp. 731-764.

Schulpen, L. and Gibbon, P. 2001. "Private Sector Development: Policies, Practises, and Problems." CDR Policy Paper. Copenhagen: Centre for Development Research. http://www.cdr.dk.

Schwartz, Hella. 2004. 'Women's Representation in the Rwandan Parliament: An Analysis of Variations in the Representation of Women's Interests Caused by Gender and Quota.' Masters Thesis, Gothenburg University, Sweden.

Scott, Joan Wallach. 2005), "French Universalism in the Nineties." In M. Friedman (ed.). *Women and Citizenship.* Oxford and New York: Oxford University Press.

Seidman, Gay. 1999. 'Gendered Citizenship: South Africa's Democratic Transition and the Construction of a Gendered State.' *Gender and Society.* 13(3): 287-307.

Seifert, R. 1992. "War and Rape. Analytical Approaches" http://www.wilpf.int.ch./publications/1992ruthseifert.htm

Selolwane, Onalenna D.. 2006. *Gendered Spaces in Party Politics in Southern Africa: Progress and Regress since Beijing 1995*, UNRISD.

_____. 1998. "Equality of Citizenship and the Gendering of Democracy in Botswana." In W.A. Edge and M.H. Lekorwe (eds.), *Botswana: Politics and Society.*

Sen, A. 1999. *Development and freedom.* New York: Alfred A. Knopf.

Sen, Gita and Caren Grown. 1987. *Women, Crises and Development Alternatives.* New York: Monthly Review Press.

Shanklin, Eugenia. 1990. "Anlu Remembered: The Kom Women's Rebellion of 1958-1961." *Dialectical Anthropology* 15.

Shaw, Carolyn Martin. 2001. "Disciplining the Black Female Body: Learning Feminism in Africa and the United States." In *Black Feminist Anthropology: Theory, Politics, Praxis, and Poetics.* Ed. Irma McClaurin. New Brunswick, NJ: Rutgers University Press.

Shayo, Rose. 2005. 'Women Participation in Party Politics During the Multiparty Era in Africa: The Case of Tanzania.' *EISA* Occasional Paper No. 34. Johannesburg: *EISA.*

Sideris, T. 2001. "Rape in War and Peace: Social Context, Gender, Power and Identity," 142-158. In Sheila Meinjtes, Annu Pillay and Meredeth Turshen (Eds), *The Aftermath: Women in Post-Conflict Transformation*, London: Zed Books.

Skjelsbaek, S. 2001. "Sexual Violence and War: Mapping Out a Complex Relationship," *European Journal of International Relations*, Vol. 7 (2), 211-237.

Skjonsberg, Else. 1995. "Documenting Women's Views Through Participatory Research: Diaries of Daily Activities in Rural Zambia." In *Women Wielding the Hoe : Lessons from Rural Africa for Feminist Theory and Development Practice.* Berg Publishers.

Smelser, Neil. 1981. *Sociology.* Englewood Cliffs, NJ: Prentice-Hall.

Smith, K.P., & S.C. Watkins. 2005. Perceptions of risk and strategies for prevention: responses to HIV/AIDS in rural Malawi. *Social Science & Medicine* 60(3), 649-660.

Smock, C. 1981. *Women's Education in Developing Countries: Opportunities and Outcomes.* New York: Praeger.

Snyder, M. 2000. *Women in African Economies: from Burning Sun to Boardroom.* Kampala: Fountain Publishers.

Sobhan, Rehman. 1993. *Agrarian Reform and Social Transformation,* London: Zed.

Solidarity Peace Trust. 2006. Operation Taguta/Sisuthi: Command Agriculture in Zimbabwe: its Impact on rural communities in Matabeleland. www.kubatana.net/docs /htm/archive/demgg/060405spt.asp?sector=AGRICdownload

Somel, S.K. 2001 in Herrera, 2004. *The Modernization of Public Education in the Ottoman Empire, 1839-1908: Islamization, Autocracy, and Discipline.* Leiden: Brill Academic Publishers.

Spring, A. 2002. "Gender and the range of entrepreneurial strategies: the 'typical' and the 'new' generation of women entrepreneurs." In A. Jalloh and T. Falola, T. eds. *Black Business and Economic Power.* Rochester. NY: University of Rochester Press. Pp.381-401.

Spring, A. 2005. "African women in the entrepreneurial landscape: Reconsidering the formal and informal sectors." Paper presented at the IAABD. Dar es Salaam, Tanzania, April.

_____. 2006. "Informal-formal sectors and the formalized-informal: New definitions of African enterprising entrepreneurs." Mimeo.

_____. 2006a. "Using the Internet to study e-commerce in Ghana." Paper presented at the annual meeting of the International Academy of African Business Development. Accra, Ghana.

_____. 2006b. "The West African Enterprise Network: Business globalists, interregional trade, and U.S. intervention." In A. Jalloh and T. Falola, T. eds. *West Africa and U.S. Relations.* Rochester. NY: University of Rochester Press.

_____. (ed.) 2000. *Women Farmers and Commercial Ventures: Increasing Food Security in Developing Countries.* Boulder: Lynne Rienner Publishers.

_____.1995. *Agricultural Development and Gender Issues in Malawi.* Lanham, MD: University Press of America.

_____. 2002. "Gender and the Range of African Entrepreneurial Strategies: 'Typical' and 'New' women entrepreneurs." In A. Jaliloh and T. Falola (eds.), *Black Business and Economic Power,* Rochester, New York: Univ. of Rochester Press.

Spring, A. and McDade, B. eds. 1998. *African Entrepreneurship: Theory and Reality.* Gainesville, FL: University Press of Florida.

Spring, A. and Trager, L. 1989. "Gender issues in rural-urban marketing networks." USAID/RHUDO. Conference on Housing and Urban Development in Sub-Saharan Africa, Yamoussoukro, Cote d'Ivoire. Mimeo.

Stacey, Judith. 1983. *Patriarchy and Socialist Revolution in China,* Berkeley: University of California Press.

Stanworth, M. 1983. *Gender and Schooling: A study of Sexual Divisions in the Classrooms.* London: Hutchinson.

Steady, Filomina, ed. 1981. *The Black Woman Cross-Culturally.* Cambridge, MA: Schenkman Publishers.

Stilgmayer, A. (ed.), *Mass Rape: The War against Women in Bosnia-Herzegovina,* 1994, Lincoln and London: University of Nebraska Press.

Susser, I., & Z. Stein, Z. 2000. Culture, sexuality, and women's agency in the prevention of HIV/AIDS in southern Africa. *American Journal of Public Health* 90(6), 1042-1048.

Sutton, Margaret. 2001. "Girls' Educational Access and Attainment" In Hodgson, Dorothy L. (ed.), *Gendered Modernities and Ethnographic Perspectives,* p. 381-396. New York: Palgrave.

Tadesse, Z.. 1982. "The Impact of Land Reform on Women: the Case of Ethiopia." In Beneria, L. (ed.), *Women and Development,* New York: Praeger.

Tadesse, Zenabaworke. 2003. "Women and Land Rights in the Third World: the case of Ehtiopia." In Wanyeki, L. Muthoni (ed.), *Women and Land in Africa,* London: Zed/Cape Town, D. Philip.

Tallis, V. 1998. "AIDS is a crisis for women." *Agenda* 39.

Tallis, V. 2000. "Gendering the response to HIV/AIDS: challenging gender inequality." *Agenda* 44.

Tamale, S. and J. Oloka-Onyango. 2004. "Bitches at the Academy: Gender and Academic Freedom in the African University." *African Development,* XXII (1):13-38.

Tamale, Sylvia. 1999. When Hens Begin to Crow: Gender and Parliamentary Politics in Uganda. Boulder: Westview Press.

Tamale, Sylvia. 2004. 'Introducing Quotas: Discourse and Legal Reform in Uganda.' In Ballington, ed. *The Implementation of Quotas: African Experiences.*

Tawil, S. 2006. "Quranic Education and Social Change in Northern Morocco: Perspectives from Chefchaouen." *Comparative Education Review* 50(3):496-517.

The Asia Foundation, Global Women in Politics information sheets: Budget Advocacy from a Gender Perspective in Uganda and Combating Violence against Women

The Economist, April 15-21, 2006, "Sudan: No help needed, thank you very much," 48&50.

The New York Times Magazine. 15 September 2002. Peter Landesman, "The Minister of Rape: How could a woman incite Rwanda's sex-crime genocide?" 83-89: 116, 125, 130-132.

The New York Times. 28 February 2006. "Refugee Crisis Grows as Darfur War Crosses a Border." Interview with John Prendergast in The New York Times" http://www.crisisgroup.org/home/index.cfm?id=39998

Thomas, Neil. 2003. "Land reform in Zimbabwe." *Third World Quarterly,* 24:4, 691-712

Thompson, K. (ed.) 2000. *Readings from Emile Durkheim.* New York: Routledge, 1985.

Toulmin, C and Quan, J.. 2001. "Evolving Land Rights: Policy and tenure in sub-Saharan Africa." In Toulmin and Quan (eds.), *Evolving Land Rights: Policy and Tenure in Africa.* London: DfID/IIED.

Townsend, Janet, Emma Zapata, Joanna Rowlands, Pilar Alberti and Marta Mercado. 1999. *Women and Power: Fighting Patriarchies and Poverty,* Zed Press, London and New York.

Tripp, A., Valodia, I., Lebani, L., Skinner, C., and Devy, R. 2006. "Low-waged and informal employment in South Africa." *Transformation:* 60: 90-126.

Tripp, Aili Mari. 2000. *Women and Politics in Uganda.* Madison, WI: University of Wisconsin Press.

_____. 2000. *Women and Politics in Uganda.* Madison: University of Wisconsin Press.

_____. 2004. 'The Changing Face of Africa's Legislatures: Women and Quotas.' In Ballington, ed. *The Implementation of Quotas: African Experiences.*

_____. 2005. "Regional Networking as Transnational Feminism: African Experiences." *Feminist Africa,* Issue Number 4.

_____. 2006. 'Uganda: Agents of Change for Women's Advancement?' In Bauer and Britton, eds. *Women in African Parliaments.*

_____. Forthcoming. 'Post-Conflict Societies, Quotas and the Representation of Women in Africa's Legislatures.' Article manuscript.

_____. 2004. "Women's Movements, Customary Law and Land Rights in Africa: the Case of Uganda." *African Studies Quarterly,* 7 (4). www.africa.ufl.edu/asq/v7/ v7i4a1.htm

_____. "Women's Movements and Challenges to Neopatrimonial Rule," *Development and Change,* 32. 2001), 33-54.

Trubek D. and M. Galanter. 1975. 'Scholars in Self-Estrangement: Some Reflections on the Crisis in Law and Development Studies in the United States,' *Wisconsin Law Review,* vol. 1974. 1975).

Tsikata, Dzodzai. 2003. "Securing Women's Interests within Land Tenure Reforms: recent debates in Tanzania." *J. Agrarian Change,* vol. 3 nos. 1-2.

Turner, S. 2000. "Vindicating masculinity. The fate of promoting gender equality." *Forced Migration Review* 9, (December 2000), 8–9.

Turshen, M. 2001. "The Political economy of Rape: An Analysis of Systematic Rape and Sexual Abuse of Women during Armed Conflict in Africa," 55-68. In Caroline O.N. Moser and Fiona Clark, *Victims, Perpetrators or Actors? Gender, Armed Conflict and Political Violence.* London and New York: Zed Books.

Turshen, M.. 1998). "Women's War Stories." In Meredeth Turshen & Clotilde Twagiramariya, *What Women do in Wartime: Gender and Conflict in Africa.* London & New York: Zed Books.

Twagiramariya, C. and Turshen, M. "'Favours' to Give and 'Consenting' Victims: The Sexual Politics of Survival in Rwanda." In Meredeth Turshen & Clotilde Twagiramariya, *What Women do in Wartime: Gender and Conflict in Africa.* London & New York: Zed Books

UN 2000. United Nations Millennium Declaration [on line]. Accessed February 2006 URL: Available on line at http://www.un.org/millenniumgoals/.

UN 2005. The Millennium Development Goals Report. Accessed February 2006: Available on line at http://www.millenniumindicators.un.org.

UNAIDS. 2003. AIDS epidemic update. http://www.unaids.org/en/Resources/ Publications/Corporate+publications/AIDS+epidemic+update++December+2003.asp.

UNAIDS. 2004a. AIDS epidemic update, December 2004. http://www.unaids. org/wad2004/ EPI_1204_pdf_en/EpiUpdate04_en.pdf)

UNAIDS. 2004b. Malawi. http://www.unaids.org/en/geographical+area/by+country/ malawi.asp

UNAIDS/WHO. 2004. Malawi 2004 epidemiological fact sheets on HIV/AIDS and sexually transmitted infections. Geneva: Joint United Nations Programme on HIV/AIDS.
http://www.who.int/GlobalAtlas/PDFFactory/HIV/EFS_PDFs/EFS2004_ MW.pdf)

UNDP, 'Evaluation of Gender Mainstreaming in UNDP,' UNDP Evaluation Office, January 2006.

UNDP. 2004. "Cultural Liberty in Today's Diverse World." *Human Development Report.* United Nations. New York.

UNDP. 2004. Malawi: Human development index going below income? http://hdr.undp.org/ statistics/data/country_fact_sheets/cty_fs_MWI.html)

UNDPI. 1986. "The Nairobi Forward-looking Strategies for the Advancement of Women." United Nations Department of Public Information, Division of Economic and Social Information.

UNECA. 1990. "African Charter for Popular Participation in Development." Arusha Declaration, United Nations Economic Commission for Africa (E/ECA/CM.16/11).

UNECA. 1990. Economic Report on Africa.

UNECA. 1999. *Post-conflict Reconstruction in Africa: A Gender Perspective* (United Nations: Addis Ababa, Ethiopia.

UNESCO 2005. United Nations Educational, Scientific and Cultural Organization. Accessed February 2006: Available on line at http://www.unesco.org

UNESCO Institute of Statistics (UIS). 1993. *Development of Higher Education in Africa: the African University into the New Millennium.* Paris: UNESCO.

UNESCO Institute of Statistics (UIS). 1998. *World Year Book on Education.* Washington, UNESCO.

UNESCO Institute of Statistics (UIS), New York.

UNESCO. 2004. "Comparing Statistics across the World." *Global Education Digest.*

UNICEF 2003. "The State of the World's Children 2004: Girls' Education and Development." United Nations Children's Fund (UNICEF). Accessed February 2006: Available on line at http://www.unicef.org.

UNIFEM. 1995. Report of the Expert Group Meeting on the Development of Guidelines for the Integration of gender Perspectives into United Nations Human Rights Activities and Programmes. Para. 13.

United Nations High Commissioner for Refugees (UNHCR). *United Nations Convention Relating to the Status of Refugees 1951.* http://www.unhchr.ch/html/menu3/b/o_c_ref.htm

United Nations Integrated Regional Information Network/All Africa Global Media via COMTEX. 14 April 2006. Soldiers Jailed for Mass Rape." http://global.factiva.com/ha/default.aspx

United Nations News Service. 9 September 2005. "People of Western Sudan Report Nightmares, Suicidal Impulses As a Result of Assaults." http://www.un.org/as/news/ story.asp?NewsID=15740&Cr=&Cr1

United Nations. June 2007. "Africa and the Millennium Development Goals: 2007 update." UN Department of Public Information. DPI/2458.

Urdang, Stephanie. 1989. And Still They Dance: Women, War and the Struggle for Change in Mozambique. New York: Monthly Review Press.

USAID. 2003. Strengthening Education in the Muslim World: Summary of Desk Study. Issue Paper Number 2 (PN-ACT-009). Bureau for Policy and Program Coordination. U.S. Agency for International Development. Washington, D.C. Accessed January 2006: Available on line at: www.usaid.gov.

Van Allen, Judith. 2001. "Women's Rights Movements as a Measure of African Democracy." *Journal of Asian and African Studies* 36 (1).

_____. 2000a. "'Bad Future Things' and Liberatory Moments: Capitalism, Gender and the State in Botswana." *Radical History Review* 76.

_____. 1976. "'Aba Riots' or 'Igbo Women's War': Ideology, Stratification and the Invisibility of Women." In N. Hafkin and E. Bay (eds.) *Women in Africa.* Stanford, CA: Stanford University Press.

_____. 2000b. "Must A Woman (Politician) Be More Like a Man? Constructing Female Political Power and Agency in Botswana." Paper presented at the African Studies Association Annual Meeting, Nashville.

VeneKlasen, Lisa. Valerie Miller, Cindy Clark and Molly Reilly, 'Rights-Based Approaches and Beyond: Challenges of Linking Rights and Participation,' IDS Working Paper 235, December 2004.

Voet, Rian. 1998. *Feminism and Citizenship.* Thousand Oaks, CA: SAGE.

Vogel, Ursula. 1991. "Is Citizenship Gender Specific?" In U. Vogel and M. Moran (eds.) *The Frontiers of Citizenship.* Basingstoke: Macmillan.

Volkmann, D. 1998. "The Militarization of Africa." In Meredeth Turshen and Clotilde Twagiramariya. *What Women Do in Wartime: Gender and Conflict in Africa.* London & New York: Zed Books.

WAEN website. 2000. http://www.waen.net.

WAEN. 1993. Facing the issues: Final Report on the Regional Conference on the West African Private Sector. Accra: The Enterprise Network of Ghana.

Wakhweya, Angella M. 1999. "Women's Health and Human Rights in Uganda: To Be or Not to Be, That is the Question!" In *Women's Activism and Human Rights in Africa* (pp.266-286). Diana Fox and Naima Hasci, eds. Lewiston, NY: The Edwin Mellen Press.

Walden, V.M., K. Mwangulube, & P. Makhumula-Nkhoma. 1999. Measuring the impact of a behaviour change intervention for commercial sex workers and their potential clients. In *Malawi. Health Education Research* 14(4), 545-554.

Walker, Cherryl. 2003. "Piety in the Sky? Gender Policy and Land Reform in South Africa." *J. Agrarian Change,* vol. 3: 1-2.

Waterhouse, R.. 1998. "Women's Land Rights in Post-War Mozambique." In UNIFEM, *Women's Land and Property Rights in situations of Conflict and Reconstruction,* Geneva: www.oxfam.org.uk/.what_we_do/issues/livelihoods/landrights/downloads/mozwomen.rtf

Weeks, J.R. 1988. "The Demography of Islamic nations." *Population Bulletin* 43(4). Washington, DC: Population Reference Bureau.

Weiss, H.A., M.A. Quigley, & R.J. Hayes. 2000. "Male circumcision and risk of HIV infection in sub-Saharan Africa: a systematic review and meta-analysis." *AIDS* 14 (15), 2361-2370.

Werbner, Pnina and Nira Yuval-Davis. 1999. "Women and the New Discourse of Citizenship." In N. Yuval-Davis and P. Werbner (eds.). *Women, Citizenship and Difference,* London and New York: Zed Books.

Werbner, Pnina. 1999), "Political Motherhood and the Feminisation of Citizenship: Women's Activisms and the Transformation of the Public Sphere," in N. Yuval-Davis and P. Werbner (eds.). *Women, Citizenship and Difference,* London and New York: Zed Books.

West Africa. 1992. *News Report,* 20-26 , 683.

Whitehead, Anne and Tsikata, Dzodzia. 2003. "Policy Discourses on Women's Land Rights in Sub-Saharan Africa: the Implications of the Return to the Customary." *J. Agrarian Change,* vol. 3 nos. 1-2.

Wiergsma, Nan. 1991. "Peasant Patriarchy and the subversion of the collective in Vietnam." *Review of Radical Political Economics:* 23 (3-4): 174-97.

Wing, Adrien (ed.). 2000. "A Critical Race Feminist Conceptualization of Violence: South African and Palestinian Women," in *Global Critical Race Feminism: An International Reader* 332.

Wing, Adrien and de Carvalho, Eunice. 1997. "Black South African Women: Towards Equal Rights," in *Critical Race Feminism: A Reader*, 387. NYU Press.

Wipper, Audrey. 1982. "Riot and Rebellion among African Women: Three Examples of Women's Political Clout." In J. O'Barr (ed.). *Perspectives on Power.* Durham, NC: Duke University Center on International Studies.

WLSA (Women and Law in Southern Africa). 1994. *Inheritance in Zimbabwe: Law, customs and practices,* Harare: WLSA Trust.

WLSA. 1997. *Paradigms of exclusion: women's access to resources in Zimbabwe.* Harare: WLSA.

Wohlmuth, K. and Wauschkunh, M. 2001. "West African Enterprise Network: WAEN." In *The African Development Perspectives Yearbook Volume B.* Africa's Reintegration into the World Economy. New Brunswick, NJ: Transaction Publishers. Pp. 841-854.

Women and Law in Southern Africa Research Trust, WLSA, http://www.wlsa.org.zm/

Women in Law and Development Africa, WiLDAF, http://www.wildaf.org.zw/prog.htm

Women, Law and Development International. *Becoming an Advocate Step by Step.* 2000.

Women's Agency in Governance, Lina Hamadeh-Banerjee.

Women's Groups Find Silver Lining in Summit, Laura Bagnetto, Women's eNews, Sept. 29, 2005.

Women's Legal Rights Initiative, http://womensnet.org.za/WLRI/index.shtml

World Bank. 2001. World Development Indicators. World Bank CD-Rom.

_____. 'Africa Region Gender and Law Program 2006 Stocktaking, Design of G&L Impact Evaluation Framework Terms of Reference.'

_____. 1988. *Education in Sub-Saharan Africa: Policies for Adjustment, Revitalization and Expansion,* Washington, D.C.: ISRD.

_____. 1994. *Higher Education: Lessons of Experience. Development Practice Series.* Washington, DC: World Bank.

_____. 1999. "Gender and transport: A rationale for action." Prem Notes 14. http://www1.worldbank.org/prem/PREMNotes/premnote14.pdf

_____. 2003. "Sustainable development in a dynamic world: transforming institutions, growth, and quality of life." *World Development Report.* New York: Oxford University Press.

_____. 2003. *Land Policies for growth and poverty reduction: a World Bank policy research report.* Oxford; World Bank/Oxford Univ. Press.

_____. 2004. "A better investment climate for everyone." *World Development Report* 2005. New York: Oxford University Press.

World Health Organization. 2004. "Maternal Mortality in 2000: Estimates developed by WHO, UNICEF and UNFPA." Department of Reproductive Health and Research, World Health Organization, Geneva 2004

World of Parliaments. December 2003. Issue N°.12. "Elections in Rwanda Produce Record Results for Women." http://www.ipu.org/news-e-/12-7.htm

Wright, G. 2005. "Understanding and assessing the demand for microfinance for broadening the access to microfinance." Challenges and Actors High Level Conference June 20. Powerpoint presentation.

Ylönen, A. July 2005. "Grievances and Roots of Insurgence: Southern Sudan and Darfur," *Peace, Conflict and Development: An Interdisciplinary Journal*, Vol. 7. http://www. peacestudiesjournal.org.uk

Young, Iris. 1990. *Justice and the Politics of Difference.* Princeton: Princeton University Press.

Youssef, Nadia. 1995. "Women's Access to Productive Resources: The Need for Legal Instruments to Protect Women's Development Rights." In Peters, Julia and Andrea Wolper, eds., *Women's Rights, Human Rights* (279-287). New York: Routledge.

Yuval-Davis, Nira and Pnina Werbner (eds.). 1999. *Women, Citizenship and Difference.* London and New York: Zed Books.

Zarkov, D. 2001. "The Body of the Other Man: Sexual Violence and Construction of Masculinity, Sexuality and Ethnicity in Croatian Media," 69-82. In Caroline O.N. Moser and Fiona C. Clark (Eds.), *Victims, Perpetrators or Actors? Gender, Armed Conflict and Political Violence*, London & New York.

Zinyama, Lovemore. 1995. "The Sustainability of smallholder food systems in Africa: the case of Zimbabwe." in T. Binns (ed.), *People and Environment in Africa*, Chichester, Wiley Pubs.

Zulu, S. 1999. "Zimbabwe Court rules that women are teenagers." *Mail and Guardian:* 7-13 May.

NOTES ON CONTRIBUTORS

Adrien Katherine Wing
Adrien Katherine Wing is the Bessie Dutton Murray Professor at the University of Iowa College of Law and a member of the University's interdisciplinary African Studies faculty. She is also the Associate Dean for Faculty Development and Director of both a summer program in France and a semester program in London. With a B.A. from Princeton, an M.A. in African studies from UCLA, and a J.D. from Stanford Law School (1982), Professor Wing spent five years in practice in New York City law firms, specializing in international law issues regarding Africa, the Middle East, and Latin America, before joining the University of Iowa's Law faculty in 1987. She has taught courses in International Human Rights, Law in the Muslim World, Constitutional and Comparative Law, Critical Race Theory, and the Legal Aspects of AIDS. She has authored more than 100 publications and is the editor of *Critical Race Feminism: A Reader* and *Global Critical Race Feminism: An International Reader*. Professor Wing has advised the founding fathers and mothers of three constitutions: South Africa, Palestine, and Rwanda. She organized an election-observer delegation to South Africa, and taught at the University of Western Cape for six summers. She also advised the Eritrean Ministry of Justice on human rights treaties.

Gretchen Bauer
Gretchen Bauer (Ph.D. University of Wisconsin-Madison) is Professor and Chair of Political Science and International Relations at the University of Delaware. She specializes in African Politics, Comparative Politics, and Women and Politics. Her current research focuses on the use of electoral gender quotas to increase women's representation in parliaments in East and Southern Africa. Recent books include *Women in African Parliaments* (2006), co-edited with Hannah E. Britton; and *Politics in Southern Africa: State and Society in Transition* (2005), co-authored with Scott D. Taylor. She has worked throughout Eastern and Southern Africa. In 2002 she was a Visiting Researcher at the Institute for Public Policy Research in Windhoek, Namibia.

Marcia Greenberg
Marcia E. Greenberg is Adjunct Professor of Law at the Cornell Law School, where she teaches "Law and Social Change: International Perspectives" and offers a seminar on "International Women's Rights." Since 1997, Ms. Greenberg has focused her international work on

women's rights and gender mainstreaming. As democracy and governance specialist for the WIDTECH project, she advised staff and partners of the US Agency for International Development on gender integration. Focused primarily on Eastern Europe and Africa—including Angola, South Africa, Eritrea and Mali—she also worked with women's groups on conflict-related issues for the five-year review of the Beijing Platform for Action. In recent years, Ms. Greenberg has undertaken gender mainstreaming evaluations for the United Nations Development Program and the World Food Programme, as well as diverse gender assessments and training. She is co-author of "Gender Dimensions of Post-Conflict Reconstruction: Challenges in Development Aid" in *Making Peace Work: The Challenges of Social and Economic Reconstruction,* published by the United Nations University.

Judith Van Allen
Judith Van Allen is a Visiting Fellow at the Institute for African Development and a long-time activist-scholar. She has been writing about African women for over thirty years, beginning with "Sitting on a Man," her article about the 1929 Igbo Women's War against the British. In the late 1980s she lived in Botswana, doing liberation support work and studying the emerging Botswana women's movement. She is currently completing a book extending the analysis in her article, "Bad Future Things: Gender, Capitalism and the State in Botswana." In addition to numerous articles on African women and politics, she has written Marxist-feminist analyses of the feminization of poverty and of reproductive rights in the U.S., and of capitalism and gendered "development" in Africa. She has taught at the University of California-Berkeley, the California State University at San Francisco, the East Bay Socialist School, and Ithaca College. Her current research interests include Christianity and cultural erasure in Africa, and a comparison of anti-racism work by Communist Parties in South Africa and the United States.

Claire Robertson
Claire Robertson received her MA from the University of Chicago in European History and her Ph.D. from the University of Wisconsin-Madison in African History. Since 1984 she has taught at The Ohio State University and is now Professor of History and Women's Studies. She is deeply committed to the use of oral history and has done fieldwork in Ghana, Kenya and St. Lucia, the present site of her research. She has published seven books and over forty articles on various aspects of African women's history, including market trade, feminist methodology

and theory, women's education, slavery, and on Caribbean history. Three of her books have received awards, including the African Studies Association's Herskovits Award for Sharing the Same Bowl.

Mary J. Osirim
Mary Johnson Osirim is Professor and Chair of the Department of Sociology and Co-Director of The Center for International Studies at Bryn Mawr College. Her teaching and research interests have focused on gender and development, race and ethnic relations, immigration, the family and economic sociology in sub-Saharan Africa, the English-Speaking Caribbean and the U.S. During the past twenty years, she has conducted fieldwork on women, entrepreneurship and the roles of the state and non-governmental organizations in the microenterprise sectors of Nigeria and Zimbabwe. She has many publications in these areas including articles in *International Sociology* and *Gender and Society*, a co-edited recent edition of *African and Asian Studies* and a book, *Enterprising Women: Gender, Microbusiness and Globalization* (Woodrow Wilson Center and Indiana University Presses, 2009). Currently, her research is focused on transnationalism and community development among African immigrants in the northeastern U.S. and will appear in her forthcoming volume, *Global Philadelphia: Immigrant Communities, Old and New*, co-edited with Ayumi Takenaka. She is the recipient of many grants and fellowships from such organizations as The National Science Foundation, The Pew Foundation and the Woodrow Wilson International Center for Scholars.

Diana J. Fox
Diana Fox is an Associate Professor of Cultural Anthropology at Bridgewater State College and the Coordinator of the Women's and Gender Studies Program. She is the founder and executive editor of the online *Journal of International Women's Studies*. Her research interests include Gender in Anglophone Caribbean societies, Feminist Anthropology, Women's Human Rights in Africa, Gender Studies, HIV/AIDS, the Anthropology of Activism, and the Anthropology of Development. She has conducted fieldwork in Eritrea, Jamaica, Trinidad and Tobago. Dr. Fox is co-editor with Naima Hasci of *The Challenges of Women's Activism and Human Rights in Africa* (1998) and author of various articles on women's human rights in Africa. She was a Fulbright fellow in Jamaica and Trinidad, associated with the Centre for Gender and Development Studies at the University of the West Indies, and in January 2006 was appointed a Senior Fulbright Specialist.

Margaret Grieco
Margaret Grieco (University of Oxford, D.Phil. Sociology) is a Professor of Transport and Society at Napier University and a Visiting Professor at the Institute for African Development, Cornell. She was a staff member of the Africa region of the World Bank and has been a consultant to the World Bank, the United Nations, and the UK Department for International Development. She served as Professor of Sociology at the University of Ghana and has recently worked with the Mitsubishi Research Institute on the Transport arrangements of the northern corridor in Kenya. She has written and edited numerous books, including *Travel, Transport, and the Female Traders of Accra* (Ashgate, 1996) and most recently two edited volumes of IAD conference proceedings titled *Africa's Finances: The Contribution of Remittances* (Cambridge Scholars, 2008) and *The Hydropolitics of Africa: A Contemporary Challenge* (Cambridge Scholars, 2007), as well as over 60 articles. Her areas of expertise include new information technology; globalization and social organization; and urban, regional and transport studies.

Jayati Ghosh
Jayati Ghosh (M.Sc., University of Calcutta, India; Ph.D., University of Waterloo, Canada) is an Associate Professor in the Division of Business at the Dominican University of California and Director of the Honors Program. Before coming to Dominican, she taught at the Wilfrid Laurier University and at University of Wisconsin-Whitewater. Her research interests are in the areas of economic development, health, and women's health in Africa and Asia from an economic and social perspective. She has written a number of articles dealing with the AIDS epidemic and economic development in India and Africa. She has recently co-edited a book entitled *HIV and AIDS in Africa: Beyond Epidemiology* (Blackwell Publishers, edited with Ezekiel Kalipeni, Joseph Oppong, and Susan Craddock, 2004). Her current research focuses on HIV/AIDS in Malawi, India, and the Indian Diaspora in eastern and southern Africa. Some of her recent articles will be published in scholarly journals such as the *Journal of Social Aspects of HIV/AIDS, Asian Profile,* and *Social Science and Medicine.*

Ezekiel Kalipeni
Ezekiel Kalipeni is Associate Professor of Geography and African Studies at the University of Illinois at Urbana-Champaign. He holds both a Ph.D. degree and a Master's degree in Geography from the University of North Carolina at Chapel Hill. He is a population/medical/environmental

geographer interested in demographic, health, environmental, and resource issues in sub-Saharan Africa. He has in the past taught at the University of Malawi (1986-1988), University of North Carolina at Chapel Hill (1988-1991), and Colgate University (1991-1994). His research interests focus on health care issues in Africa, population, the environment and medical geography. His most recent books include: *Issues and Perspectives on Health Care in Contemporary Sub-Saharan Africa* (Edwin Mellen Press, edited with Philip Thiuri, 1997); *AIDS, Health Care Systems and Culture in Sub-Saharan Africa: Rethinking and Re-Appraisal* (special issue of *African Rural and Urban Studies,* Michigan State University Press, Vol 3:2 edited with Joseph Oppong, 1996); *Sacred Spaces and Public Quarrels: African Economic and Cultural Landscapes* (Africa World Press, edited with Paul T. Zeleza, 1999); *HIV/AIDS in Africa: Beyond Epidemiology* (Blackwell Publishers, edited with Susan Craddock, Joseph Oppong, and Jayati Ghosh, 2004); *HIV/AIDS in Africa: Gender and Empowerment Issues* (special issue of *Social Science and Medicine*, forthcoming, guest edited with Assata Zerai and Joseph Oppong). He has published numerous articles in scholarly journals such as the *Geographical Review, Social Science and Medicine, Population and Environment, Africa Today, Population Research and Policy Review* and many others.

Fatou Jah
Fatou Jah is a Ph.D. candidate in Population and Development in the department of Development Sociology at Cornell University. In this period of the educational and fertility transitions occurring in the developing world, her research interests center around disentangling the nexus in the determinants of these socio-economic changes and how these militate or reinforce the inequalities and equities in society. Before coming to Cornell, she actively participated and served as a resource person in the formulation and implementation of The Gambia Population Program and its related project components. She also directed and coordinated the institutionalization of the training component of Gambia's tertiary education system.

Philomina Okeke-Ihejirika
Philomina Okeke-Ihejirika is professor of Gender, Development and Transnational Studies in the Women's Studies Program of the University of Alberta, Edmonton, Canada. Her research and teaching focus on Gender and Development in Africa as well as on Gender Issues in Migration and Settlement in Canada. Her publications in journals and books reflect a

continuing contribution to the debates in these fields, including her highly acclaimed volumes *Negotiating Power and Privilege: Igbo Career Women in Contemporary Nigeria* (Okeke-Ihejirika, Ohio University Press, 2004); *Gendering Transformations: Gender, Culture, Race, and Identity in Africa and Her Diaspora* (Korieh and Okeke-Ihejirika, Routledge 2008). Philomina Okeke-Ihejirika is actively involved in building cross-Atlantic linkages with scholars, academic institutions, and local communities. She also works with international organizations such as the Rotary International Foundation as well as various immigrant-serving organizations and social agencies in Canada.

Penelope E. Andrews
Penelope (Penny) Andrews (LL.B., University of Natal, Durban, South Africa; LL.M., Columbia Law School) is Professor of Law at Valparaiso University School of Law, where she teaches International Human Rights Law and Comparative Perspectives on Race and the Law. She was the Chamberlain Fellow in Legislation at Columbia Law School and has worked at the Legal Resources Centre in Johannesburg and the NAACP Legal Defense Fund in New York. She was on the law faculty at City University New York and at La Trobe University in Melbourne, Australia. She has taught at the University of Maryland School of Law, the University of Natal in South Africa, the University of Aberdeen in Scotland, the University of Amsterdam and the University of Potsdam (Germany). She has written extensively on constitutional and human rights issues in the South African, Australian and global contexts, with particular emphasis on the rights of economically marginalized communities, women and people of color. She is active in many international organizations and has received several honors for her human rights activities, particularly her work in South Africa.

Muna Ndulo
Muna Ndulo is Professor of Law at Cornell University and Director of the Cornell Institute for African Development. He is also Honorary Professor of Law, Cape Town University. He obtained his Bachelors of Law (LLB) from the University of Zambia, an LLM from Harvard, and a D. Phil. degree from Trinity College, Oxford University. He also holds a Certificate in Law and Development from Wisconsin University. He has been admitted to the Bar as an Advocate of the Supreme Court of Zambia. As a student, Muna Ndulo received awards including Law Society Prize for the Best Second Year Law Student and Best Graduating Law Student at the University of Zambia. Ndulo started his teaching career at the

University of Zambia as a Lecturer in Law in 1971. He later became Professor of Law and served as Dean of the University of Zambia School of Law. In 1984-1985 he was Visiting Professor at Cornell University. In 1986 he joined the United Nations and worked as Legal Officer in the Secretariat of the UN Commission on International Trade Law (UNCITRAL). From 1992-1994 he was seconded to the United Nations Observer Mission in South Africa (UNOMSA), where he served as the Chief Political and Legal Adviser to the Mission and to the Special Representative of the United Nations Secretary-General in South Africa. He has also served as Legal Adviser to the United Nations Missions in East Timor (UNAMET, 1999), Kosovo (UNAMIK, 2003), and Afghanistan (UNAMA, 2003). He has published twelve books and over 100 articles. Recent publications include *Security, Reconstruction and Reconciliation: When the Wars End* (ed., University College London Press, 2007).

Susie Jacobs
Susie Jacobs lectures in Sociology and Global Studies at Manchester Metropolitan University, UK, and is an Honorable Research Fellow at the University of Manchester, Department of Religions and Theology. Her qualifications are in sociology, anthropology and development studies. Her D.Phil, from the Institute of Development Studies at the University of Sussex, on Gender Relations and Land Resettlement in Zimbabwe, was the first substantial study of gender and land reform in southern Africa. She has also researched gender, land and agrarian issues in South Africa and more widely; and she has recently published a book, *Gender and Agrarian Reforms* (Routledge, 2009). Other research fields include gender networks and globalization; gender and violent conflicts, and 'race' and ethnicity, particularly with regard to higher education.

Anita Spring
Anita Spring (Ph.D. Cornell University) is Professor of Anthropology and African Studies at the University of Florida. She has carried out long- and short-term research and development work in Botswana, Cameroon, Eritrea, Ethiopia, Ghana, Kenya, Malawi, Senegal, South Africa, Swaziland, Uganda, and Zambia. She was Associate Dean of the College of Liberal Arts and Sciences at the University of Florida and Chief of Women and Agricultural Development and Rural Production at the Food and Agriculture Organization of the United Nations. Since 2000 she has been conducting research on the "new generation of African entrepreneurs" in the global market and how they fit into the African

entrepreneurial landscape. The countries for the study are Botswana, Ethiopia, Ghana, Kenya, Senegal, South Africa, Tanzania, and Uganda. On this topic, she wrote "Gender and the Range of Entrepreneurial Strategies: The Typical and the New African Woman Entrepreneur" in *Black Business and Economic Power* (2002); "West African Enterprise Network: Business Globalists, Interregional Trade and U.S. Interventions," in *West Africa and U.S. Relations* (2006); and with B. McDade, "The New Generation of African Entrepreneurs: Changing the Environment for Business Development and Economic Growth," *Entrepreneurship and Regional Development* (2005). She is the author or editor of eight books and over 50 articles and monographs including *Women Farmers and Commercial Ventures: Increasing Food Security in Developing Countries* (2000); *African Entrepreneurship: Theory and Reality* (with B. McDade 1998), *The Tree Against Hunger: Enset-Based Agricultural Systems in Ethiopia* (with S. Brandt et al. 1997), and *Agricultural Development and Gender Issues in Malawi* (1995).

Kabahenda Nyakabwa
Kabahenda Nyakabwa earned a B.A. from Makerere University (Kampala); an M.Sc. from the University of Manitoba (Canada); and a Ph.D. from the University of London. She currently works as an independent researcher based in Ottawa, Canada. Her academic interests focus on women's issues (gender and forced migration, women and health, violence against women, and women's human rights) with emphasis on Africa. She serves as director on the Ottawa Community Immigration Services Organization. Her publications include "Gender and Internal Displacement: Sub-Saharan Africa," (2007, in Encyclopaedia of Women & Islamic Cultures, Vol. IV, *Economics, Education, Mobility and Space)*; "Women and AIDS in Uganda and the Future of Ethno-medicine," (in Christine E. Gottschalt-Batschalk, Judith Schuler & Doris Iding, eds., *Women and Health: Ethnomedical Perspectives* Berlin: Verlag un Vertrieb); "Uganda and the Challenge of AIDS: Confronting the AIDS Epidemic," in *Confronting the AIDS Epidemic: Cross-Cultural Perspectives on HIV/AIDS Education,* edited by Davidson C. Umeh, 1997 Africa World Press); "Health Issues of African Refugee Women" (in *Association of Concerned Africa Scholars.* No. 44-45 Winter/Spring, 1995); and *Black Immigrant Women* (with Carol D.H. Harvey), in Vanaja Dhrurarajan (editor), *Women and Well Being* (McGill-Queen's University Press, 1990).

INDEX

AAWORD, xvi, 107, 111, 350, 360, 364, 366
ABC, 3
Abdoulaye, 145, 341
Abdullah, 274, 277, 292, 341
AbouZahr, 146, 147
Absharaf, 336
Accra, 77, 79, 80, 81, 83, 84, 89, 119, 302, 314, 367, 370, 374, 380
Accumulating Savings and Credit Association, 301
Ackerly, 301, 341
Adepoju, 101, 341
advocacy initiatives, 34
Afghanistan, 28, 145, 195, 205, 383
Afonja, 212, 219, 342
African Charter on People and Human Rights, 36
African entrepreneurial, 293, 294, 384
African feminism, 95
African feminist, 95, 97, 100, 103, 104, 125
African law schools, 29
African National Congress, xvi, 12, 351
African organizations, 41
African parliaments, 9, 225
African Plan for Action, 224
African rural women, 271, 367
African scholars, 94, 96, 98, 129, 134, 179, 215, 228
African women entrepreneurs, 298
African women leaders, 29
African women scholars, 94, 102, 107, 110
Africana Studies, 116
African-American, 102, 137
African-Anglophone scholars, 94
Africanist feminist, 103, 114
AFWE, xvi, 312, 314
Agbaw, 303, 342

Agutu, Mark, 90
Ahmadu Bello University, 111
AIDS, vii, xvi, 3, 4, 34, 52, 155, 159, 160, 165, 166, 167, 168, 169, 170, 171, 172, 173, 174, 175, 176, 232, 244, 335, 342, 343, 345, 346, 350, 352, 357, 359, 364, 365, 367, 370, 372, 374, 380, 381, 384
Akamba, 83
Akrofi v. Akrofi, 264
Albanese, 63, 342
Allman, Jean, 89
Amadiume, 213, 221, 342
American, 26, 29, 31, 32, 33, 38, 39, 41, 53, 56, 58, 64, 74, 77, 95, 98, 118, 137, 267, 361, 370
American law, 26, 29
American law schools, 29
American legal culture, 40
Amina Mama, 96, 98, 224, 354
Ampofo, Adomako, 98, 100, 341
ANC, xvi, 12, 13, 63, 70
Anderson, Margaret, 178, 189, 209, 215, 267, 342, 344
Anglophone-African feminist, 102
Angola, 10, 23, 145, 327, 378
Anlu, 79, 367, 368
anomie, 327, 332, 333, 334, 339, 340, 349
Anti-Corruption Bureau, xvi, 160
anti-retroviral drug, 242
Arab trade, 182
Ardener, Shirley, 89
armed combatants, 11
Arould, 300
Arusha, 222, 331, 353, 373
ASCAs, 301, 310
Asia, 53, 58, 97, 99, 145, 182, 210, 267, 342, 371, 380
Asian, 8, 122, 342, 343, 344, 348, 374, 379, 380

Asians, 304
Aspaas, 300, 343
Assie-Lumumba, N'dri, 179, 181, 206
Assoc. of African Women for Research & Dvpt., xvi, 107
Atrobus, Peggy, 55
Aubrey, 224, 343
Augustine Mojekwu, 262
Baartman, Saartijie, 113, 140
Babangida, General, 101
Bahrain, 43
Baloyi, 240, 249
Banda, 275, 288, 343
Banderage, 213, 342
Banga, 301, 364
Bangladesh, 145, 357
Banks, Taunya, 234, 246
BAOBAB, xvi, 110
Barrera, 209
Basadi, Emang, 65, 66, 68, 69, 70, 71, 75, 350
Bastian, Misty L., 89
Basu, Amrita, 224, 313, 342
Bauer, v, 8, 9, 11, 12, 16, 19, 61, 216, 343, 344, 348, 355, 359, 371, 377
Baxi, Upendra, 234, 246
Bay, Edna G., 88, 364, 374, 378
Behar, 117, 120, 344
Beijing, 1, 2, 28, 32, 106, 368, 378
Beise, 182, 344
Better Life Program for Rural Women, 101, 107
Bhe and others, 266, 270
Bikie, 276, 292, 359
Bill of Rights, 232, 235, 236, 240, 241, 242, 243
Billingsgate Market, 81
Biraimah, 215, 344
Black Caucus, 114, 137
Black feminist anthropology, 112
Black Feminist Anthropology, xvi, 113, 137, 347, 361, 369
Black woman, 96
Blavy, 313

Bloch, 215, 342, 344, 362
Boserup, 213, 344
Botswana, 10, 42, 45, 65, 66, 68, 69, 70, 72, 74, 75, 104, 159, 207, 303, 305, 346, 349, 350, 353, 359, 361, 362, 363, 368, 374, 378, 383
Botswana Democratic Party, 75
Botswana National Front, 75
Bowditch, 304, 344
Bowman, 178, 189, 209, 344
Brand, Daniel, 233, 245
Brantley, Cynthia, 89
Brazil, 182, 273, 280
British common law, 67
Britton, 9, 11, 12, 16, 19, 61, 216, 343, 344, 348, 355, 359, 371, 377
Brodsky, 291
Bryceson, 117, 119, 273, 345
Buatsi, 302, 310, 353
Bujra, 212, 214, 219, 345
Burkina Faso, 122, 145, 184, 302, 314
Burundi, 8, 22, 23, 24, 145, 327
Business Partners Ltd., 311
Butler, Judith, 62, 345
Cameroon, 79, 139, 184, 276, 292, 349, 359, 383
Cape High Court, 242
Cape Town, 96, 104, 108, 113, 243, 292, 344, 351, 357, 370, 382
Caribbean, 145, 182, 342, 379
Carillo, 336, 345
Carnell, Brian, 91
Carothers, Tom, 57, 345
CEDAW, xvi, 28, 34, 36, 48, 79, 124, 266, 269, 291
CEDPA, xvi, 43, 49, 58, 59, 346
Center for Economic Growth, 210
Central Africa, 184, 189, 193, 194, 197
Central African Republic, xvi, 141, 145, 184, 327, 328
Chad, 145, 182, 184, 328
Chama Cha Mapinduzi, 18
Chamber of Deputies, 14, 19

Charmes, 296, 346
Chauhan, Richa, 140
Chepkemei, Pamela, 90
Chernikovsky, 189
ChevronTexaco, 78
Chinsapo, vi, ix, 155, 156, 163, 164, 170, 171
Chuku, 226, 346
Cisco Systems, 104
Citizenship Act, 42
Citizenship Amendment Law, 66, 67
Civic Education and Advocacy, 47
Civil Rights movement, 40
Clark, 61, 300, 307, 308, 309, 346, 354, 359, 362, 372, 374, 376
Cliffe, 336, 346
Clinard, Marshall, 333, 346, 362
Clinton, Hillary, 74
closed list, 15
Cohen, David William, 90
Colclough, 189, 195, 196, 346
Cole, Johnetta. *See* Johnetta B., 112, 113, 117, 120, 121, 140, 341, 347, *See*
Collins, Patricia Hill, 100, 102, 103, 342, 347
COMESA, 306, 315
Commission for Gender Equality, 236, 261
Commission on Africa, 3
common practices of women's rights, 26
Communal Land Reform Bill, 20
communal property, 82
Compton Foundation, 172
conflict, 4, 9, 11, 12, 18, 23, 32, 65, 70, 85, 97, 261, 264, 286, 287, 327, 328, 329, 330, 332, 334, 336, 337, 338, 339, 349, 373, 378
constitution, 11, 12, 13, 21, 23, 24, 64, 85, 86, 100, 233, 238, 244, 262, 264, 265, 269
Constitutional Court, 232, 235, 236, 237, 239, 240, 241, 242, 243, 246, 248, 250, 261

Constitutive Act of the African Union, 55
Convention for the Elimination of all forms of Discrimination Against Women, 1
Convention on the Elimination of All Forms of Discrimination Against Women, 264
Copenhagen, 106, 368
Coquery-Vidrovitch, 307, 308, 309, 310, 347
Cornia, 212
Cote d'Ivoire, 184, 327, 370
Courts, David, vi, 210, 251, 252
Covenant on Civil and Political Rights, xvii, 85, 264, 266
Covenant on Economic, Social and Cultural Rights, 264
Criminal Code, 42
Crummey, Donald, 89
Csapo, 181, 182, 189, 193, 195, 347
Cultural Anthropology, 112, 379
cultural environment, 147, 192
cultural relativism, 40
customary law, 4, 33, 39, 45, 49, 59, 66, 100, 242, 251, 252, 253, 254, 256, 258, 259, 260, 261, 262, 263, 264, 265, 266, 268, 271, 275, 276, 277, 279, 282, 283, 285, 286, 287, 290, 291, 292
customary law system, 258
DAE, 215, 347
Dahlerup, 8, 23, 347, 361
Daily Nation, 88, 90
Danish International Development Association, **303**
Darkwah, 99, 348
Darnovsky, 116, 348
Daun, 177, 182, 183, 348
David Trubek, 38
DAWN, xvi, 109, 348
de Grazia, 333
de Marees, Pieter, 80, 89
de Sousa Santos, Boa, 234
Decade of Women, 28

Democratic Republic of Congo, 10, 145, 296, 309, 327, 328, 330, 332, 339
DeRose, 182, 348
Desai, 106, 348
Development Alternatives with Women for a New Era, xvi, 109, 348
Development Program, xviii, 37, 104, 129, 130, 378
Diaspora, 29, 57, 95, 96, 102, 136, 137, 380, 382
Dikeletso tsa Bomme mo Botswana, 75
dikgosi, 69
discrimination based on sex, 86
Domestic Relations Bill, 36
Domestic Violence Act, 20, 36, 250
Dominican University, 163, 172, 380
Donors to African Education, 347
DAE, 347
Dorsey, Nancy, 89
Dunne, 209
Durban, 292, 297, 360, 366, 382
Durkheim, Emile, 333, 334, 339, 340, 349, 371
east Africa, 13, 14, 21
East Africa, 184, 189, 192, 193, 194, 196, 197, 269, 309
East African, 12
Ecobank, 306, 315
e-commerce, ix, 295, 297, 299, 301, 302, 303, 307, 309, 310, 311, 370
ECOWAS, xvi, 306, 315
Edge, 74, 349, 363, 368
Egypt, 196, 352
Ekechi, 300, 350, 354, 367
El-Bushira, 334
El-Bushra, 331, 337, 349
electoral college, 13, 17
electoral quotas, 8, 10, 21, 226
electoral systems, 9, 10, 11, 15, 16
Eloundou-Enyegue, 191, 205, 349
Elshtain, 62
Elson, 271, 291, 350, 355

empowerment by right, 336
empowerment through adversity, 336
Engels, Frederick, 88
Friedrich, 77, 88
England, 87, 256, 257, 258, 267, 268, 356, 365
Englund, 158, 163, 350
Enugu, 101
Eritrea, 129, 305, 312, 327, 378, 379, 383
Esbin, 303, 350
Ethiopia, 57, 129, 145, 301, 304, 305, 308, 309, 310, 312, 313, 314, 318, 327, 341, 355, 370, 373, 383
European, xvi, 8, 29, 41, 57, 60, 61, 80, 84, 95, 128, 140, 144, 178, 246, 353, 358, 359, 369, 378
Fafchamps, 311
Falola, 299, 300, 308, 346, 350, 356, 369, 370
Family size, 193
family violence, 45, 334
Fatton, 221, 350
Fear Woman, 307
Feierman, Steven, 89
female education, 177, 179, 180, 182, 196, 205
Female Genital Mutilation, 115, 126, 128, 136, 140
feminism, 32, 66, 94, 95, 96, 98, 100, 101, 107, 111, 116, 117, 138, 222, 225, 342
Feminist Africa, 103, 361, 371
feminist ethnographers, 114, 119, 123, 125
Ferguson, James, 141
Fernandez-Kelly, Patricia, 98, 363
Ferrand, 303, 350
FGM, xvi, 115, 123, 125, 126, 128, 129, 134, 135, 136, 140, 141, 352
Films and Publications Act, 20
Filomina Steady, 95
Fimbo, 260, 269
Fischer, 116, 360

Fletcher School of Law and Diplomacy, 32
Ford and Hivos Foundations, 108
Ford Foundation, 38
Fortna, 180, 181, 351
Fourth UN World Conferences, 106
Fourth World Conference on Women, 28, 34
Fox, Diana, 141
France, 110, 179, 342, 365
Franceschet, 225, 228, 364
Franzer, 117
Fraser, 240, 248
Frelimo, 12, 341
French, 31, 74, 333, 368
Front for the Liberation of Mozambique, 12
Ga, 75, 79, 80, 81, 82, 119
GAD, xvi, 51, 52, 212
Gage-Brandon, 189, 194, 359
Gaitskell, Deborah, 63, 70, 351
Galanter, 38, 39, 56, 57, 372
Gambia, 47, 381
gari, 101
GAWE, xvi, 308, 312, 314
Geiger, Susan, 89
Geisler, 61, 351
Gender and Counseling, 104
gender and development, 26, 27, 29, 31, 37, 51, 54, 59, 134, 227, 337, 379
Gender and Economic Reforms, 104
Gender and Poverty Reduction, 104
Gender and Refugees, 104
Gender and Social Policy, 104
Gender Audit of laws, 36
Gender Budget, 53
gender division of labor, 72, 309, 336, 367
gender equality, 2, 3, 4, 13, 16, 17, 20, 26, 27, 28, 29, 30, 35, 38, 47, 50, 51, 53, 55, 183, 188, 189, 197, 232, 233, 235, 236, 237, 240, 243, 244, 245, 372
gender inequalities, 157, 160, 178, 181, 211, 274

Gender Links, 2, 3, 4, 9, 24, 362
Gender Links Publication, 2
gender mainstreaming, 4, 30, 55, 56, 96, 104, 378
Gender Studies Program, 104, 360, 379
gender-based violence, 45, 135, 327, 329, 330, 334
genocide, 9, 12, 330, 331, 335, 337, 371
Gerlach, 105, 351
Ghanaian Association of Professional Business, 307
Ghanaian society, 82
Gibbon, 304, 368
Gideon, 271, 291, 350
Gledhill, James, 140
global Africa, 115
Global South, 98, 106, 107, 109
Global Women in Politics, xvii, 42, 58, 371
Gluckman, 260, 269
Goebel, 278, 289, 290, 292, 351
Goedhuys, 304, 351
Goetz, 16, 61, 351, 357
Gold Coast, 80, 83
Goldblatt, 248, 250, 331, 352
Gomes, 190, 352
"good mother", 64, 70, 71
Govindasamy, 196, 352
Great Britain, 179
Grieco, Margaret, iv, v, vi, xv, 1, 144, 146, 352, 380
Grootboom, 241, 246, 247, 249
Guatemala, 182
Guinea-Bissau, 145
GWIP, xvii, 42, 46, 58
Gender & Women's Studies, xvii, 108, 109, 111
hadith, 179
Hafkin, Nancy J., 88, 364, 374
Hagos, 303, 352
Hague, 331, 332, 352
Hamza, 274, 277, 292, 341
Hanawalt, Barbara, 89
handicapped, 14

Hansen, 296, 297, 353, 357
Harare, viii, 300, 316, 353, 354, 357, 361, 366, 368, 375
Harris, Angela, 234, 246
Hart, 296, 343, 345, 353
Hassim, 8, 15, 21, 61, 351, 353, 357
Hay, Margaret Jean, 91
Hayward, 210
Headrick, 144, 353
Health Surveys, xvi, 184, 348
Helleiner, 212
Herrera, 180, 181, 351, 353, 369
Hilling, 144, 353
Hinson, 302, 310, 353
HIV/AIDS, vi, 2, 3, 74, 103, 155, 158, 159, 163, 165, 166, 167, 168, 169, 171, 172, 241, 244, 290, 339, 343, 345, 357, 359, 360, 369, 370, 372, 379, 380, 381, 384
Hobson, 60, 63, 353
Holm, 65, 74, 353
Horn, 300, 308, 309, 353, 354
Horwitz, Martin, 67
House-Midamba, 300, 308, 350, 354, 367
Hugo, 238, 239, 240, 247, 248
Human Development Report, 160, 161, 372
Human Rights Commission, 236, 245, 246, 249, 261
human trafficking, 2
Hurricane Katrina, 339
Hurtig, 117, 359
Hussein, Hubbie, 86
Hyde, K.A.L., 215, 354
Ibanez, 331, 354
ICESCR, xvii, 291
Ifeka-Moller, Caroline, 89
Igbo, 78, 79, 88, 119, 308, 364, 374, 378, 382
Igbo women, 78, 79, 119, 308
Igboland, 78
Ihonvbere, 224, 356
Ikdahl, 281, 285, 286, 287, 291, 354
Imam, 98, 110, 228, 343, 354

Ayesha, 98
IMF, 99, 107, 289, 301, 356
India, 53, 145, 274, 282, 350, 380
Indianapolis Star, 88
informal sector, 161, 162, 163, 293, 294, 295, 296, 297, 298, 299, 300, 306, 311, 312, 343
Intermediate Technology Development Group, 90
international agreements, 35
International Conference on Human Rights in Vienna, 1
Internat'l Conference on Population and Development, 106
International Covenant on Economic, Social and Cultural Rights, xvii, 55, 241, 291, 350
International Criminal Court, 338
International IDEA, 9
International Monetary Fund (IMF), 107
International Women's Year, 28
Inter-Parliamentary Union, 22, 24, 225, 337, 355
IPU, xvii, 14, 22, 24, 225, 355
Iran, 28, 180, 360
Isbister, 212, 355
Isichei, Elizabeth, 89
Islam, vi, 4, 127, 177, 178, 179, 181, 191, 197, 287, 351, 353, 357, 359, 360
Islamic clerics, 31
Islamic religion, 188, 191, 196, 197
Jackson, C., 88, 90, 246
Jacobs, vi, 271, 274, 276, 277, 278, 284, 288, 289, 292, 331, 332, 337, 349, 350, 355, 356, 363, 365, 383
Jacobson, 331, 332, 349, 355, 356, 363
Jalloh, 299, 300, 356, 369, 370
Jetter, 63, 356, 365
Johannesburg, 134, 292, 297, 305, 350, 359, 362, 369, 382
Johannesburg Stock Exchange, 305
jural minor status, 79, 87

Justice Kriegler, 239, 248
Justice Mahomed, 237
Justice O'Regan, 238
K'obonyo, 306, 356
Kabeer, 301, 357
Kadirgamar-Rajasingham, Sakuntala, 59
Kalipeni, vi, 155, 158, 159, 162, 357, 364, 365, 380
Kalu, 213
Kamba people, 263
Kampala, 104
kanyenya, 170
Kaplan, 63, 357
Kazakhstan, 182
Kazimbaya-Senkwe, 300, 357
Kelly, 213, 214, 215, 357, 367
Kenya National Council of Women, 86
Kenyan, viii, 85, 102, 132, 263, 264, 298, 301, 317, 343
Kerr, 304, 358
Keto, 114, 115, 358
Kevane, 211, 214, 358
kgotla, 65
Khalwale, Bonny, 86
Khasiani, 309, 358
Kibera, 299, 358
Kigali, 14, 18
Kikuyu, 80, 83, 89, 138, 346
King, 4, 180, 189, 346, 358, 360, 361, 364
Kiribiti, 303
Klare, Karl, 232, 233, 245
Koenig, Dolores, 318
Koran, 179
Kravdal, 182, 348
Kuada, 295, 299, 303, 311, 358
Kuala Lumpur, 28
Kuenyehia, Akua, 44, 59, 268, 358
Kyrgyz Republic, 182
Lagos Plan, 216, 364
Lamphere, Louise, 88
Latin America, 38, 145, 182, 228, 282, 348, 359, 364
Latin American, 8, 282

Lavoie, 334, 335
law and development, 26, 27, 30, 33, 37, 38, 40, 41, 49, 50
law reform, 32, 37, 51, 54
Lawrence Friedman, 39, 57
Lawyers Day, 291
Lebanese, 304
Leith-Ross, Sylvia, 89
Lekorwe, 74, 349, 363, 368
Lentin, 330, 352, 359
Lesotho, 10, 159
Lewis, 60, 100, 353, 359
liberal legal model, 29, 30, 37, 38, 47, 48, 49, 50
Liberation Movement, 329
Liberia, 327
Libya, 279, 328
Liebenberg, Sandra, 233, 245
Lilongwe, ix, 156, 158, 163, 164, 166, 169, 170, 172, 350, 352, 357, 360
Lisa VeneKlasen, 37, 57
Lister, 60, 62, 63, 359
Lloyd, C.B., 189, 190, 194, 359, 367
Logo, 276, 292, 359
Longman, 13, 14, 19, 20, 24, 359
Lumeya, 329, 335, 359
Lumley, 330
Luo, 86
Maata N Tudu, 314
Maathai, Wangari, 86
Macaulay, Steward, 39, 44, 57, 351
MacCaffey, 296
MacGaffey, 300, 309, 359
Madagascar, 184, 267, 304
Magaya, 100, 265
 Venia, 100
Magubane, 99, 359
Makerere University, 104, 360, 384
Malawi, vi, xvii, xviii, 10, 45, 48, 145, 150, 155, 157, 158, 159, 160, 161, 163, 166, 167, 169, 171, 301, 303, 304, 343, 346, 350, 352, 357, 358, 360, 363,

366, 369, 370, 372, 373, 374, 380, 381, 383
Malhotra, 181, 196, 352, 360, 365
Mali, 31, 145, 150, 151, 184, 378
Mama, 101, 107, 108, 222, 224, 343, 354, 360
Manicom, Linzi, 63, 64, 69, 360
Manu, 299, 360
Marc Galanter, 38
Marchbank, 331, 332, 349, 355, 356, 363
Marcus, 116, 282, 360
Marge Schuler, 35, 56
Married Persons Equality Act, 20
Marry Rono v. Jane Rono and William, 264
Marsden, 303, 360
Marx, Karl, 57, 350
Masiiwa, 289, 361
Mason, 4, 180, 189, 358
Matercare project, 153
maternal health, 148, 149
Maternal Mortality, vi, xvii, 144, 153, 341, 353, 376
maternity leave, 20
Matland, 15, 18
Mauritania, 145
Mauritius, 10, 305, 361, 368
Mba, 61, 221, 361
McClaurin, Irma, 347
McDade, Barbara, 294, 295, 296, 299, 300, 304, 305, 306, 308, 312, 315, 318, 348, 354, 361, 365, 367, 370, 384
McFadden, Patricia, 96, 98, 100, 361
MDGs, 2, 3, 28, 149, 177
medieval England, 79
Meintjes, 8, 15, 21, 331, 346, 352, 353
Merton, 327, 334, 362
Meru, 90
Messick, Richard E., 57
Mexican border, 97
microcredit, 107, 294, 295, 297, 299, 300, 310, 313

micro-enterprises, 101, 107, 294, 299
microfinance, 294, 295, 297, 301, 310, 312, 313, 376
micro-savings, 297, 300
Millennium Development Goals, 1, 2, 28, 146, 150, 177, 372, 373
Ministry for Gender, 48
Ministry for Women and Family Affairs, 48
modernization, 98, 196, 212, 219, 226
Moghadam, 98, 105, 106, 109, 362
Mohanty, Chandra T., 117, 118, 132, 362
Molokomme, 65, 67, 68, 362
Athaliah, 74
Molutsi, 65, 74, 353
Molyneux, 60, 77, 88, 350, 362
Momsen, 274, 288, 362
Montoya, 117, 359
Moore, Sally Falk, 40, 58, 120, 362
Morna, 10, 11, 12, 13, 15, 18, 19, 23, 362
Moseneke, D., 245
Moshi, 213, 217, 220, 362
mothers of the nation, 63
Mozambique, 8, 11, 14, 15, 16, 19, 22, 45, 46, 145, 184, 286, 287, 288, 327, 341, 344, 346, 348, 353, 373, 374
Mukta, 331, 363
Mukungu, 301, 364
multilateral and bilateral donors, 33
Muluzi, 160
Munch, 333, 363
Murambatsvina, 289
Musee d l'homme in Paris, 113
Musisi, Nakanyike, 89
Muslim, vii, viii, xviii, 110, 177, 178, 179, 180, 181, 182, 183, 185, 186, 187, 188, 189, 190, 191, 193, 194, 195, 196, 197, 199, 200, 201, 202, 203, 205, 329, 356, 373
Muslim communities, 110, 188

Muslim countries, 110, 177, 178, 181, 182, 183, 186, 205
Muslim girls' school, 197
Muslim societies, 180, 181, 182, 198
Mutharika, 160
Myerhoff, 117
Nairobi, 1, 2, 28, 77, 79, 83, 84, 85, 86, 88, 89, 90, 106, 109, 298, 348, 350, 358, 363, 364, 367, 373
Nairobi Conference, 2
Nairobi UN World, 1
Namibia, 8, 11, 15, 16, 19, 22, 46, 57, 343, 359, 377
Nasha, Margaret, 75
National Assembly, 12, 14, 17, 19, 24
National Assembly elections, 12
National Council of Women of Kenya, 102
National Democratic Institute, xvii, 42, 58, 363
NDI, xvii, 42, 46, 47, 48, 58, 363
Neier, 329, 330, 332, 363
NEPAD (New Partnership for Africa's Development), xvii, 216, 224, 363
Netherlands, 329, 330, 363
New Family Law, 20
New York Times, 328, 330, 331, 334, 335, 346, 371
Ngau, 298, 363
Ngcobo, 266
Ngwira, 161, 162, 363
Nielsen, 333, 349
Niger, 78, 145, 184
Niger Delta, 78
Nigeria, xvi
Nigeria's Structural Adjustment Program. *See*
Nigerian, 89, 98, 101, 134, 136, 262, 344, 361
Nigerian Court of Appeals, 262
Njoki, Piah, 90
Nkiwane, 221, 363
NORAD, 314

Norwegian Council for Refugees, 334
Nwauwa, 212, 214, 363
Nyakabwa, vi, 327, 334, 335, 384
Nyiramasuhuko, Pauline, 331
Nzegwu, Nkiru, 127
Nzomo, Maria, 100, 102, 364
O'Barr, 61, 364, 375
Obermeyer, 178, 179, 181, 189, 360
Obstetric Transport, 153
Occlu, 307
Odhiambo, Atieno, 90
OECD, xvii, 146, 306, 311, 341, 347, 365
Ogundipe-Leslie, Molara, 118, 362
Okeke, vi, 207, 212, 213, 217, 220, 224, 225, 226, 228, 364, 381
Okonjo, 61, 364
Okurut, 301, 364
Olomi, 303, 356, 358, 364
Orleck, 60, 63, 356, 365
Osirim, Mary J., v, 94, 98, 298, 341, 365, 379
Ossetia, 53
Oyewumi, 213
Pakistan, 145
Pala, Achola O., 114
Pande, 180, 181, 365
Pankhurst, 276, 278, 331, 365
Pare women, 79
Parliamentary women's caucus, 16
party-based quota, 10, 21
Pateman, 60, 62, 366
patriarchal state, 102
patriarchal structure, 217
patrilineage, 82, 278
patrilineal, 61, 67, 80, 252, 264, 275, 287
patrilocality, 80
patronage, 17
Pearson, R., 88
Pelosi, Nancy, 74
Penal Code, 42
Pereira, 98, 366
Pesantren Al-Muayyad, 180
Petai, 117

Petrides, 208, 209, 366
Pierterse, 116
Pietermaritzburg, 292
Platform for Action, 28, 224, 378
Pohl, 180, 205, 366
political participation, 4, 8, 48, 73, 161, 192, 227, 336, 337
polygyny, 81, 127
Population Reference Bureau, 128, 185, 366, 374
Portugal, 179
positive law, 33, 40, 50
Post-Beijing, 28
Povich, 74
powerful mothers, 63, 64, 65, 66, 67, 69, 72, 73
PR systems, 11, 23
President Bush, 205
President Mogae, 75
Presley, Cora, 61, 90, 366
Pretoria, 248, 292, 349, 363
Prevention of Family Violence Act, 239
Prophet Muhammad, 205
proportional representation, 9, 14, 24
Protocol on Women's Rights in the African Charter on Human and People's Rights, 266
Psacharopoulos, 209
Quachey, 314, 366
Quota, 343, 358, 368
racist society, 96
Rakesh, 301, 366
Rao, 209
Rathgeber, 215, 367
Razavi, 60, 292, 362
Refugees International, 329, 330, 332, 338, 367
relativism, 32, 40, 125, 130, 133
religion, ix, 33, 38, 39, 40, 82, 110, 121, 165, 177, 178, 179, 180, 181, 182, 183, 184, 185, 186, 187, 188, 189, 190, 191, 192, 193, 194, 195, 196, 197, 205, 221, 236, 247, 327, 337, 349

Republican Party, 74
Reserved seat, 21
reserved seats, 9, 13, 14, 16, 17, 18, 23
Rhodes, 302, 314, 367
rights conventions, 36, 266
Rio, 28, 106
Rist, 212
Ritzenthaler, 61, 367
Robertson, Claire C., v, 77, 89, 90, 119, 120, 126, 300, 307, 308, 356, 363, 366, 367, 378
Rodenberg, 227
Rosaldo, 78, 88
Royal, Segolene, 74, 267
Ruddick, 63, 367
Rule of Law, 57, 345
Rwanda, 8, 12, 13, 14, 18, 19, 20, 22, 24, 145, 327, 330, 331, 335, 336, 337, 357, 359, 366, 371, 372, 376
SADC, xvii, 10, 15, 24, 55, 75, 306
SAFERE, 103
Sall, 212, 368
Salo, 96, 98, 368
Samatar, 74, 368
SAP, xviii, 220
Sarajevo: A War Journal, 334
Sassen, 98, 368
Sayed, 209
Scandinavia, 8, 23, 347
Schapera, 65, 69, 75, 368
Schneider, 296, 368
Scholars in Self-Estrangement, 38, 56, 57, 372
Schulpen, 304, 368
Schultz, 208, 210
Schwartz, 18, 20, 24, 25, 368
Seidman, Robert & Ann, 11
Selolwane, 61, 66, 75, 368
Sen, 109, 161, 162, 246, 357, 368
Senegal, 52, 59, 305, 343, 354, 368, 383
Seneyaki, Pramila, 152
Setswana, 65, 70, 75

sexual harassment, 58, 102, 104, 162
Sexual Offences Bill, 36
Seychelles, 8, 22, 23
Shanklin, 61, 368
Shell and Chevron-Texaco, 99
Shettima, 229
SID, xviii, 27
Sideris, 331, 336, 369
Sierra Leone, 95, 145, 327, 356
Simm, 60
Singh, 301, 366
Sleuwaegen, 304, 351
Smelser, 105, 369
Smock, 213, 215, 369
Society for International Development, xviii, 27
Solidarity Peace Trust, 289, 369
Somalia, 135, 145, 327, 336
Somanya, 314
Somel, 180, 181, 369
Soumare, 215, 342
South Africa, 8, 11, 13, 14, 15, 16, 19, 22, 34, 42, 44, 53, 58, 59, 66, 96, 100, 101, 108, 134, 140, 157, 162, 207, 228, 232, 233, 234, 237, 239, 240, 243, 244, 245, 246, 247, 248, 249, 250, 261, 267, 272, 273, 277, 282, 284, 292, 296, 297, 302, 304, 305, 344, 345, 346, 349, 351, 352, 353, 356, 360, 361, 362, 363, 368, 371, 374, 378, 382, 383
South African Bill of Rights, 234
South African Human Rights Commission, 246, 261
southern Africa, 13, 14, 21, 86, 103, 159, 271, 285, 346, 357, 365, 370, 380, 383
Southern African Development Community, xvii, 2, 10, 14, 23, 306
Sowutum Mothers Association, **314**
'special' seats, 14
Spring, vi, 89, 90, 274, 293, 294, 295, 296, 297, 299, 300, 301, 302, 304, 305, 306, 307, 308, 309, 310, 312, 315, 318, 322, 324, 325, 326, 346, 348, 352, 354, 358, 361, 365, 366, 367, 369, 370, 383, 384
St. Kizito, 90
Stanworth, 214, 370
Stellenbosch, 292
Stephen Lewis, 3
Stokes, 205, 349
structural adjustment policies, 98
sub-Saharan, 96, 98, 101, 105, 106, 144, 155, 157, 159, 177, 182, 183, 197, 207, 215, 228, 273, 275, 345, 348, 353, 371, 374, 379, 381
Sudan, xviii, 123, 124, 125, 126, 128, 327, 328, 329, 330, 331, 334, 335, 336, 337, 340, 342, 352, 354, 355, 371, 373, 376
sunna, 126, 179
supply-driven assistance, 37
Sutton, Margaret, 214, 215, 370
Sylvia Tamale, 12, 364
Syrians, 304
Taguta/Sisuthi, 289, 369
Taliban, 195
Tallis, 155, 370
Tanzania, xviii, 8, 12, 14, 17, 18, 20, 22, 24, 53, 58, 79, 89, 145, 179, 182, 184, 222, 264, 269, 285, 286, 290, 303, 305, 310, 313, 331, 345, 353, 361, 369, 372, 384
Tanzania Gender Networking Project, 13, 18
Taylor, 61, 343, 356, 366, 377
Termination of Pregnancy Act, 20
terrorism, 177
TFN (transnational feminist networks), 105, 108, 109, 110, 111
The Rape of Nanking, 333, 346
The Women's Manifesto, 71, 75, 350
The World of Parliaments, 337

Thomas, Barbara, 57, 90, 246, 289, 345, 371
Thompson, 333, 339, 371
Thuku, Harry, 79, 89
Toner, 74
Tostan, 52, 59
Trager, 309, 370
Transnational feminist movements, 105
Treatment Action, 241, 249
Tripp, Aili, 8, 10, 12, 17, 20, 23, 61, 108, 224, 225, 273, 274, 290, 291, 371
Trubek, 38, 39, 56, 57, 372
Tsikata, 285, 286, 290, 372, 375
Tswana, 65, 66, 67, 71, 75, 368
Tunisia, 180, 360
Turshen, 329, 330, 331, 332, 335, 336, 339, 346, 352, 369, 372, 374
Tutsi, 23, 329, 331, 335
Twagiramariya, 329, 330, 335, 336, 339, 352, 372, 374
U.S., xviii, 37, 38, 40, 41, 56, 58, 59, 61, 64, 74, 77, 84, 87, 88, 95, 97, 100, 110, 112, 114, 125, 134, 135, 137, 148, 195, 205, 302, 356, 370, 373, 378, 379, 384
U.S. Agency for International Development, xviii, 37, 373
Uganda, xviii, 8, 12, 13, 14, 16, 18, 19, 20, 22, 24, 36, 58, 79, 99, 104, 130, 145, 151, 157, 184, 275, 276, 283, 285, 286, 288, 298, 299, 305, 307, 310, 327, 336, 337, 343, 344, 345, 351, 355, 357, 361, 364, 367, 371, 372, 374, 383, 384
UN peacekeepers, 332, 338
UN World Conference on Women, 106
UN World Conferences on Women, 106, 111
UNAIDS, 155, 159, 161, 162, 372
UNDP, xvi, xvii, xviii, 37, 52, 53, 55, 90, 104, 129, 130, 157, 160, 161, 227, 360, 372, 373

UNECA, 220, 223, 373
UNESCO, 207, 208, 210, 214, 215, 347, 373
UNFPA, xviii, 150, 151, 376
UNHCR, xviii, 328, 373
UNIFEM, 59, 207, 314, 358, 373, 374
United Nation's Decade for Women. *See*
United Nations, xvii, xviii, 3, 9, 37, 55, 104, 129, 130, 150, 177, 208, 214, 222, 269, 283, 328, 332, 338, 339, 341, 345, 364, 366, 372, 373, 378, 380, 383
United Nations Mission, 383
United States, 28, 29, 30, 32, 33, 38, 40, 55, 56, 57, 104, 112, 114, 118, 137, 138, 234, 250, 314, 369, 372, 378
Unity Dow, 66, 68, 349
universal citizenship, 61
Universal Declaration of Human Rights, 55, 264
university administration, 217, 218
University of Cape Town, 96
unrecognized assumptions, 37
Unterhalter, 63, 70, 351
Elaine, 63
USAID, xviii, 37, 41, 42, 43, 104, 159, 205, 286, 306, 311, 370, 373
Ussher Town, 81, 90
UWONET, 36
Uzbekistan, 182
v. Magaya, 265
Vaa, 296, 297, 353, 357
Valodia, 297, 371
Van Allen, v, xv, 60, 61, 65, 66, 88, 374, 378
virilocality, 80
Vogel, 60, 374
Voland, 182, 344
Wambui Waiyaki Otieno, 85
Wauschkunh, 305, 375
WB, 280
Weeks, 177, 178, 182, 183, 189, 196, 374

Weiss, 156, 157, 374
Werbner, 60, 63, 343, 375, 376
West African, xvi, 79, 152, 276, 306, 308, 315, 342, 365, 370, 374, 375, 384
Whitehead, 290, 375
WHO, 145, 159, 162, 289, 372, 376
WID, xviii, 51, 98, 212
widow, 34, 85, 253, 255, 259, 264, 268, 275, 278
WiLDAF, xviii, 41, 55, 375
Wilson, 214, 379
Wipper, Audrey, 61, 89, 375
WLRI, xviii, 41, 42, 44, 45, 46, 59, 375
WLSA, xviii, 41, 283, 375
WLUML (Women Living under Muslim Law), xviii, 110
Wohlmuth, 305, 352, 368, 375
Women and Law in Southern Africa, xviii, 41, 283, 375
Women in Development, xviii, 98, 342
Women in Law and Development in Africa, xviii, 41
Women's Legal Center, 242
Women's Legal Rights Initiative, xviii, 41, 43, 375
Women's Legal Rights program, 31
women's movements, 8, 9, 21, 105, 224, 283, 288
women's rights advocacy, 26, 28, 29, 30, 34, 35, 37, 38, 41, 49, 50, 54
Women's rights are Human rights, 28
women's rights programs, 26, 44, 47, 50

Women's Studies, xvii, 89, 108, 133, 135, 141, 218, 352, 356, 359, 360, 364, 378, 379, 381
women-in-development, 51
Woodhall, 209
World Bank, 1, 42, 44, 49, 57, 58, 99, 107, 129, 146, 148, 154, 158, 161, 180, 209, 211, 214, 215, 272, 274, 280, 281, 306, 315, 345, 350, 354, 358, 360, 375, 376, 380
World Conference on Human Rights, 4, 106, 267
Wright, Marcia, 91, 301, 317, 376
WTO, xviii, 101
Yale University, 210, 366
Yoruba, 308, 350
Youssef, Nadia, 376
Yoweri Museveni, 12
Yulek, 313
Yuval-Davis, 60, 63, 351, 375, 376
Zambia, 10, 119, 184, 252, 255, 257, 258, 267, 268, 269, 270, 272, 282, 290, 297, 310, 345, 347, 356, 357, 363, 369, 382, 383
Zanzibar, 14, 17, 24, 179
Zarkov, 330, 331, 332, 376
Zegoua, 150, 154
zibolibori, 170
Zimbabwe, 10, 96, 100, 103, 106, 139, 145, 153, 159, 184, 260, 265, 275, 276, 277, 278, 279, 283, 289, 290, 297, 298, 302, 304, 314, 348, 351, 353, 354, 355, 356, 358, 361, 363, 365, 366, 367, 368, 369, 371, 375, 376, 379, 383